AF695599

MENTALIZATION-BASED TREATMENT FOR CHILDREN
A TIME-LIMITED APPROACH

Mentalization-Based Treatment for Children, Second Edition stands as a compelling articulation of how reflective functioning and mentalization can be cultivated in children whose early relational experiences have disrupted their capacity to make sense of minds—their own and those of others. Grounded in developmental and psychodynamic theory, and animated by careful clinical attention, this volume shows how thoughtfully held therapeutic relationships can restore meaning and emotional coherence, and encourages psychological growth. It is an indispensable work for clinicians committed to igniting children's curiosities about their internal worlds in the service of relationship building and repair.

—**Miriam Steele, PhD,** Alfred J. and Monette C. Marrow Professor in Psychology, New School for Social Research, New York, NY, United States

I very warmly recommend this book to clinicians, and to anyone interested in learning about helping troubled children. It is very clearly written and organized, with reference to the broader background of theory and work with adults, and presents the great progress made in working with children, since the first edition. The authors are international leaders in this field, and this book is a major contribution.

—**Mary Hepworth (formerly Mary Target), PhD,** Professor, Research Department of Clinical, Educational and Health Psychology, University College London, London, United Kingdom

This second edition offers a wonderfully nonstigmatizing and deeply respectful look into the inner worlds of children, especially at a time when COVID's aftereffects and rapid technological change make reflective thinking harder to sustain. The authors bring the model to life through rich case studies and thoughtful attention to cultural context, giving clinicians a clear and robust framework they can trust. It's a timely, humane, and genuinely practical guide for anyone who wants to help children reclaim their capacity to make sense of themselves and others.

—**Francine Conway, PhD,** Distinguished Professor, Rutgers University, New Brunswick, NJ, United States

This inspiring second edition of *Mentalization-Based Treatment for Children* transforms cutting-edge science into a practical, developmentally attuned response to today's urgent child and family mental health needs. It stands out through its vibrant synthesis of developmental theory, attachment research, mentalization-based treatment scholarship, and the realities of everyday clinical work—all held within a flexible and evidence-informed framework. With its focus on the building blocks of mentalizing, the role of parents, and time-limited goals, this manual becomes an indispensable resource for clinicians committed to nurturing children's emotional growth and resilience.

—**Nicole Vliegen, PhD,** clinical psychologist and psychodynamic child psychotherapist; Professor of Clinical Psychology, Leuven University, Leuven, Belgium

This book provides a very clear, well-organized, and integrated presentation of how and why to practice a brief, structured approach of mentalization-based treatment with children. It demonstrates the utility of a developmental approach to therapy and is brought to life with vivid examples. It should be an invaluable resource to any clinician or educator involved in the care of children.

—**Efrain Bleiberg, MD,** Professor of Psychiatry and Child and Adolescent Psychiatry, Menninger Department of Psychiatry and Behavioral Sciences, Baylor College of Medicine, Houston, TX, United States; Educational Consultant, Houston Center for Psychoanalytic Studies

MENTALIZATION-BASED TREATMENT FOR CHILDREN
A TIME-LIMITED APPROACH

Second Edition

Nick Midgley, Karin Ensink, Karin Lindqvist,
Norka Malberg, and Nicole Muller

AMERICAN PSYCHOLOGICAL ASSOCIATION

Copyright © 2026 by the American Psychological Association. All rights, including for text and data mining, AI training, and similar technologies, are reserved. Except as permitted under the United States Copyright Act of 1976, no part of this publication may be reproduced or distributed in any form or by any means, including, but not limited to, the process of scanning and digitization, or stored in a database or retrieval system, without the prior written permission of the publisher.

The opinions and statements published are those of the Authors, and do not necessarily represent the policies of the American Psychological Association. The information contained in this work does not constitute personalized therapeutic advice. Users seeking medical advice, diagnoses, or treatment should consult a medical professional or health care provider. The Authors have worked to ensure that all information in this book is accurate at the time of publication and consistent with general mental health care standards.

Published by
American Psychological Association
750 First Street, NE
Washington, DC 20002
https://www.apa.org

Order Department
https://www.apa.org/pubs/books
order@apa.org

Typeset in Meridien and Ortodoxa by Lumina Datamatics, India

Printer: Gasch Printing, Odenton, MD
Cover Designer: Gwen J. Grafft, Minneapolis, MN

Library of Congress Cataloging-in-Publication Data

Names: Midgley, Nick, 1968- author | Ensink, Karin author | Lindqvist, Karin author | Malberg, Norka T. author | Muller, Nicole (Psychotherapist) author
Title: Mentalization-based treatment for children / by Nick Midgley, Karin Ensink, Karin Lindqvist, Norka Malberg, and Nicole Muller.
Description: [Second edition]. | Washington, DC : American Psychological Association, [2026] | Previous edition: 2017. | Includes bibliographical references and index.
Identifiers: LCCN 2025046662 (print) | LCCN 2025046663 (ebook) | ISBN 9781433844980 paperback | ISBN 9781433844997 epub | ISBN 9781433850110 pdf
Subjects: LCSH: Mentalization Based Therapy | BISAC: PSYCHOLOGY / Psychotherapy / Child & Adolescent
Classification: LCC RJ504 .M53 2026 (print) | LCC RJ504 (ebook)
LC record available at https://lccn.loc.gov/2025046662
LC ebook record available at https://lccn.loc.gov/2025046663

https://doi.org/10.1037/0000486-000

Printed in the United States of America

10 9 8 7 6 5 4 3 2 1

CONTENTS

FOREWORD TO THE SECOND EDITION

Almost 10 years have passed since the first edition of this highly successful book. The world has changed, particularly for the children at the heart of this treatment guide. The pandemic, with its enforced isolation, has been catastrophic for school-age children. Even before COVID-19, child mental health was in crisis, with waiting lists for children and young people's mental health services (CYPMHS) in the United Kingdom growing, despite increased investment. In 2023, around one in five children aged 8 to 19 in England had a probable mental disorder, up from 12.5% in 2017 when the first edition was published (Newlove-Delgado, Marcheselli, et al., 2023). New in-year referrals to CYPMHS rose by more than 50%, from 821,734 in 2020/2021 to 1,288,653 in 2022/2023 and 1,290,913 in 2023/2024, with increases across all regions (NHS Digital, 2025). Eating disorder services are now supporting 47% more children and young people than before the pandemic, reflecting the escalating demand for mental health services.

This rising trend is not unique to the United Kingdom, as similar increases have been documented globally. Although COVID-19 exacerbated existing challenges, including disrupted routines, reduced social development, and delayed access to support (Wolf & Schmitz, 2024), other evidence suggests the pandemic's impact may have been modest (Newlove-Delgado, Russell, et al., 2023). Increased mental health awareness may also play a role (Foulkes & Andrews, 2023), but it cannot fully explain the rise (Armitage et al., 2024). The prevalence inflation hypothesis suggests that increased reported prevalence may arise as a self-fulfilling prophecy, where mild symptoms escalate to a diagnosable level due to changes in behavior and self-image (Foulkes & Andrews, 2024). Rising rates of disorders such as attention-deficit/hyperactivity disorder and autism may also reflect evolving diagnostic standards (Kazda et al., 2021), identification of previously undetected cases (Banaschewski et al., 2023), and shifts in societal understanding (Morris, 2024). But the increase in CYPMHS prevalence is large and has been consistently observed across countries and reported by professionals, parents, and teachers. Children diagnosed with disorders in 2017 already faced greater difficulties than those in previous decades, highlighting the growing severity of the issue (Armitage et al., 2024).

I do not suppose anyone truly knows what has happened to children's lives over the last decades, although there is little shortage of hypotheses and speculations. Some not readily modifiable factors that may have contributed to increased prevalence include national and global pressures, economic outlook, climate change, international conflicts, and inequalities. The widening gap between the richest and poorest and the cost-of-living crisis have undoubtedly contributed, as children living in households in the lowest 20% family income distribution are four times more likely to be identified by their parents as having severe mental health problems compared with the highest 20% (Gutman et al., 2015).

Since 2012, concerns about widespread smartphone use and social media exposure have grown (Haidt & Allen, 2020). These technologies may impact how children and young people manage stress, with some experiencing increased exposure to bullying and harmful content, whereas others benefit from reduced social isolation (Twenge et al., 2020). Observational studies show moderate links between high screen media use and poor mental health, although some researchers argue these associations lack societal significance (Orben & Przybylski, 2019). A randomized controlled trial reducing leisure-time screen use to 3 hours per week for 2 weeks demonstrated significant benefits, including 45 additional minutes of nonsedentary leisure time daily, reduced internalizing symptoms, and improved prosocial behavior (Schmidt-Persson et al., 2024). These findings suggest limiting screen time can alleviate behavioral difficulties, particularly internalizing issues, and enhance social interactions. Social media's impact remains divisive. A Harris Poll found 60% of Generation Z believe it harms society, with many wishing platforms such as TikTok (47%), Snapchat (43%), and X (50%) had never been invented (The Harris Poll, 2024).

There are those who believe the recent generations are just less resilient. Young people's reduced ability to cope with stress may partly stem from changes in parenting practices (Skenazy, 2021). A shift from intensive caregiving in early years could activate epigenetic mechanisms, increasing lifelong stress reactivity (Tarsha & Narvaez, 2022). Overprotective "helicopter" parenting, reduced unsupervised play, and fewer risk-taking opportunities limit children's ability to develop resilience, often leaving them unprepared to navigate life's challenges without trusted adult support (Gray et al., 2023).

Why begin the foreword to the second edition of the mentalization-based treatment for children (MBT-C) guide with what may seem like journalistic alarmism about children's mental health? For four compelling reasons:

- First, the current crisis in children's mental health is undeniably tied to the diminishing agency afforded to children by adults. MBT-C provides a crucial framework for supporting the social development of vulnerable children.
- Second, there has rarely been a more urgent need for a nonstigmatizing, strength-based, generic, transdiagnostic approach in children's mental health services. MBT-C offers a nonstigmatizing, accessible, and transdiagnostic approach to addressing children's mental health challenges.
- Third, adverse caregiver-related early environments play a causal role in childhood psychopathology. MBT-C demonstrates particular utility in tackling adversity-associated posttrauma reactions.
- Fourth, and building on the theme of mediation, emerging research highlights the critical role of mentalizing impairment for parents who have their own history of adverse childhood experiences. MBT-C holds promise in addressing the persistent issue of transgenerational trauma.

I will elaborate on each of these points.

DIMINISHING AGENCY AFFORDED TO CHILDREN BY ADULTS

Rutherford's insightful analysis of early 20th-century popular magazines published in the United Kingdom highlights a striking contrast with today's reality. At that time, magazines frequently depicted children as the heroes who solved puzzles and captured villains. But children as young as 5 also regularly walked or biked independently and meaningfully contributed to household tasks. By age 11, many had part-time jobs, reflecting a perception of children as competent, responsible, and resilient (Rutherford, 2011). From the 1960s, and particularly since the 1980s, an implicit societal shift has occurred. The understanding of children evolved from viewing them as capable individuals to a focus on their need for supervision and protection. Children's freedom to engage in activities that involve risk and personal responsibility has declined significantly. Research on children's independent mobility documents stark reductions across Europe between 1970 and 1990 (B. Shaw et al., 2015). In England, the percentage of primary school children walking home alone fell from 86% in 1971 to 35% in 1990 and just 25% in 2010. Similarly, the proportion of children licensed by parents to use public buses independently dropped from 48% in 1971 to 15% in 1990 and 12% by 2010.

This reduction in children's autonomy has been compounded by structural changes in schooling. Between 1981 and 2003, primary school hours in the United Kingdom increased by 11.4 hours per week, effectively adding a full day to a child's working week. This shift is significant because mentalizing—the ability to understand and reflect on the thoughts and feelings of oneself and others—develops most robustly in later childhood and adolescence through peer interactions (Fonagy et al., 2017a, 2017b). Evidence demonstrates the transformative impact of adding recess time in primary schools, with consistent findings of improved social and emotional well-being and, in some cases, enhanced academic performance (Burson & Castelli, 2022). Play is a critical context in which children cultivate social understanding. Longitudinal studies link children's ability to engage in social pretend play, create shared narratives, and symbolize with the development of reflective functioning later in life (Tessier et al., 2016).

The erosion of play opportunities has stripped children of a vital context for sharing their minds with peers. With this loss, we have undermined a key avenue for fostering resilience and mental well-being. This second edition of this MBT-C guide seeks to address these deficits through a developmental focus that is both therapeutic and resilience building. Mentalizing contributes to meeting three basic psychological needs (Ryan et al., 2016) essential for a child's well-being: autonomy, or the sense of agency to choose one's path; (social) competence, the confidence to feel skilled enough to pursue those paths; and relatedness, the need to feel connected to and supported by others. By restoring children's capacity for autonomy, competence, and relatedness, MBT-C aims not only to support mental health but also to build the resilience needed for a fulfilling, connected life.

This revised second edition also introduces an important evolution of the mentalization-based treatment (MBT) model, tailored specifically for children. It incorporates a focus on the foundational "building blocks" of mentalizing—such as attention control and emotion regulation—while also addressing explicit mentalizing in a way that aligns with typical developmental milestones. This approach reflects a nuanced understanding of children's needs, combining therapeutic intervention with their natural developmental priorities. Unlike the adult MBT model, which centers primarily on reactivating mentalizing and addressing its breakdowns, the MBT-C model adds a developmental perspective. It recognizes the importance of not only helping children recover mentalizing when it falters but also actively supporting their capacity to develop this essential skill. By addressing both the developmental cultivation of mentalizing and the repair of its breakdowns, MBT-C provides a comprehensive framework for fostering resilience, emotional well-being, and social competence in school-age children. At the heart of the MBT-C approach outlined in this well-constructed manual is the understanding that, in each of us, our emerging capacities for envisioning actions in terms of thoughts and feelings crucially depend on the support we are offered by our families, our social networks, which are essential to us if we are to develop and maintain this stance. The therapist is an obvious partner and, during the treatment process, will be able to sustain a child's mentalizing and help them experience the value of mentalizing in social relationships and self-recognition. When the therapist is no longer there, a child who has not yet recruited peers and adults to help them sustain such a contemplative stance will struggle to retain their developmental achievements.

The clarity with which this dialectic process is depicted and illustrated by this guide is one of the valuable contributions of Midgley et al.'s work.

THE NEED FOR A NONSTIGMATIZING, STRENGTHS-BASED, TRANSDIAGNOSTIC APPROACH FOR TREATING CHILDREN

Evidence from randomized controlled trials (e.g., Harvey et al., 2023) demonstrates that structured interventions designed for specific mental disorders can lead to negative outcomes when administered to asymptomatic or mildly symptomatic populations. MBT-C, with its developmental focus, avoids medicalizing problems and instead empowers children through targeted techniques. These techniques are applied flexibly, incorporating specific exercises and activities that support work at different developmental levels. The time-limited MBT-C model also places parents at its core—not as a secondary consideration but rather as an integral part of the therapeutic process.

A personalized approach lies at the heart of MBT-C, requiring careful assessment to ensure that interventions are pitched appropriately to the child's developmental stage and needs. This is achieved through a shared "focus formulation," which might take the form of a story or picture to help children and families cocreate a therapeutic focus. The model also highlights the cultural contexts shaping mentalizing capacity, recognizing that the therapist's stance in MBT-C is influenced by cultural factors. This edition places greater emphasis on concepts such as embodied mentalizing and the development of epistemic trust (Fonagy & Allison, 2014, 2023), fostering a collaborative and trusting therapeutic relationship.

Crucially, MBT-C addresses the general vulnerability factor in childhood mental health, often referred to as the *p* factor, which accounts for more than 50% of the variance in childhood psychopathology (Caspi et al., 2020). This understanding moves beyond viewing comorbidity as a diagnostic nuisance and underscores the importance of transdiagnostic approaches such as MBT-C. Rather than prematurely narrowing the focus to specific diagnostic categories, MBT-C is uniquely suited to addressing the wide range of clinical challenges faced by families and children in real-world settings, offering unparalleled generalizability.

Parent collaboration in MBT-C is not only psychoeducational but also therapeutic. By helping parents overcome distortions or inhibitions in their mentalizing about their child, the therapy enhances the child's own mentalizing development. The dialectical model of self-development underpinning MBT-C suggests that when parents can see their child as an intentional being, this clarity profoundly supports the child's mentalizing capacity (Fonagy et al., 2007). This raises a compelling question: Could adult therapies also be more effective if key relationships were integrated into the therapeutic process to support the recovery of balanced mentalizing?

THE DETRIMENTAL EFFECTS OF CHILDHOOD ADVERSITY

Over the past decade, mentalizing has emerged as a central framework in developmental psychopathology (Fonagy et al., 2024), particularly in addressing transdiagnostic vulnerabilities such as childhood maltreatment. Early adversities are among the most significant environmental risk factors for lifelong mental illness, with far-reaching impacts on functioning, including prolonged susceptibility to poor physical health (Bellis et al., 2019) and mental disorders (Cicchetti, 2016; Danielsdottir et al., 2024; DePasquale et al., 2019; Gilbert et al., 2009). These adversities are consistently linked to earlier onset of symptoms, greater severity of challenges, and diminished treatment responses (Nelson et al., 2020).

The disruption of the parent–child relationship is a common thread in all maltreatment experiences, affecting emotional behaviors and shared pathways that extend to other domains, such as academic performance. Despite the diversity of maltreatment types, children perceive these experiences in relatively uniform ways. A comprehensive umbrella review by Coughlan et al. (2023) examined 570 effect sizes across 11 million participants, confirming evidence of equifinality (different forms of maltreatment leading to similar outcomes) and multifinality (a single form of maltreatment leading to various outcomes; Coughlan et al., 2023). The review identified the severity of maltreatment, rather than its specific type, as the critical factor. This underscores the importance of focusing on the disruptions that maltreatment causes, particularly in interpersonal and affective domains, and their implications for physical and mental health problems.

Childhood maltreatment also profoundly impacts social experiences, extending beyond mental health to difficulties in forming and maintaining social bonds. A major study of more than 150,000 participants found that individuals reporting maltreatment during childhood experienced greater loneliness and social isolation in adulthood (Hanlon et al., 2020). These disruptions affect well-being and impede the chain of social communication necessary for cultural transmission, contributing to what has been described as "epistemic dysfunction." This dysfunction mediates and moderates the long-term consequences of maltreatment by impairing trust and disrupting the processes of social learning governed by epistemic trust.

MBT-C directly addresses the social challenges faced by children who have experienced early adversity. If there is a common pathway linking adverse childhood experiences to mental disorders, it likely lies in the challenges such adversity creates for the development of mentalizing. Studies have found significant mentalizing impairments among children with histories of sexual abuse (Ensink, Bégin, Normandin, & Fonagy, 2017; Ensink, Normandin, et al., 2014). A systematic review and meta-analysis confirmed this association but noted the heterogeneity of findings (Yang & Huang, 2024). Substantial evidence supports the role of mentalizing as a mediator between adversity and posttrauma symptoms, including posttraumatic stress (Ensink et al., 2023), posttraumatic stress disorder (Ensink et al., 2023; Huang et al., 2020), dissociation (Wagner-Skacel et al., 2022), identity diffusion (Penner et al., 2019), general psychopathology (Martin-Gagnon et al., 2023), and personality disorders (Chiesa & Fonagy, 2014; Sharp & Vanwoerden, 2015).

The rationale for MBT-C includes its capacity to address a range of mentalization challenges. Impaired mentalizing carries significant costs, making it harder for children to distinguish who can be trusted and undermining their ability to engage in social learning. This is perhaps the most compelling justification for a MBT approach for children. They have so much to learn, and profound difficulties in mentalizing can prevent them from recognizing trustworthy sources of knowledge, thereby obstructing their socialization into the world they inhabit.

Although this guide focuses on treating children with mental health problems, its broader mission is to improve the quality of mentalizing in children, enhancing their ability to adapt to an increasingly complex social world. By strengthening children's mentalizing capacities, MBT-C not only addresses mental health challenges but also equips children to fully benefit from the rich social and educational opportunities that shape their development and future.

THE DETRIMENTAL EFFECTS OF PARENTS WITH MENTALIZING IMPAIRMENTS

Accumulating evidence indicates that a parent's capacity to mentalize moderates the impact of their own childhood abuse and neglect on their children's development. For instance, sexually abused mothers with strong mentalization abilities related to their trauma were better able to break intergenerational cycles of sexual abuse (Borelli et al., 2019). A Canadian study of 111 mothers found that childhood abuse and neglect in their own history predicted developmental challenges in their children, mediated by impairments in maternal reflective function. Notably, mothers with higher capacities to mentalize their own trauma were less likely to expose their children to sexual abuse (Garon-Bissonnette et al., 2022).

Clear examples of intergenerational transmission also come from studies involving individuals diagnosed with borderline personality disorder. A large community study of nearly 400 adults (average age 66) with a history of maltreatment and borderline personality disorder pathology revealed key findings: The transmission of maltreatment was tied not to specific types of abuse but rather to broader adverse experiences; there was a homotypic association between parental emotional neglect and similar experiences reported by their offspring; and, most importantly, parental borderline traits mediated the relationship between childhood maltreatment in one generation and maltreatment in the next. These traits increased the likelihood of offspring maltreating their own children (Paul et al., 2019).

In recent years, mentalization-based interventions have been developed specifically for foster, adoptive, and residential care settings. Many focus on enhancing caregivers' reflective functioning (Adkins et al., 2022; Downes et al., 2022; Midgley, Irvine, et al., 2021; Midgley, Sprecher, & Sleed, 2021). Others aim to educate residential care staff, equipping them with mentalization-based tools to support the children in their care (Domon-Archambault et al., 2020; Hagelquist et al., 2023; Jacobsen et al., 2015). Although the quality of evaluations varies, findings consistently support the hypothesis that improving caregiver mentalizing capacities can positively affect both children and adults, potentially interrupting intergenerational cycles of maltreatment.

MBT-C may be especially beneficial for children who are developing mentalizing skills but whose progress is halted by the challenges this emerging capacity creates. For some children, understanding human motivation "in the raw" can be overwhelming, especially when they lack the emotional armor—such as robust affect regulation—to cope with the discovery of malevolence or hostility in others. This biological or experiential vulnerability can lead to an emotional response that undermines their capacity to understand others, leaving them increasingly vulnerable to misinterpret intentions and beliefs. Neither biology nor social context alone suffices as a cause; rather, the failure of mentalizing represents a "mind in body" failure.

Importantly, MBT-C offers an opportunity to disrupt the pattern of parent blaming that persists among some psychotherapists. Mentalizing is inherently intersubjective: We find our own mind reflected in others' thoughts and feelings about us. Responsibility is shared across the parent–child dyad. If a child, for biological or experiential reasons, hides their mind from their parent, the parent's apparent failure to mentalize cannot be seen as a fault. Yet, this limited understanding of their child puts the child at a disadvantage, depriving them of the critical experience of being understood. Children contribute significantly to shaping the quality of their environment, and parents of children predisposed to be "difficult" or "unavailable" require support to break the vicious cycle of unmentalized relationships.

MBT-C provides a framework to help children make their minds available while equipping parents to take an active interest in their child's mental state. This dynamic fosters a relationship in which the child internalizes the parent's understanding, using it to develop a self-sustaining capacity for mentalizing. By addressing both the child's and parent's roles in the relationship, MBT-C offers a powerful means of breaking cycles of adversity and fostering healthier developmental trajectories.

WHY THIS GUIDE TO TREATMENT?

I have presented four reasons why MBT-C is valuable. Now let me explain why you should read and treasure this book. One of the most admirable aspects of this book is how the authors' commitment to understanding different perspectives is reflected in its design. Written in an engaging style, the book employs a series of fictional case studies to introduce the various elements of the MBT-C model, such as assessment, parent work, and working with endings. These case studies vividly portray the messy reality of therapeutic practice, with theory woven in as a reflective tool. The approach allows readers to consider the therapist's choices, their grounding in the MBT model, and their practical applications.

This second edition, building on developments in MBT theory (Fonagy et al., 2022), places an even greater emphasis on the cultural contexts of parenting and their influence on work in MBT-C. The authors' extensive experience in training thousands of clinicians shines through in their elaboration of the assessment process, particularly their guidance on integrating structured assessment tools into clinical practice. These refinements reflect the authors' deep understanding of the complexities of working with children and families.

The message is simple yet profound: MBT-C is a therapeutic approach with immense promise, and this book is the definitive guide to its implementation. Although the first edition was excellent, this updated version is sharper, deeper, and more focused, making it an invaluable resource for practitioners. Its style and presentation mirror the therapeutic approach itself: friendly, accepting, insightful, and, ultimately, profoundly helpful. For anyone seeking to implement MBT-C, this guide is indispensable.

—Peter Fonagy, Professor,
University College London, London, United Kingdom

ACKNOWLEDGMENTS

We would like to thank the editorial team at the American Psychological Association, especially Susan Reynolds, Emily Ekle, and Beth Hatch, for steering this book through from conception to publication (and the creation of a second edition!) so expertly. The anonymous reviewers of the manuscript for the American Psychological Association made a range of helpful suggestions, which helped us to "see ourselves from the outside" and modify the text with our readers' needs better held in mind. Clare Farrar at University College London (UCL) provided invaluable help with referencing!

All of us would like to thank the many talented individuals who have contributed to the development of mentalization-based treatment—a wide range of practitioners from around the world, including Peter Fonagy, whose contribution is reflected in the huge number of references we have made to his work and who generously wrote the preface to this book.

We also thank all the families we have worked with, who share their pain, trust, and hopefulness in the context of this work. The photograph of "Belinda's" calendar in Chapter 10 is taken from a child seen at YOUZ (formally known as DeJutters CAMHS) Clinic in the Netherlands and is reproduced with permission. The painting in Chapter 7 by Ruth Zuilhof was created especially for this book.

Karin Ensink would like to thank Peter Fonagy and Mary Target for giving her the opportunity to learn about the development and assessment of mentalization in children. She would also like to thank Lina Normandin for many years of collaboration and elaborating clinical research and interventions focusing on mentalization in children and parents, especially in the context of trauma.

Karin Lindqvist would like to thank the Erica Foundation in Stockholm, and especially the members of the mentalization-based treatment for children

(MBT-C) team, including Jan-Olov Karlsson, Anders Schiöler, and Helena Vesterlund, as well as Agneta Thorén for her contributions to research on MBT-C.

Norka Malberg would like to thank her colleagues in Spain, Latin America, Norway, Poland, Finland, and Australia for the support and enthusiasm they have shown for the MBT-C model throughout the years. Teaching and supervising in diverse cultural settings has enriched the MBT-C model and also strengthened her conviction of its value.

Nick Midgley would like to thank Mary Target and his many colleagues (and former colleagues) at University College London and Anna Freud, who have worked together on the development of mentalization-based treatment for children and young people, as well as the international collaborators who have so enriched the journey. He also offers his thanks to the staff at the Parliament Hill Cafe for keeping him caffeinated while working on the manuscript!

Nicole Muller would like to thank her old team at CAMHS YOUZ and her current colleagues at Centrum Hecht, Holland, especially Masja Juffermans, Merlijn Rutten, and Hanneke van Aalst with whom she has been teaching about MBT-C for many years.

A version of Chapter 5 was first delivered as a lecture by Nick Midgley on "The mentalizing stance in working with children" at a symposium in Lucerne, Switzerland, in 2015. We thank Roland Muller, who organized the symposium and gave helpful feedback.

An earlier version of Chapter 6 was first published in 2015 as an article by Nicole Muller and Nick Midgley, "Approaches to Assessment in Time-Limited Mentalization-Based Therapy for Children (MBT-C)," in *Frontiers in Psychology*, Volume 6. This is an open access journal whose articles are distributed under the terms of the Creative Commons Attribution License.

MENTALIZATION-BASED TREATMENT FOR CHILDREN
A TIME-LIMITED APPROACH

Introduction

Why We Developed Time-Limited Mentalization-Based Treatment for Children

It has been estimated that, at any one time, almost 15% of children and adolescents around the world are suffering from a mental health disorder (Bruha et al., 2018). Among the most common mental health difficulties in children are conduct problems, antisocial behavior, attention-deficit/hyperactivity disorder, depression, and anxiety—with emotional disorders more common in girls and behavior problems more common in boys. As Hagell and Maughan (2017) pointed out, such mental health problems "have important implications for every aspect of young people's lives including their ability to engage with education, make and keep friends, engage in constructive family relationships and find their own way in the world" (p. 28). We might add that they therefore have important implications for family members, friends, schools, and wider society.

Although there are now a wide range of evidence-based treatments available for children and families, a significant proportion of children still either drop out of therapy or are not able to make use of the treatments available (Fonagy et al., 2015). Moreover, many of the evidence-based treatments have been developed for very specific populations, making it unrealistic for child therapists to be trained in a vast assortment of treatment models relevant to the extensive array of presenting problems that may bring children to child mental health services. Paradoxically, faced by the many manualized therapies for specific childhood disorders, an increasingly narrow range of approaches are actually made available to children and families, with many child mental health services primarily offering interventions based on a cognitive behavioral therapy (CBT) approach.

https://doi.org/10.1037/0000486-001
Mentalization-Based Treatment for Children: A Time-Limited Approach, Second Edition, by N. Midgley, K. Ensink, K. Lindqvist, N. Malberg, and N. Muller
Copyright © 2026 by the American Psychological Association. All rights reserved.

Although CBT has a good evidence base for a range of childhood disorders (Stallard, 2022) and has clearly benefited many children and families, a "one-size-fits-all" approach is always dangerous, especially when the evidence suggests that client choice and preference should be at the heart of all good clinical practice. Moreover, many practitioners have had experiences where parents and children have difficulties using the kind of strategies that may be offered to manage their problems more effectively, often because they do not have the affect regulation skills or capacity to make use of guidance that is a prerequisite for benefiting from such therapeutic approaches (e.g., Scott & Dadds, 2009).

We hope that the approach described in this book therefore fills an important gap by offering a short-term, focused intervention for school-age children (roughly age 5–12), which not only draws on traditional psychodynamic principles but also integrates them with the findings from attachment theory, the empirical study of mentalization, as well as features of other evidence-based approaches.

In the remainder of this introductory chapter, we define and conceptualize mentalization, explain how mentalization-based treatment (MBT) was developed and adapted for children, and present an overview of this book.

DEFINING MENTALIZATION

The term *mentalization* has emerged as a key concept in the world of psychotherapy since being used in an article written by Peter Fonagy (1991), which sets out a new way of thinking about borderline states of mind in adults. Fonagy referred to "the achievement of a representation of mental events," which he noted had been referred to in the psychoanalytic literature as the "capacity for symbolization." This term, he suggested, had become "over-burdened with meanings, particularly in psychoanalysis" (p. 641). So, he proposed: "For the sake of brevity I would like to label the capacity to conceive of conscious and unconscious mental states in oneself and others as the capacity to *mentalize*" (p. 641, italics in original).

In other words, *mentalization* refers to the ability to "make sense of" and interpret the meaning of others' behavior by considering their underlying mental states and intentions. In addition, it involves the capacity to understand our own emotional reactions and their impact on others (Bateman et al., 2023). In simpler language, mentalizing is about understanding oneself and others on the basis of what is going on inside us; it involves seeing oneself from the outside and others from the inside. Mentalizing is particularly important because it facilitates interpersonal interactions and supports self and emotional regulation.

Indeed, when we are mentalizing well, we are likely to be able to

- have an awareness of what we are feeling as well as a sense of our personalities or qualities as people, which helps us have a sense of how we "look from the outside" to others, so that it is, in turn, easier to understand their reactions to us;

- have a solid ability to consider the emotions and motivations of others and see their reactions and behaviors from this perspective;
- have some awareness of the limits of our ability to know what is in the minds of others;
- have curiosity about how the world looks from other people's perspectives and how our own perspective may influence what we do or color how we see someone else's behavior; and
- be mindful that we might get it wrong when we try to understand why others behave in the way they do and that trying to make sense of these misunderstandings can enrich our interpersonal relationships.

When we are able to make sense of the behaviors of others (and ourselves), the interpersonal world becomes a more predictable, safe, and meaningful place. But when we misread the intentions of others, or struggle to make sense of our own internal states, this can lead to confusion, misunderstanding, and difficulties in interpersonal relating, contributing to escalating conflict or bottled up anger and fear. How we interpret why people are behaving in the way they do has a huge impact on the way we think and behave.

We see how, as Fonagy et al. (2002) put it, mentalization is central to the sense of self and emotion regulation. Being able to mentalize, even in a fairly stressful situation, helps a person to stay emotionally regulated. It helps them make sense of a stressful situation, so they can see it in perspective and remain focused on the priorities. J. G. Allen and Fonagy (2006) described this function of mentalizing as like having a pause button, which can be used to help regulate our emotional reactions. As Fonagy and Allison (2014) noted, the stakes are highest in close interpersonal relationships, especially attachment relationships in which general emotional understanding is not enough and a more nuanced understanding of others, as well as of our own feelings and personalities and the impact of this on others, can have important implications for the quality of these relationships.

THE DEVELOPMENT OF MENTALIZATION-BASED TREATMENT

What began in 1991 as a term used for "the sake of brevity" has taken off in a spectacular fashion in the years since those words were written. In a 2013 review article about MBT (Bateman & Fonagy, 2013), the authors note with evident pride that the use of the term "mentalizing" in titles and abstracts of scientific papers on the Web of Science increased from 10 in 1991 to 2,750 in 2011, with a whole range of authors now using the term, "from psychoanalysts to neuroscientists, from child development researchers to geneticists, from existential philosophers to phenomenologists" (Bateman & Fonagy, 2013, p. 595). Although the figures since 2013 are not available, it is likely that the number has continued to rise exponentially.

The 1991 article situates the development of the concept of mentalizing at the interface of a number of domains, including research on theory of mind (Premack & Woodruff, 1978) and attachment and reflective functioning (Fonagy et al., 1991). But it is perhaps best known as a development in the clinical sphere and, in particular, a way of approaching the treatment of borderline personality disorder (BPD), which Fonagy and Bateman came to reconceptualize as "a disorder of mentalizing" (Bateman & Fonagy, 2004). From the early 1990s, Bateman and Fonagy began to describe certain modifications to the technique of psychodynamic therapy that would follow from a focus on the capacity to mentalize, leading them to finally propose a new model of therapy for adults with BPD: MBT (Bateman & Fonagy, 2004). Since this key article on MBT was published, the approach has come to be seen primarily as a model of treatment for adults with BPD, which, in its development, was strongly influenced by research in the fields of attachment, social cognition, and (to a lesser extent) neuroscience. But in recent years, modifications of MBT for work with children and families have also taken place (Midgley & Vrouva, 2012; Volkert et al., 2022). Many of the early approaches focused on open-ended or longer term interventions, often targeted at children with severe histories of neglect and maltreatment and explicitly integrating mentalizing approaches with psychodynamic child therapy (A. J. E. Verheugt-Pleiter et al., 2008). Developments in MBT have also taken place for both younger and older children, including mentalization-based interventions for parents and infants, adolescents, and families (Byrne et al., 2020) as well as in schools and children's social care settings (Midgley, Sprecher, & Sleed, 2021). Empirical studies examining what therapists actually do in the consulting room (looking beyond the brand name of therapy) have demonstrated how promoting mentalizing is a feature of psychodynamic therapy, CBT with children, and play therapy (Goodman et al., 2015, 2016). Given the links between attachment, trauma, and mentalizing (see Chapter 2), it is not surprising that a number of interesting developments have also taken place exploring how ideas about mentalizing can helpfully inform work with children in the context of fostering and adoption (for a review, see Midgley, Sprecher, & Sleed, 2021).

Although seen as an adaptation of MBT work with adults, clinical work with children can also be viewed as having played an important role in the development of MBT and should not be considered as only an "adaptation" of MBT to a new clinical field (Midgley, 2024). As early as 1966, Anna Freud herself recognized that using traditional child analytic techniques for treating children with "developmental disturbances" was likely to be unsuccessful, and she called for new developments in the technique of child analysis (Freud, 1966). She gave her clinical staff at the Hampstead Child Therapy Clinic (renamed the Anna Freud Centre after her death) considerable freedom to experiment with different ways of working with these complex cases, resulting in the groundbreaking papers on technique with borderline children written by her colleagues Rosenfeld and Sprince in the early 1960s (Rosenfeld & Sprince, 1965). Following Anna Freud's death in 1982, Fonagy, Moran, Bleiberg, Target, and others continued this strand of work, demonstrating how the lack of a fully formed theory of mind can underlie the kind of developmental disturbances that are so common in referrals to child mental health services, and they offered the outlines of a clinical approach to child treatment under the umbrella term of "psychodynamic developmental therapy" (Fonagy & Target, 1996).

In their 1998 article on the changing aims of child analysis, Fonagy and Target focus on three elements in particular that they suggest are of particular importance in psychodynamic developmental therapy: a capacity for playfulness, a focus on enhancing reflective functioning, and the need to work in the transference. All three of these elements are elaborated on in the book edited by Anne Hurry in 1998, *Psychoanalysis and Developmental Therapy*, which along with Stanley Greenspan's work on developmentally based psychotherapy (Greenspan, 1997) is perhaps the most complete early articulation of what a mentalization-based, psychoanalytic, developmental child therapy could look like. This led to the important work by A. J. E. Verheugt-Pleiter et al. (2008; A. Verheugt-Pleiter & Zevalkink, 2021), *Mentalizing in Child Therapy*, which systematically explored how a mentalizing approach could be seen as central to the process of long-term psychodynamic psychotherapy with children. These were all elements that significantly influenced the model of time-limited mentalization-based treatment for children (MBT-C) set out in this book. (For a more detailed account of the relationship between child analysis and MBT, see Midgley, 2024.)

TIME-LIMITED MENTALIZATION-BASED TREATMENT FOR CHILDREN

The idea for developing a time-limited model of MBT for school-age children originated at a meeting in London in 2011, which brought together a range of clinicians who were interested in thinking about clinical developments of MBT for children and families. Several members of that group met again in London in the following year and for a third time in Stockholm in 2013. Working closely with colleagues in this group was the impetus for developing our thinking about MBT-C. In particular, our ideas about working in a time-limited way were influenced by the Norwegian work on time-limited developmental therapy (e.g., Haugvik & Johns, 2008; Svendsen et al., 2012). So, when the American Psychological Association offered us an opportunity to write a book about MBT for children, five members of the original working group came together, drawing on our experience in a number of clinical settings and in close collaboration with each of our clinical teams, to develop and describe a model of time-limited MBT-C in a form that we hope can speak to child therapists from a range of clinical and conceptual backgrounds, applicable to work in a range of settings with a wide variety of children and parents.

In their foreword to the 2006 publication of the *Handbook of Mentalization-Based Treatment*, Allen and Fonagy wrote,

> In advocating mentalization-based treatment we claim no innovation. On the contrary, mentalization-based treatment is the least novel therapeutic approach

> imaginable: it addresses the bedrock human capacity to apprehend mind as such. Holding mind in mind is as ancient as human relatedness and self-awareness. (p. ixx)

Although this statement might be seen as somewhat disingenuous, there is no doubt that much of what has been described as MBT will be familiar to therapists coming from a range of different backgrounds—perhaps especially those, like us, who have trained in the psychodynamic tradition. At the same time, we do believe that some new ideas have crept in, whether deliberately or accidentally. When running MBT training at the Anna Freud Centre in London, Dickon Bevington added a typically playful addendum to Allen and Fonagy's statement, warning: "This product may contain traces of originality. These are only trace contaminants, occurring as part of the production process, and should not spoil your enjoyment of the product."

In this book, we describe an approach to working therapeutically in a time-limited way with children, which we hope will be both familiar and common-sensical while at the same time offering clinicians a few "traces" of originality that we hope will add something of value to the child therapist's toolbox. We describe the work as a "treatment guide" because we set out a particular model of treatment, but one that can be adapted and fitted to the local contexts in which therapists are working and which can be flexible enough to be of use when working with children presenting with a range of difficulties.

By focusing on a core capacity that may promote resilience in a wide range of children, with a variety of presenting problems, MBT-C aims to be a generic therapy that can be adapted to the particular needs of a range of children in middle childhood—roughly between the ages of 5 and 12. MBT-C as described in this book is a time-limited, focused intervention that draws on fundamental psychodynamic and attachment principles but which can be easily integrated and used alongside a range of psychosocial treatments. The overall aim of MBT-C is to promote mentalizing and resilience in such a way that the family and child are better equipped to tackle the problems that first brought them to therapy. In doing this, MBT-C aims to increase the child's capacity for emotional regulation and support parents to best meet the emotional needs of their children.

The basic MBT-C time-limited model is 12 individual sessions, with separate meetings for the parent(s) offered alongside it. Although some therapists may view short-term and time-limited therapies as a "necessary evil" in the era of managed care, a significant body of research has suggested that short-term interventions in child mental health can be effective (McLaughlin et al., 2013), including short-term psychodynamic interventions (Midgley, Mortimer, et al., 2021). Time-limited work, when effective, is clearly in the interests of children and families because it allows children to return to their daily lives without too much disruption. Nevertheless, there are some children for whom a brief intervention may not be indicated. In certain cases, where a longer-term intervention is appropriate (e.g., for those children whose early relational trauma or attachment insecurity makes trusting an adult a real challenge), it is possible to offer up to three "blocks" of 12 MBT-C sessions (i.e., up to a maximum of 36 sessions). These additional blocks of treatment are based on a review process that weighs up the pros and cons of additional treatment. In these cases, the treatment is never open-ended but rather continues to be time limited, with a clear focus and aims.

Like all mentalization-based interventions, the fundamental aim of MBT-C is to enhance skills in mentalizing, both in the parent and in the child. For both parents and children, this would include opportunities not only to practice good mentalizing but also to pay attention to the places where mentalizing breaks down or to work on areas where there are deficits in the capacity to mentalize. Such a focus is justified by the fact that research is increasingly demonstrating that the capacity to mentalize contributes to a positive sense of self, healthy relationships, and better emotional regulation (Kumpasoğlu et al., 2025). Targeting such capacities is likely to be of value to children (and their parents) with a range of presenting problems, even if the underlying mental health disorder is not "caused" by a failure of mentalization.

As the above description implies, the focus of MBT-C is more on process than on content: The aim is not primarily for either parent or child to gain insight into their difficulties or to develop an understanding of where their difficulties may have come from; rather, it is to enhance their capacity to use their mentalizing capacity to manage emotions and relationships and to increase the child's capacity to make use of relationships for emotional learning. As such, the ultimate aim of MBT-C is to help the child to make better use of helping relationships after the therapy has ended and for the parents to be better equipped to support their child's development outside and beyond therapy.

WHAT IS NEW IN THIS EDITION?

The first edition of this book was published in 2017 and drew its inspiration from a number of different settings and contexts, building on work being done by the authors in clinics in the United Kingdom, Europe, Scandinavia, and North America. What we shared was a background and training in psychodynamic therapy with children, and all had been influenced by the development of MBT work that has taken place at the Anna Freud Centre in London and elsewhere in the United States and Europe. But the contexts in which we had developed our ideas were somewhat different, and the approach described in this book tried to provide a synthesis of what we (and the teams that we had each been part of) had learned.

This second edition builds on the original work in a number of ways. We have updated and integrated new developments in both MBT theory and research, including greater attention to the role of epistemic trust and how cultural differences can be thought about in time-limited MBT-C. We have included a number of new assessment tools that we hope will be of benefit to practitioners, and we have expanded (and split into two chapters) the section on direct work with children to reflect emerging thinking about this core aspect of the model. This includes more explicit attention to how MBT-C therapists can work with the "building blocks" of mentalizing: attention control and emotion regulation. We are also delighted to be able to add a new chapter on the empirical evidence for MBT with school-age children. Although still a new field, this is an area that has developed significantly since the first edition was published, and it is exciting to be able to share the findings of the first clinical trial of time-limited MBT-C for children with emotional and behavioral difficulties.

In working on a second edition of the book, we drew not only on the exponential increase in research about mentalizing, early development, and psychotherapy that has been published in the past 10 years but also on the experience we have gained in running training for practitioners based on the time-limited MBT-C model, including in parts of the world such as East Asia and South America, which have expanded our understanding of MBT in different cultural contexts. In presenting this updated account of MBT-C, we acknowledge the vital input we have had from colleagues working in each of our teams, and around the world, in developing and sharpening our thinking.

AN OUTLINE OF THIS BOOK

This book is divided into two parts: the first primarily theoretical and empirical, the second mostly clinical. Readers who are already familiar with the concept of mentalization and the empirical and developmental research around it may wish to skip the first part of the book. However, even for those whose interest is purely clinical, we would encourage you to engage with the theoretical section first. After all, MBT is based on the idea that learning a set of behaviors (e.g., mentalization-promoting therapeutic techniques) is not sufficient in itself; rather, what is important is the intentions that inform those behaviors—intentions that ultimately depend on a way of thinking about the world—in other words, theory. For this reason, Chapter 1 provides an overview of the concept of mentalizing, specifically focusing on mentalization in children and what we might expect to see during middle childhood. In Chapter 2, we describe the situations in which a child's mentalizing might be underdeveloped, or how to recognize when mentalizing has broken down. We offer some thoughts on the links between these mentalizing difficulties and the kind of clinical problems that often bring children and families to seek help. Chapter 3 summarizes the empirical support for MBT. These first three chapters are intended to offer a conceptual background to the model of time-limited MBT-C that is described in the remaining parts of the book.

The second part of the book presents clinical guidance for providing MBT-C. Chapter 4 provides a general introduction to time-limited MBT-C, setting out the basic model and the framework and outlining who may be suitable for this way of working. Chapter 5 presents the "mentalizing stance" as a foundation for all the clinical work in MBT-C, whether in working with children or their parents. Chapter 6 describes the process of assessment of children in MBT-C, discussing aspects especially relevant to assessment from a mentalizing perspective as well as the practicalities of the assessment of both child and parents. Chapters 7 and 8 describe the therapeutic interventions used in the direct work with children, including interventions focused on supporting the "building blocks" of mentalization (Chapter 7) and interventions focused more on explicit mentalizing and breakdowns in mentalizing (Chapter 8). Chapter 9 describes clinical work with parents from an MBT-C perspective. Chapter 10 explains how to work toward ending treatment, and Chapter 11 presents a case study illustrating a complete case in time-limited MBT-C. The concluding chapter provides some final thoughts on possible future developments for MBT-C.

This book is a guide for clinicians rather than a full treatment manual, and it is intended to be used flexibly according to the setting and contexts in which the reader may work. Throughout the book, we make use of clinical vignettes, which we hope will help the reader to get a sense of how the MBT-C model looks in practice. These vignettes are based on composite cases, which draw on our clinical experience but which do not describe actual children or families. Although using such fictionalized cases always comes with the risk that the work can be presented in an idealized form and that the messy reality of clinical practice can be airbrushed out, we have made an effort not to present these as examples of "perfect" therapy but rather to portray usual clinical practice with all its imperfections and improvisations.

THEORETICAL FRAMEWORK AND EVIDENCE BASE

1

The Development of Mentalizing

This chapter introduces mentalizing and the role it plays in the early development of the child. We draw on developmental research to demonstrate how the capacity to mentalize emerges across the course of childhood and early adolescence. We outline the development of children's understanding of self and others as intentional mental agents and use empirical research to show the importance of this for emotional well-being and mental health. Because this book focuses on middle childhood (roughly between the ages of 5 and 12), we try to set out the particular features of mentalizing at this stage of life and attempt to address some common questions that clinicians may have about mentalizing. In doing so, we hope this chapter will provide a conceptual foundation for the model of time-limited mentalization-based treatment for children that is set out in the later chapters of this book.

MENTALIZATION, SOCIAL COGNITION, AND THEORY OF MIND

As we have set out in the introduction to this book, the modern use of the term *mentalizing* owes much to the work of Peter Fonagy, Antony Bateman, Mary Target, and their colleagues, who, since the 1990s, have made a unique contribution in pulling together diverse lines of inquiry and bridging the divides across disciplines to develop an integrated, developmentally based model of mentalization. This emerged out of work on understanding the process of change in child psychoanalysis (Fonagy & Target, 1998; Midgley, 2024) and developments in the treatment of adults with borderline personality disorder (Bateman & Fonagy, 2004). Although we sometimes feel that the term is not always easy to explain to

https://doi.org/10.1037/0000486-002
Mentalization-Based Treatment for Children: A Time-Limited Approach, Second Edition, by N. Midgley, K. Ensink, K. Lindqvist, N. Malberg, and N. Muller
Copyright © 2026 by the American Psychological Association. All rights reserved.

children and families, the oddness of the word *mentalizing* can be helpful as a way of "marking" this capacity as something that we try to focus on in therapy.

Those who are familiar with developmental research literature may ask us how the concept of mentalization relates to terms such as "theory of mind," "mind-mindedness," or even "social cognition," and there is indeed a lot of overlap between these different concepts. In particular, the terms mentalization and reflective function are often used interchangeably, although reflective function was initially considered to refer to the verbal expression of mentalizing, since assessment of mentalization is sometimes based on narratives regarding attachment relationships (see Appendix A). In this book, we use *reflective functioning* to refer to the capacity to mentalize, especially explicit mentalizing—that is, the conscious ability to stop and reflect on the states of mind of self and other.

DIMENSIONS OF MENTALIZING

Mentalizing contains within it a number of dimensions that can be helpful to disentangle when working clinically (Luyten, Malcorps, et al., 2019). There are two that we have found especially helpful when thinking about our work with children: the difference between implicit (or automatic) and explicit (or controlled) mentalizing and the difference between the mentalizing of self and other.

First, mentalization has both implicit/automatic and explicit/controlled dimensions. Most of the time, mentalization goes on automatically, without us needing to put things into words. Without consciously thinking about it, we infer people's mental states, often based on the expressions in the eye regions of the face, and feel that we know when they seem to be angry, happy, sad, frightened, interested, or bored. From an evolutionary perspective, rapid processing of social information was essential in identifying whether others were potential friends whom we could cooperate with to increase the chances of success in complex tasks and survival or potential foes who were a threat to our security. Speed of processing is of essence where detection of threat is concerned because it is a matter of life and death, but this automatic processing has the disadvantage of being based on, and therefore biased by, previous experience. It is not adapted for more complex social situations in which slower consideration and figuring out possible motives are necessary to make accurate inferences. Neuroscience researchers have studied this kind of automatic, implicit mentalizing and found that it seems to be subserved by a set of brain circuits that rely primarily on sensory information and that, from an evolutionary perspective, are quite primitive (Luyten & Fonagy, 2015b). These include the amygdala, basal ganglia, and the dorsal anterior cingulate cortex, all of which are primarily involved in rapid detection of threats and social information related to the fight-or-flight response.

Although our implicit or automatic mentalizing may be quick and agile, it may not always be accurate. Considering that automatic mentalizing is largely based on prior experience, when past experiences have been overwhelmingly negative, this processing tends to be negatively biased. In these cases, past experience suggests that a high level of vigilance toward potential threat is needed and that it is potentially dangerous to trust others. However, this is unlikely to be appropriate in social contexts of low threat. There are times when children may feel suspicious and have a sense, for example, that someone might be trying to trick them, and they will need to stop and consider whether that judgment is correct. In other words, there are times when we may need to make use of more explicit mentalizing, a process that requires more conscious and explicit reflection on the emotions, thoughts, and intentions of others. Interestingly, neuroscientists suggest that this capacity is subserved by newer brain circuits, which are more linked with symbolic and linguistic processing, such as the lateral prefrontal cortex and the medial prefrontal cortex (Luyten & Fonagy, 2015b). These are parts of the brain that are commonly activated by tasks involving reasoning, effortful control, and perspective taking. Such processes may be slower than the more automatic modes of mentalizing, but they make it possible for us to more carefully and deliberately make attributions about the emotions, thoughts, and feelings of self and others. This allows us to consider whether our immediate reactions are actually warranted after we have considered the situation, and then we can override or adjust our first impressions to be in line with these reflections.

We often make use of more controlled or explicit mentalizing when there has been a difficult situation that demands some kind of active reflection to help make sense of it. Although this often involves trying to mentalize others—that is, make sense of what mental states are behind someone else's behavior—mentalizing also takes place in relation to the self. Sometimes, it is important to turn the mentalizing capacity inwards and be curious: "What made me behave in this way at this moment? Why am I feeling like this after what has just happened?" The capacity to explicitly mentalize about one's own thoughts and feelings is an essential part of managing relationships and modulating one's own emotional responses.

When children show no evidence of mentalizing or only think about themselves and others in physical and behavioral terms, this is obviously a cause for concern. As a broad guideline, we ideally hope to see school-age children show a basic understanding of themselves, others, and relationships in mental-state terms (what the Reflective Functioning Scale refers to as Level 4 or 5; see Table 1.1). If a child shows some capacity to identify feelings or mental states (Level 3), this is an indication that they could benefit from additional help in elaborating a more solid, even if incomplete, mental understanding of self, others, and relationships. When a child appears to be functioning below Level 3, this could be a cause of concern in terms of them being able to use basic mentalizing to deal with the challenges of life.

FACTORS THAT PROMOTE THE CAPACITY TO MENTALIZE

Although the capacity to mentalize is partly innate, with its own biological underpinnings (Kovács et al., 2010), the development of our ability to mentalize also depends on the quality of the social learning environment

TABLE 1.1. Different Levels of Child Reflective Functioning

Level	Description
−1	Bizarre, disorganized response in which mentalizing is actively avoided or there is an aggressive refusal to mentalize: *When Mom gets cross? There is an angel dancing on her shoe.*
0	Absence of mentalization: *I don't know, it just is.*
1	Descriptions in terms of physical or behavioral nonmental characteristics: *Mom says, "Go to your room."*
3	Unelaborated references to mental states when describing relationships: *I like it. It's fun.*
4	References to mental states but with gaps that have to be filled in: *When I feel sad, my Mom like ... comforts me.*
5	Clear description showing a solid mental-state understanding, even if fairly simple: *When Mom gets angry, she shouts, and I don't like it, but I know she doesn't really mean what she says and that I am a little bit to blame.*
7–9	Increasingly sophisticated mental-state understanding, with "9" denoting exceptional mental-state understanding: *When Dad gets angry, I also get angry at first, but then I feel guilty because I know he helps me a lot. And when I forget my books at school, trying to finish my homework takes much longer, and he gets tired and has work to do too.*

Note. Adapted from "Maternal and Child Reflective Functioning in the Context of Child Sexual Abuse: Pathways to Depression and Externalising Difficulties," by K. Ensink, M. Bégin, L. Normandin, and P. Fonagy, 2016, *European Journal of Psychotraumatology, 7*, p. 4. Copyright 2016 by Karin Ensink, Michaël Bégin, Lina Normandin, and Peter Fonagy. Adapted with permission.

and attachment relationships in which we are raised. In their major work, *Affect Regulation, Mentalization and the Development of the Self,* Fonagy et al. (2002) proposed a developmental model in which awareness of mental states emerges in the context of early attachment relationships. Because infants are born without their own capacity to reestablish emotional regulation when faced with distress, they rely on their caregivers to help them regulate when they are frightened or overwhelmed. Through this process of dyadic regulation, in which parents repeatedly help the infants to reestablish self-regulation, children gradually learn to regulate themselves (Trevarthen et al., 2006). Because they are unable to articulate their feelings and distress, infants and young children depend on their parent's interest in their subjective experience and their capacity to make the child's behavior meaningful by interpreting it in terms of underlying mental states. Reflective functioning is seen as underlying sensitive responding by helping parents to imagine the infant's experience (Fonagy & Target, 1997).

Fonagy et al. (2002) showed how children learn to identify and mentally represent their own affects through the parent's interest in the child's subjective experience and the parent's emotional displays focusing on the child's mind and feelings. In this model, the parent's capacity to imagine the subjective experience of their infant or young child is considered to facilitate the development of emotion regulation and self-control.

NATURAL PEDAGOGY AND THE EARLY ROOTS OF MENTALIZING, THE SELF, AND EPISTEMIC TRUST

One of the questions that has intrigued both developmental researchers and clinicians is the ways in which parents communicate an interest in infants' mind and feelings and thereby help them to develop their own capacity to recognize and know their feelings and regulate emotions. From infancy onward, children are progressively building a type of autobiographical narrative of self in relation to others that is presymbolic and procedural, and involves nonverbal memories of sensory and affective experiences (Fonagy & Target, 1996). But what is the mechanism through which this development takes place?

Fonagy and colleagues drew on the work of Csibra and Gergely (2009) to propose that there are a set of recognizable ways through which caregivers transmit knowledge about the way relationships work to their offspring, known as "natural pedagogy," referring to the various means that we as humans have—in a way that is quite specific to our species—for engaging in a quite extraordinarily rapid process of social teaching and learning. But how do babies know what information is important for them, and how do parents manage to signal to their infants that what they are communicating is of importance? Csibra and Gergely suggested that we do this through a series of ostensive cues, which for parents of babies might include things such as eye contact, turn taking, and a special vocal tone ("motherese"), all of which help the infant to preferentially attend to what is being communicated. In more recent work, Fonagy and Allison (2014) suggested that these cues also serve to moderate what they called "natural epistemic vigilance"—that is, "the self-protective suspicion toward information coming from others that may be potentially damaging, deceptive or inaccurate" (p. 373). In other words, certain ways of verbal and nonverbal communicating (and, building on this, certain relationships) communicate to infants not only that this information is of value but also that the person communicating with them is someone who is trustworthy—someone they can learn from.

Although the names used for these processes may seem confusing to some, we think these concepts are valuable not only for developmental researchers but also for clinicians, as we try to demonstrate in later chapters. In particular, we find it helpful to understand how parents' contingent and congruent marked affect mirroring is central in the early development of recognition of self and affective states and self-regulation. By this, Fonagy and Allison (2014) mean the way that, in interactions with their distressed infant, parents

- partially reflect the infant's affect but at a lower level of intensity;
- fairly accurately reflect the infant's state of mind (congruent);
- reflect the infant's affect in a timely manner, after the infant's affective display (contingent); and

- mark it, for example, with an exaggerated facial display or vocalization to signal to the infant that they recognize the feeling (e.g., fear or distress) but are not experiencing it themselves in the same way.

The "marked" nature of this mirroring, which may have something of a playacting quality, is especially important. By this, Fonagy et al. (2002) were referring to the exaggerated facial expressions and vocalizations that parents intuitively use when interacting with infants that makes it clear that they are trying to describe what the infant is feeling but in a way that also communicates that it is the child's own feelings that are being shown, not the adult's. For example, when a baby starts to cry, the caregiver may respond with an exaggerated facial reaction marked with a quizzical look and accompanied with calming words that name the infant's affect and possible mental states: "You look a little sad. Are you getting tired or feeling hungry? Don't worry, it won't be long." Insofar as the infant's feelings are being "marked," it is clear that it is not the caregiver who is feeling upset or hungry.

It is frequently said that infants find themselves in the loving gaze of the mother, who sensitively picks up and mirrors the moment-to-moment changes in their affect states (Winnicott, 1967). By having their affects mirrored in this way, infants receive feedback that helps them develop basic representations of what their feelings look like, a building block for later being able to mentalize about oneself. Infants, in turn, appear exquisitely sensitive to this communication from the parent, as has been observed in microanalytic studies of mother–infant interaction (Beebe et al., 2012). Stern (2010) described this as a dance between parent and infant in which the rhythm and "feeling" of what it is like to relate is established. Some things that we take for granted, such as infants' need to be held, touched, and cuddled, may also play quite a central role in helping develop a sense of feeling comfortable and secure in one's body.

In sum, the affective core of the self (Panksepp & Biven, 2012) can be seen as constellating around these early experiences of being held (Fonagy & Target, 2007a, 2007b). Furthermore, through these early experiences, the child develops an ongoing expectation of sensitive responding from others and of epistemic trust—that is, a "willingness to consider new knowledge from another person as trustworthy, generalizable and relevant to the self " (Fonagy & Allison, 2014, p. 373). Such expectations can help to reduce our natural epistemic vigilance, so that children can open themselves to learn from those around them and turn to them when in need. The establishment of epistemic trust can be seen as a precondition for the transmission of all knowledge that is culturally transmitted.

Through repeated experiences of marked affect mirroring, children learn to recognize their feelings, first how they look and then what they are called, contributing to an early sense of self. What start as undifferentiated states of discomfort or tension become recognized as affects. At the same time, when parents mirror their infants' affect at a lower intensity, this is believed to help infants downregulate their affect until it is regulated. Insofar as infants experience themselves as initiating this interaction, they gain a sense of perceived control and agency (Fonagy et al., 2007) and gradually become less reliant on the caregiver to help them regulate, until they are no longer dependent on dyadic regulation but have internalized a pattern of self-regulation.

THE IMPORTANCE OF REFLECTIVE PARENTING AND THE PEDAGOGICAL STANCE

Reflective parenting (Cooper & Redfern, 2015) can be seen as an orientation in which the child's mind is kept in mind by their primary carers (Slade, 2005). A reflective parenting stance is implicit in interactions and might include the following features:

- a benign interest in the mind of the child and emotional availability to help the child make sense of their own reactions and those of others;
- a capacity to look past the child's behavior to determine what it communicates about their experience, feelings, and difficulties;
- a capacity to play, joke, and imagine with the child;
- a motivation to consider the meaning and sense of a child's thoughts and feelings, even if one cannot be exactly sure what is in the child's mind;
- availability to help the child put feelings into words and elaborate autobiographically meaningful narratives;
- a motivation to see the child's perspective and awareness that the child's experience may be very different from one's own;
- an ability to have a sense of one's own thoughts and feelings when interacting with the child and modulate one's own aggression; and/or
- an appreciation that one's own feelings and moods will have an impact on one's children.

Parental reflective functioning is often divided into two different aspects of mentalizing: being able to mentalize the child (i.e., reflecting on the child's inner experiences, motives, and reactions) and being able to mentalize oneself as a parent (i.e., reflecting on one's own experiences and reactions when parenting, and how this influences interactions with the child and the impact one has on the child). This second part is closely related to being able to regulate emotions when parenting and being able to modulate reactions and responses in interactions with the child. For example, self-focused mentalizing may help a parent realize that they need to control their anger because their child is becoming frightened or more dysregulated.

As with children, clinical researchers have developed a way of assessing reflective functioning in parents by using the Reflective Functioning Scale, which is used to code the Parent Development Interview (Slade et al., 2004). Using this scale, Slade and her colleagues have been able to code the way a parent speaks about their relationship with their child to assess explicit parental reflective functioning. Table 1.2 shows the different ratings that can be given (from −1 to 9) and examples of the way a parent might speak that would lead to such a rating. Although the Parent Development Interview is not a clinical tool, it can be helpful for clinicians to have this system of coding in mind when thinking about what

TABLE 1.2. Different Levels of Parental Reflective Functioning

Level	Description
−1	Bizarre, disorganized response in which mentalizing is actively avoided or there is an aggressive refusal to mentalize: Parent: *When I am talking on the phone with friends, she provokes me by running up and down, and the only thing that helps to calm her is to hit her.*
0	Absence of mentalization: Parent: *He just does it for no reason; he's just like that.*
1	Descriptions in terms of physical or behavioral nonmental characteristics: Parent: *He just keeps twirling around—he never stops.*
3	Unelaborated references to mental states when describing relationships: Parent: *He gets irritable.*
4	References to mental states but with gaps that have to be filled in: Parent: *When we are preparing for an exam and he messes around, I know it is going to take so much longer. I get so angry.*
5	Clear description showing a solid mental-state understanding, even if fairly simple: Parent: *I get angry because he loses everything—his gloves, his books—and when we arrived at school, and he had forgotten his gloves again and we had to turn back, I realized I was going to be late for work, and I lost it. But I realize that I need to find a way to help him become more responsible, and it doesn't help to shout.*
7–9	Increasingly sophisticated mental-state understanding, with "9" denoting exceptional and complete mental-state understanding: Parent: *I don't often get angry with him, but sometimes when he becomes very excited and maybe because he wants to show off in front of his friends, he behaves in a way that he would not usually, becoming defiant, and I feel a little foolish and frustrated. He does not realize that he actually risks losing his friends' respect, and it makes them feel uncomfortable. I don't know how to explain this without hurting his feelings.*

Note. Adapted from "Maternal and Child Reflective Functioning in the Context of Child Sexual Abuse: Pathways to Depression and Externalising Difficulties," by K. Ensink, M. Bégin, L. Normandin, and P. Fonagy, 2016, *European Journal of Psychotraumatology, 7*, p. 4. Copyright 2016 by Karin Ensink, Michaël Bégin, Lina Normandin, and Peter Fonagy. Adapted with permission.

good (or poor) mentalizing may look like in the way parents speak about their relationship to their child.

Fonagy et al. (1991) first proposed that mentalizing underlies sensitive parenting. Consistent with this, there is evidence that parents' reflective functioning about their attachment relationships, both past and present, underlies sensitivity in interaction with infants. Higher reflective functioning in parents is associated with fewer negative behaviors in children (Ensink, Bégin, Normandin, Biberdzic, et al., 2016; N. E. Suchman, DeCoste, Leigh, & Borelli, 2010). In an important study of intergenerational patterns of attachment, Fonagy et al. (1994) were able to show how mothers with a history of deprivation who are able to acquire a capacity for reflective functioning are more likely to have infants with a secure attachment. In line with this, Nijssens et al. (2020) showed that the effect of parents' attachment style on children's socio-emotional development was at least partly mediated by their reflective functioning—in other words, the fact that parents' own attachment styles seems to impact on their children can be explained by the degree to which parents tends to operate in a "prementalizing" mode.

The value of mindful or reflective parenting in the development of emotion regulation and secure attachment in the child has been demonstrated in a number of empirical studies (e.g., Ensink, Bégin, Normandin, & Fonagy, 2016). For example, reflective functioning in mothers has been associated with maternal sensitivity (Dollberg et al., 2022; Ensink, Berthelot, et al., 2016; Ensink et al., 2019; Gagné et al., 2021) and infant attachment (Ensink et al., 2019; Gagné et al., 2021). When it comes to school-age children, reflective functioning in parents has been associated with less externalizing difficulties in children as well as higher socio-emotional competence (Bianco et al., 2021; Charpentier Mora et al., 2022; Ensink, Bégin, Normandin, & Fonagy, 2016; Lindblom et al., 2022; Nieto-Retuerto et al., 2025). In fact, evidence from one study suggests that in the context of child sexual abuse, which disrupts emotion regulation and triggers children's needs for security, maternal reflective functioning may have a particularly important role because it appears to counterbalance the effect of abuse (Ensink, Bégin, Normandin, Biberdzic, et al., 2016).

Parental reflective functioning is thought to promote sensitive parenting by helping parents look beyond behaviors to what the child is feeling and inhibit negative interactions by helping parents regulate their own negative reactions and remain focused on the child's needs. Even when their baby is distressed, these parents are able (at least most of the time) to remain relatively calm and not take it personally when their infant is dysregulated. This, in turn, helps the infant to become regulated (Ensink, Normandin, et al., 2016). These patterns of feeling secure in the belief that others will be there when in distress or, alternatively, trying to rely on the self to regulate have been shown to have long-term implications for the way individuals regulate distress. It also underlies the feeling that it is safe and rewarding to express and share feelings with others when distressed and, in turn, be available and supportive of others when they are in distress (Ensink, Bégin, Normandin, & Fonagy, 2016).

MORE THAN WORDS—EMBODIED MENTALIZING

Research on mentalizing has primarily focused on verbal manifestations of mentalizing, often studied by researchers by assessing "reflective functioning." However, mentalizing is a construct that is manifested not only verbally but also in nonverbal interactions. Shai and Belsky (2011, 2017) introduced the term "parental embodied mentalizing" (PEM), which entails the parent's ability to both read and understand the child's inner mental states based on their nonverbal expressions (e.g., body language, facial expressions, tone of voice) and to adapt their own bodily expressions accordingly. This is seen as particularly important in infancy, as communication with infants is primarily nonverbal. However, as will become clear throughout the book, in mentalization-based work with children and parents, we emphasize the importance of embodied mentalizing throughout childhood, as it plays an important role in promoting attention control and emotion regulation. Although it is still a relatively new area of research, studies point to the importance of embodied mentalizing for secure attachment (Gagné et al., 2021; Shai & Meins, 2018) as well as language and cognitive development (Shai et al., 2022). Some studies even suggest that PEM predicts secure attachment above and beyond verbal manifestations of mentalization (Gagné et al., 2021; Shai & Meins, 2018). Others have theorized that PEM and reflective functioning are different manifestations of the same capacity (mentalizing), but as yet, the few studies that exist investigating the relationship between verbal and nonverbal measures of mentalization show mixed results, with, at best, modest relationships between the two (Aras et al., 2024).

SECURE ATTACHMENT RELATIONSHIPS AND THE DEVELOPMENT OF MENTALIZING

As the research makes clear, a parent's capacity for mentalizing, even when assessed before the child is born, can predict infant-initiated interaction at 7 months of age (Foley et al., 2022) and is part of what provides the optimal conditions for infants and babies. In a longitudinal study (Bernier et al., 2017), mothers' capacity to mentalize (assessed as "mind-mindedness") when their children were aged one predicted school readiness for the child when they were aged 5. Although much of the research has focused on parents of infants and very young children, parental reflective functioning has been shown to remain important for school-age children's psychological adjustment (Ensink, Bégin, Normandin, & Fonagy, 2016) as well as for parents of adolescents (Benbassat & Priel, 2012). In sum, the family is the key context in which children develop their capacity to mentalize, especially in relation to negative or distressing situations. Socio-emotional and cognitive development is closely intertwined in childhood. One could say that one of the most important tasks of parents is to transmit a mentalizing stance and help their children become aware of their feelings and behaviors and use mentalizing to enhance and deepen their close relationships.

ATTENTION CONTROL, EMOTION REGULATION, AND MENTALIZING

As one of the building blocks of mentalization, the concept of attention control will be found in this book, as we believe it to be helpful in clinical work with school-age children. The term was used in a particular way by Fonagy and Target (2002), who argued that the development of self-regulation in infancy depends on the development of mechanisms to react to stress (emotion regulation), maintain focused attention (attention control), and interpret mental states in self and others (explicit mentalizing). When operating in combination, these three mechanisms are "probably responsible for self-regulation in social relationships" (Fonagy & Target, 2002, p. 309). Their development is "arguably the most important evolutionary function of attachment to a caregiver" (p. 313). Although each can be thought of separately, in reality, their functions are interdependent, with each impacting the others.

Emotion regulation and explicit mentalizing are described elsewhere in this chapter, but it may be helpful to say a few words about the concept of attention control, which links directly to the ability not only to control impulsivity but also to function adequately in interpersonal contexts (Fonagy & Bateman, 2007). We use the term *attention* in a somewhat broader sense than in the research literature. Normally, it is used to refer to the capacity to deliberately focus on some stimuli while deliberately excluding other types of information by controlling impulses to react to distracting stimuli. In the clinical literature about mentalization, attention regulation is described by Zevalkink et al. (2012) as the "ability to gain control of impulsiveness—something that can be learned in a safe relationship" (p. 145). During the first year of life, attention capacities are evident in the infant's capacity to orient and direct attention and, later, in "effortful control" (Beebe et al., 1997), which makes a developmental leap during the second year of life. Later in childhood, as the child becomes increasingly self-regulating, attention control will take the form of a capacity to focus attention and to inhibit inappropriate responses.

Parents can be viewed as organizers of attention systems (Fearon & Belsky, 2004), with the infant initially depending on the caregiver's regulatory capacity, or what has been called the "dyadic regulatory system" (Tronick, 2007). Kochanska et al. (2001) demonstrated how higher levels of mutual responsivity in mother–child dyads in the third year of life predict greater self-control and reduced need for maternal control. Attention control is seen as important in the development of the capacity to mentalize because "the ability to gain control of impulses that arise from within is an essential condition for the capacity to mentalize" (Zevalkink et al., 2012, p. 110).

THE CAPACITY TO MENTALIZE AT DIFFERENT STAGES OF CHILDHOOD

Mentalization-based treatment is a developmentally informed approach to therapy. Therefore, it is useful for clinicians to have some sense of the typical course of the development of emotional understanding and the sense of self in children across the early years, as these are key dimensions of mentalization. By "typical," we mean the capacities that children have usually achieved by different ages based on developmental studies, although, of course, there is great variation in when any particular child may do so. Nevertheless, if we consider what typically developing children are able to do from early on, it can help us to identify and appreciate the sometimes severe difficulties of the children *and* parents with whom we work, who may not have developed these basic abilities.

Children's understanding of mental states and emotions has consistently been related to their present and future social competence (Eggum et al., 2011). For example, children with better emotion and mental-state understanding are generally responded to more positively (Cassidy et al., 2003), and are more likely to engage in positive play and cooperative pretend (Dunn & Brown, 1994).

Age 0 to 1 Year

During the first few months of life, infants are thought to begin to organize their experience and differentiate emotions by their valence (Widen & Russel, 2008), crystalizing around physical sensations of pleasure or pain and distress and how the parent responds to these. Infants appear to be biologically wired to be receptive to dyadic communication (Csibra & Gergely, 2009), attending to their parents' reactions and showing that they are sensitive to emotional communication. We know from microanalytic studies of mother–infant communication that infants are tuned in to the facial and physical reactions and tone of voice of the parent (Northrup & Iverson, 2020) and that they react with disorientation and distress to inappropriate responding, such as when the parent laughs when the infant gets hurt or when the carer fails to respond to the infant's bids for communication (Beebe et al., 2012). By the age of 8 months, most infants are able to follow their parents' gaze and engage in joint attention (Moore & Dunham, 1995). This will become increasingly important in the development of attention control, cognitive development, and mutual and self-regulation strategies. This is because it makes it possible to help infants self-regulate by distracting them from the source of distress and focus on something neutral or interesting. By 12 months of age, infants also show the ability to use the caregiver's reactions to know whether a new situation is safe and whether they can proceed and engage (Vaish et al., 2008)—for example, glancing at the mother to see whether she nods or shows a fearful face.

Age 1 to 3 Years

At around 15 to 18 months of age, a well-researched attachment milestone is reached, and distinct attachment patterns are evident in the way toddlers respond during separations and reunions in the context of the strange situation paradigm (Ainsworth et al., 1978). In this procedure developed to assess attachment, toddlers are observed during separations and reunions with their caregiver, and their responses are coded. Research using the strange situation has demonstrated that most toddlers have developed distinct patterns of regulating their distress based on repeated experiences of whether the mother was available and responded sensitively to their distress. These patterns form the well-known attachment strategies that have been validated across a range of cultures (van IJzendoorn & Kroonenberg, 1988). The experiment shows that toddlers have developed an internal model based on whether they can expect the parent to be available or unavailable to help them regulate distress or, alternatively, expect her to be frightening and increase distress.

At around 18 months of age, toddlers are also beginning to engage in pretend play and show an early capacity for self-awareness evident in their ability to recognize, when they look in the mirror, that the image in front of them is a reflection of themselves (Bukatko & Daehler, 2004).

During the toddler years, rapid strides are made in self-regulation and mentalizing. At an individual level, cognitive and attentional processes mature, language skills emerge, and play with peers stimulates the development of a range of prosocial abilities. Fonagy and Target (1996) theorized that between the ages of 2 and 3 years, play becomes an especially important realm where the child, entering a pretend mode, can discover the representational aspects of thoughts through the elaboration of different fantasy play scenarios. Especially when the parent is able to engage in playing and pretending with the child, this not only encourages the process of imagining but also provides an opportunity for the child to see and learn something about how mental reality works.

Play is widely recognized to have an important developmental role in trying out roles, developing skills, and learning social abilities. Playing and suspending reality, while imagining and creating a realm of make-believe, appears to be fertile ground for learning about mental states and developing emotion regulation and empathy. Creating play narratives and finding different endings through play is thought to contribute to the sense that subjective experience can be expressed, transformed, and represented in different ways by the child. From a clinical perspective, children's fantasy play is an early mental activity that helps them integrate experience and make sense of their own and others reactions, and thus it facilitates self- and emotion regulation (Berk et al., 2006; McMahon, 2009). Indeed, pretend play, where children are able to complete play narratives, has been found to predict both children's later reflective functioning (Tessier et al., 2016) and children's psychological adjustment 3 years later (Normandin et al., 2023). It has even been suggested that pretend play has an important evolutionary function for the human race and culture, as it fosters our capacity to move between imagination and reality (Gleason & White, 2023)—in other words, to move on from prementalizing modes and show a capacity to "play" with ideas.

Furthermore, we know from developmental research that children learn to think about mental states in the context of families where they have opportunities to learn and, through relationships, where they experience others as mentalizing and get help to develop these capacities themselves (Fishburn et al., 2022; Luyten et al., 2017). Initially they may require active scaffolding by parents, but, with practice, most children internalize this as part of their own repertoire. Most likely without thinking about it consciously, reflective parents teach children to adopt a mentalizing stance themselves in the context of a range of everyday activities—for example, when a parent comments on the emotional reactions of a storybook character or uses conflict between siblings as a way to teach children to take each other's perspective. Furthermore, parents spontaneously engage in reminiscing about emotionally challenging and significant experiences and, in this way, help children to develop the capacity to elaborate a series of narratives around significant events that can be linked up into an autobiography.

With emerging language capacities opening doors to learning and exchanges about emotions, children's ability to express, understand, and communicate about feelings develops rapidly. By the age of 2 or 3 years, most children make reference to and recognize facial expressions of basic emotions such as happiness, sadness, fear, and anger in their everyday communication (Weimer et al., 2012).

During this period, children go from an implicit knowledge of emotions to a conscious knowledge of them (Southam-Gerow & Kendall, 2002), and they also begin to use words such as "want," "wish," and "pretend," reflecting the early use of language to express agency and self. However, the ability to recognize emotions from other cues, such as vocal cues, usually develops slightly later (Chronaki et al., 2015).

Age 3 to 4 Years

Children now start to show the ability to identify how others will feel in emotion-provoking situations. They know that others can want, like, dislike, and feel, and how this is linked to how people will react. They can predict the reactions of others based on what they know about the likes and dislikes or desires and intentions of others (Denham et al., 2014). Children at this age usually show an awareness that the emotions of others can be different in the same situation, showing that they no longer egocentrically assume that others will feel the same way they do and suggesting that they can imagine the emotions of others, even before they are able to pass theory-of-mind tasks (discussed subsequently). For example, they know that although they will be happy to find a new toy, the child who lost it will be sad (Pons et al., 2004). From around the age of 3 years, words such as "thinking" and "knowing" also become part of the child's expressive vocabulary, showing an emerging implicit awareness of self as a mentalizing agent.

Age 4 to 5 Years

At this age, most children pass another well-researched milestone: the theory-of-mind or false-belief task (Happé & Frith, 2014). In this task, the child sees Maxi's mother moving the cookies from where they are usually kept in the blue cupboard to a green cupboard and has to predict where Maxi will look for the cookies. Correctly predicting that Maxi will have a false belief and look in the blue cupboard shows that the child has developed the capacity to imagine and represent the mental perspective of someone else. This demonstrates that children are no longer egocentric in their thinking, as younger children are, who simply assume that others will think like they do and know what they know. At this age, some children who have specific difficulties (e.g., slightly more impulsive or aggressive temperaments) may develop an even better knowledge of emotion in this area if they have access to people who use situations where there are disagreements or conflict as opportunities to teach them about the impact of their behavior (Laurent et al., 2020). This is thought to help them make interpersonal adjustments to compensate for their temperaments through other prosocial behavior so that they may not necessarily be less popular.

At this age, children also begin to be able to describe themselves, but this is still mainly in terms of physical characteristics and their likes and dislikes—for example, "I am a boy, I have blue eyes, and I love dogs and playing soccer." At this age, self-representations are often overly positive and infused with fantasies about what they want to be or qualities that they wish to have (Trzesniewski et al., 2010), which may contrast with their actual feelings of vulnerability.

Age 5 to 6 Years

When children start school and their social world becomes increasingly rich, this provides further opportunities and challenges to developing self- and interpersonal understanding in the context of making new friends and finding their place in the social structure of the school. This also leads to better understanding of more complex social rules and dealing with issues of acceptance, inclusion, and exclusion.

With regard to their sense of self, the development of their autobiographical memory and its increasing sophistication around the age of 5 years also contributes to children's evolving capacity to describe themselves in terms of their own experiences and to begin to be able to give concrete examples (Music, 2011). By representing memories about the self and others more coherently and richly, children develop a sense of continuity, which, in turn, facilitates the development and integration of identity. At this age, children frequently describe themselves in terms of their abilities and tend to use comparisons with others (Harter, 2012), but they might frequently find it difficult to distinguish between the superpowers that they wish to have and may have in fantasy and play (e.g., having magic rays that can freeze or shrink an enemy) and their real self, who, in fact, does not have these powers (Harter, 2012). In line with this, young children tend to overestimate their knowledge and skills. Children around this age still tend to overvalue their abilities, but then gradually become more accurate in their self-perception during the early school years (Shin et al., 2007).

Age 6 to 7 Years

Six-year-olds have usually established the capacity to know what they and others will feel in different situations because the capacity for explicit mentalizing becomes established during the school years, building on the emotional understanding developed during the preschool period. However, during the early school years, children still need help from adults to explain and help them understand the reactions of others (e.g., when school friends react in ways that they don't understand and cause them distress due to exclusion, criticism, or being tricked). At the same time, they begin to develop the capacity to understand and make reference to emotions that require self-evaluation, such as pride, guilt, and shame, which imply a certain awareness of social norms and expectations (Thompson et al., 2006). They start to know that feelings can be disguised not to hurt the feelings of others, as when someone is disappointed with a gift (Weimer et al., 2012). At this age, children may begin to be able to use simple self-descriptions that capture something about their qualities, such as "I am kind and like to help," and they begin to be able to describe something about the quality of their close relationships.

Age 7 to 12 Years

At these ages, most children have developed sufficient cognitive sophistication to be able to think of themselves and others more in terms of individual personal qualities and mental states (Ensink et al., 2015), although for children at the lower end of this age group, this is generally simple, and they may struggle to find examples without some scaffolding. As children progress through elementary school, mentalization rapidly becomes more sophisticated, enabling children to begin to see their own qualities in terms of what they are like as people and their personalities, and also to think about their attachment figures and describe their relationships in ways that capture the unique qualities that characterize these relationships. By this time, most children should have a well-established capacity to say what they feel and express complex and mixed emotions as well as ambivalent feelings (Southam-Gerow & Kendall, 2002). They will have a well-developed understanding of a repertoire of more complicated interpersonal reactions built around previous experiences and explanations so that they only require help to understand interactions or situations that fall outside of this range.

From the age of 8 years, children become increasingly able to describe themselves in terms of personal characteristics such as "popular," "helpful," and "caring," and they are able to capture something about themselves that remains stable across different contexts (Ensink, Berthelot, et al., 2014). Self-descriptions become more coherent, and autobiographical memories are more integrated with the particular experiences of the child. They begin to consider both positive and negative attributes of the self and to differentiate between the actual self and the self they wish to be (Harter, 2012). They have also developed in what is called "epistemic humility," meaning the capacity to acknowledge one's limitations in terms of knowledge and understanding, and so be open to the input of others (Viana et al., 2023). Children at the age of 5 to 7 years tend to be more rigid in their own thinking and tend to stick to their own thinking in conflicts with others, while children at this age show more capacity to take in the perspective of the other ("I see your point"). However, their growing self-awareness and capacity for self-evaluation also makes them more vulnerable and can have an impact on their self-esteem, and they may need help to integrate these observations in a way that can help them appreciate their strengths while acknowledging their weakness. At the same time, the capacity to see their own personalities and those of others helps them to increasingly make sense of interpersonal relations and understand the reactions of others who have personalities that are different from their own.

Finally, early adolescence is also an important period in the consolidation of identity and an awareness that one may have different selves expressed in different contexts (e.g., the self with one's parents differs from the self with friends). However, this change often comes without a child being able to recognize how these different aspects of the self are linked and what the common unifying characteristics underlying them are (Harter, 2012). For example, whereas a young adolescent may be quite outspoken and confident when with her parents, she may be shy and anxious when socializing with peers. However, she may not yet be able to clearly account for these differences and how this is linked to her sense of self. Later, she may be able to do this, for example, saying,

> I enjoy being around people, but I am not as extroverted as my friends and can get a little anxious when around a lot of people I don't know. I feel most at ease and confident when I am with people I know, like my family and close friends. Then I can actually be quite loud and funny at times.

CULTURAL ASPECTS OF THE DEVELOPMENT OF MENTALIZING

As with many psychological theories, the theory of mentalizing has been largely developed in Western countries, and it has been questioned whether the theory is cross-culturally valid (e.g., Aival-Naveh et al., 2019). For example, when it comes to empathy and perspective taking, there seem to be differences between people who have grown up in "individualist" or "collectivistist" cultures, even though research shows mixed results regarding the nature of these differences. Most research points to a greater emphasis on perspective taking and empathic accuracy in people from collectivist cultures (Aival-Naveh et al., 2019). However, when looking at emotional reactivity, which would be closely linked to affective mentalizing, results are more mixed. One study indicated that East Asian participants (usually considered to be part of more "collectivist" cultures) reported less empathic concern and personal distress than British participants (considered to be more "individualist") when looking at video clips showing people in painful situations; however, they were more accurate in inferring mental states correctly (Atkins et al., 2016).

In broad terms, it has been suggested that people from more individualist cultures have a greater focus on mentalizing the self than others, with the opposite pattern in people from collectivist cultures (Aival-Naveh et al., 2019). It should also be noted that differences in mentalizing, especially in empirical studies of theory of mind, are primarily found in verbal measures than in nonverbal measures. This opens up several possible interpretations. One is that people from collectivist cultures are more focused on implicit rather than explicit mentalizing. Another is that the verbal display of mentalizing (or theory of mind) is rooted in language, and whether a language has words for indicating false beliefs, or grammatical means of marking certainty of beliefs, will affect the way people are able to convey these concepts verbally (Aival-Naveh et al., 2019). It seems from the cross-cultural research that has been done in this area that parenting styles are associated with mentalizing, with "authoritarian" parenting being related to lower theory of mind in the child, and greater use of mental-state talk by parents (an aspect of "authoritative parenting") being related to higher theory of mind in the child (see Aival-Naveh et al., 2019, for a summary of studies).

When thinking about cultural influences on the development of mentalizing, we need to consider value systems, norms, and expectations in the cultural context. We will return to this more explicitly in the chapters concerning parental mentalizing, and how we not only can think about mentalizing capacity as an internal phenomena but also need to take contextual and cultural factors into account.

CONCLUSION

In this chapter, we have presented a model of the development of mentalizing in the contexts of reflective parenting and described empirical evidence in support of this model. In the last part of this chapter, we have set out what we might expect mentalizing to look like in the course of early child development, from birth to age 12, and have specified the key developmental achievements in this regard as mentalizing unfolds. This "story" is only partial and draws largely on research that has been conducted in what has been called the "WEIRD" world (Western, educated, industrialized, rich, and democratic; Henrich et al., 2010). We hope that this developmental story will continue to evolve as the research develops and diversifies. However, for now, we hope that it can provide a helpful context for the clinical model that is described in this book.

2

When the Capacity for Mentalizing Is Underdeveloped or Breaks Down

In the previous chapter, we described how the capacity to mentalize develops throughout childhood and the role that mentalizing plays in the development of affect regulation, a sense of self, and supporting interpersonal relationships. We also explored the importance of reflective parenting in supporting children's development and looked at the ways in which children, in the context of secure attachment relationships, can be helped to establish a curiosity about minds, which lays the foundation for epistemic trust and the capacity for social learning.

In this chapter, we turn to the ways in which mentalizing can go awry and the consequences this may have for children's development. We begin by stating clearly, however, that we do not believe all childhood emotional and behavioral problems are caused by mentalizing difficulties. Modern developmental psychopathology research shows that various interacting factors contribute to risk and resilience processes so that different roads lead to similar psychological symptoms (Pollak, 2024). From this perspective, we see mentalizing as one of a number of important risk factors that need to be considered. However, we do believe that it is an important one to focus on, not only because difficulties with mentalizing can be seen in a range of childhood disorders but also (and more importantly) because we believe that a focus on promoting mentalizing in therapy—both for parents and for children—may have significant clinical value. Whatever challenges and difficulties contribute to psychopathology,

https://doi.org/10.1037/0000486-003
Mentalization-Based Treatment for Children: A Time-Limited Approach, Second Edition, by N. Midgley, K. Ensink, K. Lindqvist, N. Malberg, and N. Muller
Copyright © 2026 by the American Psychological Association. All rights reserved.

mentalizing, we argue, may be central in the process of potentially overcoming such difficulties, or at least living with them more adaptively (Bazzi et al., 2024).

A clear model is thus needed of how underdeveloped mentalizing, as well as mentalizing breakdowns and failures, may be implicated in a variety of psychological disorders. For this reason, we focus specifically on difficulties, deficits, and distortions in mentalizing as they relate to self- and affect regulation—in relation to both children and their parents. In this chapter, we briefly outline our developmental model of breakdowns and failures in mentalizing before presenting in more detail how this is connected with the kind of difficulties that often bring children to the attention of psychological services.

A FRAMEWORK FOR THINKING ABOUT MENTALIZING DIFFICULTIES

First of all, we want to be clear that difficulties or breakdowns in mentalizing are perfectly normal and occur frequently in everyday interactions, so there is nothing inherently pathological when we speak about problems with mentalizing. It is an inevitable part of human interactions that we misread people's intentions or make attributions that later turn out to be wrong. Fonagy (2015), building on the work of Tronick, noted that miscommunication and "messiness" lie at the heart of the development of the self and self-regulation. "Miscommunication creates negative affect, but, when interactive errors are repaired, the negative is replaced by positive affect in both infant and mother" (Fonagy, 2015, p. 361). It is no accident that "understanding misunderstanding" is one of the most important definitions of mentalizing because misreading the intention of others, then recognizing this and repairing it, is a crucial element of all lasting relationships.

Furthermore, our capacity for mentalizing is a fragile one, liable to break down at least temporarily, especially when we are under stress or in a state of emotional arousal. We would probably all recognize some of the ways in which our capacity to reflect on the mental states of self and others becomes far more limited when we are highly stressed; this is both normal and expected. Nevertheless, in a certain respect, difficulties and breakdowns in mentalizing can create problems for both parents and children. Sometimes, we may simply be faced with challenges we have not encountered before, such as a sudden loss or a difficult situation with peers. In such situations, ordinary or even good mentalizing that has been developed to deal with everyday situations may not be enough. An analogy here could be that of a pilot who knows how to fly a small plane but will be at risk when flying in a storm without specific knowledge about the storm winds raging in a specific area and without particular skills in being able to fly based on the radar only.

In general terms, mentalizing difficulties can be considered from two broad perspectives. On the one hand, we can think of problems arising from an underdeveloped mentalizing capacity. This may be the result of children growing up in family environments where they have had few opportunities to learn about their own mentalizing or that of others. As a result, many children (and some adults) may have limited capacity to know what they are feeling and then use this understanding to guide self- and affect regulation. For example, they may show little capacity to think about themselves and relationships in mental-state terms or may describe themselves and others only in physical and behavioral terms. In such cases, there may be a therapeutic benefit in helping to build or better establish a capacity for mentalizing or, in some cases, to focus on supporting the "building blocks" of mentalizing and self- and affect regulation, including a capacity for attention control (Fonagy et al., 2002; Sharp & Bevington, 2022).

There are times, however, when difficulties may be more clearly associated with a breakdown of mentalizing, either temporary and context specific or more chronic (see Table 2.1). Often, this may take the form of a switch away from more controlled, explicit mentalizing, usually in the context of heightened emotional states of stress or arousal. From an evolutionary perspective, this switching makes good sense because explicit mentalizing relies on slower neural processes and a capacity for effortful control. A switch to more automatic forms of mentalizing is quicker but less accurate and may take the form of what Bateman and Fonagy (2009) referred to as prementalizing or nonmentalizing modes of experiencing the self and others. These are described in more detail later in the chapter. Another reason why there may be a breakdown in mentalizing is that a child may be emotionally overwhelmed by a situation such as a parental separation or divorce, or a sudden move where the child is faced with the loss of their familiar school and social environment. Faced by such situations, their mentalizing capacities may be temporarily unavailable to them at a time when they need them the most.

WHEN PARENTS STRUGGLE TO MENTALIZE

However good our capacity to mentalize may be under normal circumstances, there is no doubt that family life and being a parent place huge strains on our capacity to mentalize. Fonagy and Allison (2012) wrote,

> There is no context more likely to induce a loss of mentalizing than family interactions. It is within the family that relationships tend to be at their most fraught, their most loving and their most intense emotionally; in other words, the family is an environment with the potential to stimulate a loss of mentalizing in one or more members of the family, on a daily basis. (p. 24)

Even parents who are generally sensitive may not know how to guide their children when they are faced with really difficult situations. Mentalization may break down when parents are overwhelmed with financial or other difficulties or are faced with challenges such as immigration or divorce; in such stressful and overwhelming contexts, they may not be able to keep their children in mind or be emotionally available for them or may struggle much more to do so. Parents who have more chronic difficulties with mentalizing may well have had parents

TABLE 2.1. Underdeveloped Mentalizing Versus Specific Mentalizing Difficulties and Breakdowns

Underdeveloped	Breakdown and difficulty
These children have ongoing deficits in mentalizing.	Emotional or behavioral difficulties occur for these children in the context of an established basic capacity for mentalizing.
These children may be unaware of how they are reacting or have limited capacity to identify feelings and express them verbally. They struggle to consider the feelings and intentions of others, to understand their behavior, and to predict their reactions.	These children have age-appropriate abilities to think about their reactions and those of others in terms of underlying feelings and motivations.
These children may have difficulty with self-regulation and find it difficult to be aware of their reactions and those of others.	These children are able to self-regulate at a level expected for their age, express feelings and thoughts about themselves and others, and use this knowledge to understand interpersonal reactions. This ability may be lost when distressed or angry or when overwhelmed by difficult experiences or situations.
Affects may be acted out physically or behaviorally, and these children have little ability to reflect about this or put the experience into words. Not knowing what they feel, or being unaware of the impact of their actions on others, leaves them unable to use explicit mentalizing to modulate their reactions and contain affects.	These children may be unable to express and think about certain feelings, or struggle with contradictory or "unacceptable" feelings. They may lose their capacity to mentalize when overwhelmed, afraid, or angry, or they may need help to elaborate their reactions in the context of a safe relationship.
These children may have no clear sense of self and their attributes, abilities, and weaknesses. Others are often seen only in terms of current behavior and utility and whether they are a source of frustration or gratification.	These children have a sense of self, their personalities, and who they are and can see others in terms of both their good and bad qualities. They are able to relate to others appropriately, although there may be difficulties in some specific contexts or with specific people.

who, in turn, were not reflective in their style of parenting, even if their childhood was not overtly abusive or traumatic (Stuhrmann et al., 2022). For example, their own parents might have given them the message that "crying is for babies" and that sad or vulnerable feelings should be either ignored or mastered. On becoming parents themselves, it may, in turn, be difficult for these parents to tolerate or actively mirror their own infant's more vulnerable feelings.

In *Anna Karenina*, Tolstoy wrote, "All happy families are alike; each unhappy family is unhappy in its own way." Likewise, Bateman and Fonagy (2016) noted that although "good mentalizing takes just one form, non-mentalizing may be indicated by a wide range of possible manifestations" (p. 66). When parents are struggling to mentalize, it may appear in a number of ways, such as:

- a focus on their child's behavior, without attention to their mental states or internal experience;
- excessive blaming or fault finding;
- trying to control their child's behavior through authoritarian styles of parenting;
- exhibiting unmodulated mental states themselves, without awareness of the impact these may have on their child; and/or
- demonstrating negative distortions and attributions to their child (e.g., asserting that their child is crying "because she wants to punish me").

At times, parents struggle to see beyond children's behaviors and consider the feelings underlying them. In those circumstances, they may not be able to see the child's distress and may react to the child's behavior in ways that are likely to escalate them rather than help the child feel understood. At times like this, parents and their children may get into nonmentalizing vicious cycles in which a powerful emotion in one family member may reduce their capacity to mentalize, which, in turn, makes it harder for them to understand the other's behavior or intentions (N. Malberg et al., 2023). Figure 2.1 illustrates such a vicious cycle, in which Person 1's powerful emotions lead him to temporarily lose his capacity for mentalizing, so that he struggles to understand the intentions or feelings of the other person. This can then make the other person's behavior seem incomprehensible, which can, in turn, trigger an attempt to try and control the other person. Such controlling behavior can be frightening or distressing for the other person, which therefore creates powerful emotions in Person 2. The same cycle of responses is then triggered in her, leading to a vicious cycle of nonmentalizing interactions. For example, when a child is upset, she may think that her father's attempt to calm her down is "just trying to make me be quiet" (misreading of her father's intention). This, in turn, can lead the child to become more controlling in her behavior—for example, by kicking or pushing her dad away. This may create distress and heightened emotional arousal in the girl's father because people do not like feeling misunderstood, and when this happens, it can create powerful

FIGURE 2.1. Vicious Cycles of Mentalizing Problems Within the Family

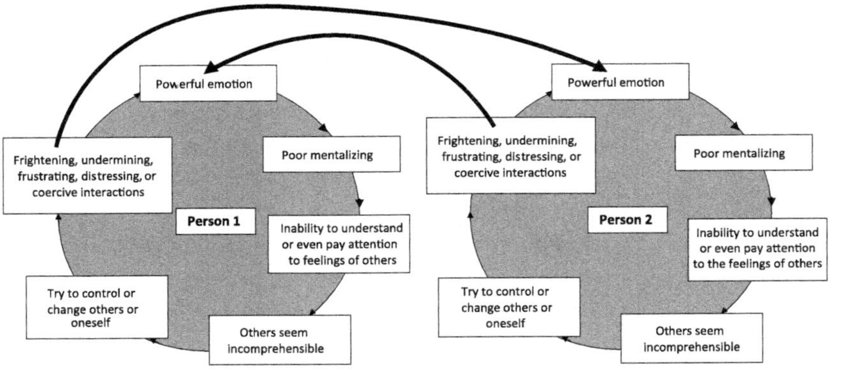

Note. From "Mentalizing-Based Treatment With Adolescents and Families," by E. Bleiberg, 2013, *Child and Adolescent Psychiatric Clinics of North America, 22*(2), 295–330 (https://dx.doi.org/10.1016/j.chc.2013.01.001). Copyright 2013 by Elsevier. Reprinted with permission.

feelings of hostility and rejection. The girl's father may thus become less mentalizing and less well equipped to reflect on his daughter's behavior. For example, the father, in his frustration, may think "she's just doing this to be difficult because she knows I need to cook supper," and this misattribution will, in turn, make him behave in a more controlling way, shouting at his daughter or telling her, "That's it then, no television today!" This controlling behavior is likely to make his daughter even more angry and upset, thereby increasing her emotional arousal and reducing her capacity to mentalize. And so the vicious cycle continues.

In other circumstances, there may be various reasons why parents may struggle to maintain a reflective capacity in relation to their children. For example, when parents are substance abusing or prone to dissociation, they may psychologically withdraw from their children and not engage in the interactions and communication essential to help them develop their own mentalizing capacities. Parents with certain types of temperament may be good at mentalizing when not emotionally activated but may be unable to step back and see themselves from the outside when they lose control, and so they fail to see the impact of their own behavior (Gölcük & Berument, 2021). The bottom line is that parents with difficult temperaments need to be particularly adept at mentalizing about themselves in order to help them to gain perspective and develop strategies to protect their children and modulate their own aggression.

Serious failures in parental mentalizing are sometimes associated with parental mental illness, personality disorder, or unresolved trauma in the parent's own history. Mentalization regarding trauma is particularly challenging, and failures in mentalizing about trauma and its impact on one's development, personality, and parenting leave people particularly vulnerable to failures in monitoring and modulating inappropriate trauma-related affects in relationships with partners and children (Berthelot, Ensink, et al., 2015; Ensink, Berthelot, et al., 2014; Ensink et al., 2023). For these parents, mentalization may be so distorted that they are constantly in a state in which they are sure that what is in their own mind is what the child is really feeling or thinking. Some parents may not be particularly reflective about themselves and may not be aware when they are aggressive, especially when it is a reaction to anxiety or fear or when it is linked to personality or trauma.

As the literature on mentalization has expanded, a broad range of prementalizing styles have been identified. For example, some parents talk about their child's problems by only focusing on behavior and describing what is physically observable. This has been described as concrete mentalizing and reflects a general failure to appreciate that internal states can provide a way to understand behavior. Parents functioning in this way may display no curiosity as to what their child's behavior could say about their feelings, wishes, or needs. Often, emphasis is placed on external social factors such as school or the neighborhood. The child's behavior may be explained in terms of "he was born this way" or "this is just the way he is," and labels such as "he is an ADHD child" might be used as explanation. Phrases such as "he always" or "she never" are cues that a parent may be short-circuiting the process of trying to understand their child's behavior and instead relying on fixed explanations. This often has a blaming quality rather than showing true acceptance of the child's individual qualities or a potentially important understanding of something central about the child's nature.

In other situations, parents who at times can be thoughtful and reflective about their child's experience may suddenly shift when faced with certain situations. Such context-specific loss of mentalizing may be because their child's behavior has been a trigger that inhibits their own capacity for mentalization (Berthelot et al., 2024). For instance, consider a mother who has a history of sexual abuse and does not want her daughter to stay overnight at her friend's house because she fears her daughter might be sexually assaulted. In this situation, depending on the age of the child, it is not surprising that this mother might find it difficult to differentiate her need to protect out of fear and her child's need for peer interaction. To her daughter, who may not be able to understand the intention behind her mother's behavior, she may come across as insensitive and rigid.

UNDERDEVELOPED MENTALIZING IN CHILDREN

Some of the children who are referred to child mental health services may have a limited capacity to mentalize about themselves or others, evidenced by them being unable to know what they feel and unable to use reflections on feeling states to facilitate self- and affect regulation. Indications that such children are likely to have an underdeveloped capacity to mentalize may be when they

- do not know and cannot identify what they are feeling;
- cannot use knowledge of affects to self-regulate;
- cannot see themselves from outside (e.g., how angry they are);
- cannot identify their reactions to hurt, sadness, fear, and anger;
- cannot describe what they are like as people (i.e., their personality);
- cannot tell a story of their lives (i.e., their autobiography);
- demonstrate difficulties related to extreme temperament; and/or
- ruminate (i.e., have difficulties with thinking too much).

In some cases, this underdeveloped capacity for mentalizing may be primarily attributable to genetics. For example, children with autism spectrum disorder (ASD) may have limitations in basic mentalizing abilities that others take for granted, such as the ability to read the minds of others by analyzing their facial expressions (Charki & Adnane, 2024). To compensate for difficulties with implicit mentalizing, they may develop explicit mentalizing strategies over time, but painfully and sometimes with little help from others (N. T. Malberg, 2021). Other children who are brought for psychological help may not have had sufficient support and opportunity to develop representations of themselves in terms of personal characteristics and personality. This can contribute to difficulties in the capacity to see themselves through others' eyes and think about the impact their behavior has on others. Not having a basic sense of themselves, in terms of what they and their personalities are like, also makes it difficult for these children to make choices that are well matched to their personal qualities and abilities, which will help them build on their strengths and develop them further.

Many children who are referred for help have few opportunities to learn to identify what they are feeling and to express this when they are in pain, are afraid, or want something. Children growing up with parents who struggle to take a reflective stance, are behaviorally focused, and punish behaviors they consider problematic have few opportunities to learn to think about themselves and their behaviors as being motivated by underlying mental states (Zhou et al., 2025). Without a parent with whom the child can reflect on experiences (e.g., rejection or teasing by a group at school), few children are able to develop a more nuanced mental-state understanding on their own. These children may not have had the opportunities to learn and develop basic capacities to identify their own feelings and be aware of their own reactions and their impact on others, or to understand the feelings and motivations that may underlie the reactions of others. They may have difficulty noticing the intentions of others and have insufficiently elaborated or unbalanced mental representations of self and others. For example, when a teacher reacts with anger when provoked, children with underdeveloped mentalizing may only be able to see the reaction of the teacher and may react as if the teacher is nasty and they are being unfairly victimized, without considering how they have provoked the teacher, who is normally patient and tolerant. These children also often have difficulties with affect regulation, poor social capacities, and weak attention regulation. They are likely to have an insecure or disorganized attachment style (Fonagy et al., 2002), and there is sometimes a history of neglect or trauma.

Children who grow up with parents with psychiatric disorders or substance abuse that have affected their capacities to parent, or children who are traumatized, adopted, or in foster care, frequently have underdeveloped mentalizing capacities. This is because the multiple processes through which children develop these abilities have been negatively influenced by the ongoing experiences of neglect, disruption, and maltreatment (Ostler et al., 2010; Wagner-Skacel et al., 2022).

For children with particularly sensitive, fearful, or difficult temperaments or personalities, it may be especially important to develop the capacity to see themselves from the outside with a benign and playful regard that will help them understand not only their strengths but also their challenges. Ordinary mentalizing may not be enough, and ideally the parents of these children need to be more reflective than other parents to help their child understand why others might react to them in certain ways. Children with temperamentally based extreme fearfulness, anxiousness, or sensory processing sensitivity may need additional help from reflective parents (or therapists) and may be vulnerable when parents are unable to adjust their parenting based on an empathic understanding of the child's psychological experience. A reflective stance may be particularly important for parents to understand and respond in ways that are sensitive to the specific challenges these children face.

Some children, with or without histories of abuse, have extreme difficulties with affect regulation because of their temperamental sensitivity. For example, a child in a special school might regularly be sent to a "quiet room" (isolation) when they become dysregulated because this is the only way the school can think of to try to help them regain regulation. However, these sanctions probably contribute to the child becoming even more disorganized. Children with temperaments like this, where they have more negative affectivity, impulsivity, or aggression, need to be better than other children at mentalizing about themselves and the impact of their behavior on others if they are to modulate their negative behavior and limit damage to interpersonal relationships.

DIFFERENT MODES OF PREMENTALIZING

Having described various ways in which children may have an underdeveloped capacity to mentalize, we now turn to the various modes of prementalizing that clinicians and researchers working in this field have identified. In their work on understanding and treating adults with borderline personality disorder (BPD), Bateman and Fonagy (2004) began by noticing a set of key deficits that were characteristic of this particular disorder: impulsiveness, difficulties with emotional regulation, relationship problems, and problems of identity formation. In their seminal work on BPD, they argued that all of these difficulties could be understood as a result of difficulties with mentalizing—in particular, in perceiving the mental states of self and others with sufficient accuracy. On the basis of their clinical experience with such patients, they identified certain patterns of prementalizing thinking, which seemed to be activated in their patients when in a state of stress or tension or when the attachment system was highly aroused, as was often the case when forming a therapeutic relationship.

Bateman and Fonagy (2004) went on to describe three typical patterns or modes of prementalizing, which they hypothesized may be part of normal development but for most people are rapidly replaced by a more mature capacity for slow and reflective mentalizing. They named these modes the teleological, psychic equivalence, and pretend modes. Although these modes were identified in the context of work with adults with BPD, we believe that they can be of help when working with mentalizing difficulties in children and parents, so we introduce each of them briefly here.

In the teleological mode (which, because the word is rather technical, we sometimes simply refer to as "quick-fix thinking"), "changes in mental states are assumed to be real only when confirmed by physically observable action contingent upon the patient's wish, belief, feeling or desire" (Bateman & Fonagy, 2016, p. 23). In other words, when operating in a teleological mode, only an immediate action seems like a possible solution and is thus aggressively or anxiously demanded. The assumption that action is needed, or interpersonal difficulties or distress can only be solved through action, can be problematic. Rather than having a notion of feelings in the self that can be thought about, understood, and resolved, there is a conviction that mental states can only be "solved" by means of physical action. When someone is operating in a teleological mode, a quick solution or specific actions are demanded, and there is a refusal to consider mental states underlying behaviors. If a child says, "When my mom gives me money, that's how I know she loves me" or a parent says, "The only solution is for my son to be on Ritalin," then they may be operating in a prementalizing, teleological way. The teleological mode increases the risk for abuse—for example, where a parent thinks that they have to stop a child's behavior, their frantic interventions may actually escalate the child's dysregulation and can increase the risk for increasingly coercive physical interventions and abuse (Jessurun, 2021).

In the psychic equivalent mode (which can more simply be described as "inside-out thinking"), the perception of external reality is distorted by internal states; there is no interest in internal states in the self or in others, and any attempt to draw attention to them may be angrily rejected. The child may be convinced that others always get preferential treatment and that he is unfairly treated, and because that is what he thinks, he sees it as a fact. In younger children, this may be developmentally appropriate (e.g., if a young child imagines that there may be a monster under the bed, she may believe there really is a monster there); in older children (or adults), this kind of "mind–world isomorphism" makes it difficult for the person to take another perspective or to see his or her thoughts as something that can be explored and thought about or treated with curiosity. In extreme cases (as in BPD), this may take the form of "rigid inflexible thought processes, inappropriate conviction of being right, extravagant claims of knowing what is on someone else's mind or why certain actions were performed" (Bateman & Fonagy, 2016, p. 21). As most parents will acknowledge, however, this description is fairly recognizable from arguments with a typical teenager, which only confirms that all of us are likely to fall into nonmentalizing ways of thinking under stressful circumstances. Parents also manifest psychic equivalence in their thinking when they are convinced that children are being manipulative and intentionally doing something to provoke them (even before the young child is developmentally able to be manipulative), when, in fact, the infant or child is displaying genuine distress. Often, this is as a result of the parent "projecting" their own feelings such as anger onto the child and misattributing this to the child. This results in a situation where the frustrated, angry parent, rather than being aware of their own frustration and anger, attributes to the child their own emotions. They might be thinking, "You know that I am exhausted, and you are intentionally doing this to push me to my limit," even though, from a developmental perspective, the child is too young to be intentionally doing so. The parent then responds to the child as if they are bad, manipulative, and aggressive when, in fact, the infant is afraid or in distress (N. Malberg et al., 2023).

The third form of prementalizing thinking that Bateman and Fonagy (2016) described is the pretend mode (or what we might call "elephant-in-the-room thinking"). When operating in this mode, there is "a separation between psychic and physical activity to a point where the connection between the two can no longer be achieved" (pp. 21–22). When the mental world is decoupled from reality and becomes more real than reality, this interferes with and undermines normal development. A person operating in pretend mode may even use a lot of mental-state language but without this being meaningfully linked to their reality (e.g., having grandiose and self-serving descriptions of their abilities and plans and how much others admire them but not engaging with the real issues of their failing grades or risking expulsion from school for bullying). With parents, the pretend mode can sometimes leave the listener with a sense that there has been endless inconsequential talk about thoughts and feelings but without any genuine quality. Often, it is an indication that something else may be going on, which is not being sufficiently attended to (hence the elephant in the room).

Pretend mode is also the favored mode of prementalizing for some therapists and can usually be spotted when we find ourselves using clever and internally coherent words that have no connection to the actual feeling states of the people in the room (Muller & Midgley, 2020). As with most prementalizing modes, we are most likely to fall into this when we are anxious or stressed (e.g., when feeling that we need to come up with a clever response when faced with an angry parent demanding that we make the situation better), and as with all prementalizing modes, the first step in addressing it in others or in ourselves is to notice it.

ATTACHMENT AND BREAKS IN MENTALIZING

As we have tried to emphasize throughout this chapter, not all childhood psychopathology, and not all difficulties with mentalizing, can be traced back to the early parent–child relationship. Severe autism is a case in point: Even the most loving parenting cannot resolve the many severe difficulties these children present with, and parents need all the help and support they can get to continue dealing with the challenges of providing loving care in difficult circumstances. In addition, we know little about children at the far end of the spectrum of temperament, who display extreme reactivity, impulsivity, or hypersensitivity, and to what extent parental care can be effective in modulating these vulnerability factors over time. Nevertheless, in many cases, early childhood experiences are important, and an attachment perspective can provide us with a clinical tool that is useful for understanding certain kinds of mentalizing breakdowns. It also helps to understand how strong feelings or stress in parents and children can trigger dramatic breakdowns in mentalizing, even in individuals who can be reflective at other times.

As we set out in the previous chapter, when children are securely attached, they are more likely to see their caregivers as reliable sources of knowledge and to show curiosity about mental states in themselves and others. These children are more likely to accurately read the intentions of others and to show empathy and emotional attunement. In their relationships with others, they are often better at resolving conflict situations because they are able to make use of their perspective-taking skills to see the views of others and to regulate their own affects by using explicit, controlled mentalizing. Secure attachment facilitates mentalizing and can be seen as organizing the brain in a way that promotes social cooperation and strong relationships (Parada-Fernández et al., 2021; Tanzilli et al., 2021). This is not to say that children (or adults) with a secure attachment are not vulnerable to mentalizing breakdowns; rather, in most cases, these children will be able to recover their capacity to mentalize relatively quickly and use it to effectively downregulate their stress levels. As Luyten and Fonagy (2015a) put it, individuals who predominantly use secure attachment strategies when faced with adversity "have the ability to turn to (internalized) secure attachment figures in times of need, they find interpersonal contacts rewarding, and they have the capacity to keep controlled mentalizing 'online' even when faced with considerable stress" (p. 373).

For children with more insecure attachment patterns, the picture is different (Taylor, 2012). Children with insecure avoidant (or dismissive) attachment styles have learned to use deactivating strategies in which they minimize and deny attachment needs and dependency as well as their feelings. They generally show avoidance of mentalizing about relationships and low mentalization regarding others, taking a cognitive route to thinking about relationships that may be disconnected from affect. This can often present as underdeveloped mentalizing—that is, children give a reduced mental-state account of events, and the emotional impact of interpersonal behaviors is not considered. In such cases, children may simply seem not to pay attention to what others think or show a lack of interest in what others feel about them. They may emphasize their own independence, working on the belief that others cannot provide support or comfort to them.

In some respects, children with avoidant attachment states of mind may look like those with more secure forms of attachment in terms of their mentalizing. They may be able to think about others' mental states and also, to some extent, their own because attachment deactivation strategies allow controlled mentalizing to stay "online" (Vrtička et al., 2008). However, this mentalizing will often be overly cognitive and can sometimes have the quality of pretend-mode thinking, with their words lacking emotional resonance. Furthermore, in situations of high stress, these children may not be able to recover their mentalizing capacity in the way that more securely children can usually do, leaving them overwhelmed by affect (Mikulincer & Shaver, 2007).

Children with insecure preoccupied (or ambivalent) attachment styles are also at a particularly elevated risk for psychological difficulties, so it is clinically useful to be aware how this tends to present. Whereas children with an insecure-avoidant attachment style have learned to use deactivating strategies to minimize and deny attachment needs and dependency, these children are more likely to use attachment hyperactivating strategies. This means that they have a fairly low threshold, when faced with stressful situations, for switching from more controlled, reflective mentalizing into prementalizing modes and become dependent on others to regulate them (Fonagy et al., 2016).

When asked to think about attachment relationships, as in the Child Attachment Interview (Target et al., 2003), these children often focus on the failings of others but are unable to "finish the story," as if mentalizing cannot contain the emotion. Instead, preoccupied anger drives an endless unsuccessful search for alternative mental solutions. In structured attachment interviews, this is evident in long, rambling narratives that are difficult to follow and where there may be a great deal of pseudomentalizing, but the listener ends up feeling confused. These children usually understand that there are feelings and thoughts behind people's actions, but they are likely to misunderstand both, leading to inaccurate assumptions about other people and their intentions (Yang & Huang, 2024). When asked to describe situations with a parent, such children often seem unwilling to think of why the parent may have behaved in a certain way, even when it is evident to the listener, or, alternatively, they may be unable to wrap things up mentally by saying, for example, "I don't know why my mom behaved that way" rather than trying to reflect or becoming curious.

Preoccupied attachment styles are relatively rare in low-risk populations but more common in children with histories of abuse and neglect and also in youth with emerging personality disorder (Santoro et al., 2021). In the context of abuse and neglect, preoccupied styles (compared with avoidant styles) are costly in terms of functioning because these children remain emotionally entangled and focused on a parent whose behavior they are unlikely to change or understand, and this interferes with self- and affect regulation. These children can sometimes come across as controlling or manipulative, which, in turn, reduces the likelihood that the adults around them will respond in a reflective way.

In children who have disorganized attachment styles, we often observe a complete breakdown of mentalization under stress, just at the moments when they are most in need of their mentalizing capacities. These children often show features of both hypermentalizing and catastrophic breakdowns in mentalizing, which are also seen in young people with emerging personality disorder (Bogdanović et al., 2023; Fonagy et al., 2016). Drawing on his extensive clinical experience with children in foster care, Taylor (2012) carefully described how children with disorganized attachment styles, as they reach school age, may make superficial judgments about other people based on how they appear and have little capacity for perspective taking. For these children, interpersonal stress, such as conflict, rejection, or criticism, can easily activate disorganized states, especially in attachment relationships, and when facing apparently simple challenges that may be experienced as overwhelming. So, when asked if he will help set the table, a child with a disorganized attachment may react with fury because he misread this request as a criticism that he does not help enough around the house. Such violent reactions can, in turn, challenge the caregiver's capacity to remain reflective, leading to the kind of prementalizing vicious cycles described earlier in the chapter.

Whereas children with secure attachment styles are able to maintain mentalizing or rapidly regain their ability to regulate, children with disorganized attachment lack strategies for regaining regulation when they become distressed. This may be linked to earlier experiences in which, when distressed as an infant, the parents failed to respond or responded in ways that increased, rather than decreased, the infant's distress, thus undermining the development of organized strategies for regaining and achieving self- and affect regulation. Failures to respond to infant distress are most apparent in contexts of abuse and neglect, where parents manifest extreme withdrawal so that the infant may be left for long periods in states of distress or where parents react in ways that induce fear (e.g., by becoming angry and aggressive). However, attachment disorganization is also observed in low-risk mother–infant dyads where it has been linked to a history of unresolved loss and trauma in the parent and where the infant's distress triggers trauma-related affects so that the mother reacts with fear or shows fear-inducing behaviors.

Berthelot, Ensink, et al. (2015) proposed that risks associated with disorganized attachment can be understood in terms of a failure in parental mentalizing and marked affect mirroring. In early infancy, caregivers may have responded with their own trauma-related affects completely disconnected to the infant rather than responding sensitively to the infant's distress. This is thought to leave the infant with a sense of being trapped with distress that cannot be related to and thus with a desperate sense of being "bad" and totally alone or abandoned when they are at their most distressed and most in need of help. These experiences of unmetabolized distress can lead to experiences of incoherence of the self that are so painful, they trigger dissociation or acting out.

It is argued that the kind of attachment strategies children use may have implications for their capacity for epistemic trust. Children who are securely attached are more likely to have confidence in their own experience, so that they are able both to learn from trusted adults and to know when to trust their own judgment. An anxious attachment is more likely to create a sense of epistemic uncertainty ("Is it safe to learn from this person and have confidence in what she says?"), whereas an avoidant attachment may be more associated with epistemic mistrust ("I don't think it is safe to believe what the other person is teaching me."). For disorganized attachment, there is an even greater extreme, epistemic hypervigilance, which is based on the unresolvable question "Who can I trust?" (Fonagy & Allison, 2014, p. 374). These children may even mistrust their own experience. This can lay the groundwork for a potentially interminable epistemic search in which such children seek others to confirm or deny their own understanding and feeling, yet find it impossible to trust the information once it has been received. The implications of this for assessment and therapy are explored in later chapters of this book.

FAILURES IN MENTALIZING RELATED TO TRAUMA, ABUSE, AND NEGLECT

Trauma, especially relational trauma in the context of early abuse and neglect, is recognized as a key factor in increasing the risk for all types of psychiatric disorders (Cicchetti & Banny, 2014; Dorahy et al., 2016; Li et al., 2023). This appears to be the case not only for depressive and anxiety disorders and personality disorders such as BPD but also for psychotic disorders such as schizophrenia, which, until recently, was considered primarily genetically determined (Berthelot, Paccalet, et al., 2015). Early trauma, such as child abuse and neglect as well as harsh or affectionless parenting, is considered an important stress factor that undermines and disrupts normal development of self- and affect regulation and acts as a general diathesis that can activate underlying genetic risks for psychopathology.

In addition, specific types of abuse, such as attachment or betrayal trauma (B. Allen, 2008; Fonagy et al., 2023), in which a child has been abused by an attachment figure who should have been a source of protection and security, are known to have especially negative consequences in terms of undermining trust. Such experiences profoundly disrupt development because they leave children with the sense that others cannot be trusted, learned from, or confided in when in trouble or in distress. At the same time, their attachment systems may be permanently activated by a sense of fear and distress, leaving these children with few self-regulation strategies.

Children who have experienced attachment trauma and grow up in contexts of abuse and neglect frequently present with underdeveloped capacities to think about themselves and others. They also tend to focus mainly on behavior and use automatic modes of mentalizing adapted to detect threat and need help developing slower, more reflective mentalizing. They frequently have an underdeveloped capacity to know what they feel and how to use this knowledge to facilitate self-regulation (Fonagy et al., 2023).

We believe that mentalizing is especially vulnerable to *relational trauma*—that is, trauma or abuse that happens in the context of primary relationships (Luyten et al., 2021; Muller et al., 2025). It is proposed that children growing up in a context in which caregivers cannot be trusted adapt by constantly being in a state of hypervigilance (Ensink, Berthelot, et al., 2014; Fonagy & Allison, 2014). As a result, they become closed to the minds of others, in contrast to the normal curiosity of children about the motivations and intentions of others. Furthermore, they habitually use automatic modes of mentalizing that are predominantly concerned with detection of threats to survival, so it becomes increasingly difficult to break this pattern and engage in more reflective, explicit mentalizing (Ensink, Bégin, Normandin, & Fonagy, 2016). Children may actively avoid mentalization to protect an attachment relationship or because they are frightened to think about the (possibly malevolent) intentions of others.

Maltreated children manifest a range of socio-cognitive and mentalizing difficulties (Ensink, Normandin, et al., 2014), including being less likely to express empathy with other children in distress and having challenges in thinking about themselves and attachment relationships in mental-state terms (Schwarzer et al., 2024). This has been associated with depressive as well as externalizing symptoms (Ensink, Normandin, et al., 2016). Young, maltreated children elaborate and complete fewer play narratives than other children; interestingly, the capacity to elaborate play narratives predicts their later mentalization capacities and mediates the relationship between abuse and mentalization (Tessier et al., 2016). Maltreated children engage in less symbolic play and are less likely to initiate dyadic play (Valentino et al., 2011).

Furthermore, in the context of abuse, low mentalization appears to further increase the risk of dissociation in children (Ensink, Bégin, Normandin, Biberdzic, et al., 2016). Maltreated children are particularly vulnerable to dissociation because processes that contribute to metacognitive integration and mental-state understanding, such as the capacity to suspend reality in the context of pretend play, may also contribute to dissociation (Wagner-Skacel et al., 2022). Because dissociation undermines the development of strategies for tolerating and integrating affect and thinking about the consequences of actions (Fonagy, 2004), dissociation increases the risk of manifesting maladapted behaviors.

One of the consequences of early experience of maltreatment, trauma, and abuse is often an increase in "epistemic hypervigilance." In Chapter 1 in this volume, we discussed epistemic trust and its development in children. In order to learn about the (social) world, we need to rely on others as sources of information. Therefore, from an early age, we need to be able to distinguish reliable and benevolent people as sources of information from others who may not wish us well, may not know our best interests, or may be ill-informed. One of the most powerful cues for humans that it is safe to learn is that we feel accurately perceived, understood, or, in other words, mentalized. However, Fonagy et al. (2019) suggested that adversity and deprivation can cause both chronic mistrust by inhibiting mentalization and inappropriate trust, stemming from the same inability to judge other people's perceptions of us. People with chronic epistemic mistrust will have difficulties using others as sources of regulation and knowledge—about the world, about others, and about oneself—meaning that they will function more like "closed systems." This will have implications for how we work in therapeutic settings, as the establishment of epistemic trust will be a core objective when working with children who have experienced early maltreatment and abuse (Muller et al., 2025).

MENTALIZING DIFFICULTIES IN CHILDHOOD DISORDERS

Many researchers and clinicians have strong views on the value (or lack of value) of a psychiatric diagnosis when trying to make sense of children's mental health (e.g., Timimi, 2002). In the context of mentalization theory, Fonagy and Campbell (2015) noted the limited explanatory power of more descriptive, category-driven approaches to psychopathology. They pointed out that in a longitudinal study by Caspi et al. (2014) that examined the structure of psychopathology from adolescence through to adulthood, psychiatric disorders were best explained by one general psychopathology factor, which the authors called the "*p* factor." Fonagy and Campbell suggested that this mysterious but determining *p* factor may turn out to be epistemic trust and speculated that "an individual with a high p factor score [which predicts greater lifetime risk of a range of psychopathologies] is one in a state of epistemic hypervigilance and epistemic mistrust" (p. 243). Although such lines of inquiry are intriguing, in this section, we take a more conservative position and describe what the empirical research suggests so far about the role of mentalizing difficulties in various psychiatric disorders in children. This knowledge is inevitably tentative but expanding rapidly.

As indicated earlier, difficulties with mentalizing may contribute to a wide range of childhood disorders, and strengthening mentalization can therefore have a positive effect for children presenting with diverse symptoms or behaviors. This is not to say, however, that all childhood mental health difficulties should be thought of as "mentalizing disorders" in the way that could be argued, for instance, in the case of BPD (Fonagy & Bateman, 2007). What is presented here is only a snapshot, but the literature has been reviewed in more detail elsewhere (e.g., Ensink, Berthelot, et al., 2016; B. N. Johnson et al., 2022; Nieto-Retuerto et al., 2025; Sharp & Venta, 2012).

Much of the original impetus for examining the role of mentalizing in childhood disorders came about as a result of the increasing interest in understanding ASD. Most of the empirical research in this area draws on a narrower, more cognitive idea of mentalizing—in particular, theory of mind (see Chapter 1, this volume). Baron-Cohen et al. (1985) were the first to suggest that children with ASD were less able to pass the false-belief task than age-matched children either with Down syndrome or who were typically developing. On this basis, Baron-Cohen et al. postulated that children with ASD suffer from "mindblindness." Subsequent research has suggested that the picture is less black and white than was first suggested, and in his later work (e.g., Baron-Cohen, 2009), Baron-Cohen has suggested that all children are on an "empathizing continuum," and children with ASD are usually at the lower end of this spectrum. In reviewing a considerable body of empirical work in this area, Sharp and Venta (2012) concluded that "a solid body of literature suggests reduced mentalizing capacity in autistic children and adolescents across all developmental stages" (p. 38). Recent literature from the neuropsychological field of study continues to explore this issue and influences the approach to therapeutic interventions with this population (Liu et al., 2023; N. T. Malberg, 2021).

Internalizing (Emotional) Disorders

The role of mentalizing (and mentalizing difficulties) is gradually becoming clearer with other common childhood disorders, including the internalizing disorders such an anxiety and depression. There is evidence that lower understanding of emotions and strategies to hide and change emotions (Zandpour et al., 2023) is associated with an increased risk of anxiety disorders, although not all anxious children have mentalization difficulties. In reviewing research on anxiety disorders, Sharp and Venta (2012) quoted Banerjee (2008) in concluding that there is now a substantial amount of empirical evidence to support the view that anxious youth experience "difficulty with understanding and effectively managing social situations involving multiple mental states" (p. 253). These difficulties may be associated with both the social skills deficits and hypervigilance with regard to the minds of others that are features of anxiety. On the basis of clinical experience and given the links between emotional dysregulation and mentalizing, it is easy to imagine that when children's baseline anxiety is high, it takes little additional arousal to push them over the edge into prementalizing (Haslam-Hopwood et al., 2006). Although breakdowns in mentalizing may not be the cause of anxiety, it is easy to imagine that helping children become better able to recognize their triggers for overarousal and anxiety states could be one benefit of a better capacity to mentalize for those suffering from anxiety.

Like many early-life stressors, trauma and intrapersonal conflicts may contribute to depression in childhood, and children's mentalizing about themselves and others appears to be an important potential resource in the context of depressive symptoms. There is evidence that by the age of 7 to 12 years, children's mentalizing about themselves and attachment figures is inversely associated with depressive symptoms (Ensink, Normandin, et al., 2016). This is in line with findings that major depressive disorder in adults is associated with lower reflective functioning in general (Fischer-Kern et al., 2013) and also with lower reflective functioning specifically regarding experiences of rejection and loss (Staun et al., 2010). Vulnerability to depression has been linked to insecure attachment, especially to preoccupied and avoidant attachment (Bifulco et al., 2002; Caldarera et al., 2022), and the symptoms of depression may be caused by impaired mentalizing and, in turn, lead to further disruptions in mentalizing (Luyten, Lemma, & Target, 2019). Haslam-Hopwood et al. (2006) suggested that those with depression are likely to lack the incentive to mentalize others ("why bother?"). They noted that the self-absorption and social isolation that can be features of depression may lead those with the disorder to be out of touch with the mental states of others or indeed to be unaware of the impact of the self on relationships. Moreover, distortions in mentalizing are likely to underlie the negative cognitive bias that is a well-known feature of depression—not so much failing to read the intentions of others but rather misreading those intentions (e.g., "He's probably just playing with me to be kind; he doesn't really want to be here.").

Externalizing (Behavioral) Disorders

Childhood externalizing difficulties have also been shown to be linked to low child mentalizing as well as parental mentalizing (Ensink, Bégin, Normandin, & Fonagy, 2016; Ensink, Bégin, Normandin, Godbout, & Fonagy, 2017). Child conduct disorders, as well as oppositional defiant disorders, have been shown to be associated with lower maternal mindedness—that is, where mothers use fewer mental-state comments when interacting with young children (Centifanti et al., 2016). In terms of the mechanisms linking low parental mentalizing and child externalizing behaviors, the parent's focus on behavior rather than on trying to look past the behavior to what this may say about what the child is feeling and struggling with may contribute to dysregulation. Furthermore, insensitive reactions to a child's oppositional and externalizing behaviors, and the parent's own difficulties in regulating infant distress, likely contribute to escalating conflict and oppositional behaviors. This may then contribute to the child becoming increasingly dysregulated and disorganized, in turn reducing the parent's capacity to mentalize.

For children who present with externalizing difficulties, interpersonal difficulties are a key feature, and Dodge et al. (2002) showed that these children often demonstrate a range of social-cognitive deficits, including in emotional understanding and theory of mind (C. Hughes & Ensor, 2008). They also have a tendency to attribute hostile intentions to others when a situation is ambiguous, a form of distorted mentalizing that Sharp and Venta (2012) described as a "theory of nasty minds." Sharp et al. (2011) showed that children with behavioral problems show anomalies in their trust behavior, especially in situations in which the emotional intensity of the situation was heightened. Compared with other children, they tend to read malevolence in the intentions of others, creating a kind of epistemic hypervigilance that might prevent them from being able to make use of others in a social learning context.

In the case of callous and unemotional traits, when children may have the cognitive knowledge that someone else is suffering or in pain but lack an empathic response, it is much more difficult to determine the nature of the relationship between such problems and mentalization. There is evidence that lacking empathy and showing callousness may be partly genetic (with some overlap with some difficulties on the autism spectrum) and that this may underlie psychopathic tendencies (Mariz et al., 2022). On the other hand, social experiences have also been shown to activate the development of empathy, so that young children who lack empathy need to be given the chance to develop it through therapeutic relationship interventions designed to encourage perspective taking and identification and that challenge and make them aware of and question their unempathetic responses. For some children with the most severe forms of externalizing problems, including those who bully or demonstrate psychopathic tendencies, there is some evidence that they are actually quite adept at reading the minds of others but that they use this skill to manipulate and control and have difficulty feeling positively connected and attached to others. J. G. Allen et al. (2008) described this as *pseudomentalizing*, meaning there is a lack of true curiosity, empathy, or respect for the minds of others, even when someone may appear to be skilled at reading the mind of others. Such pseudomentalizing may develop in response to environments characterized by harsh and inconsistent discipline (Sharp & Venta, 2012).

Although this way of relating to others may be difficult to change in adults, the verdict is still out in terms of whether youngsters with such tendencies can be helped, if not necessarily to change, to become more aware of their difficulties in these areas so as to protect their close relationships.

Furthermore, recent research on adolescents with features of BPD has suggested that *hypermentalizing*—that is, overinterpretative mental-state reasoning—is highly characteristic of individuals with BPD, many of whom have experienced trauma and abuse in their early lives (Sharp et al., 2011; Sotomayor-Enríquez et al., 2024). These young people tend to overinterpret social signs and make overly complex inferences based on social cues. For example, a young girl might respond to a peer offering her support by imagining that the peer is doing this to earn her trust so that she can take advantage of her. Sharp and Venta (2012) concluded that such hypermentalization in young people with BPD is "not the result of mind-blindness; rather, individuals with BPD tend to struggle with the integration and differentiation of mental states, especially under conditions of high emotional arousal" (p. 40).

CONCLUSION

As we hope this chapter has made clear, breakdowns in mentalizing play a role in numerous childhood difficulties and are also an important concern for parents, who play a significant role in supporting their children's emotional and psychological development. Although not all problems that lead parents and caregivers to seek psychological help for their children are necessarily caused by breakdowns or deficits in mentalization, it seems likely that developing mentalizing capacities—in both parents and children—may help them develop the internal resources to face such difficulties more effectively. Moreover, recognizing the ways in which mentalizing may go awry, as well as the prementalizing patterns that we are likely to see in clinical settings, is important to clinicians as we begin the challenging work of providing effective therapeutic interventions.

3

The Evidence Base for Mentalization-Based Treatment

As the introduction to this book made clear, the development of mentalization-based treatment (MBT) was first seen most clearly in the work of Bateman and Fonagy (2010) on the treatment of adults with borderline personality disorder (BPD). These clinicians recognized that some of the core features of BPD—including affect dysregulation, impulsivity, and unstable interpersonal relationships—could potentially be understood as consequences of difficulties in the capacity to mentalize, and so they developed a treatment for adults with BPD focusing on promoting mentalizing capacities. Much of the initial research evaluating the effectiveness of MBT was focused on is this initial population of adults with BPD, although in more recent years, the adult MBT world has also started evaluating whether this therapy can be effective for other clinical groups (Luyten et al., 2024). In this chapter, we will briefly review how the research on MBT for adults with BPD developed, before turning to the more recent studies of MBT with children and adolescents. As a relatively new field of research, the number of studies is still quite small, but an important step was taken in 2024 with the publication of the results of the first full-scale randomized controlled trial (RCT) of time-limited mentalization-based treatment for children (MBT-C) for children with emotional and behavioral difficulties (Halfon et al., 2024). We will therefore give a more detailed summary of that study, before ending with an examination of the research on mentalizing as a change mechanism in child therapy.

https://doi.org/10.1037/0000486-004
Mentalization-Based Treatment for Children: A Time-Limited Approach, Second Edition, by N. Midgley, K. Ensink, K. Lindqvist, N. Malberg, and N. Muller
Copyright © 2026 by the American Psychological Association. All rights reserved.

MENTALIZATION-BASED TREATMENT FOR ADULTS DIAGNOSED WITH BORDERLINE PERSONALITY DISORDER

Given that MBT (like other new approaches to therapy) emerged out of this impulse to make what we offer more effective, it was natural that a subsequent question should be posed: Is MBT more effective than how people had worked with clients with BPD previously? Although the question is natural and important, how we try to answer this question is more complicated. Should the answer depend on our own clinical experiences ("now that I have started doing this, I'm finding that the work I am doing is more helpful to my clients")? Or does the approach need to be evaluated more systematically? And if so, what counts as "systematic" evaluation? Should we be asking clients what their experience of this therapeutic approach has been? Or should we introduce some questionnaires or other forms of assessment before and after therapy to see whether there has been improvement? Or since such pre–post evaluations do not necessarily show that one type of therapy is more effective than others, do we need to do comparative evaluations of two or more types of treatment using designs such as the RCT? And maybe to be sure that a particular study is not just a one-off result, do we perhaps need to look across a number of RCTs and other evaluation studies, in the form of a "systematic review," to see whether a clear pattern of effectiveness has been established? But even here, showing that MBT is more effective than another type of treatment does not necessarily tell us whether it is the focus on mentalizing that makes MBT effective. So, do we perhaps also need process studies, or studies that explore moderators and mediators of change, in order to be confident that any additional benefits of MBT as a treatment are actually due to the mentalization-focused interventions?

In the case of MBT for adults with BPD, all of the above approaches have been reported. Individual practitioners have written about the benefits they have seen in their work because of using MBT (e.g., Drozek & Unruh, 2022), and teams have collected assessments pre and post treatment to explore whether clients with MBT appear to have benefited from treatment (e.g., Bo et al., 2017). Studies have also explored the experience of adults who have engaged with MBT and identified some of what clients have found helpful or unhelpful (e.g., Barnicot et al., 2022; Morken et al., 2019). In terms of "gold standard" research, Bateman and Fonagy (2008, 2009) have reported on the findings of RCTs, which have included extended follow-up periods to establish whether any differences in effectiveness between MBT and other approaches could be identified and whether these changes were sustained beyond the end of treatment. With several different studies using different approaches to evaluate the effectiveness of MBT for clients with BPD, there have now been a number of systematic reviews (e.g., Vogt & Norman, 2019), which have looked across a range of studies and concluded that "mentalization-based therapy can achieve significant reductions in BPD symptom severity and the severity of comorbid disorders as well as increase quality of life" (Vogt & Norman, 2019, p. 441). However, this review adds a caveat that there is still a need for better quality research and that there is a paucity of studies that demonstrate potential mediators of effectiveness in MBT—a paucity that has only begun to be addressed in more recent years (e.g., Luyten et al., 2024).

MENTALIZATION-BASED TREATMENT FOR CHILDREN AND YOUNG PEOPLE

As with the MBT work with adults, it is important to ask similar questions about whether any innovations in our ways of working with children actually lead to better outcomes. As is often the case, the amount of research in the field of psychological therapies with children is less than that with adults. In the first edition of this book, we were able to describe how MBT-C builds on a large body of research on the role of mentalizing in child development and in the parent–child relationship (see Chapter 1, this volume), but we had to acknowledge that the evidence base for the effectiveness of time-limited MBT as a therapeutic approach to working with school-age children still had to be developed. Although that is still the case to some degree, this second edition has given us the opportunity to add this new chapter and provide some update on progress—what we know and what we do not (yet) know.

To begin with, it is worth reviewing what the evidence shows regarding mentalization-based interventions more generally with children and young people. To date, two systematic reviews have been published, which help provide a general overview of the state of our knowledge. Byrne et al. (2020) and Midgley, Sprecher, and Sleed (2021) provided systematic overviews of a range of studies that have evaluated various MBT formats for children and young people, such as parent–infant interventions, parenting programs, school-based interventions, and individual therapies. For parent–infant therapy, many mentalization-based interventions target mothers from vulnerable populations, such as those with histories of drug abuse (e.g., Pajulo et al., 2012, N. Suchman et al., 2008; N. E. Suchman et al., 2017), those who are homeless (Bain, 2014), or those who are imprisoned (e.g., Baradon et al., 2008; Sleed et al., 2013). Generally, these interventions lead to increased capacity for mentalizing (reflective functioning) in the mothers who take part, although the impact on the mothers' mental health generally is less clear. Evidence from some of these studies also suggests that there are positive impacts on child development following mentalization-based parent–infant interventions, such as improvements in motor, speech, and intellectual development (Bain, 2014; Sleed et al., 2013), as well as improvements in the quality of attachment (Sadler et al., 2013; Slade et al., 2020) to their caregivers, although some studies have not showed these changes compared with control conditions (Longhi et al., 2020; N. E. Suchman et al., 2017).

Mentalization-based parenting interventions have also been evaluated for several groups, such as foster and adoptive parents (Dalgaard et al., 2023; Midgley, Besser, et al., 2019; Midgley, Cirasola, et al., 2019), parents of children with autism (Enav et al., 2019), parents with children at risk of maltreatment (Byrne et al., 2019; Gervinskaitė-Paulaitienė et al., 2023), and parents who are experiencing interparental conflict (Hertzmann et al., 2016). Several studies show significant improvements in parental reflective capacity following these interventions, but not all results are consistent (Camoirano, 2017). Some studies show that parenting programs decrease parental stress and increase self-efficacy, but again findings are not consistent across all studies. Improvements in child difficulties following parenting programs have been found in some studies, mainly indicating reductions in externalizing behaviors, but not all studies show such improvements.

The evidence base for individual mentalization-based treatment for adolescents (MBT-A) has mostly focused on young people with emerging borderline symptoms and/or self-harm behaviors. The findings show that MBT-A, through increasing the young person's mentalizing capacity, leads to decreased symptoms of personality disorder and depression, as well as improvements in general symptomatology and well-being (e.g., Bo et al., 2017; Laurenssen et al., 2014; T. I. Rossouw & Fonagy, 2012). However, a study where MBT-A was delivered solely in a group format failed to find effects on either personality symptoms or psychological well-being (Beck et al., 2020), suggesting that a group format alone is insufficient to activate change.

When it comes to time-limited MBT with school-age children specifically, research on outcomes and effectiveness is still only starting to be carried out. However, some important developments have taken place since the first edition of the book was published. One pilot study of time-limited MBT, based on the treatment of 18 school-age children referred to mental health services, examined outcomes for children with severe emotion regulation problems, including internalizing and externalizing and disturbed parent–child interactions (van Aalst et al., 2023). Using an assessment of "clinically meaningful change," this pre–post evaluation showed that 15 of the 18 children had shown "clinically meaningful change" by the end of treatment and that behavioral problems had decreased to the point that the children were comparable to a nonclinical population of children of the same age. Building on this, a pilot quasi-RCT of MBT-C for children aged 4 to 11 with a range of childhood mental health difficulties reported on a small study (n = 17) comparing 12 weeks of time-limited MBT-C, with parallel parent sessions, to a waitlist control group (Thorén et al., 2025). Compared with the waitlist control group, those in the MBT-C arm showed significant improvements in child pathology, therapist-rated global functioning, parent-perceived overall distress and impairment, and child-perceived emotional distress, although no significant effects were observed for parent-perceived symptoms (d = 0.41, p = .28). Improvements were maintained and even further improved at 6- and 12-month follow-ups.

As mentioned above, the "gold standard" for evaluating the effectiveness of psychological therapies is generally considered to be RCTs. Although there are a range of practical challenges to this type of research, the feasibility of conducting such a study in the context of child mental health services has been established (Midgley, Besser, et al., 2019). The first full-scale RCT evaluating time-limited MBT for school-age children focused on children with a broad range of emotional and behavioral problems (Halfon et al., 2024). The study included 222 children aged 5 to 12, with clinical levels of externalizing and/or internalizing problems, as assessed using the Child Behavior Checklist. Of the 222 children, 42% presented with internalizing problems, 17% presented with externalizing problems, and 41% presented with mixed internalizing and externalizing problems, with a large proportion of the children (79%) presenting with insecure patterns of attachment.

Participants in the RCT were randomized to 12 weeks of MBT-C with parallel parent sessions or 12 weeks of group-based parent and child social skills intervention. The impact of the interventions was assessed both at the end of treatment and at 6-month follow-up. At the end of treatment, both groups improved on overall symptomatology, as assessed by parents on the Child Behavior Checklist, with no statistically significant group differences. However, when looking at the children's own views of what had changed (using the Me and My Feelings questionnaire), those in the MBT-C arm showed significantly better outcomes at the end of treatment compared with those in the control group. When assessments were repeated at the 6-month follow-up stage, children who attended MBT-C showed a steeper improvement than those in the control arm of the study. The children in the MBT-C arm of the study showed larger improvements in parent-reported emotion regulation, as well as in overall problems, and their parents showed greater improvement than those in the control arm of the study in terms of their own capacity for emotion regulation.

These are important findings, which provide the first evidence for MBT-C as a transdiagnostic intervention for school-age children with a mixture of both internalizing and externalizing difficulties. The therapists delivering the MBT-C treatments were clinical psychology trainees (and some newly qualified clinical psychologists) who attended a 3-day training course and were provided with regular group-based supervision in MBT. Levels of treatment fidelity were high, suggesting that the MBT-C approach is one that can be learned (and delivered "on model") by mental health professionals after relatively brief training. It will be important to see to what degree these findings are replicated in a second full-scale RCT currently taking place in the United Kingdom: the Emotion Regulation in Children Study (Midgley et al., 2023). This is a large-scale RCT comparing relatively short-term MBT (6–8 sessions) with treatment as usual for children (aged 6–12) referred with emotional and/or behavioral difficulties. It will also be important to see whether studies evaluating MBT-C for other specific populations, such as neurodiverse children or those who have experienced early relational trauma, demonstrate whether this model of working is effective for them.

THE EVIDENCE FOR MENTALIZING AS A CHANGE MECHANISM IN CHILD THERAPY

The studies reported above set out the emerging evidence base for the effectiveness of mentalization-based interventions with children and young people generally as well as more specifically for time-limited MBT for school-age children. However, these studies do not directly address the question of whether mentalizing is the core change mechanism in this type of therapy—or, indeed, in therapy with children more widely.

Despite the complexity of conducting research studies to answer this question, some studies have succeeded in showing that a focus on mentalization may be a core therapeutic process in a range of child therapies (Goodman et al., 2015). An important set of studies conducted by Sibel Halfon and her colleagues, using detailed analysis of video-recorded sessions of psychodynamic therapy for children, alongside the use of a range of pre–post measures, have allowed an empirical investigation of what role mentalizing plays in the therapeutic process, what actually happens in sessions, and how this relates to change. In one study, focusing on therapy with children aged 4 to 10 years with mixed problems, the team looked to see how closely child therapists used different types of interventions (including those based on a mentalization-based approach). The findings indicate that techniques focusing on mentalizing were associated with better affect regulation in the child and an increased capacity to make use of symbolic play for children with externalizing disorders (Halfon & Bulut, 2019). In other words, it seems that the therapist's use of mentalization-based interventions has positive impacts on the psychotherapy process, at least for this group of children. In another study on a subsample of the same psychotherapies, again with both internalizing and externalizing disorders (Halfon et al., 2019), it was shown that therapists' use of the mentalizing stance in sessions helped children process and regulate difficult emotions. This provides some initial evidence that when therapists take a mentalizing stance and use MBT techniques that focus on improving mentalizing, it leads to improvements in the child's capacity for play and their ability to manage and regulate emotions.

Halfon and Besiroglu (2021) also explored how the mentalizing capacity of both children and their parents may impact on their capacity to make use of therapy. Outcomes for school-age children in therapy were better when parents showed (at the time of referral) a higher level of reflective functioning and the children demonstrated a greater capacity for "mental-state talk" (which can be seen as a proxy measure of child mentalizing). These findings highlight the importance of assessment and creating a "mentalizing profile" to adapt treatment according to the mentalizing capacities of both parents and their child. In line with this notion, Coşkun et al. (2024) showed that in (online) psychodynamic child therapy, children who struggled more with emotion regulation were helped by therapists' interventions addressing attention control, whereas children who entered therapy with a better capacity for emotion regulation were helped more when therapists made greater use of explicit mentalizing interventions. These findings demonstrate the importance of adapting interventions to the individual profile of the child, including the "level" of mentalizing capacity as well as their profile in terms of the "building blocks" of mentalizing—that is, attention control and emotional regulation. Individualizing therapy in this way may be an important element of effective therapy. As the chapters in this book discuss, MBT is not about using a fixed set of techniques with all children but rather about using the mentalizing stance as a fundamental base and then adapting one's interventions to the level that fits the child's needs.

CONCLUSION

When the first edition of this book was published in 2017, it did not include a chapter on the evidence base for time-limited MBT with children, as the model was a new one and studies had not yet been conducted. As the chapters in this book make clear, the development of the model itself was heavily informed by research, but this was mostly developmental research, exploring the role of mentalizing in the development of the self as well as the role of parental mentalizing in supporting the child's development.

At the end of the first edition of this book, we wrote that "there is an urgent need for well-designed evaluations of the [MBT-C] approach, to better understand 'what works for whom, under what circumstances, and when?'" At the point of preparing this second edition, is that still the case? The evidence base is still in its infancy, but enough has been done to justify including this new chapter reviewing the current evidence. Encouragingly, the research on interventions with children, young people, and families is generally indicating positive effects for both children and parents from various types of MBT. However, there is still a lot to be discovered. More high-quality outcome trials on MBT-C are needed, ideally also addressing research questions related to what works for whom. The voices of children who have attended MBT-C have not yet been included in the studies of MBT-C. We need the research to tell us more about whether there are particular groups of children whom this treatment is particularly suited for—or not suited for—and we need to have more evidence for what elements of MBT help to make it effective. Such a focus on what is called the "mechanisms of change" in time-limited MBT-C could help us not only to have greater confidence in the effectiveness of our work but also to learn more about the treatment process and the factors that lead to meaningful change for children and their families.

II

THE THERAPEUTIC APPROACH

4

The Structure and Aims of Time-Limited Mentalization-Based Treatment for Children

As the chapters in the first part of this book have set out, when a child fails to develop a sufficient capacity to mentalize, they are deprived of one of the most valuable tools available to the developing child: a skill that is at the heart of both the capacity to self-regulate and to manage an increasingly complex, interpersonal world. Entering middle childhood, the capacity to mentalize is for interpersonal relations what a healthy diet might be for physical health: It creates resilience in the face of hardship, and internal resources in the face of a demanding external world.

For many clinicians working in both public and private health care settings, it is essential to be able to offer relatively brief interventions that can be of benefit to a wide range of children and families. Although we have an increasing number of evidence-based treatments in child mental health, most are designed to treat specific diagnoses or symptoms, often with a behavioral focus on offering children and their parents "strategies" to manage their problems more effectively. Although such strategies can be very helpful, many of those working in child mental health have probably had experience of working with parents and children who struggle to use such strategies, often because they do not have the affect regulation skills or the epistemic trust that is prerequisite. By focusing on a core capacity that may promote resilience in a wide range of children, with a variety of presenting problems, mentalization-based treatment for children (MBT-C) aims to be a generic therapy that can be adapted to the particular needs of a range of

https://doi.org/10.1037/0000486-005
Mentalization-Based Treatment for Children: A Time-Limited Approach, Second Edition, by N. Midgley, K. Ensink, K. Lindqvist, N. Malberg, and N. Muller
Copyright © 2026 by the American Psychological Association. All rights reserved.

children in middle childhood—roughly between the ages of 5 and 12 years. When discussing the concept of resilience, Fonagy et al. (2016) wrote,

> Studies suggest that the ability to continue to mentalize even under considerable stress leads to so-called "broaden and build" (Fredrickson, 2001) cycles of attachment security, which reinforce feelings of secure attachment, personal agency, and affect regulation ("build") and lead one to be pulled into different and more adaptive environments ("broaden"). (p. 730)

This is precisely the aims of MBT-C, a time-limited, focused intervention that draws on fundamental psychodynamic principles but which can be easily integrated and used alongside a range of psychosocial treatments. The overall aim of MBT-C is to promote mentalizing and resilience in such a way that a developmental process is put back on track, and the family and child feel in a position where they are better equipped both to tackle the problems that first brought them to therapy and to learn how to make better use of supportive relationships. In doing this, MBT-C aims to increase the child's capacity for emotional regulation and to support parents to best meet the emotional needs of their children.

Working with parents alongside the time-limited therapy with the child is seen as an essential element of MBT-C, not only in the short-term but also to give the best chance of the parents continuing to support the child's development after the therapy has ended. For some children, time-limited MBT-C may be all that is needed; for others, it can be seen as a start, in order to develop reflective and regulatory capacities, which may need further, longer term support or therapy to ensure that development stays on track. As in many other time-limited therapies, we do not always expect an entire process of change to take place within the therapy; rather, we aim to start change processes that can continue after the therapy has ended (J. G. Allen et al., 2012).

In this chapter, we will begin by setting out our views on which children may benefit most from time-limited MBT-C, before going on to describe the overarching aims of this therapy in relation both to the direct work with children and to the parallel work with parents. We will then give an overview of the main treatment phases in MBT-C, each of which will be described in more detail in subsequent chapters.

WHICH CHILDREN MIGHT BENEFIT FROM TIME-LIMITED MENTALIZATION-BASED TREATMENT?

Time-limited MBT-C was developed for children aged between 5 and 12 years, presenting with a wide range of emotional and behavioral difficulties. In Chapter 3 in this volume, we provided an overview of the current evidence base for this approach, which provides preliminary support for seeing time-limited MBT-C as a transdiagnostic approach but does not (as yet) provide definitive empirical evidence for which types of children (and families) may benefit most from this way of working. As such, what we hope to offer here are some clinically useful guidelines on when to offer time-limited MBT-C. However, as with all guidelines, these will need to form the basis for more systematic research and evaluation, which will, in turn, inform our ongoing understanding of "what works for whom."

Because of its focus on promoting a core developmental process, MBT-C has not been developed specifically for treating one type of clinical presentation. In Chapter 2 in this volume, we outlined what the empirical research suggests about the role of mentalizing in a range of childhood disorders. Informed by that research, as well as our own clinical experience, we suggest that MBT-C appears especially suitable for children presenting with some combination of emotional (e.g., affective or anxiety disorders) and/or mild or moderate behavior problems, those with adjustment reactions, or those who need help dealing with a particular life challenge such as parental divorce or bereavement. Time-limited MBT-C may also be recommended for those who have experienced trauma and attachment difficulties, as we have tried to indicate through the case studies that we use throughout the book. In all cases, a careful consideration of the child's particular circumstances should inform any treatment recommendation, and specific adaptations can be necessary.

Although nonbehavioral therapies generally report less successful outcomes for children with externalizing problems, there is a particular reason why we do not rule out time-limited MBT-C as a treatment for all children with behavioral problems. In many cases of externalizing and aggressive children, parents as well as clinicians often focus on the "noisy" symptoms, thereby missing co-occurring internalizing symptoms, such as anxiety, depression, or low confidence (Goodman et al., 2012). Many children with conduct problems have received little help in understanding and integrating aspects of their temperament such as impulsivity, aggression, competitiveness, or desire for dominance, and they may benefit enormously from the opportunity to think about this with someone who is curious rather than judgmental. Conduct problems might also be a result of traumatic experiences. In these cases, therapists can help children to understand their reactions in the context of traumatic experiences, develop self- and bodily awareness, promote a sense of agency, and support affect regulation. Therapists can also help children to explore more adaptive ways of integrating aspects of their temperament or personality, or their traumatic experiences, to help facilitate self-esteem and affect regulation.

We are more hesitant to make claims that this treatment can be effective in cases where a lack of empathy underlies aggressive behaviors (such as children with callous–unemotional traits) or where there is a sadistic quality to the aggression. However, it may be worthwhile to attempt to stimulate the development of empathy and an awareness of negative impacts on others, given that there is much to gain and little to lose by intervening.

For children with experiences of trauma or loss, the extent and severity of the trauma needs to be assessed when possible. Often, this only comes to the surface while creating a safe therapeutic environment. Sometimes, longer term therapy is needed, and working in a time-limited way is not suitable or sufficient for children who need an extended period to build up enough sense of trust and safety to make use of the therapeutic setting. On the other hand, for some chronically traumatized children, the time-limited nature of the work may help them to commit to the process, since engaging in a shorter-term therapy can appear less threatening.

Likewise, for children with multiple experiences of separations and disruptions, there may be reason to reflect on whether a time-limited model is appropriate. For most children, the separation from the therapist after a time-limited intervention is an opportunity to work through a well-prepared ending, as we discuss more fully in Chapter 10 in this volume. However, for some children who have had multiple rejections—for example, those who have had multiple moves between different foster families—ending and separating so soon after establishing a bond, perhaps for the first time, may not be therapeutic. With these children, it is recommended to make a careful clinical evaluation and embark cautiously on time-limited psychotherapy, with the notion that more extended treatment may be needed.

Neurodevelopmental disorders such as autism spectrum disorder are not necessarily counter-indications for time-limited MBT-C. On the contrary, working with children with neurodiverse functioning from an MBT-C model can represent an act of epistemic justice (N. T. Malberg & Gori, 2024) in that it potentially offers children a chance to experience a sense of agency in the therapeutic context. Neurodiverse children can benefit from this way of working with some modifications (e.g., N. T. Malberg, 2021). The scaffolding nature of MBT-C facilitates the coconstruction of realistic therapeutic goals that seek to meet the child and the family where they are in the developmental line of mentalization. Often, treatment goals for this group of children will focus on the building blocks of attention control and affect regulation. This is in response to the need to increase the motivation to connect interpersonally and manage the emotional impact of relational stress that these children often experience. Regarding goals for parents, it is often important to focus on the process of mentalizing the experience of having a child who speaks a "different relational language," as well as further exploring the need for acceptance of their child's functioning.

As the paragraphs above make clear, making treatment recommendations based purely on psychiatric diagnosis has only limited value, and it is important to take into account the wider family context when considering suitability of treatment rather than focusing exclusively on the child's presenting problems. We consider instead that MBT-C is suitable for children with a wide range of clinical difficulties and that MBT-C is flexible so that the therapist can adjust how they will work to be appropriate for a particular child, taking into account their level of functioning and the limits of their capacities. Given what we have said in earlier chapters about the importance of epistemic trust, a factor to consider when thinking about suitability for MBT-C is the nature and quality of the child's capacity to consider new knowledge from another person as trustworthy, generalizable, and relevant to the self (Fonagy et al., 2015). When there is a fundamental capacity for epistemic trust, the child and parents are open to the therapist and open to learn. This is most often found in children and parents with specific/temporary mentalizing breakdowns, who have perhaps faced situations that have challenged their functioning, such as parental separation or a significant loss.

When children and/or their parents have a greater degree of epistemic distrust, more time may be needed to build a relationship with the therapist(s), but the argument for offering a more mentalization-focused intervention is stronger because the work explicitly focuses on addressing what may stop the child or parent from being able to learn from others. However, the process of generalizing what is learned in therapy may take longer because of the mistrust that can only gradually change into trusting oneself and others. As described in the previous chapter, this is more often the case for children with insecure attachments, where helping to address the child's epistemic vigilance and suspicion toward others may be a core part of the therapeutic work. When parents share such suspicion, it is especially important to engage them meaningfully in the work.

Children who have experienced chronic trauma, such as neglect or abuse, or who have disorganized patterns of attachment often show epistemic hypervigilance. When presenting to services, these children may display a combination of internalizing and externalizing problems. For many of these children, three rounds of 12 sessions of time-limited MBT-C may not be enough. However, this is not to say that offering open-ended, long-term work is necessarily the better option. Haugvik and Johns (2008) pointed out that offering focused, time-limited intervention can help families with more complex problems to engage in therapy. Offering an initial period of time-limited work can be extremely helpful, but it is also important to be realistic and modest about the aims of the work. When the parents themselves have severe psychiatric difficulties, careful consideration needs to be given as to how their mental health may be impacting on the child's well-being. However, in these cases, we have found that an MBT-C trajectory can give an impetus for parents to decide to work on their own mental health if the MBT-C treatment has been experienced as helpful.

THE OVERARCHING AIMS OF TIME-LIMITED MENTALIZATION-BASED TREATMENT FOR CHILDREN

Although the clinical presentations of children entering time-limited MBT-C may vary, there are certain aims of the work that are likely to be common. The general aim of MBT-C is to help develop and enhance mentalizing processes in the child as well as the parents, which will, in turn, help the child to become aware of and regulate emotions and/or develop explicit mentalizing skills that can help manage key difficulties. These key difficulties can be addressing trauma, parental mental illness, or other family and life difficulties, or developing better mentalizing about aspects of self, such as temperament or specific emotional difficulties and concerns. Related to this is helping the child create a narrative and develop a more coherent sense of self, which can lead to a better, more positive self-image. When children have the capacity to mentalize about their reactions and those of others, this should facilitate emotion regulation and contribute to a feeling of self-agency.

A central aim of the individual work with the child is to develop their capacity to pay attention to, recognize, endure, and regulate emotions. This capacity is enormously helpful in attuning toward others and understanding complex social situations, as well as experiencing self-control, a sense of self, and agency. Children brought to therapy may be either under- or overregulated, meaning that feelings can be experienced and expressed too little or too much. It is not unusual for children to be underregulated regarding certain affects and overregulated regarding others. For example, a child may overregulate their anxiety about separation, appearing to be dismissive of attachment needs, yet underregulated when it comes to their capacity to control aggression. The aim in therapy is to help the child develop the capacity to connect with their body, identify bodily signals, become aware of sensations and emotions, regulate these, and express emotions in age-appropriate ways.

A metaphor that might illustrate this, and which can be helpful for parents, is to talk about affect regulation as a form of volume control. When children have limited capacities for affect regulation, we may think of it in terms of them needing to learn to use their volume control more effectively. Sometimes, the volume is too low, so that their feelings cannot be heard by themselves and those around them; sometimes, the volume is too high, so that their feelings take over and it is impossible to hear anything else, such as their own thoughts. In order to use their volume control effectively, first, they need to recognize that there is something there that they may need to modulate; second, they need to find the volume control; and third, they need to use the volume control, regulate, and modulate.

For children who have experienced breakdowns in mentalization due to trauma, loss, or other specific triggering situations or events, an additional aim can be to create a coherent narrative about the event, as well as exploring related thoughts, feelings, and experiences and how this narrative has impacted their self-image. A crucial element of this is mentalizing the affect (Jurist, 2005), which is at the heart of regulating emotions. This means reflecting on emotions linked to traumatic events or losses and accepting the existence of feelings without being overwhelmed by them. The aim is not to create insight into the trauma per se, although understanding the link between some automatic reactions and trauma can be helpful. The aim is more about learning and understanding in the here and now how to endure and regulate the emotions associated with the traumatic event.

Another aim common to most MBT-C work is to strengthen and deepen the child's ability to form and maintain relationships. Related to this is working with affective interaction—being able to regulate and express emotions in relationships. This can also entail seeking comfort and care from attachment figures when in distress.

Alongside the direct work with the child, the fundamental aim of the work with parents is to strengthen their parental reflective functioning (Slade, 2005) and capacity for assuming a reflective stance as parents (Ensink et al., 2017). This includes helping them to develop a capacity to think about the child's psychological experience and to focus on the child's mind—to see their child as a separate person with their own thoughts and feelings, with a sense that being curious about their child's mind can help them to give meaning to behaviors. A secondary, but important, component is also to help the parent develop the capacity to see their own affects and behavior from the perspective of their child, as this might affect their parenting in important ways. When parents can explicitly mentalize about themselves and their child, this helps them respond to the child's needs and emotions in more flexible and attuned ways.

Inevitably, parents of children referred for therapy, like all of us, will have their own mentalizing difficulties, whether temporary or more pervasive. Helping parents reflect on how their own emotions affect their behavior toward the child and, in turn, their child's emotions will then be an important part of the work. Developing, for example, some empathic awareness of when their own anger may be overwhelming, disorganizing, and scary (for the child but also perhaps for themselves) or how fear and anxiety make them withdraw or become intrusive and controlling may have crucial implications for their capacity to limit potentially harmful interactions with their children (Cooper & Redfern, 2015). Parents who have experienced neglect or abuse in their own childhood may also need extra help to address real or imagined concerns around intergenerational patterns that may affect their parenting.

In light of work related to the concept of epistemic trust, it is possible to think about the general aims of MBT-C in an additional way. Fonagy and Allison (2014), in writing about their work with adults who have personality disorders, go so far as to suggest that learning to mentalize in treatment is not, in itself, a sufficient therapeutic aim. Instead, they argue that mentalizing in therapy is only of value insofar as it is a way of establishing epistemic trust: "The very experience of having our subjectivity understood—of being mentalized—is a necessary trigger for us to be able to receive and learn from the social knowledge that has the potential to change our perception of ourselves and our social world" (p. 372).

In light of these ideas, Fonagy and Allison (2014) go on to describe the key processes that they consider to underlie all meaningful therapeutic change:

- creating of a therapeutic context in which the patient feels understood, which allows them to reduce their sense of epistemic mistrust or hypervigilance;
- the reemergence of the patient's own capacity to mentalize, as they find themselves in the mind of the therapist, leading to a greater sense of self-coherence and agency; and
- the recovery of a "capacity for social information exchange" (p. 377), which allows the patient to discover new ways of learning from, and about others, beyond the therapy context.

Although these authors are writing about therapeutic work with adults with personality disorders, we find these ideas helpful when thinking about time-limited MBT-C as well. This is partly because they make explicit why work with parents (and often the wider network) is such a crucial part of the model. Fonagy and Campbell (2015) noted, when speaking about work with adult patients, that "reopening epistemic trust in a therapeutic context is merely one part of a process of social learning . . . that needs to be supported in the patient's wider social environment for there to be any chance of sustained or meaningful change" (p. 243). If this is true of adults, it is even more the case in work with children, whose ongoing dependence on their caregivers makes it essential to help create the kind of context(s) in which the child is able to continue to benefit from the changes that, we hope, can begin in therapy. Each child is part of a family, but they also live in a neighborhood, and a country, with wider sociocultural influences that impact their way of being, thinking, and feeling (Fonagy & Allison, 2023). These aspects will influence the level of epistemic trust and social learning, and shape the attachment between parents and children.

Although time-limited therapy may not be sufficient to fully restore a sense of epistemic trust, it is possible to address or make children aware that certain early experiences may have affected their trust in others and in life and thereby begin a process of epistemic unfreezing. It may be helpful for children to feel how a lack of trust may manifest in their interpersonal relationships with peers and family—for example, always wanting to lead and being afraid to let go, which might make them come across as domineering toward other children. An important experience when a child lacks this sense of epistemic trust is starting the process of daring to trust others. This can happen when another person (initially the therapist but also the other adults or caregivers in the child's life) reacts with respect and curiosity toward them. In other words, the process of restoring epistemic trust and social learning, and hence creating a greater sense of resilience, can be started in a time-limited therapy.

THE STRUCTURE AND FRAME OF TIME-LIMITED MENTALIZATION-BASED TREATMENT FOR CHILDREN

In order to be able to explore, we need a secure base that we know we can return to if necessary. In therapeutic work with children and families, we strive to help parents to become the secure base from which their child can explore the world, and we invite the child to develop a curiosity about their own mind as well as the minds of others. In order to feel safe to do so, the child requires a secure external world where they feel in control (Blake, 2008). Many children and parents with mentalizing problems do not experience the outer, or the inner world, as safe enough for this exploring to take place. In MBT-C, the therapist strives to create an atmosphere of safety. A clear, transparent, and predictable therapeutic frame is one important factor in order to achieve that.

The specific practicalities of the frame include a time limitation with a predefined number of sessions, a calendar, a focus formulation, and parallel work with the parent(s). The standard duration of time-limited MBT-C is 12 weekly sessions, with sessions offered in parallel for the child and parents.

We aim not to be overly prescriptive, as the practicalities of the treatment can be organized in several different ways, depending on clinical setting as well as the severity of the problems of the child and parents. What is important is that the therapeutic contract is clear and coherent from the beginning for the parents as well as for the child. This is a way of creating a sense of safety and collaboration, and avoiding a scenario where the therapist makes decisions that the family is unaware of. This transparency is part of the mentalizing stance, described more fully in Chapter 5 in this volume, and contributes to a sense of shared ownership of the therapeutic process.

The notion of "phases" in therapy is, to some degree, an artificial one, given that the underlying aims and techniques of the work continue from the beginning to the end of therapy. Nevertheless, part of the structure of time-limited MBT-C is a predictable shape to the treatment, which can be thought of in terms of key phases, each with its own particular tasks (see Exhibit 4.1).

Assessment Phase (3–5 Meetings)

All therapeutic work with children and their families should be based on a thorough assessment leading to some provisional understanding of the presenting problem(s), as well as a formulation of how those problems may be linked to the proposed intervention. Depending on the context in which therapists work,

EXHIBIT 4.1

Phases of Treatment in MBT-C

Outline of an MBT-C time-limited treatment
• Assessment phase (3–5 meetings) Assessment meetings with family, child, and parents Reviewing the assessment phase (feedback on the assessment, making decisions about continuing with MBT-C, sharing and discussing the focus formulation and goals)
• Sessions 1 to 3: Initial phase With child: Introduce calendar and therapy box for the child, focus on engaging child in treatment, explore whether the child can play around the focus formulation With parent(s): Focus on engaging parent(s) in treatment, work with the parents around the focus formulation and supporting "reflective parenting"
• Sessions 4 to 8: Middle phase Focus of work with parents and child is on stimulating and developing mentalizing capacity in relation to the focus formulation and the issues that brought the child to therapy
• After Session 8: Review meeting Joint meeting with both therapists and parents to review progress of therapy and to make a decision about whether to move toward ending, offer a further block of sessions, or recommend alternative approaches
• Sessions 9 to 12: Ending phase Where therapy is due to end, the focus is on preparing for the ending and exploring how best to maintain gains that have been made, beyond the end of therapy Where therapy is due to be continuing, work with parents and child will be ongoing.

Note. MBT-C = mentalization-based treatment for children.

there may already be particular approaches to how an assessment is conducted, but in Chapter 6 in this volume we set out a model of assessment that focuses on developing a "mentalizing profile" of the child and family. The aim of such an assessment is to explore if and how mentalizing difficulties may be linked to the child's presenting problems, and whether a mentalization-focused intervention is likely to be of help.

The model of assessment set out in this book shows how the MBT-C therapist can assess the capacity to mentalize in both children and parents; offer feedback on the assessment; and make decisions with families about whether to continue with MBT-C. If work is going ahead, a focus statement will be formulated, and the child, parents, and therapists will agree on a set of goals for the treatment.

Sessions 1 to 3: Initial Phase

Although it can be thought of as a separate phase of treatment, much of what is done during the first few sessions in MBT-C builds on the work already done in the assessment phase (Chapter 6, this volume) and makes use of techniques that are also part of the ongoing sessions with the child (Chapters 7 and 8, this volume). With children, the primary aim of this initial phase is to establish a therapeutic alliance, primarily by means of empathic attunement and genuine engagement with, and curiosity about, the child's world. As discussed more fully in Chapter 7 in this volume, play is central to this process of engagement and is a marvelous way to socialize the child to the way that therapy works. This will include introducing the calendar and the therapy box for the child and exploring whether the child can play around the focus formulation. With parent(s), engagement and establishing a therapeutic alliance is also paramount as the parent–therapist begins to support "reflective parenting" (Chapter 9, this volume). Empathic attunement with the parent's experience, even when the therapist may have different views on how a parent is responding to their child, is key at this stage.

Sessions 4 to 8: Middle Phase

The middle phase of the work (approximately sessions 4–8) is where the core work on developing the child's mentalizing capacity takes place, drawing on a wide range of therapeutic techniques and in relation to the focus formulation (see Chapters 7 and 8, this volume). Meanwhile, the sessions with parents can increasingly focus on promoting the various elements of "reflective parenting." In the work with both parents and children, if affects can be regulated in a way that makes explicit mentalizing possible, then empathic attunement can increasingly be complemented by a focus on promoting perspective taking and seeing things from others' points of view. In some cases, the focus will be more on promoting the underdeveloped capacity for mentalizing and/or paying attention to the situations in which explicit mentalizing breaks down.

Review Meeting

After the first eight sessions, a review meeting is offered with the child and his parents where the initial focus and treatment goals are reviewed, and it is decided if the first block of sessions seems sufficient and work should come to an end or whether work needs to continue further (see Chapter 10, this volume). When it is felt that the therapeutic work will need to go on for longer than the initial block of sessions, it is still possible to work in a time-limited way using an "open-ticket model." In this case, another block of 12 sessions can be offered, up to a maximum of 36 (i.e., three blocks of 12) sessions. This flexibility facilitates using the time-limited approach for children with more complex disorders, such as those who have experienced trauma or have attachment disorders. However, we would not necessarily subscribe to the idea that more complex difficulties always benefit from longer (or open-ended) therapies. Our experience is that working with a time limitation and a focus can be helpful, but that children with more complex problems often need more than one block of 12 sessions.

Sessions 9 to 12: Ending Phase

Where therapy is due to end, the focus is on preparing for the ending and exploring how best to maintain gains that have been made beyond the end of therapy. As described more fully in Chapter 10 in this volume, the time-limited nature of MBT-C means that endings are kept very actively in mind throughout the work, and the use of a calendar helps the child to be aware of how many sessions they have had and how many are left. Because one of the aims of MBT-C is to ensure that the child and parents end the therapy with a better capacity to make use of other relationships outside therapy, a particular focus of the ending phase is on translating what has been learned in therapy to other supportive relationships.

Checking-In or Booster Sessions

At whatever point the time-limited therapy ends, the MBT-C model includes a checking-in or booster session, which is arranged for anywhere between 3 and 12 months after finishing. The timing of this meeting and how it should be planned are discussed in Chapter 10 in this volume.

THE PHYSICAL SETTING FOR THERAPY

When thinking about an optimal setting for therapy with children, there are no clear prescriptions. We recommend that the therapy is planned in the same room for all sessions and that this room does not change too much. Sometimes, however, there may be reasons for changing the room when there is reason to believe that the child needs a specific context. For example, in some settings, there may be an outdoor space that is available to the therapist, or a gym in which the child is able to engage in more physical activities. Moving the therapy at certain points into such a setting can be helpful for children with attention regulation problems, such as those who are very hyperactive or aggressive, or those who are quickly overwhelmed by incentives from the outside and lack regulation capacities.

A child's therapy room does not necessarily need to contain a lot of toys or play material. On the contrary, children with regulation difficulties may become overwhelmed in rooms with too much play material to choose from. When the arousal level is too high, the child will not be able to play or pay attention to what he is experiencing. Likewise, some children may feel safer in a smaller room, whereas others may need the space of a bigger room in order not to feel restricted. Ideally, the room needs to have at least some floor space large enough for the child to move around in and play more physical games such as looping a ball into a basket, playing mini hockey, or simply throwing and catching a ball. For some children, it can be helpful if there are some personal things in the room because they might recognize aspects of the therapist in the way the room is styled, as well as creating an atmosphere that is not too institutional (Slijper, 2021). At the same time, some children may feel anxious or get feelings of rivalry toward other children when a room is too personal.

When selecting playroom material, the therapist aims to create the optimal space for children to play and express themselves. It is recommended to have some sensory or sensopathic play material that stimulates or awakens the senses, such as water on the skin or the rich textures of clay. As Stern (1992, 2004) pointed out, such materials are often very important for children with attention and affect regulation problems. This can be a sand tray or kinetic sand, clay, finger paint, water, bubbles, or different sizes and types of balls. In order to stimulate fantasy and role-play, dolls, animal figures, cars, bricks, and dress-up clothes are often used, and it is valuable to have dolls with a variety of skin tones and of different genders and ages. It is also a good idea to have a few games as part of the playroom material. Almost all therapists have some art supplies, and some therapists also have other creative materials such as music instruments. Of course, as therapists, we do not always have much control about what kind of space is available or what materials are provided, but even so, it can be helpful to think with the child and parents about how the space may be experienced and how it may affect the child's behavior in sessions. The aim is for the child to feel invited and at ease to play following their impulses (within certain limits) and to express themselves freely.

TIME AS A FRAMEWORK FOR THERAPY

The British child psychotherapist Monica Lanyado (2012) wrote,

> Child psychotherapy is about holding and letting go. The balance between holding and letting go is an important issue in life and is a reciprocal process. Just as parents

> have to learn how and when to let go of the child and when to hold the child in mind more, so the child also needs to learn when it is safe to let go of the parents as well as when to seek the parents' presence, internally and externally. (p. 117)

Time is an aspect that is addressed throughout therapy, and its importance is emphasized by the time limitation, supported by the use of a calendar (see below). The time limitation can be a motivational factor to work with the most urgent issues, and it reminds us that the family will need to have the capacity to address difficulties themselves in the future. Every therapeutic intervention in MBT-C has the ultimate aim of encouraging and increasing the ability to mentalize in a way that can help parents and children to manage their difficulties more constructively once the treatment is over. In this way, the ending is built into the process from the very beginning of therapy (see also Chapter 10, this volume).

Being transparent about the time limitation and the number of sessions remaining also gives the child an opportunity to prepare for and work through the separation that comes with the end of therapy. Many children in therapy have experienced multiple separations in their lives, but they may not always have had the time to prepare and work through them, making this a new experience where feelings about endings can be addressed together with the therapist. Since MBT-C is process focused, the time frame can also serve as a port of entry in terms of activating relational dynamics. For example, when a child (or indeed a parent) complains "You don't give me enough time!" this can be used to explore triggers of nonmentalizing moments, or may reflect issues of fairness for some children and families that can be helpfully explored.

Inspired by developmentally directed time-limited psychotherapy for children (Haugvik & Johns, 2008; Røed Hansen, 2012), one of the ways in which the MBT-C therapist actively works with the time limitation as part of the therapy is using a calendar together with the child. The aims of the calendar are to stimulate a sense of ownership of the therapy in the child, to encourage a reflective stance, and to help the child have some sense of the time-limited nature of the work.

Calendars can look different but should always consist of a (preferably large) piece of paper marked with as many rectangles or circles as there are sessions. The therapist introduces the calendar during the first session. As part of establishing the framework of the therapy, the therapist tells the child that at the end of each session, they will draw something in the calendar, and that this is a way for them to keep track of the sessions and reflect together on what has happened that day. A good idea may be to let the child number the spaces in the calendar to establish it as a way to give some sense of the length of the therapy from the beginning. The child can also decorate the back of the calendar in order to make it more personal, thereby enhancing the sense that it belongs to them.

When there is approximately 5 to 10 minutes left of each session, the child is asked to draw something in the calendar. The main rule for this is that anything is okay. The calendar belongs to the child, and they decide what to draw in it. There may be times when the therapist feels an urge to help the child by suggesting certain things to draw or even helping, but unless the child explicitly asks for this, the therapist should refrain from this. Sometimes, however, the therapist needs to take responsibility for the calendar in the sense of not letting the child tear it apart, paint all over the different spaces, or in other ways ruin it.

As mentioned previously in this chapter, one aim of MBT-C is to help the child create a coherent narrative. Using a calendar, the child and the therapist create their own story—a narrative about the therapeutic process that can be created and visualized together. The calendar can also be a powerful tool for addressing the ending of the therapy and the forthcoming separation. By looking at the calendar together, the child and the therapist can keep track of the number of sessions they have left and prepare for their farewell. At the end of the therapy and in the booster sessions, the calendar can be used for looking back and reviewing the work that has been done together (Røed Hansen, 2012).

FOCUS FORMULATION

Another core aspect of the therapeutic frame, also inspired by developmentally directed time-limited psychotherapy for children (Haugvik & Johns, 2008; Røed Hansen, 2012), is formulating a focus for the therapy, which should emerge out of carefully observing and listening to what the child and parent(s) conveys during the assessment sessions, verbally as well as nonverbally. The focus formulation should be a short phrase or a story, shared with the child and parents at the start of treatment. In a way, it can be related to Stern's (1985) concept of a "key metaphor," representing core relational and emotional themes (Johns, 2008). One of the main aims of the focus formulation is to speak with the child and convey that the therapy has something to offer them. Many children are brought to therapy by parents or other adults with little notion of why they have come or with a sense of being there simply in order to please the adults around them (Johns, 2008). When time is limited, the task of engaging the child becomes more urgent, and the focus can be seen as functioning as an invitation to the child to engage in the therapy process. Using material from the assessment with the child in formulating the focus can strengthen the child's sense of agency in the therapy—something they have contributed to the encounter becomes a focus for the treatment.

Another aim with the focus formulation is to stimulate mentalizing by directing the parents' attention to central experiences, thoughts, and feelings in the child—keeping the child's mind in mind and, at the same time, stimulating the child's self-reflection around their own inner states. The therapist's formulation becomes a model for keeping someone else's mind in mind. The focus creates joint attention toward what the child presents as central experiences, thoughts, and feelings. It shows that the therapist has taken in something from the parents and child and invites a meaning-creating dialogue around the problems that brought the child to therapy. The process of formulating a focus is presented more fully in Chapter 6 in this volume. Sometimes, it can be helpful to create a separate focus formulation for the parents and for the child. This can be especially helpful in building epistemic trust and for the parents also to feel seen and mentalized.

ONE THERAPIST OR TWO?

As set out above, work with parents or caregivers (and, where needed, with the wider network around the child) is considered a key component of time-limited MBT-C. The basic model is that two therapists work together, one with the child and one with the parents. Ideally, the sessions are scheduled at the same time. This gives both the parents and the child their own space, but they still come together to the clinic, creating a sense that this is something they are doing together as a joint family effort. It is also helpful practically, as it means that parents do not need to make separate visits for their own meetings. When working in pairs, the two therapists can work as a team, helping each other to keep their mentalizing "online." The collaboration between the therapists can serve as a model for the family of how it is possible to mentalize together. It can also decrease concerns regarding confidentiality for the children, especially the older ones, who may have concerns that what they speak about in their own sessions will be shared with their parents.

In some cases, of course, there may be practical or therapeutic reasons for working with only one therapist. First and foremost, in many private practices or clinics, therapists lack opportunities to work in pairs. But even when this is an option, there may be some situations where one therapist is preferable. Some parents find it difficult to trust their child with anyone whom they do not know and can be more supportive of the child's therapy if they have some direct access to their child's therapist. For children to be able to use the therapeutic space themselves and to trust the therapist, they need to feel agreement from their parents that they are allowed to do so. When this is not possible, loyalty conflicts may arise. Although these can create opportunities to explore mental states, such loyalty conflicts can also threaten the work and obstruct the therapeutic process. In these cases, it may help the parents if they feel that they know and have a trusting relationship with the person working with their child. Furthermore, in families where there are very different views of the child and/or the problems, intense conflicts, or a great deal of blaming, having the same therapist may become a uniting factor. A therapist who works directly with the child can sometimes bring the child to life in their meeting with the parents in a way that is not so easy for a separate parent therapist, who inevitably focuses to a much greater extent on the child in the parent's mind.

INTRODUCING THE CASES

In the remaining chapters of this book, the model of time-limited MBT-C will be illustrated using vignettes from six cases. As outlined in the introduction, these are composite cases that draw on our clinical experience but which do not describe actual children or families with whom we have worked.

We have selected these cases because we think they represent a range of children who might be seen in time-limited MBT-C, in terms of both their ages and the presenting problems that brought them to therapy. The children demonstrate a range of attachment strategies (some more avoidant, others more preoccupied or disorganized) and capacities for mentalizing. They are also varied in the nature of their family contexts and the capacity of their carers to mentalize the child. Other than the chapter on assessment, where we follow one particular child (John) through the entire process, the vignettes from different children are combined in each chapter.

Anne, Age 6 Years

Anne was referred to therapy because of temper tantrums, oppositional behavior, and separation anxiety. She is an only child, and her parents divorced when she was 2 years old. She now lives with her mother, Mrs. H. Anne's tantrums mostly happen at home, but lately her mother has started getting calls from Anne's school regarding Anne's tendency to push and kick other children in her class when frustrated. When trying to leave her at school, Anne often clings to her mother and does not want her to leave. She has a high level of activity, and the adults around her have noticed that it seems difficult for her to relax and be calm. Mrs. H can sometimes feel so helpless that she locks herself in a room at home while Anne is left screaming downstairs.

Mohammed, Age 7 Years

Mohammed was in a severe car accident 6 months ago and badly injured his leg. His parents are divorced, and he lives primarily with his father, Mr. D, who has a new partner. After the accident, Mohammed began having aggressive outbursts at home and school. He has always been an active and smart boy who likes getting his way, but his father says he has become especially difficult to negotiate with since the accident. He has difficulties sleeping and complains of nightmares. Mr. D describes how Mohammed used to be an "easy" and well-tempered child but lately has been highly irritable and unpredictable in his behavior.

Belinda, Age 7 Years

Belinda's mother, Mrs. C, contacted the clinic, worried that Belinda was often very sad. Belinda lives with her mother and grandmother and has no contact with her father or half sister. The school reports no difficulties, but Mrs. C says there is a struggle every morning to get Belinda out of bed and dressed and to go to the school bus. Belinda says that she does not like school, and when her mother or grandmother try to talk her "into a better mood," she can become quite cruel. Both mother and grandmother say that they feel very controlled by Belinda and rather hopeless about how best to help her.

John, Age 8 Years

John was referred for therapy because of severe aggressive outbursts and difficulty controlling his impulses. He acts out verbally and physically at school as well as at home. His aggressive behavior makes him isolated at school and he has no friends. John lives with a foster family composed of a foster mother, a foster father, and two foster sisters, having been removed from his biological mother at 2 years of age. His father disappeared when he was a baby, and his mother suffers from severe, ongoing psychiatric difficulties. John sometimes visits his biological mother, who has a new partner and lives with John's biological brother. He has previously lived with two other foster families.

Liza, Age 11 Years

Liza has always been shy but lately has increasingly struggled with any kind of separation from her mother. She has stomach pains and headaches when going to school and calls her mother several times a day. She is withdrawn in school and has few friends there. Liza lives with her mother, father, and brother (age 15). Her brother can sometimes behave quite violently outside the home, has been involved in street crime, and frequently argues with his parents. There is a lot of conflict in the family related to her brother, and the parents describe that they are under a lot of stress due to his behavior. They worry that Liza's needs have been somewhat neglected because, over the years, they have had so much difficulty with her brother, who is now supported by a specialist youth offending team.

Ruth, Age 12 Years

Ruth comes to therapy with her foster parents, two women whom she has been living with for the past 2 years. Ruth was born in prison, and her biological parents are both still incarcerated. During her childhood, she has lived in several different foster homes. In one of the foster homes, she witnessed a sexual act between her foster siblings, which had a traumatic effect on her and led to her being moved to her current foster parents. Ruth has temper tantrums and difficulties eating, and she experiences mood swings. At times, she can be bossy and aggressive; at other times, she can become sad and withdrawn.

CONCLUSION

Time-limited MBT-C has been developed for use with children with a range of presenting problems and is not a therapy that was developed to treat only children with one specific diagnosis. When assessing suitability and planning the treatment, a comprehensive review of the child and family functioning is needed—one that pays attention not only to symptoms and behavior but also to the nature and severity of the mentalizing deficits and the attachment relation between the parents and the child. In deciding if working in a time-limited way is appropriate, it can help to assess whether there is a global underdevelopment of mentalizing or if the breakdowns in mentalizing are more specific/temporary in both the child and the parents.

The overarching aim of time-limited MBT-C is to help develop and enhance mentalizing processes, helping the child to become aware of and regulate emotions as well as to mentalize about difficulties that the child might face. This, in turn, can help to reduce epistemic mistrust, so that the child is better able to make use of supportive relationships, both within and beyond therapy. The aim of the parental work is to enhance the carers' ability to mentalize regarding their child's experiences and the parents' own emotions related to parenting and how they influence family interactions. When these two can be achieved side by side, children with a range of presenting difficulties may be meaningfully helped. The standard model for MBT-C is 12 sessions for the child with simultaneous sessions for the parents, but it leaves room for adaptations. The use of a calendar and the focus statement become means for the child to develop a sense of participation, ownership, and agency in the therapeutic process, as well as being helpful instruments for keeping track of time and creating coherency in the therapy. In time-limited MBT-C, structure and focus are seen as important therapeutic factors. Everybody knowing and agreeing on the setting of the therapy from the start enhances the sense that the therapeutic endeavor is a shared one and that the therapists do not have information or make decisions on their own. By discussing aspects of the therapeutic setting together with the family, the therapists can model a reflective stance as well as negotiating an appropriate frame and a focus statement for therapy. Nevertheless, many aspects of the therapeutic frame, such as working with one or two therapists, can be tailored according to the needs of the family, the preferences of the clinicians, as well as the opportunities provided in the clinical setting.

5

The "Therapist Stance"

Successful mentalizing is not so much the capacity to always accurately read one's own or another's inner states, but rather a way of approaching relationships that reflects an expectation that one's own thinking and feeling may be enlightened, enriched, and changed by learning about the mental states of other people. In this respect, mentalizing is as much an attitude as it is a skill, an attitude which is inquiring and respectful of other people's mental states, aware of the limits of one's knowledge of others and reflects a view that understanding the feelings of others is important for maintaining healthy and mutually rewarding relationships.

—ASEN AND FONAGY (2012A, P. 107)

When teaching mentalization-based treatment (MBT) to therapists who are new to the approach, there is often a temptation to focus on acquiring specific techniques, as if they are the heart of any therapeutic approach. But as most people working in this field would probably agree, any specific model of therapy—whether MBT, cognitive behavioral therapy, or interpersonal therapy—is not simply a set of tools or techniques that can be "applied" when working with children and families; it also implies a stance, or way of being, that informs every aspect of the therapeutic work.

When researchers ask adults or children to look back on what it was like going to therapy, very few of them say much about what kind of techniques the therapist used—they do not often comment on the quality of the cognitive reframing or whether the therapist's interpretations were accurate. Instead, they tend to begin by speaking about the therapist—what he or she was like, whether he or she was nice, whether they felt comfortable with him or her. Of course, this does not mean that the techniques the therapist uses do not matter—just that all such techniques always take place in the context of a relationship, and that the therapist's "way of being" may be as important as the particular techniques used.

https://doi.org/10.1037/0000486-006
Mentalization-Based Treatment for Children: A Time-Limited Approach, Second Edition, by N. Midgley, K. Ensink, K. Lindqvist, N. Malberg, and N. Muller
Copyright © 2026 by the American Psychological Association. All rights reserved.

EXHIBIT 5.1

Key Elements of the Therapeutic Stance in MBT-C

- The "therapeutic presence" of the MBT-C therapist (including basic helping orientation, being authentic, nonjudgmental, genuine, accepting, respectful, responsive, present, empathic, supportive, and willing to self-disclose where appropriate)
- An interest in the mind, not just behavior
- Curiosity and the not-knowing (inquisitive) stance
- Monitoring misunderstandings (alliance ruptures)

Note. MBT-C = mentalization-based treatment for children.

The stance in MBT is not just a background to the real work of therapy—it is at the core of what MBT is and how it works, and it is for this reason that we introduce it here, before setting out the specific details of the mentalization-based treatment for children (MBT-C) model itself. The stance is crucial because it is both an aim of MBT-C, insofar as we are trying to help the families we work with to develop a capacity to mentalize, and the means by which we can achieve this aim by trying to model this stance ourselves.

This chapter therefore sets out the key components of the therapeutic stance in MBT-C, which are summarized in Exhibit 5.1. Most importantly, we describe the ways in which the therapist's own mentalizing capacity can break down and the importance of identifying these moments and using them for therapeutic ends. We end by making some comments about the role of supervision in supporting the therapist's mentalizing stance, and we describe an approach to supervision that focuses explicitly on helping the therapist to maintain their own capacity to mentalize.

THE THERAPEUTIC PRESENCE OF THE MENTALIZATION-BASED TREATMENT FOR CHILDREN THERAPIST

Belinda, Age 7

Belinda started time-limited MBT-C because she was anxious and withdrawn, and had difficulty making friends at school. She has lived with her mother and grandmother since her parents divorced after years of arguing, shouting, and recriminations. Her parents felt that they had protected Belinda from witnessing this, but it was clear that Belinda's own needs had been somewhat neglected amid all the acrimony, and both her mother and grandmother conveniently saw her as a child who "just kept herself to herself and didn't need friends."

When the therapist first meets Belinda, he is struck by how little eye contact she makes. At the first individual meeting, Belinda follows the therapist to the playroom but sits rather listlessly, drawing circles on a piece of paper. When the therapist invites her to play a game of catch, Belinda looks rather surprised but accepts. She throws the ball a few times, but her coordination is poor, and one of her throws knocks a plastic cup off the table, rattling onto the floor. Belinda glances quickly at the therapist and appears scared. The therapist smiles at Belinda and gets down to floor level, picking up the cup. "Don't worry—not broken," he says, and he

> shows Belinda the cup. Then, he goes on: "I don't know what you're like, but when I go somewhere new, I'm always a bit nervous about what people are going to think of me. I don't know if they're going to like me or not." Belinda looks at the therapist, with a bit of curiosity. "Know the feeling?" asks the therapist, but Belinda doesn't reply. Instead, she picks up the ball, and they carry on playing catch. The therapist starts adding in different tricks, and soon they are laughing. "Good catch!" says the therapist, when Belinda reaches a ball that is quite high. And when he misses one and the soft ball bounces off Belinda's nose, the therapist goes "Ouch!" in a playful, somewhat exaggerated manner. "Did that hurt?" he asks, but Belinda shakes her head.

In the opening part of this session, there is nothing much that the therapist is doing that may look like mentalizing therapy. He is not using any sophisticated techniques or trying to invite explicit mentalizing ("What did you think I was thinking when the cup got knocked off the table?"). Instead, he is acting like a fairly regular person, meeting a rather anxious girl on her own for the first time in an unfamiliar place.

This natural, human therapeutic presence is at the heart of time-limited MBT-C therapy, just as it is for most therapies. But as there is always a danger that it gets overlooked, or taken for granted, we begin this chapter by emphasizing the importance of this fundamental therapeutic presence. As Rogers (1957) set out, in his seminal work on humanistic (person-centered) therapy, this therapeutic presence includes empathy, genuineness, and nonjudgmental, positive regard. In his actions and behavior, Belinda's therapist presents himself as an interested, well-disposed adult, who engages with Belinda in a reciprocal way and shows some interest in understanding how Belinda is feeling. He is not a "blank screen" but instead speaks about feelings and discloses a little of his own personal experience and what goes on in his own mind. The MBT-C therapist can answer questions from the child or parents as well as practice judicious self-disclosure. A survey of experienced therapists suggests that only a small minority make use of self-disclosure in their work with children, and that few view it as contributing to the aims of their work (Capobianco & Farber, 2005). But as Taylor (2012) wrote, when working from a mentalizing stance, it is helpful to have "a clear, [but] perhaps a little flexible, boundary between the personal and the private domains" (p. 93), so that we can be genuine while at the same time mindful not to disclose personal information that we may not feel comfortable sharing. Speaking openly about oneself can often help to engage children, especially in the early stages of therapy, and can help to create a sense that the therapist is friendly, interested, and noncritical (Barish, 2009). In this way, the therapist brings herself in as a person with her own mind and perspective, and models honesty and courage in relation to the children and families she works with.

For example, when Belinda knocks the cup off the table accidentally, her therapist first reassures her that no damage has been done—and, implicitly, that he is not angry and that Belinda is not going to be punished. He shows empathy with how Belinda might be feeling but also behaves in a supportive way. He is not detached, aloof, or inscrutable—but as Bateman and Fonagy (2016) pointed out, neither is he bubbling over with emotion in a way that might overwhelm the child. He is helping to create a (relatively) safe context in which levels of arousal can be modulated (neither too high nor too low) and in which there are two human beings in the room, both with their own thoughts, feelings, and histories. Both are probably anxious, and both expectant.

The therapist brings not only their thoughts and feelings into the room but also their embodied self. Geller (2013) described therapeutic presence as "bringing one's whole self into the encounter with a client, being completely in the moment on a multiplicity of levels, physically, emotionally, cognitively, spiritually, and relationally" (p. 209). Child development research now shows that a parent's nonverbal, body-based interactions with their child are also a part of parental mentalizing and contribute to the emotional and cognitive developmental of the child (Shai et al., 2022). So too, when a therapist is able to bring their "embodied mentalizing" into the therapy setting, this can contribute to the way in which a child can experience their therapist as actively trying to make sense of their thoughts and feelings, even at a nonverbal level. When Belinda accidentally knocked over the cup, it was not only the therapist's words ("Don't worry, not broken") that conveyed his understanding of her actions but also the whole way his bodily state (his shape, the relaxation of his muscles, tone of voice, as well as his smile) that Belinda was responding to.

Fonagy and Allison (2014) described MBT for grown-ups as a means of "establishing epistemic trust in relation to social learning in an attachment context" (p. 372). In other words, the relationship with a therapist, when there is a sufficient level of relational safety, offers an opportunity for the individual to "consider new knowledge from another person as trustworthy, generalizable, and relevant to the self" (p. 373). This, they suggested, is only marginally important in terms of the particular content that individuals may learn within the therapy itself (e.g., a new way of understanding why they have always been scared of meeting new people). Instead, the real significance lies in the fact that the reduction in epistemic vigilance brings about change in rigidly held beliefs and opens up the capacity for "social learning"—that is, the possibility of having different kinds of interactions and experiences in the world. This, in turn, helps changes that have taken place within therapy to be sustained beyond therapy.

All of this is perhaps just a sophisticated way of saying that the therapeutic presence of the adult who is offering MBT-C is a crucial element, and we should not underestimate the importance of this personal quality. It is not a set of fixed behaviors, because each of us is different, so that being jokey, for one therapist, might convey a real authenticity, whereas for another, it would be forced and unnatural. These individual differences can easily be accommodated in MBT-C. What is important is the sense the child gets of being with an adult who is genuine, nonjudgmental, empathic, and comfortable with a certain level of self-disclosure as a person. Given what we know from developmental research (e.g., Schore, 1994) about the role of positive affect, including joy and delight, in normal child development, it is perhaps not surprising that we share Barish's (2009) view that the therapist's "enthusiastic responsiveness" to a child's own interests is a key but neglected element of work with children. This, in itself, may not be sufficient for therapy to be effective, but without it, the chances of success are certainly much slimmer.

AN INTEREST IN THE MIND, NOT JUST BEHAVIOR

Anne, Age 6

Anne is sitting at a low table, intensely focused on a set of farm and wild animal toys in front of her. Her therapist is sitting at a right angle to her, on a low chair, so that she is close but without intruding on Anne's space. On the table, a set of sheep are huddled behind a fence, and Anne is holding a lion. "You be the sheep!" Anne demands excitedly as she picks up the lion herself and stealthily moves it across the table, letting out a low growling sound. As she does so, she looks up at her therapist, with a look of pleasure on her face. Her therapist's eyes widen, with an exaggerated look of shock at the growling sound, although her face and eyes glint, showing pleasure in the game. The therapist picks up one of the sheep, lets out a baa-ing sound, and moves the sheep backwards, fearfully. "Oh no! Here comes that nasty lion—I hope it's not going to eat me!" she says. Anne enjoys this and moves her lion forward in a menacing way, this time letting out a full roar. The therapist now does an exaggerated "Aaargh! I'm scared! Help me!" and notices that Anne glances up at her face, as if checking to see whether this is real fear or just pretend. Seeing it is playful, she roars again.

After repeated scenes where Anne takes pleasure in the lion intimidating the sheep, the therapist tries to introduce some more flexibility and a potentially protective figure, bringing in a dog, which she places in front of the sheep, as if protecting them (see Figure 5.1). "Grrr," she says assuming the dog's voice, "I'll keep you safe." At this, Anne immediately lashes out and flicks the dog off the table, turning to her therapist with a look of anger. "No!" she yells, "that's not in the game!" Her therapist, somewhat taken aback by the force of Anne's reaction, leans back a little, then says, "I'm sorry, Anne, I got it wrong!" Anne's mood slightly softens, but she still looks displeased. The therapist says, in an exaggerated voice, with her eyebrows furrowing together, "Oh, it is soooo annoying when grown-ups

FIGURE 5.1. Anne's Farm Animals

Note. Image created by Nicole Muller.

get it wrong! I feel so cross!" Anne repeats, "You got it wrong!" "Yes," replies the therapist, now looking away, in a way that demonstrates she's reflecting to herself on what happened. "I didn't mean to spoil the game, but I can see now that you may have felt a little frustrated when I put the dog there. I wonder why I did that?"

In the first chapter on the developmental origins of the capacity to mentalize, we discussed the way in which an infant's sense of affective self is built up through repeated experiences of contingent responses and marked mirroring, so that what starts out as a set of undifferentiated tension states can be gradually transformed into second-order representations of affect states—for example, an awareness of being "angry," rather than some undifferentiated, negative state of tension. We described how, over time, this helps to establish an ongoing sense of an affective self—one that can develop a certain level of self-control, as emotions are not simply experienced in an undifferentiated, potentially overwhelming way. Gergely and Watson (1996, 1999) described the process by which this gradually happens as the "social biofeedback theory of parental affect-mirroring," and emphasized the importance of ostensive cues, contingent responsiveness, and marked mirroring to this process.

For many of the children who are referred for time-limited MBT-C, there may be limitations in the degree to which they have been able to explicitly develop a language of feelings to speak about body-based, affective states, resulting in them lacking a capacity to manage strong emotions. They may not have had sufficient experience of being responded to as a child with a mind, and as they grow older, their increasingly challenging behaviors (often developed as a way of managing uncontained emotional states) further invite controlling or punitive responses on behalf of the adult—for example, "If you do that again, then I'm going to have to ground you for two weeks!"

In time-limited MBT-C, as in many other forms of child therapy, pretend play can be an opportunity for continuing (or beginning) a process of helping a child to develop a sense of themselves as a person with a mind by finding themselves in the mind of the therapist. Although not all children referred for MBT-C have a capacity for pretend play, Anne is able to make use of play as a means of expressing some internal experience while maintaining an awareness that the play is "not for real." When Anne's therapist joins in the play with the sheep and the lion, she is using—in a developmentally appropriate form—many of the ostensive cues that parents use with infants in the process of social biofeedback. These include appropriate eye contact (enough to stay engaged but not too much to be overwhelming), the raising of eyebrows in a quizzical or inquiring way, changes in vocal tone (especially to mark emotional states as pretend), and shifts in posture, such as tilting the head or looking up in the distance to mark the act of reflection. The therapist can use an exaggerated (and sometimes slowed-down) voice to help make clear that she is not actually experiencing these emotions (such as the sheep's fear) but rather is presenting them back to the child in a saliently marked manner (Fonagy et al., 2022). Anne's attentive look at her therapist's face when she first voices her fear ("I'm scared!") demonstrates the vulnerability that children like her may have to finding expressions of emotion overwhelming when the "as if" quality is lost and they are experienced as real—hence the value of the pretend play, in which the whole setting is marked as make-believe, allowing the exploration of a range of affective states that might otherwise be felt as too intense, too immediate.

When the pretend play breaks down, as it did for Anne when her therapist introduced the protective dog, the therapist's first response was not to focus on Anne's behavior or to try and help Anne learn more appropriate ways to engage in reciprocal play. If the therapist had done so, she would likely have got into the kind of nonmentalizing vicious circle described in Chapter 2 in this volume, where a child's nonmentalizing actions are met by equally nonmentalizing responses. However, Anne's therapist also avoids what might appear to be a more mentalizing response, such as trying to talk about why Anne behaved in that way. As Bateman and Fonagy (2016) pointed out, forcing someone to try and think why they behaved in a certain way when they have just "acted out" (whether that is throwing a toy or attempting to self-harm) is almost never productive:

> Rather, it forces them to focus on the behavior they engaged in that itself is a consequence of a failure of mentalization. The mentalizing therapist knows that this is precisely what the patient is incapable of doing: finding and giving a reason for their action. (p. 107)

When Anne knocks the toy dog off the table (breaking the play, in a nonmentalizing state), the therapist's primary aim is to try and help to down-regulate the affect, as without this, there is little chance of starting a more mentalizing interaction. But from a mentalization-based perspective, it is equally important to help the child to express so-called negative feelings in a safe way. As Gergely and Watson (1996) emphasized, the marked mirroring of negative affect states is especially important in the development of the self, and so the therapist also uses an exaggerated voice to name the cross feeling (but being careful to take on the first person, "I feel cross," rather than directly saying to Anne that she was cross, which might have again been overwhelming). Once Anne's affective state is more modulated, the therapist can go one step further, introducing the idea of an intentional state of mind ("I didn't mean to spoil the game") and inviting some curiosity about why the therapist's own behavior had evoked such a powerful reaction from the child. Rather than focusing on Anne and her mind, the therapist shows some curiosity about her own mental states ("I wonder why I did that?"), inviting Anne to be curious about why the therapist decided to introduce the dog into the game at that particular moment. The focus, then, remains on the mind (of both child and therapist) and not only on behavior.

CURIOSITY AND THE NOT-KNOWING (INQUISITIVE) STANCE

Liza, Age 11

In the initial family meeting, the therapists are exploring different ideas about the anxiety that Liza suffers from. Her parents don't think it is related to the arguments that they often have with her older brother, late at night, as "she is always asleep at the time." Her dad thinks that Liza may be putting on her anxiety in order to get attention, whereas her mom says that she herself had been very anxious as a child, so it is "probably something genetic," and that she is sure Liza will grow out of it in the same way that she had.

During the meeting, one of the therapists explains that she does not know for sure why Liza gets so anxious, but she is really interested to hear the different ideas that people have. When dad says that he thinks Liza is just trying to get attention, the therapist turns to Liza's mom and asks her if she has any thoughts about why dad sees it that way? Liza's mom says that dad doesn't like it when Liza clings on to her, especially in the evenings, before bed, when her husband wants to have a bit of quiet time with his wife. "So let me check that I've understood," says the therapist. "Do you mean that he might want to be spending that time with you—and gets frustrated when Liza won't leave the two of you alone?" "Yes, that's right," says Liza's mom. The therapist then turns to the dad, and asks what he thought about his wife's idea. "Yes, that's true I guess," he says, sounding a bit more thoughtful than he had earlier, "but I don't think it's just me who gets frustrated by it—my wife does too." "How can you tell?" asks the therapist. The dad replies, "Oh, she's got a special face she puts on—you can always tell when she's annoyed by that face!" Liza giggles, and the therapist turns to her and asks her if she knows the face that dad is talking about? Liza nods, looking a little shy. The therapist asks Liza if she could show her what the face looks like, and Liza pulls a face—half quizzical, half cross. Both Liza's parents laugh, and the therapist turns to the mom and asks, "Has she got that right?" Liza's mom nods, looking at her daughter with some curiosity. "Did you know that Liza knew about that face?" the therapist asks. Mom says no but glances at dad. The therapist noticed this and says, "I just noticed that glance between you, but I don't know what it means." The parents look at each other again, and then dad says, "I think it means—I don't want to talk about this." The therapist looks across at mom, who then turns to the therapist, asking, "Is this really relevant? I thought we'd come here to talk about Liza's anxiety." The therapist thanks her for asking this and says, tapping the side of her head, "Yes, perhaps I should explain what was going on in my head that made me ask—I can see that perhaps otherwise it may not make much sense. Let me see. I have only just met you. I guess we were all sharing our ideas about why Liza sometimes gets anxious, and it seems that there were different perspectives on what is going on when she becomes anxious and clingy in the evening. I guess I had a feeling it was important and wanted to follow this idea and see where it led, but I did not have a preconceived idea. Would that be okay for you if we sometimes try following an idea and see where it leads us, even if it sometimes takes us down a dead end?"

While saying this, the therapist makes a mental note that Liza's mother may feel anxious about trying to meet the expectations of her husband while also responding to Liza's needs for reassurance, and she wonders whether this may make her less patient with Liza in the evening. She thinks that this is a potentially sensitive subject, which may be important for the parents to discuss when they have their own meetings with the therapist.

When trying to define the essence of the mentalizing stance, a number of authors have rightly emphasized the centrality of not knowing. As Bateman and Fonagy (2016) were quick to clarify, describing the MBT therapist as taking a not-knowing stance is not synonymous with the therapist having no knowledge or no ideas of her own. As mentalizing therapists, we are not supposed to ignore our theoretical knowledge and clinical expertise, nor are we supposed to refrain from forming our own hypotheses about what might be going on in the clinical setting. These hypotheses should, however, be seen as mental constructs rather than absolute knowledge, and they should be explored together with the child or parents in therapy. The not-knowing stance implies starting from an assumption that knowledge of the other (or indeed of the self) is not a straightforward process, and that we always have to work hard to try and understand the experience of others. Being inquisitive, as manifested in a process of active questioning, is a key component of MBT-C. This stance clearly has similarities to the approach taken by systemic practitioners (with the process of circular questioning) or indeed to the model of "collaborative inquiry" that is a hallmark of third-wave cognitive behavioral therapy. What is specific about the mentalizing stance, however, is that the curiosity is specifically focused on mental states and how they may link to behaviors.

As Arietta Slade put it, when speaking about working with parents from a mentalizing perspective, in being curious, the therapist is trying to model a reflective stance (Slade, 2008, p. 223), which can include the following:

- struggling to imagine the child's experience,
- talking about feelings and linking them to behaviors,
- coming to realize that feelings change over time, and
- remaining aware that we can have a sense of what someone else feels but we can never be 100% sure—but that we are curious and open to discovering it.

One of the core features of good mentalization is this notion of the mind's opacity: that one cannot ever be sure of what another person thinks or feels. J. G. Allen et al. (2008) referred to it as "a nonjudgmental attitude of curiosity, inquisitiveness and open-mindedness" (p. 160). The MBT-C therapist tries to avoid any sense of being an expert who knows better or who knows for sure what is going on in the mind of the other. If you hear an MBT therapist start a sentence with the words "When you say that, what you are really meaning is . . . ," then you can be sure she is in a nonmentalizing frame of mind!

In most cases, taking on an expert position—giving advice or telling the patient what to do—does not promote mentalization. By modeling a not-knowing stance and by stimulating curiosity and motivation to inquire into mental states, the therapist tries to help the child and the parents to become curious about the child's experiences and promote an understanding that they are separate from the parents. When Liza's therapist starts exploring the different ideas that family members have about Liza's anxiety, she is already marking these thoughts as just that—different perspectives, which are worth taking seriously, worth understanding better, but not absolute truth. In this way, the therapist is working from an inquisitive stance based on the understanding that mental states of others are opaque and that where one attempts to imagine what the other thinks and feels followed by recruiting the other to figure it out, this often results in improvement of affect regulation and overall quality of interpersonal relationships. When Liza's dad first suggests that Liza was anxious and clinging just to get attention, the therapist does not directly challenge this idea, as doing so might have led to a cognitive debate about whether dad was right or wrong. Although the therapist thought it this was unlikely to be the real reason for Liza's behavior (i.e., the therapist did have her own ideas), by asking mom for her views about why dad saw Liza's behavior that way, she showed that she was accepting this view of Liza as dad's perspective and implicitly modeling a view that there are probably good reasons why each of us holds the ideas that we do—reasons that can best be understood if we are curious about where they come from. When Liza's therapist brings in her own perspective, there is a regular process of checking. The therapist tries not to assume anything with regards to feelings and reaction in the child or the parents. Rather, she actively checks if she has understood things correctly and uses the process of checking to acknowledge when she has got something wrong or to "thicken" (to use a systemic term) the narrative around a particular incident.

In this case, showing (and inviting) curiosity about the different perspectives that each of the family members have regarding Liza's anxious behavior seems to facilitate a more open discussion between the parents, and for a period of time, it creates a more thoughtful and reflective atmosphere. However, at a certain point, the discussion moves into an area where Liza's mother appears to feel uncomfortable, and she challenges the therapist about why this is an important topic for discussion. Once again, the therapist, rather than treating this as a manifestation of "resistance," uses it as an opportunity to try and spell out her own thinking, her own intentional states that led her to take the discussion in this direction. She makes it clear that she does not necessarily fully understand the intentions behind her own behavior (our minds and intentions are somewhat opaque, even to ourselves). She uses this as an opportunity not only to share her way of working with Liza's parents but also to check out how this is experienced by them in order to build a more collaborative approach. The therapist, in a double sense, is trying to be *open minded*—that is, not only in the sense of being open to the idea of changing her mind but also in the sense of opening up her own mind as an object of curiosity for the family. By tapping the side of her head, the therapist is actively demonstrating that what had been going on was a thinking process, one that she both wanted to share with the family and one that she was curious to explore herself.

Maintaining an open-minded and curious approach has been recognized as a particularly important element of working within and across cultures. Building on earlier work around cultural competencies in psychotherapy, Owen et al. (2011) introduced what they described as the multicultural orientation framework as a way of examining how cultural dynamics can influence the process of therapy. The approach emphasizes the importance of three elements in particular: cultural humility, cultural opportunities, and cultural comfort (Davis et al., 2018). The first of these aligns particularly well with the "not-knowing" stance in MBT, insofar as it emphasizes the need to approach others with the intention of honoring their beliefs, customs, and values and not assuming that you necessarily understand these. The idea of "cultural opportunities" also aligns well with the concept of taking a curious stance and looking for opportunities to explore and understand different perspectives.

Liza's parents have entered this therapeutic space with a wide range of cultural values and assumptions that will inevitably shape how they engage with this meeting, just as the therapist does. When Liz's mom asked if the discussion they were having was really relevant, the therapist (rather than being defensive or taking an authoritative position) was able to see this as a "cultural opportunity" to explore different sets of values and ideas about what therapy is and the role parents may have in it. She may only have been able to do this because of a degree of "cultural comfort" in exploring her own, and others' values, which may partly come from gaining experiences in training and supervision (as well as daily life) to think openly about her own and other people's cultures. By demonstrating humility and curiosity about that culture, the therapist hoped to model a "not-knowing" (or "wanting-to-know") attitude.

Maintaining a curious and inquisitive stance is both the simplest and the most challenging element of mentalizing therapy. After all, when working in a field where there has often been a great deal of trauma, and in which emotions run high, the capacity for the system to become a nonmentalizing one should never be underrated. When working across cultures, there is a particular risk of losing one's capacity to mentalize. So, the MBT-C therapist will often investigate observed or reported interactions in a seemingly naïve, if not stupid and rather slow way. The therapist may mentalize aloud, entering the arena of safe uncertainty (Mason, 1993), sharing hunches and observations as she tries to understand what is going on. The therapist might say, "I can see this makes perfect sense to you, but I'm not quite following—can we just go over that again bit by bit, so I can get my head around it?" Slowing things down is a powerful way of bringing in new perspectives, which might otherwise get missed.

One child, for example, was referred to a clinic because he was urinating everywhere, both at home and at school. The school was finding this behavior intolerable, and his foster carers had introduced a whole series of rewards and punishments based on the assumption that he was "doing it on purpose" and needed to better control his behavior. Having not yet been fully caught up in this system of thinking, the MBT-C therapist took the opportunity, on first meeting with the social worker and foster carers, to show some curiosity about how this boy's experiences might relate to this symptom. After a bit of exploration, his social worker mentioned (rather matter-of-factly) that this boy had first been taken into care after a fire in his home, during which his younger brother had been burned to death. The therapist interrupted and checked that he had heard that right. The social worker stopped for a moment and then said, more thoughtfully, that he had heard it correctly. "Gosh, what must it be like having that on your mind?" wondered the therapist aloud. There was a long silence in the room—but one that had a very different quality to the rather mechanical recounting of incidents that had taken place up until then. Somehow, no one had ever made a connection between this incident and the boy's compulsive need to urinate. As they sat there, the faces of the social worker and the foster carer changed, and when they began speaking about the boy again, their voices had a different quality. They were now, to use a helpful definition of mentalizing, "looking at the other from the inside, and seeing themselves from the outside." The following week, when the professional network met again, the foster carer reported that the urinating had stopped. Yet, no one had spoken directly to the boy about their conversation, and no new "strategies" had been implemented. As Sally Provence put it so well (quoted by Slade, 2008, p. 225), sometimes it is enough to just say, "Don't just do something. Stand there and pay attention!" (It should be added, just to be absolutely clear, that MBT-C does not often lead to these kinds of miracle cures and that the process of change is as slow, messy, and gradual in MBT-C as any other effective therapy!)

MONITORING MISUNDERSTANDINGS

Ruth, Age 12

There was only one more session until the end of the time-limited MBT-C with Ruth. During this time, she had formed a close relationship with her therapist, and in this penultimate session, they were playing one of the games that Ruth had invented. As the therapist took his turn, Ruth took out her mobile phone and started filming what was happening. Her therapist felt suddenly anxious and told Ruth that this was a private space and that it wasn't appropriate for her to be filming. Ruth apologized and said she quite understood, and they carried on playing.

When the session was over, the therapist found that he kept thinking about what had happened. He talked it over with a colleague, who asked the therapist why he thought Ruth had decided to film at that particular moment. The therapist thought about it and wondered whether it was connected to the sessions coming to an end and whether Ruth had perhaps wanted to find a way to "hold on" to the link with him. He realized that he had been feeling quite bad about holding the firm line on ending therapy because he knew that Ruth liked coming to see him. However, he also recognized that they had made good progress and that stopping at this point was probably appropriate. He was going to miss her, however, as she had been a child whom he had enjoyed working with.

In using this supervisory space to reflect on his response to Ruth and to be curious about what had motivated Ruth to get out her camera at that point, the therapist felt that he had made a mistake in stopping her from filming. Although he was just following his usual rules, in this case, he felt that his anxiety had made him overlook what might have been in Ruth's mind. So, the following week, when he saw Ruth for their last meeting, the therapist went back to what had happened and apologized to Ruth, saying that he thought he had perhaps been a bit hasty in how he had responded and that he had wondered whether there might have been a good reason why Ruth had wanted to film them together. This led to an unusually open discussion between them, about what it was like to have to say goodbye to people just as you were getting to know and like them. The therapist then wondered if they could go back and think how they could create a record of what they had shared together. Together, they decided to make a photo record of some of the important things they had done together, and Ruth agreed that this was something that she would keep at home but not put online. The central image was a "selfie," of Ruth and her therapist standing together, holding a game that they had often played.

When working from the not-knowing stance, the therapist keeps an open mind to the fact that there are times (quite often, in fact) when they may not understand things correctly. Sometimes, this can be quickly dealt with by the simple act of checking: "Let me see if I got this right. . . ." Even more important is to model honesty and openness by acknowledging one's own misunderstandings. The therapist tries to convey to the family that misunderstandings are great opportunities to revisit, in order to learn more about contexts, experiences, and feelings.

When Ruth's therapist asked her to stop filming in their session, this was not a mistake in any absolute sense—it is clearly quite appropriate to have certain rules about what can and cannot happen in a therapy room, and there are good reasons why, as therapists, we might not want to find a video of ourselves in session appearing on YouTube! But from a mentalizing perspective, it is possible to see what happened in this interaction as a mistake or a misunderstanding on the therapist's part, insofar as he had probably mistaken the intention behind Ruth's actions and so had quickly moved to controlling Ruth's behavior (asking her to wipe the video and put her camera phone away) rather than holding on to a curiosity about what had made her start filming in the first place.

That the therapist had slipped into a nonmentalizing response is perfectly understandable in this context if we remember that all of us struggle to stay mentalizing when our anxiety levels are raised. For the therapist at this moment, seeing the camera not only raised professional anxieties about boundaries and confidentiality but also probably linked to his own difficult feelings about ending the therapy and his struggle to acknowledge the depth of loss that Ruth was likely to feel about this significant relationship. As with all of us, the therapist benefited from having space and time to reflect on this, and his colleague did an inspired piece of mentalizing supervision when she avoided telling the therapist how he should have handled the situation, instead inviting him to be curious about Ruth's mental state at the moment that she got out her camera phone. In doing so, the therapist was able to regulate his own emotions better and could also become more curious about his own emotional reactions, some of which belonged to the specific relationship with Ruth and some to his more personal feelings about his professional competency and how people would look on him if they saw that he was "just playing" in sessions with a child.

Once his capacity to mentalize had been re-established, Ruth's therapist was ready to go back and acknowledge this misunderstanding and also apologize to Ruth for his hasty response. Such apologies—when genuine—can be a powerful component of the mentalizing stance, as they model a way of being that is able to reflect on what has happened and acknowledge that we can all get things wrong when we are not able to mentalize. When working with clients of color, recognizing and apologizing when microaggressions have occurred may be especially important, and doing so is part of the multicultural orientation described above (MacIntosh et al., 2022). Being able to acknowledge and seek to address one's own mistakes introduces a model of rupture and repair, which Schore and others (e.g., Schore, 1994, 2003) showed to be central to the building up of the early parent–infant relationship, just as Safran and Muran (2000) and others showed its centrality to building a therapeutic alliance in work with adults.

In acknowledging his error and showing an interest in going back and understanding what had been going on in Ruth's mind the previous week, the therapist also contributed to creating a safe enough space for a different kind of discussion to take place, one in which the experience of loss—so central to Ruth's life—could be put into words and thought about rather than seemly repeated. The therapist was able to share with Ruth some ideas he had about why Ruth may have wanted to film them, but he did so from a not-knowing position, simply sharing his ideas as one perspective. He was also able to reflect with Ruth on his own emotional reaction and how it led him to react in a controlling way ("I think I felt a bit put on the spot, and didn't feel comfortable, so I just wanted to make it stop—by telling you to stop!").

Some might question whether it was really necessary to go on from that to literally allow Ruth to take photos in the room. Certainly, there is a teleological quality to this ("I can remember you because I've got a photo to prove it"), but as Bateman and Fonagy (2016) pointed out, in work with adults with borderline personality disorder, sometimes "being kept in mind has to be manifest in physical reality" (p. 96). For children whose capacity to symbolize is still fragile, there may be times when the mentalizing therapist is also the doing therapist, finding concrete ways to help the child feel that they are kept in mind—and are able to keep the other in mind too. Ruth was a child who already had a certain capacity to recognize thoughts and feelings, and reflect on how they might link with behavior. When the therapist first asked her to stop filming, she was able to self-regulate and carry on as if apparently unaffected. (In fact, we could say that she was overregulated, like many children who have a pattern of dismissive attachments.) However, when working with children who have rarely been seen as separate individuals by their caregivers, the misunderstandings, mistakes, and alliance ruptures can be far more dramatic. It is not uncommon for the therapist to feel provoked by the child's behavior and reject the child. Although it is not always easy to do so in the moment, the way to handle these situations as a mentalizing therapist is to take responsibility for any misunderstandings and mistakes and to return to the not-knowing stance. By taking responsibility for the interaction, the therapist validates the child's experience. By admitting to not knowing, the therapist normalizes and models an understanding of the opacity of minds.

Quite often, the mentalizing therapist might find herself taking responsibility for a mistake long before she understands what she has actually done.

Mohammed, Age 7

Mohammed is only just starting his time-limited MBT therapy when the therapist gets news just before a session that Mohammed has been temporarily excluded from school because of an incident where he had tried to poke another child in the eye with a pencil. Mohammed's father, who has been called away from work in the middle of the day to take him home, is extremely angry about what has happened, and he arrives at the session in a very bad mood. He insists on joining the meeting, but the therapist suggests that she first have a bit of time alone with Mohammed and that she would then invite Mohammed's father to join them a little later.

The therapist begins the session with Mohammed, who, at first, makes no reference to what had happened that day but begins a game in which a doll is being

> picked on by all the other dolls. At one point, the doll kicks back and tells the others to go away. The therapist says, with some feeling, "It seems like she wants them all to get out of her face!" Mohammed turns round, abruptly, and throws the doll toward the therapist's face, at the same time screaming at her, "I hate you! I hate you!" The therapist had not expected this at all and immediately moves backwards, away from Mohammed, breaking eye contact. As she does so, she says, "Mohammed, I'm really sorry. I'm not sure quite what I've done, but I can see that I've really upset you. I'm so sorry." At that point, Mohammed bursts into tears.

When Mohammed's therapist apologized in this way, she had no idea what it was about her words that had produced such a violent reaction. The first step, from a mentalizing perspective, is simply to acknowledge that something the therapist has done has affected the child, and for that she was genuinely sorry. The tone of her voice made this absolutely clear, and by breaking eye contact, she was trying to help reduce the emotional intensity of the situation. To have tried to guess what it was in Mohammed's mind that had provoked this reaction might be seen as a mentalizing response (curiosity about mental states), but it would most likely have been entirely ineffective, given that the capacity for explicit mentalization is almost certainly lost when affect is this high. The first priority, when working in MBT-C, is to help regulate the emotional temperature, and at this point, the therapist's apology was simply an acknowledgment that something had gone wrong between them and that the therapist had not intended to do this.

It was some time before Mohammed's therapist actually came back to this interaction, and she never fully came to understand what it was that had provoked Mohammed's powerful emotions. But simply in going back to the event, the therapist demonstrated to Mohammed her wish to understand the intentional states underlying behavior, and modeled a stance that misunderstandings offer opportunities to revisit to learn more about contexts, experiences, and feelings. One of our colleagues in the field of MBT with children and young people, Dickon Bevington (personal communication, October 2016), goes as far as telling the adolescents he works with, in their first meeting, that he is almost certainly going to misunderstand them as the sessions go on and make mistakes. He asks them, if they can, to let him know when he has got something wrong, explaining that he will not always realize it himself. (The opacity of minds—we do not always realize when we have said or done something that has upset someone else.) And he adds,

> I hope my next mistakes will not be hurtful, but will give us a chance to take a step back and learn how to talk about how to work out our mistakes, mis-readings and all the resulting hurt and anger.

USING SUPERVISION TO SUPPORT THE MENTALIZING STANCE

In MBT-C, we try to help parents and children to understand themselves and each other better by offering them a therapy where they learn a way of exploring and talking about thoughts and feelings that helps them to be better attuned. For the therapists working with this model, it is equally important to actively mentalize and to notice when our mentalizing (inevitably) breaks down. In some clinics, therapists will be working in larger teams, and in some settings, the therapist may work with a single colleague or even alone. The most important factor, regardless, is to create a working environment that is safe and secure to allow mental states to be explored from a curious, not-knowing position. When we as therapists feel safe and supported, we are usually better able to ask for help and speak freely about experiences while working with challenging clients. However, a sense of safety is not always easy to maintain. We may work in an organization that sets up prerequisites for our work that may not always be completely congruent with our ideals. Furthermore, different patients will challenge our capacity to remain reflective, and some children or families may trigger feelings and conflicts in the therapist, affecting the mentalizing capacity in the therapist.

One of the main "tools" used by therapists to keep their ability to reflect and stay on track is supervision. The therapist's supervision needs to provide a place of psychological safety, where the therapist can bring doubts, anxieties, thoughts, and anger and, last but not least, celebrate the work they do and the progress their patients make. Reflective questions about the therapist's own assumptions and beliefs can be helpful in order to unravel implicit aspects of the relationship between the therapist and the child/parents. When making the work explicit in a supervising context, aspects that are not directly observable can be discovered. The MBT-C Adherence Scale (see Appendix B) can also be used as a way of reflecting on which aspects of the MBT-C model the therapist is making more (or less) use of during a particular session. The therapist may want to complete the scale themselves after the session as a way of identifying aspects of the approach that they want to think about in supervision, or else a supervisor (if available) could watch a video recording of the session and rate the scale as the basis for shared reflection in supervision itself.

At the heart of the MBT-C Adherence Scale is not a set of techniques but rather the mentalizing stance itself. Given that most therapists work in relatively high-stress conditions and that much of what goes on in therapy happens in physical isolation behind closed doors, it is not surprising that the mentalizing stance can be hard to sustain for us as therapists. As Bevington and Fuggle (2012) noted, there can be "a tendency to move into nonmentalizing states such as teleological thinking (preoccupation with what to do) or with psychic equivalence (the belief that how the worker thinks/feels is actually how it is)" (p. 176). In the light of such (normal) challenges, Bevington and Fuggle proposed a particular format for supervision, which draws on our natural ability to regain our capacity to mentalize through contact with attachment figures (our colleagues and supervisors) while avoiding the risk that supervision becomes a simple narrative of dramatic events or an opportunity for the supervisor to demonstrate a "better" understanding of the child than the therapist. The latter, in particular, is likely to result in reduced mentalizing in the therapist, even when the insights about the child may be quite brilliant!

In order to keep the focus of supervision on maintaining (or reactivating) the therapist's mentalizing stance, Bevington and Fuggle (2012) proposed a four-step process, which they referred to as "Thinking Together" (Bevington et al., 2015, see Diagram 5.2):

- Stage 1: Marking the task: Rather than beginning with a detailed narrative of a session, the supervisor is encouraged to invite the therapist to briefly consider what they need from the conversation. This question, like time-limited therapy itself, can help to ensure that a focus is maintained in the supervision.
- Stage 2: Stating the case: The therapist is invited to share enough information about the case and the current situation, without slipping into overlong storytelling. The supervisor helps the therapist to stay focused on the "simple bones" to avoid slipping into lengthy or overly detailed recounting of background history or what happened in the session.
- Stage 3: Mentalizing the moment: This is the heart of "Thinking Together," where the supervisor invites the therapist to explicitly reflect on the case and the issues that they have brought to supervision. The aim of supervision at this stage is not to find the "right" answers but rather to mentalize about the process, the child, the therapist, and their relation. It is important to find a balance between being self-critical and being reassuring toward others or oneself. Every clinician has her own style, and it is a challenge for all of us not to become stuck in a position or in one model but instead to stay curious, open, flexible, and creative, challenged by colleagues in a safe space.
- Stage 4: Returning to purpose: Having actively mentalized the moment and (hopefully) helped the therapist to regain their mentalizing stance, it is important to return to the task that was set at the beginning of the supervisory discussion, so that the active mentalizing can be used to help address the issue at hand. As such, this mirrors the therapeutic process itself, where improved mentalizing is not an end in itself but rather a tool that can help us to develop more creative and flexible approaches to the challenges we face, so that we are able to manage them better.

When thinking about our own understanding of the psychotherapeutic processes we engage in, we keep in mind that everything we see, understand, and react to has to do with our own lives. We have our own ways of seeing and interpreting things around us, depending on our cultures and histories. We also have our own bodily histories, with unique sensibilities that can become actualized in interactions with others. These subtleties are often difficult to put in words. Using video-recorded material can often reveal these interactions, as well as other implicit dynamics outside the therapist's explicit awareness. For this reason, we strongly recommend working with recorded material at least sometimes in supervision in order to be able to reflect on important processes that might otherwise go unnoticed.

Where possible, we have also found that it can be helpful to arrange the timing of sessions so that the therapist has the chance to sit down after the session and take some time to reflect on thoughts and feelings in the moment. Going beyond writing summary notes for a file, we have found that it can be valuable to reflect on one's own emotions and bodily experiences. Often, a lot of information is "hidden" in the interaction or felt by the therapist, which might be helpful to reveal the nature of the interaction with the child and the parent(s). For example, the therapist may note that they suddenly felt very sleepy during a session for no apparent reason, or felt annoyed about something a parent said when there was no clear logic for why they felt like that. Noting and then reflecting on such emotional or bodily experiences (what might be called "the embodied countertransference") can sometimes throw light on an important element of the interaction that, at the time, could not be fully mentalized.

For those working as part of a team, it may be useful to have a routine in supervision of briefly monitoring the work with each child and family. Whatever the context in which the work may be happening, a mentalizing approach emphasizes the importance of having a team around the practitioner, which can help keep the practitioner's mentalizing on track (Talbot, 2023). The team helps the clinicians involved understand what any obstacles are and how they may be related to the pattern of interaction that is typical in the family or plays in parallel in the treatment relationship. Risks regarding dropout and destructive interaction patterns can be assessed as well as the progress of treatment. Additional interventions (e.g., calling after a session or sending an email) are discussed in the light of the therapist's reflections on their own thoughts and feelings following the most recent meeting(s). This helps the practitioner to clarify implicit aspects of their inner world in order to promote mentalizing.

CONCLUSION

In this chapter, we have tried to describe the therapeutic stance in MBT-C based on four key elements: the therapeutic presence of the MBT-C therapist; an interest in the mind, not just behavior; curiosity and the not-knowing (inquisitive) stance; and monitoring misunderstandings. Several elements of this stance may be shared with other approaches—for example, there is significant overlap with the emphasis on playfulness, acceptance, curiosity, and empathy to be found in dyadic developmental psychotherapy (D. A. Hughes, 2004). What is specific about the mentalizing stance, we would argue, is the particular focus of the therapist's curiosity on understanding intentional mental states.

As a complement to this, J. G. Allen et al. (2008, p. 166) helpfully set out a number of things that are not characteristics of the mentalizing therapist's stance. These include the following:

- striving to be clever, brilliant, or insightful;
- offering complicated, lengthy explanations;
- making up an authoritative answer when you do not really know;
- assuming you know what the other is thinking;
- being rigid in your thinking; and

- focusing only on behaviors and actions rather than on the intentional states that underlie those behaviors.

All of these are forms of nonmentalizing, as described in Chapter 2 in this volume. You may notice that most of these are things that the therapists were doing at one time or another in several of the clinical vignettes described in this chapter. That is because all of us—patients, parents, therapists, and children—lose our capacity to mentalize at certain moments, often because we are anxious, under pressure, or in some state of high arousal. All of this is normal and an inevitable part of clinical work. But the mentalizing therapist strives to notice when she is operating from such a nonmentalizing stance, and (where possible) tries to become aware of these breakdowns in mentalizing and take steps to restore the mentalizing stance. Sometimes, we may be able to do this ourselves, but often supervision, especially in the context of a secure relationship that can help to regulate our own levels of emotional arousal, plays an essential part.

It is because finding, losing, and re-establishing a mentalizing stance is so central to clinical work that we argue that the stance is the foundation of all therapeutic work in MBT-C. It may seem like a daunting task for a therapist to always be mentalizing—which is why it is important to underline that that is not the point and is not possible. No one can keep a mentalizing stance all the time. In later chapters, we will discuss some of the ways in which the therapist can try and restore a capacity for mentalizing. But for now, we end this chapter with four points to be kept in mind when mentalizing seems hard:

- You can enhance mentalization by doing it yourself.
- When you are aware of nonmentalizing interventions, you are mentalizing.
- Moments where mentalization stops (in you or in the child) are possibilities for change and new learning opportunities.
- Just as we recognize that children develop a capacity for mentalizing in the context of relationships, so too we as therapists can use supervision, as a form of relational learning, to help us keep our mentalizing on track.

6

The Process of Assessment

In this chapter, we describe a clinical approach to assessment, formulation, and the identification of a therapeutic focus statement and treatment goals in the context of time-limited mentalization-based treatment for children (MBT-C). This is necessary not only to identify children who are most likely to benefit from this approach but also to develop a clear formulation that can help the family think about and understand the problem and how it links to the therapy being offered. Being clear and realistic about the focus and goals is an important start to working collaboratively with children and families, and it provides an opportunity to stimulate the mentalizing process. A specific emphasis is on the assessment of both the parents' and the child's capacity to mentalize and a formulation about how this is linked to the child's presenting difficulties. In many ways, the focus formulation serves as framework that creates a common language and guides the therapist's interventions. In order to provide a clear sense of how the different stages of the assessment link together, we present the assessment of one child, John, and his foster carers.

THE STRUCTURE OF THE ASSESSMENT PROCESS

There are different ways of initiating a time-limited MBT-C assessment, and it is important for the therapist to be flexible in how to respond to any request for help. Normally, the assessment phase will start with a family session, offered jointly

---

An earlier version of this chapter was first published in 2015 by Nicole Muller and Nick Midgley, "Approaches to Assessment in Time-Limited Mentalization-Based Therapy for Children (MBT-C)," in *Frontiers in Psychology, 6*, Article 1063 (https://doi.org/10.3389/fpsyg.2015.01063). This is an open access journal, and its articles are distributed under the terms of the Creative Commons Attribution License.

https://doi.org/10.1037/0000486-007
Mentalization-Based Treatment for Children: A Time-Limited Approach, Second Edition, by N. Midgley, K. Ensink, K. Lindqvist, N. Malberg, and N. Muller
Copyright © 2026 by the American Psychological Association. All rights reserved.

(when working in pairs) by a child therapist and a parent therapist, followed by two or three individual sessions with the child and parallel sessions for the parents. Alternatively, when working alone, the therapist can meet with the family, followed by individual parent and child sessions. After these initial meetings, the therapists, child, and parents come together again to have a review and feedback session, where the outcome of the assessment can be discussed and a decision made about whether to continue with time-limited MBT-C. The assessment may need to be combined with psychiatric or pediatric and educational assessments and liaison with outside agencies that play a significant role in the child's life.

Starting with a joint meeting with the parents and the child together communicates a number of important MBT-C principles, including

- that MBT-C does not work on the assumption that problems are simply "inside" the child,
- that difficulties for one person are usually embedded within key relationships, and
- that solving those problems often involves work on the part of the whole family.

There are times when this format may need to be modified—for example, when parents feel that there is something that may be contributing to the child's difficulties, such as difficulties between the parents or the mental health difficulties of a parent, and are appropriately reluctant to discuss this in front of the child.

Whatever the specific format, the overall aims of the assessment in time-limited MBT-C are to develop a *mentalizing profile* of the child and the parents or family and to explore what links this might have with the difficulties that brought the child to treatment. If, at the end of the assessment, the child is to be offered time-limited MBT-C, the assessment process is also used to help reach an agreed focus for the work and set goals (see Exhibit 6.1). At the same time, the assessment process can be therapeutic in itself, giving opportunities for the clinicians to assess the child and family's capacity to make use of this particular way of working.

EXHIBIT 6.1

Outline of the MBT-C Assessment

- Initial meeting with child and family or carers

When working with two therapists, both therapists will meet with the child and parents together to learn more about what led to the referral and how each person sees the problem. At this session, the therapists make an initial assessment of the family's mentalizing profile and gain a sense of the interaction within the family.

- Two or three meetings with the parents or carers

When working with two therapists, these meetings take place with the parents' therapist in parallel with the child's assessment meetings. They provide an opportunity to establish a therapeutic alliance with the parents and gain a better understanding of their perspective of the child and the presenting problem(s). During these sessions, the therapist formulates an initial assessment of parental reflective functioning (strengths and weaknesses) and how this may relate to the presenting problem(s).

(continues)

EXHIBIT 6.1

Outline of the MBT-C Assessment (*Continued*)

- Two or three meetings with the child

When working with two therapists, the child's therapist meets with the child to begin to establish a therapeutic alliance and gain a better understanding of the child's perspective. The therapist formulates an initial assessment of the child's capacity to mentalize (strengths and weaknesses) and how this may relate to the presenting problems.

- Feedback and review session

In this joint meeting with both therapists, the parent, and the child, the group reviews how the assessment has gone. The therapists share their formulations with the family. On this basis, a joint decision is made about whether to continue with time-limited MBT-C and, if so, to agree on the focus formulation and the treatment goals.

Note. MBT-C = mentalization-based treatment for children.

MEETING THE CHILD AND FAMILY FOR THE FIRST TIME

John, Age 8

For the initial meeting, John attends with both of his foster parents, Mr. and Mrs. F. John has been referred to the service because of severe aggressive outbursts and attachment trauma, and it is the first time he has come to the clinic. The two therapists who will be working with the family meet them in the waiting room together and take them through to the consulting room. They explain briefly what will happen in the first meeting. The therapist who is going to be meeting with the foster carers says that she has heard from the social worker that they are worried about the outbursts that John has been having recently. But before she asks more about that, she wonders if they can begin by introducing themselves. Everyone nods, and the therapist adds that she has a slightly odd way of doing this and that she would like everyone to select a toy animal from the basket in the center of the room, which they think represents each person in the room: Would they be okay to do that? Everyone agrees, albeit with a mixture of curiosity and some apprehension on their faces.

When he is asked to choose an animal for each person, John begins by choosing a chimpanzee for himself. The therapist is curious about this choice and looks around the room to see if anyone has any thoughts about it. Mrs. F guesses he chose this because he can sometimes be quite cheeky, like a monkey. Both John and his foster father laugh at this, as if in recognition. When the therapist checks this out with John, he nods, but he adds that chimpanzees also have sharp teeth. The therapist wonders aloud why that might be important to John, and John's foster father says that chimpanzees sometimes have to protect themselves when things don't feel safe. John looks intently and somewhat thoughtfully at his foster father and then says that he wants to select an animal for his foster parents. Before he does so, the therapist suggests that each of the foster carers guesses which animal John might choose for them but tells them to keep their guesses to themselves for now. When they've done so, John tells everyone that he has chosen a gorilla for his foster father. The therapist asks Mr. F if that was the animal he was expecting, and he laughs and says no, he thought he'd be an elephant! The therapist asks if he can guess why John might have chosen a gorilla, pointing out that gorillas and chimpanzees are both monkeys but from different families. "They belong to the family of the apes, they belong to each other but they also have their own family," John says with a lot of feeling. Mr. F responds to this in a warm and genuine way, gently putting his arm on John's shoulder and adding, "Just like us."

In starting with an initial family meeting, the therapists convey that they really want to understand what has brought the family to seek help, that they would like to hear everyone's views and experiences, and that they will listen to these in a respectful and nonjudgmental way. One of the aims is to introduce the family to some of the components of a mentalizing approach, both by explaining the core elements of MBT-C and by demonstrating the mentalizing stance from the very start, in the way the therapist interacts with family members. Throughout the first meeting, the therapists aim to develop a shared understanding of what has brought the child and family to seek help, representing the different perspectives that different family members might have, and to link this to their hopes and expectations about therapy. Seeing the family together also allows the therapists to observe something about the quality of attachment relationships in the family and to identify both strengths and weaknesses in the family's capacity to mentalize together and areas where the family's capacity to mentalize appears to be vulnerable. All of this is used to try and develop a preliminary formulation about the links between the family's mentalizing strengths and weaknesses and the issues that brought them to seek help.

A lot can be learned from listening to what family members say about each other, but as much can also be learned from observing nonverbal, relational patterns between the parents and child (Ensink, Leroux, et al., 2017; Fonagy, 2015; Shai & Fonagy, 2014)—what Stern (1985) called "ways of being together." For example, what parents do in interaction with their children and whether they are emotionally available, able to listen to the child, and can imagine their internal experience is as important—if not more important—than the parents' capacity to describe the child in an interview. These patterns of nonverbal, implicit relational knowledge (Lyons-Ruth et al., 1998) are important to observe in the initial family meeting.

The first family meeting is usually somewhat structured, drawing on ideas developed in the context of systemic and family-based mentalization-based treatment (MBT; Asen & Midgley, 2025; Asen & Fonagy, 2021; Keaveny et al., 2012) and can include the following elements:

- family introductions;
- clarifying how different family members see the difficulties that brought them to seek therapy and what they have tried so far to address these problems;
- a family activity or game; and
- checking in and reviewing the session and explaining what might happen next.

Inviting the Family to Introduce Themselves

First, each member of the family is invited to introduce one of the others and to say a little bit about them as a person (e.g., what they like, the kind of person they are, etc.). Starting with this, rather than going directly into the reasons why the child has been referred, helps to avoid too quickly focusing on the child and his or her problems. It also gives an opportunity, in a playful way, to discover something about the family relationships, and from the beginning, it introduces the idea that we are interested in different perspectives—to see ourselves from the outside and others from the inside. While listening to these introductions, the therapist may want to keep certain questions in mind, as this will help in coming to make an assessment of the family's capacity for mentalizing:

- Are the family members able to describe each other in terms of personal qualities, mental states, and how they relate, or are their descriptions more concrete, focusing primarily on behavior?
- What is the emotional quality of the descriptions? Are they very negative and overly idealized, or are they nuanced?
- How do the family members being described respond to the description that others give of them?

After (or sometimes instead of) this verbal introduction of each family member, the therapists sometimes ask the family members to select an animal for each other and invite some discussion about these choices, looking for more implicit information about how different members of the family see each other and themselves (Muller & Midgley, 2015). As in the example with John and his foster carers above, there can often be a playful quality to these introductions, as family members surprise themselves (and each other) with the way they are introduced or the images that others have of them. This can help move away from too great an emphasis on "the problem" and can introduce the value of seeing other people's perspectives.

Using the animal figures as a way for the family to describe each other can result in a more structured way to get to know each other. This is especially helpful when working with families where there are high levels of stress or a tendency to focus on moving to quick solutions, without allowing much space to think together. The following is a way of introducing such an activity:

> There are all these animals here. I want [child] to choose an animal that reminds them of you, how you are as a person [give an example if possible], then pick one for each member present here today. Now, I want you to write it on this paper or ask me to help you. In the meantime, your parents and siblings [if present] will write down what they imagine/guess you will choose. After that, you will share with us what you picked for each member, and we can see what the others thought you would pick.

The idea behind this exercise is

- to identify the capacity of the child and family members to think of others in the family in terms of their mental states and personality traits, not only physical appearance;
- to introduce the idea that we never really know how others see us or think of us unless we ask and think together; and
- to highlight the reactions of each member of the family to the attributions made about them and highlight the importance of different perspectives.

Finding Out About the Problem

After everyone in the room has been introduced (including the therapists, who can be asked to introduce each other), family members are asked about what brings them to seek help and are given the opportunity to express their own ideas about the problems that have brought them to therapy. There is a focus from the start on the idea that different people may have different perspectives, and that the therapists are not interested in establishing who is right or wrong. Rather, they want to see how things look from everyone's position. Areas to explore may include the following (Asen & Fonagy, 2021):

- Focus on context and history of difficulties: This includes the nature and development of the problem(s); the contexts in which they present, how the family have tried to deal with the problem(s) and how they have tried to understand them, the effects on family and others, and the history of previous treatment and help sought.
- Exploring differences: This involves finding out whether family members might have different ideas about the difficulties, or if they have different understandings of what has caused them.

Often with younger children, the parents will talk about their child's problems; children may find it hard to speak about their problems themselves. However, they are also asked to give their views, as they can often surprise their parents by showing that they have their own perspectives on the issues that brought them to therapy. The aim is to get a clear picture of the existing problems of the child, when and in what context the problem first developed, when it manifests now and what occurs, and the ideas everyone has about the meaning or history of the problems. Although the child's problems are treated as an important topic, we also try to see the difficulties of the child from an interpersonal or systemic perspective and underline the interpersonal nature of the therapy, explaining that an effort will be made to find a way of addressing the problems together.

Using Structured Activities Within the Assessment Process

John, Age 8

During a family session, the therapist shows the foster parents and John a picture of a home. The therapist asks all present to look at the names of emotions written at the bottom of the house: fear, happiness, pride, envy, anger, sadness, and loneliness. Then, the family is asked, "In the home that you all share, the family that you are making together right now, which of these emotions are in the middle? This means that when someone feels them, they feel comfortable sharing them because they feel safe to do so. If they feel like that sometimes but other times they are not sure, they can place half of the word inside the house and half outside. If they feel that usually it is best to keep these feelings to themselves, they will write them outside the house."

Once the foster parents and John have written their words, a conversation starts in which the family is able to say if they are surprised or not by the other's perceptions. The therapist facilitates a conversation regarding the importance of checking and communicating that it is okay to express such emotions. More importantly, John is able to listen to his foster parents' experience and is able to feel their genuine interest in learning how different members of the family can learn to share a common language about emotions and let each other know when they do not feel understood or accepted. The therapist also learns about which emotions feel safer or less safe to share in the context of this family, and how the family are able to share and listen to each other's experiences.

Where appropriate, the first assessment session with families can include a family game or structured task, giving the therapists the opportunity to see how the family members interact with each other when carrying out a shared task. The therapist may introduce this by explaining that some families can easily speak about the strengths and difficulties they have and some families are better at showing things to us by doing something together, so we always try to combine talking and doing things together. The activity suggested can be an interaction task, like the squiggle (Ensink, Leroux, et al., 2017; Winnicott, 1996), where the parent and child make a story together by completing each other's squiggles. A squiggle is a mark or beginning of a drawing started by one person, which the other person then completes and makes into a complete drawing. It provides an opportunity to observe whether the parents express an interest in the child's experience, can imagine the child's internal world, and are receptive to their affective communication and can elaborate and coconstruct a story with them that captures something that is of personal salience to the child. One could say that it is a test of the parent's capacity to imagine the child's experience and make it meaningful and turn something that, in the beginning, is no more than a squiggle into a meaningful story with the child. Alternatively, the therapists can suggest a relatively free task such as drawing or creating something out of clay or blocks—for example, asking the family to make their dream family house or a family zoo.

One reason for doing this is to see how the family relates to each other in a play-based situation—the process of doing this is as important as (if not more important than) what is actually created. In some families, especially where the initial interactions have been quite chaotic or where there is a lack of spontaneity in the family, the therapist may feel that the family needs more structure in order for the game or task to be a good experience for everyone. The therapists may then choose a more structured task, such as asking the family to build a tower with a set of blocks.

Where the child and family give consent and do not feel too anxious, it can be helpful to get permission to video record the family task or game. This can be introduced by explaining that during a subsequent meeting with the parents, the video will be watched together to try to better understand the communication and relations within the family.

Checking In and Explaining What Might Happen Next

The first session usually ends with the therapists checking in with each person about how they have experienced the meeting. The therapists may also share with the family what they feel they have heard and check whether they have understood what the family has tried to convey and that they have not missed anything important. The therapists will also discuss with the family if they want to proceed and, if they do, explain the assessment process. This is also an opportunity to explain something about what is meant by a "mentalization-based treatment" and what might happen next.

How one explains the concept of "mentalizing" will depend on the age and level of understanding of the child (and the parents!), and there are different views on whether it is helpful or necessary to use the term "mentalization" with children or families (N. Malberg et al., 2023). If you do, there is always the danger of becoming a bit abstract or using too many words. Our experience is that it works best if you can link an explanation of the term to something that has happened in the room together, to a story from your own life, or to something that the child and family are likely to know. (If children have seen it, the Pixar film *Inside Out* can be a great way to talk about what mentalizing is.) Each person has their own style, but it can be helpful to start by saying something like the following:

> In our meetings together, you might sometimes hear me using a slightly odd word: "mentalizing." This is a word we sometimes use as a way of trying to notice something that might be really helpful to you in sorting out the issues that brought you to therapy. "Mentalizing" is about trying to get interested in what might be going on in people's minds when they say or do something. For example, I'm talking now, but you might be thinking "Why's he telling me this?" That's mentalizing because you're trying to figure out what the intention is behind what I'm saying. If you get why I'm telling you this, things can make a lot more sense. But when we can't do that or when we get it wrong, it can lead to all kinds of problems.

At this point (if eyes have not glazed over already), it can be helpful to link this explanation to something that has happened in the room or, failing that, to tell a story from your own experience. The story can be about how helpful good mentalizing can be. For example, you might say to a child,

> Like today, do you remember when dad said to you, "That must have been really hard when we left you on your own"? I noticed that a tear came into your eye, and you gave him a big hug? That was dad mentalizing well. He was thinking what it felt like to be you at that moment when you were left alone in hospital, and I'm guessing that it made you feel good when he did that?

Or sometimes, it can be about what happens when mentalizing goes wrong and why fixing it can be helpful. For example, you might say to a child,

> Do you remember how you told me today how angry you were with dad because you thought he'd brought you here today as a punishment for behaving badly? And that made you sulk with him, and then he started getting irritable with you? But when we all talked about it, dad explained that the main reason he brought you here today was because he was really worried about you—and when you understood that, I think it changed how you felt, didn't it? That's the power of mentalizing!

Once you have explained a bit about what mentalizing is and how it might link to the issues they came here to get help with, it is time to decide whether to continue with the assessment. Sometimes, a family may want to go home and think before deciding about whether to continue with the assessment. Often, at this stage, a sufficient level of trust has been built for the child to agree to meet with one of the therapists separately at the next meeting and for the parents to be comfortable with this. If they are not, then the structure of the assessment can be adapted. The important thing is not to follow the exact process but rather to keep in mind the aims of the MBT-C assessment and decide how best to achieve them in each case.

It is also helpful to contact the school to hear their thoughts and observations about the child. Sometimes, children, especially children with trauma or attachments problems, behave differently at school and at home, and as a result, they will most likely evoke different reactions that can help to inform the assessment (N. Malberg et al., 2023; Muller et al., 2012).

ASSESSMENT MEETINGS WITH THE CHILD

The assessment of the child is usually conducted over two or three sessions, and the aim of these meetings is to develop a profile of the functioning and abilities of the child, their personality, and way of relating, as well as an understanding of how the child's capacity for mentalizing may be linked to their presenting problems and difficulties. In addition, the therapist will be attentive to areas where the child's mentalizing may be underdeveloped or situations in which an existing capacity to mentalize might break down. The aim of these assessment sessions is not just to give information to the therapist but also to create a relationship and a working alliance with the child. Rather than following a prescribed formula, the therapist uses their own creativity and clinical knowledge to find ways of engaging the child, selecting activities that facilitate a playful engagement and the opportunity to mentalize about self and other.

As part of the assessment phase, the therapist may decide to use both structured activities and free play. More structured tasks initiated by the therapist will give information regarding the child's ability to accept limits and follow instructions; free play will give information about the child's ability to handle lack of structure, to take initiative, and to use fantasy. Free play also provides an opportunity to observe whether the child is able to play and make play narratives with a beginning, a middle, and an end (Normandin et al., 2023; Tessier et al., 2016), as well as to identify traumatic play (Chazan et al., 2016) or whether there is play inhibition where the capacity to play is disrupted.

Projective tasks can be incorporated for some assessments—for example, asking the child to tell a story using pictures, such as the Narrative Story Stems (Hodges et al., 2003; Kelly & Bailey, 2021). It may also be useful to use drawings by asking the child to draw different emotions or by providing the child with drawings that are to be finished. In line with the MBT approach, during these sessions, the therapist uses their clinical judgment to actively respond and engage in play if that is considered helpful.

During the individual meetings, the therapist can express curiosity about what the child knows about why they have come to the service or whether they can articulate some of their problems using their own words. When children can express their own problems in a few words, it makes it much easier to find the right focus in MBT-C. Children might say something like "I am always anxious" or "I have no friends—no one wants to play with me," indicating that they themselves consider that there is a problem and have a sense of what it is. At the end of the assessment phase, the therapist and child will try to agree about one goal that coming to therapy may be able to help them with, as well as formulating a "focus statement" for the therapy.

In addition to understanding the problem, the therapist should also try to look for the "vital spark" in the child (Winnicott, 1971b)—something that seems like a strength or a little burning flame that might help in the therapy. It can be things the child likes to do or is good at or something that they are curious about. This vital spark can be helpful as a source to go back to and maintain motivation when difficult moments in the therapy arise.

Furthermore, we want to assess a child's temperament and consider the impact it might have on the quality of the relationship with their family and beyond. We could consider characteristics such as the child's emotionality, sociability, level of activity, and impulsivity. Does the child present as inhibited and introverted or as extroverted, highly expressive, and active? How do these temperamental characteristics interact with their caregivers' own temperamental profiles?

Assessing Attention Control and Basic Self-Regulation in the Child

John, Age 8

During his first individual assessment meeting, John has a limited attention span that is very dependent on his own motivation. For example, when he chooses an activity himself, he can start playing and sustain it for a while but generally quickly loses concentration, being unable to complete activities. Activities suggested by his therapist are even harder to focus on, and he is very easily distracted. He ignores the therapist when she asks him to do something, in a similar way that to what the therapist has heard can be problematic at school and at home, with John not listening to instructions. Sometimes, during the session, the therapist feels that John seems not to hear, either going into a dissociated state or simply tuning out. It soon becomes apparent that John has very little ability to regulate impulses. He is also hypervigilant in the way he reacts very sensitively to sound. The therapist notices that John is listening to others talking in the adjoining room and that he is immediately distracted by the sound of doors slamming in the distance. Furthermore, it seems that, time and again, he becomes disrupted by chaotic themes and emotions emerging from within, not contained and expressed in the play but actually disrupting the play. He can be playing peacefully when suddenly there is a big crash, objects fly about the room, and things get broken, and he genuinely seems to have no idea what is happening or a sense of being able to control it. In these situations, it is very difficult to make contact with John, and attempts to ask him what was happening do not work at all. The therapist is aware that the same things happen at school, where John has sudden violent outbursts (as the staff perceive it). He cannot talk about it afterwards.

Regarding his fine motor skills, the therapist notices that John uses the tweezers grip when holding the coloring crayons and actually has reasonably good fine motor coordination while coloring and drawing. He is not yet able to write the letter

"J" of John, his own name, and inverts the direction of the little hook at the bottom of the letter J.

Making an assessment of a child's basic capacity for attention control and self-regulation is an important part of MBT-C. When there has been a good enough start in the early phase of life, children develop some sense of their body and skin, where their skin is a natural limit of the body, supporting a sense of an internal and external world (Aras et al., 2024; Stern, 1992). Not only is being held and cuddled and offered physical comfort a central part of parent–infant interactions, it is also considered to underlie a feeling of being comfortable in one's body and skin. The first sense of self crystallizes around experiences of sensory stimulation, such as touching and being touched, hearing, seeing, smelling, and tasting (Gagne, Liew, & Nwadinobi, 2021; Stern, 1985), and forms the affective core of the self (Panksepp & Biven, 2012). This contributes to a sense of the embodied self and how one feels within oneself (Aras et al., 2024; Ensink, Berthelot, Biberdzic, & Normandin, 2016). Furthermore, mirroring helps the child to pay attention to what is felt on the inside. However, some children—including those who have experienced early neglect, such as John—are not used to having a curiosity or awareness directed to what their body tells them. These children may have elevated pain thresholds (e.g., drinking hot chocolate without noticing that they are burning themselves) or reduced perception of bodily signals (e.g., difficulty recognizing when they are feeling hungry or when they need to visit the bathroom Robinson & Skårderud, 2019).

When a child grows up in difficult circumstances (e.g., in an orphanage or with a parent with psychiatric problems) and has had little help to develop the capacity to put feelings into words, especially painful and difficult feelings, they frequently express feelings physically and act them out through their bodies. For example, prolonged institutionalization presents a set of risks associated with severe early deprivation and reduced stimulation that has marked negative effects on sensory, cognitive, and linguistic development (Invitto & Moselli, 2024; D. E. Johnson, 2002). Such children can be easily aroused and hypervigilant, making it harder to regulate their attention and emotions. They seem to be more focused on signals from the outside world. Therefore, the therapist tries to look for unusual reactivity to sound, light, touch, temperature, as well as disturbances in moving in space, gross motor skills, and fine motor skills. By school age, most children have managed to develop a way of attending only to important information and being able to cut out distractions from the environment by simply not paying attention to them. It is thus clinically significant when a child appears to be hypersensitive and distracted by everything around him. Being able to manage impulses from the inside is an essential basis that supports explicit mentalizing because there has to be room for mentalizing rather than this getting drowned out by physical action (Fotopoulou & Tsakiris, 2017; Zevalkink et al., 2012). In other words, a child has to be able to endure a feeling without immediate action in order to be able to mentalize explicitly.

In exploring the basic capacity for attention control and basic self-regulation of a child, the therapist asks herself a number of questions:

- Can the child focus attention?
- Can the child listen to others/you?
- Does the child "live in their body"?
- Does the child have normal sensorimotor regulation capacity regarding sound, light, touch, temperature, movement in space, and gross and fine motor skills?
- Is the child hypervigilant?

Assessing Affect Regulation in the Child

John, Age 8

In the assessment session, John and the therapist are working with clay, and the clay lion John is making gets stuck to the table. As he tries to remove the lion from the table, it comes apart. John's face turns red, and he utters little swear words. Despite his frustration, he shows he has some internal control and also that he is able to accept limits. He shows that he takes pleasure in playing with water during the clay sculpting, but he holds back from doing this right away and waits for the therapist to give the go-ahead, seeking eye contact with the therapist and asking for approval first in this way.

When he is emotionally touched by a topic, the therapist notices that John has difficulty saying why it touches him or what is happening inside him. Instead, he shows it by wanting to do something else, standing up, or starting to talk about something else. When the therapist underlines his behavior by saying it might be painful for him not knowing where he belongs, he doesn't show a reaction. When he sees a seashell in a corner of a table, he briefly mentions that this must be a naughty shell, having to be put in the corner. When the therapist asks him if he himself sometimes has to stand in a corner because he has been naughty, John nods sadly.

During this brief interaction, John shows a range of emotions: frustration, sadness, and pleasure in what he is doing. He can express these feelings, and he stays in contact with the therapist and does not appear to become overwhelmed by any one feeling. He is able to regulate some emotion by himself—for example, by standing up when he becomes frustrated and saying that he wants to do something else. However, he appears unable to identify and verbalize his feelings about his relationships with the key figures in his life. In these relationships, he expresses his feelings through behaviors rather than words, and he appears unable to put into words what he feels inside. Nevertheless, he is connected with what he experiences inside himself, while staying in contact with the therapist. The therapist notes that, compared with her first session with John, she is beginning to feel that everything is there to start MBT-C as soon as John, his foster carers, and the therapists have agreed on a focus.

Other children have more difficulty expressing themselves. In such cases, the therapist must look for other ways of obtaining information about the child's emotional world. She might read a picture book with the child in which all kinds of feelings are depicted and ask the child if they can recognize how the bear, fish, or child in the book feels. Perhaps the most important part, however, is to look at the child while he is playing and to ask oneself a number of questions in order to get some indication about the affect regulation capacity of the child:

- Which emotions does the child show in play or in the contact?
- Is the child able to play or use fantasy, and is this connected to the child's emotions?
- Which emotions does the child recognize/know?
- Which emotions seem to be difficult to express?
- How does the child handle difficult emotions in the session?
- What are the antecedents of the problematic behavior or antecedents of difficult feelings during the session?
- Does the child accept limits?
- Does the child ask for or accept help?
- Can the child be comforted when upset or accept positive remarks?

Explicit Mentalizing Capacity and Where Mentalizing Breaks Down

John, Age 8

During the last assessment session, John wants to play with the clay again. He starts making a bowl for his birth mother, in the shape of a heart, because he says he loves her very much. He then wants to make a Donald Duck bowl for his younger brother (who lives with his biological mother), but while working on this, he starts thinking that the heart bowl could very well be for everyone. Looking at the leftover clay, John spontaneously comes up with the idea that he would like to make a bowl for himself. He wants to make the Donald Duck bowl for himself and not for his brother.

The therapist thinks to herself that it is difficult for John, as his brother lives with his biological mother, and he probably has jealous feelings about it. John tells her that the bowl he is making for himself must be very strong. He reinforces the edges of the bowl well. "It must be able to hold water—that is very important," he tells her. The therapist wonders aloud if John wants to become strong himself, not being angry all the time, being able to keep his feelings inside him. John nods and says that he worries his foster parents wouldn't want to keep him when he gets angry all the time. The therapist is not quite sure how "authentic" this comment is, as John says this as if these may be words that someone has told him and he is just repeating them back, but it could also be that he takes the feeling out of these words because he is really scared of engaging with the affects that the thought and fear of losing his foster parents evoke in him.

To get a sense of the explicit mentalizing capacities of a child and their representations during the assessment phase, the therapist observes whether the child is able to think in mental-state terms when describing themselves and others. The therapist should also be alert as to whether the child shows sign of any stable representations of self and others. When possible, the Child Attachment Interview (Bizzi, Charpentier-Mora, Bastianoni, et al., 2022; Shmueli-Goetz et al., 2008) can be used and rated with the Child and Adolescent Reflective Functioning Scale (Bizzi, Charpentier-Mora, Cavanna, et al., 2022; Ensink, Berthelot, et al., 2014; Ensink et al., 2015), as these provide an opportunity to obtain information about self and other representations as well as mentalizing capacities. As a general rule of thumb, children in middle childhood should have some ability to think about themselves and others in mental-state terms rather than only in behavioral terms. If they are able to think in mental-state terms, difficulties in particular domains may be more easily addressed in short-term treatment, as they already have some of the tools that may be useful to do so. When time and resources are limited, drawing on questions from the Child Attachment Interview, the therapist can ask children for three words to describe themselves and their relationship with attachment figures and then ask for an example of each adjective (e.g., "You said 'angry'—can you tell me about a time when you were angry?"). The therapist tries to look at whether the child has a capacity for explicit mentalizing or whether the child is able to think only in behavior terms. She is finding out whether the child is able to use some basic identification of mental states or has a more developed capacity to think in terms of mental states and link behaviors with underlying feelings and other mental states (Ensink et al., 2015; Sprecher et al., 2023; Vrouva et al., 2012).

Furthermore, the therapist is sensitive to contexts in which mentalizing appears to break down, as the therapist can then try and help the child become aware of this and develop mentalizing strategies specific to these contexts. In thinking about John, it is evident that he has the potential to mentalize, as seen in his play and the story of the gorillas and chimpanzees, but he does not yet spontaneously use mental-state language to communicate how he feels and talk about his predicament and difficulties in the way that other 8-year-old children may be able to do. The therapist has the sense, however, that this can be achieved and developed with some scaffolding and that, if working with John, he could relatively easily develop a certain proficiency in naming his feelings and developing a mental-state language. The therapist also looks at the presentations that children may have of themselves and their parents. For example, if John had an overly negative representation of himself, we would be concerned, as in the contexts of normal development, children usually have largely positive self-representations (Target et al., 2003). Furthermore, if parents are represented in overly idealized or split and polarized ways, where one parent is idealized while another is represented in extremely negative terms, this may be cause for concern and will be noted by the therapist.

In the vignette above, John is able to use the clay to create some kind of representation of himself and others, and as such, he shows some capacity for mentalization. However, it seems that this capacity may go offline when his attachment system is activated, at the point at which the therapist asks him about his worry that he may not be able to stay with his foster carers if he gets angry. Although John might appear to be mentalizing here, when he talks about his worry that his foster carers may not want to keep him, the emotional quality of his words may indicate that John is operating in pretend mode—that is, the words are not really connected to a deeper level of emotional reality. It may also signal to the therapist that John feels afraid that he will not be able to control his anger, so essentially he might feel that he is bound to fail, and this makes him quite anxious and he wants to avoid talking about it. At the same time, he tries to use words but disconnects himself from his feelings when he does so because they are too overwhelming. One way that John's therapist becomes aware of this is by noticing that she finds herself rather unengaged when John speaks about his worry that the foster carer will not want to keep him, which is not how the

TABLE 6.1. Modes of Prementalizing Thinking

Prementalizing mode	In the child, we might see	In ourselves, we recognize
Psychic equivalence (inside-out thinking)	Play is often wild, chaotic, and destructive	Feeling lost or confused
	The child acts as if they know everything for sure	Noticing in oneself an inclination to set limits
Pretend mode (the elephant in the room)	The child's play has a rigid or monotonous character	Feel bored, start operating on autopilot
	The child is not in contact with feelings; incongruent or low affect	Feeling cut off or uninvolved Finding your mind wandering, or interruption of odd affects
Teleological mode (quick-fix thinking)	The child demands a quick solution	An intense wish to do something
	The child demands that you do something *now*!	Feeling controlled or under intense pressure Starting to give practical advice or offer coping strategies

Note. Data from Ten Kate et al. (2016) and Zevalkink et al. (2012).

therapist usually responds when a child speaks about such an emotional topic. She wonders if this might be because John himself does not sound entirely authentic—as if he is saying the words but is not quite emotionally engaged himself. In time, the therapist may be able to help with this by explaining that it is scary to think that one may be rejected and lose the family that he is growing to love because of something that he does not know how to control, such as anger.

Table 6.1 (based on ideas from Ten Kate et al., 2016; Zevalkink et al., 2012) offers a description of a range of child behaviors that a therapist might see during an assessment, as well as some typical emotional responses that therapists may notice in themselves, and suggests how this relates to the different prementalizing modes described more fully in Chapter 2 in this volume.

ASSESSMENT MEETINGS WITH THE PARENTS

John, Age 8

A week after the initial meeting with John and his foster carers, one of the therapists meets with Mr. and Mrs. F on their own. The therapist begins by reflecting on how the meeting had been the previous week and whether the foster carers have seen any reaction in John since then. The therapist then explains that, in this meeting, she wants to find out more about how things are from their perspective and to get to know them a bit as John's foster carers. She also reminds them about the joint activity that they filmed together and says that they will try to make time to review that together in this meeting or the next one.

Quite quickly, Mr. and Mrs. F begin to speak about the importance of healthy food. After John visited his mother recently, he had told them stories about all the candy and the snacks he had eaten. Once back with the foster family, he had trouble eating everyday food, which irritated the foster parents a lot, since John spoke so extensively about everything he had eaten when he was with his mother. They tried to explain to him that the food his mother gave him was not really healthy and that the food in their family was, and they instructed him not to eat too much candy while visiting his mother because of his weight problems. But after they had done this, they explain to the therapist, John stopped telling them about what he ate when he visited his mom, although they guessed he was probably still eating a lot of candy. Mrs. F speaks of her frustration about this and says she can't understand why John doesn't listen to their advice. "It is almost like he is deliberately doing it to upset us," she says. The therapist listens and empathizes with their frustration, and says that it sounds as if healthy eating is something that is really important to them. After further exploration, it becomes clear that Mrs. F had problems with being overweight herself when she was a child and is very worried that John will be bullied in the way she had been. Her voice becomes softer as she remembers her own experiences.

At this point, the therapist invites them to think whether John's reasons for eating the junk food might be similar to or different from the foster mother's when she was a child. Mr. and Mrs. F begin to think about how, for John, what he ate might feel like a question of which "parents" he is loyal too. Feeling sympathy with his situation, they think about whether they should stop talking to him about the unhealthy food and instead react positively to his enthusiastic way of telling and respond to his happiness about the contact with his mother. The therapist asks what they think this would be like for John. Mr. F thinks that he might be a bit suspicious at first and not sure if they really mean it. He remembers how John would often say "Really? Are you sure?" as if doubting what they told him. But they think that if they persist, then John might feel safer to talk to them about how he feels. They decide to try and change their way of speaking to John, wanting to emphasize instead that there are differences in the way things go in the two families, but that it is okay to enjoy these differences. Mrs. F, in particular, recognizes that this wouldn't be easy for her, but that that is more her problem than John's.

The two or three sessions with the parents or carers usually take place while the child is being seen by a separate therapist, and in these sessions, the therapist tries to make an appraisal of the problems that the family sought help for as well as the mentalizing capacities and difficulties of the parents or carers themselves (N. T. Malberg, 2024; Muller & Bakker, 2009; Muller & ten Kate, 2008). By that, we mean their capacity to think of children as separate people, with minds of their own, and to see the child's behavior (and their own, as parents) in terms of intentional mental states (Slade, 2006). During initial sessions, the therapist seeks to observe and listen for the ways in which the parents think, manage, and try to understand and explain the child's behaviors and emotional states. Furthermore, the therapist should be interested in the parents' own emotional reactions and their ability to reflect on those. Based on an initial assessment, the therapist can then define where she thinks she can "meet the parents best" in terms of their current reflective functioning capacities.

There are several structured and reliable instruments for assessing mentalizing capacity in parents and carers, such as the Adult Attachment Interview (George et al., 1996) or the Parent Development Interview (Slade et al., 2004; Slade & Sleed, 2024). However, when there is neither the time nor resources to use these structured interviews, certain questions that are part of these interview schedules can be useful in more clinical ways. For example, in the assessment meeting with the parents, the therapist can say, "Can you choose three adjectives that you feel reflect the relationship between you and your child? Does an incident or memory come to mind with respect to each of these adjectives?" or "Tell me about a time in the last week or two when you felt really angry as a parent. What kinds of situations make you feel this way? How do you handle your angry feelings?" Where appropriate, the therapist might also ask, "How do you think your own experiences of being parented affects your experience of being a parent now?" This last question helps the therapist to identify possible "ghosts in the nursery" (Fraiberg et al., 1975; N. Malberg et al., 2023) or "angels in the nursery" (Lieberman et al., 2005)—that is, traumatic or positive experiences from the parents' own histories that may be influencing the way they relate to their child. For parents who have experienced childhood abuse and neglect, being able to mentalize about these experiences (Dollberg & Hanetz-Gamliel, 2023; Ensink, Berthelot, et al., 2014) and the impact it has had on their development and parenting appear to be particularly important in terms of child outcomes and relationship functioning. Sometimes, as in the case of John's foster carer, these issues may come up more spontaneously, but if not, there may be times when it is helpful to explicitly ask about them while being clear why this is relevant to the issues that brought their child to therapy.

As in all aspects of MBT-C, the therapist tries to use the core features of the "mentalizing stance," including empathy, curiosity, and an interest in different perspectives. When John's foster mother spoke about her frustration that John did not listen to their advice on healthy eating, the therapist did not challenge her on this and avoided focusing on the behavior per se or whether it was right or wrong. By showing empathy with the foster mother's frustration, it seemed that she felt safer to speak about her own experiences as a child. Her softer voice was an indication to the therapist that the foster mother's mentalizing capacity was more "online" because the level of arousal had decreased. At that point, the therapist began to use some questions that invited explicit mentalizing: What did they think it would be like for John when they asked him about what he had eaten with his mom? In what way might John's reasons for eating junk food be similar to or different from the foster mother's reasons when she was a child? By asking these questions, the therapist was encouraging the foster carers to take an inquisitive stance about John's mind and his experiences. For example, John's foster carers were able to imagine that, when talking about food, John might feel as if he had to say which parents he liked best. But the word "might" was important—they did not express absolute certainty about this, although seeing it from this perspective helped them to make better sense of the way John sometimes behaved with them. Features such as this capacity to hold a position of "safe uncertainty" and be aware of the opacity of minds are helpful indicators of the parents' capacity to be reflective, to sustain a stance of mind-mindedness (Meins et al., 2002), even in the face of their child's difficult behavior. Asen and Fonagy (2012b) suggested that the therapist asks themselves the following questions as part of a "mentalizing checklist for parents":

- Does one parent feel the urge to speak for the other parent or their child in the family session?

- Do parents refer to their own thoughts or feelings?
- Do parents refer to feelings or thoughts of others in the family?
- Do parents consider the perspective of others?
- Do parents sometimes say, "I might be wrong, but I think she . . ." (opaqueness)?
- Do parents often use all-or-nothing or black-and-white words, such as "always" or "never"?
- Are the parents playful, or do they use humor?
- Are there special feelings or thoughts that seem to be avoided in the conversation or that often lead to escalation?
- When parents talk about their behavior, do they sometimes connect this to intentions?

Depending on their own histories, parents may vary greatly in their capacity to mentalize their child's experience—or they may be able to do this in some areas but be vulnerable to mentalizing breakdowns in others. For example, a parent may have the capacity to explicitly mentalize in the here and now as a result of the questions the therapist asks or because they start to think about what they are telling in a way that shows they can reflect on what they are saying at the same time. The capacity to modulate, tolerate, and name affects as well as to empathize with the experience of the child is rooted in the capacity to reflect on one's own experiences, so if emotions are familiar to the parent and known, then they can probably recognize and respond to them in a coherent, organized, and meaningful way.

Parents who have their own histories of insecure attachment may have more difficulties symbolizing the experiences of their children and making sense of their children's communication because their child's emotions can easily make them dysregulated themselves. When parents have their own histories of childhood trauma, in order to help them most effectively, special attention should be paid to understanding when mentalization breaks down and what situations are particularly challenging, even when they have good reflective functioning in general. For parents who have underdeveloped reflective function and cannot see beyond their child's behavior, the therapist may see developmentally inappropriate, unpredictable, or chaotic and contradictory regulation strategies.

In this assessment meeting with John's foster carers, it was apparent that they were able to use the space provided by the therapist to explore John's experiences and to separate their own needs and wishes from his. In doing so, they were able to think how they could best provide him with a sense of security and safety. As such, their capacity to mentalize was fundamentally good, but like for all of us, there were certain areas and contexts where they were vulnerable to mentalizing breakdowns, and at those points, Mrs. F seemed to operate in more of a psychic equivalence mode—that is, being sure that what was in her mind (about John) was how things actually were, out there. But when the therapist recognized this and offered empathy rather than challenge, her capacity to become curious about John's experience and to imagine things from his perspective quickly revived.

This is not always the case with the families seeking help. As Fonagy and Campbell (2015) put it, therapeutic change for an individual child "can only be sustained ... if the patient is able to use, and even to change their social environment in a way that allows them to continue to relax epistemic hypervigilance and foster their mentalizing strengths" (p. 245). But when there is no safe haven at home, an intervention to take the child out of the threatening situation, or to support the family's functioning, might be necessary before thinking about treatment for the child.

GATHERING IMPRESSIONS INTO A CASE FORMULATION

John, Age 8

In their final assessment session, the therapists thank John and his foster carers for coming and explore how they have found the process so far. All three agree that it has not been what they expected, and when the therapists ask what they had expected, they say that they thought the therapist would be more like a doctor telling them what is wrong! One of the therapists tells them that she's been thinking a lot about all they had shown and told her, and that she has made a small story, which she would like to share with them. John looks very pleased about this, and he leans in against his foster mother's body as if waiting to hear a story at bedtime. The therapist then begins: "There was once a little chimpanzee. He lived for a while with his mother in a group but had to leave her when he was really little because she couldn't take care of him anymore. That was sad because the chimpanzee hadn't learned all the words and rituals that are used in a chimpanzee family. After traveling around and staying in different places, the little chimpanzee came to a family of gorillas. This looked a bit like home, but sometimes he felt out of place and worried if the gorilla family would let him stay. He often lacked the words to describe what he thought or felt. He sometimes felt very alone because he missed his mother and because he had lived so long with others where he had felt like an outsider. When he felt sad, he sometimes became angry because that helped him feel a bit bigger. At the gorilla family, it often did feel like home, but sometimes it didn't. He was a chimpanzee after all. So he decided he wanted to find his own words and rituals to become stronger and not so angry anymore, and he decided he wanted to live with the gorillas and visit the chimpanzee family once in a while. The gorillas loved the little chimpanzee, and they were willing to learn more about what it is like to be chimpanzee." The therapist shows the family figures of three gorillas and a chimpanzee to represent the family (see Figure 6.1).

When the story finishes, John's foster carers turn to look at John's face, and he smiles back at them. Pointing out the interaction, the therapist wondered if Mrs. F wants to let John know what is in her mind right now. She replies, "Just that we care about him a great deal and know that he's a lovely boy—even if he does sometimes drive us crazy!" This leads the therapist and the family back to thinking about their plans, and all agree that John should begin a block of 12 MBT-C sessions and that the foster carers will also attend, although they prefer to attend fortnightly rather than every week. John himself agrees with this plan.

The final session in the assessment phase is usually with parents and the child together and is an opportunity for the therapists to try and share their thinking in a way that can be understood by both parents and the child.

FIGURE 6.1. The Family of Gorillas and a Chimpanzee

Note. Image created by Nicole Muller.

This shared formulation should ideally include the following:

- some thoughts about the mentalizing strengths in the child and family;
- some of the areas where mentalizing is underdeveloped or may break down;
- provisional thoughts on how the above links to the issues that brought the family to seek help; and
- a recommendation about whether time-limited MBT-C could be an appropriate intervention to address these issues.

When putting together a mentalizing profile, it can be helpful to ask oneself two questions:

- How well can this person mentalize when at their best—and when is that?
- How much difficulty does this person have with mentalizing when it breaks down the most—and when is that?

With this in mind, mentalizing problems can be put on a spectrum, with underdeveloped mentalizing at one end of the spectrum and specific/temporary breakdowns in mentalizing at the other.

Developing and coconstructing a shared formulation, as elaborated by T. Rossouw (2012) in the context of MBT with adolescents who self-harm, appears to be particularly useful. Rossouw points out that the aim of a formulation is "to explain the current difficulties in mentalizing and relational terms . . . [and] also to present to the young people and their families an image of themselves that will make them feel understood" (p. 137). The value of a formulation is also in its capacity to shape plans and give a focus to the work—and to link the capacity to mentalize with the problems that the family is seeking help for. Sharing such ideas with children and their parents is not always easy, and it is important to avoid using overly technical language. A case formulation can be given in the form of a little story, which can contain a metaphor that speaks to the possible implicit and explicit features of the problems, or it can be a sentence.

In the case of John, described above, the therapist's assessment indicated that John's foster carers had a good capacity to see John as a boy with thoughts and feelings, which could help them to make sense of his behavior. Although there were areas where their mentalizing capacity could break down, possibly due to issues deriving from their own histories (e.g., the foster mother's response to John not being careful about his diet and putting on weight), they were able to make use of the therapeutic space provided in the assessment to reflect on their own mental states and thereby separate out what belonged to John and what belonged to them. In doing so, they were able to think about John's loyalty conflict in a different way and modify how they responded to his behaviors accordingly.

Likewise, in his individual assessment meetings, when the circumstances were right, John demonstrated a capacity to regulate both his attention and affects. For example, over the course of the three meetings, he showed some capacity to regulate his emotions and to make use of the therapeutic relationship to support this. He also showed some evidence of potentially being able to use mentalizing to make sense of his own behavior and the reactions of others; to engage in simple symbolic play, although the play narratives were not well elaborated; and to make use of the metaphor of the chimpanzee and the gorillas. However, it was also apparent that John's ability to mentalize was underdeveloped in a number of areas: He used little explicit mentalizing in his descriptions of himself and significant relationships. In addition, even the abilities he did have easily broke down when John felt anxious or afraid. It seemed likely that John's vulnerability to such disruptions was, in part, related to his early history, where he may not have experienced the type of sensitive responding to distress, mind-mindedness, and marked affect mirroring associated with the development of self and affect regulation (Fonagy et al., 1991; Riazi & Manouchehri, 2024; Slade, 2005). Given his many foster placements, John may have had few experiences of reflective parenting and caregivers looking beyond his behavior and imagining what this communicated about his internal experience. He may have had little support to articulate his feelings and concerns, and develop self-regulation strategies. In short, John would have had few opportunities to experience the kind of benign interest in his mind considered to facilitate the development of mentalizing regarding self and others (Ballespi et al., 2021).

In John's case, the decision about whether to continue with time-limited MBT-C flowed naturally out of the therapist's sharing of what they learned from the assessment meetings and the working relationship that had been established with both John and his foster carers. Sometimes, this is less straightforward and needs to be given more time. But in all cases, once there has been a chance to think together about what brought the child and family to seek help and how their difficulties can be understood, it is a natural step to think "what next?" and, in particular, whether it is appropriate to proceed with time-limited MBT-C. This should be seen as an opportunity for shared decision making (Abrines-Jaume et al., 2016), where the perspectives of all those involved can be taken into account. In many cases, children and families will have little idea about what "seeing a therapist" actually involves before seeking help, so the assessment period is an opportunity for them to get a feeling for who the therapist is and how they work so they can make a better judgment about whether this feels like the right way to proceed. If the family has had an experience of feeling understood and the assessment has created a sense of trust in this way of working, then this is an important factor in deciding whether to proceed—or not.

In some cases, the assessment may also lead the therapist to consider that another type of help may be more appropriate or that the offer of mentalization-based help needs to be adapted. The therapist may need to provide the family with information with different ways of working (including the role of medication) and give them space to better understand the different options before deciding how to proceed. The therapist may also feel, on the basis of the assessment, that a different approach is needed. For example, when the assessment suggests that the child has a loving and supportive family but is suffering from specific posttraumatic symptoms (e.g., as the result of a car accident), then it may be that an approach such as eye movement desensitization and reprocessing may be more appropriate (Raissouni et al., 2023). Or when the assessment has highlighted that the parents are in high conflict, we may suggest that a period of work is done with the parents first before deciding whether the child has their own therapy. Likewise, if the difficulties are clearly due to complex family dynamics, it may be better to work with the whole family together rather than seeing the child and parents separately. As with the approach to working with parents described in Chapter 9 in this volume, "reasoned flexibility" (Slade, 2005), informed decision making, and a genuinely collaborative approach are key to successful therapy.

DEVELOPING A FOCUS STATEMENT

If a decision has been made to proceed with time-limited MBT-C, then the next step is to develop a shared focus statement. The focus formulation should be easy to understand for both the child and the parents. Themes of the focus are often related to self-esteem, regulation, autonomy, dependency, and developmental forces. The focus formulation aims to be exploratory and/or affect regulatory and formulated in a nondramatic, playful way. An important notion is that the focus formulation is different from a problem formulation. Instead, it points to the work that can be done in therapy, with emphasis on hope, curiosity, and resources (Haugvik & Johns, 2008; Røed Hansen, 2012). The therapist can choose to formulate the focus as a short sentence or as a short story. When formulating a shorter focus, the therapist needs to explain more of her thinking in formulating the focus, whereas a story can include more of the dynamics observed in the assessment, thereby being more self-explanatory.

It is important that both the child and the parent feel represented in the stories, focusing on the quality of their relationship. Mentioning examples from the interactions during the assessment phase as well as special facts about the child and the parents is very important to achieve that goal. It is helpful to present the formulation first to the child and ask them for help in case the therapist misunderstood something or missed an important objective. Following that, the child and therapist present it to the parents, who can give their own opinions and contributions. In this way, this exercise facilitates the coconstruction of the therapeutic goals and context.

Sharing the focus formulation with the family is one of the most important parts of the assessment and will conclude the assessment phase and introduce the treatment. When presenting the suggested focus formulation, it is helpful to explain the thinking behind your suggestion, thereby modeling how you can keep someone in mind, wonder about them, and think about them from different perspectives—for example, "We've thought about you a lot and what a suitable focus could be. I thought about how you told us . . . and I wondered a lot about. . . ."

When formulating a focus, there are some *focus traps* to avoid. The aim of the focus is to stimulate curiosity and mentalizing. However, some formulations can have the opposite effect. Contrary to many other models, a focus in MBT-C does not have to be well operationalized or easy to measure—it is actually preferable if it is not! The reason behind this is that we want to avoid a focus that is easy to fail (e.g., "fight less at home," "dare to be more brave"), as these are based on achievement or on unwanted behavior or symptom reduction (e.g., "worry less"). By contrast, the focus aims more at stimulating reflection and curiosity. Since we aim at looking more at internal processes and not just at behavior, the focus needs to be formulated in line with that.

When thinking about John, his therapist suggested that a proposed focus formulation for the work could be: "What does a little chimpanzee need to be happy in a family of gorillas?" Sometimes, the proposed focus does not feel right to the child or the family. It is important to offer the focus as just one option that can be negotiated, conveying the message that you are not necessarily right and not an expert, and that they can correct you or help identify another focus. Sometimes, you might have to go back to the drawing board. It can be a constructive and therapeutic task to think together about what the focus should be.

For example, when discussing this case formulation with the foster carers, John's therapist noticed that the focus that she had proposed focused more on desired changes in his behavior (and feelings), which perhaps reflected a pressure to try and sort out John's difficult behavior. Perhaps something more exploratory, such as "Getting to know the chimpanzees and the gorillas better" or "Finding out what chimpanzees need to be proud and happy," would have encouraged more of a sense of curiosity and interest in mental states and their link to how we feel and behave.

SETTING GOALS

It is increasingly common, when offering therapy to children, not only to use standardized pre and post measures but also to make use of individualized treatment goals, such as the Goal Based Outcome measures described by Law and Wolpert (2014). Setting a specific goal can help children and their parents focus on one central issue in the "sea" of problems. Progress toward a specific goal is both more attainable and visible and can contribute to a sense of much-needed motivation and achievement, in turn stimulating further change. It may appear as if such goal setting may contradict what has been said above about the importance of having a focus for treatment that is not behaviorally oriented. However, it is our experience that using goals and formulating a treatment focus can sit comfortably alongside each other, and both contribute to working effectively with time-limited MBT-C. It also allows the child and family to set goals that are not easily captured by standardized outcome measures. This includes underlying factors, such as building confidence, resilience, and coping skills, which regularly appear as important targets for treatment when children and families are invited to set their own treatment goals (Jacob et al., 2023).

Goal setting following the initial assessment should be clear and realistic and facilitate the ongoing evaluation process. When the therapists and the family agree and work toward these shared goals, the chances of achieving them will be higher, and the family are likely to be more motivated to attend treatment. Furthermore, specific and individual goals are helpful in order to be able to evaluate the treatment and the process, as well as make decisions regarding whether the child needs further treatment. The goals set do not necessarily become the focus of the work in sessions, but they can be used as important indicators that the therapy is impacting on life in a meaningful way for the child and parents.

Since MBT-C is not primarily symptom focused (although it can be problem focused) but rather emphasizes the promotion of mentalizing and emotion regulation, this informs the goal-setting process. When formulating goals, we recommend that this is done on a relational and regulatory level rather than being purely behavioral and symptomatic. On one hand, if the goals set are too concrete, this may be incongruent with our wish to promote mentalization; on the other hand, if the goals are too nonspecific, they will be difficult to assess and to follow up, and it may not be clear to the family how the work in therapy links to the difficulties that led them to seek help in the first place.

In the assessment phase, it is important to give sufficient time to have a conversation, where both child and parents are present, to talk about why they have sought therapy and what they are hoping for by coming to treatment. It should be clear to the child that the therapist knows about their specific problems and wants to try and help with them. When sharing the assessment, the therapist tries to share with the family, at a level that both the parents and the child can understand, a little about how she understands the problems in terms of mentalizing, regulatory difficulties, and family dynamics.

Where possible, we would encourage the use of goals jointly set by the child, the parents, and the therapist. When parents and children set goals separately, research suggests that parents tend to focus more on managing specific difficulties, whereas children also include goals related to personal growth and independence (Jacob et al., 2023). The process of jointly agreeing on goals invites discussion about the different views of each person, and so can facilitate a mentalizing process in itself, as the therapist and family members take on board each other's perspectives in trying to reach a shared set of goals. A shared agreement on goals can happen alongside agreeing a focus statement for the therapy. These goals can, and should, be returned to at review meetings as well as when the therapy comes to an end and at any booster sessions. It is our experience that the process of agreeing goals can be as important as the goals themselves, and that having this discussion up front helps to reduce the likelihood of treatment dropout at a later stage.

CONCLUSION

In this chapter, we have described the assessment process in time-limited MBT-C. It is always important to complete a comprehensive assessment of the child and the parents in order to be able to

- formulate a clear understanding of the nature and severity of the problems, their development, and key causal factors and maintaining factors;
- consider whether the impact on the child's functioning is specific to one area or is general and affecting multiple domains;
- develop an understanding of the mentalizing strengths and difficulties of the child and the parents and whether failures in mentalization are central to the difficulties;
- consider what treatment goals are realistic and identify what the potentially most productive or most central issue is to focus on; and
- form an impression about whether the child or parents recognize that there is a problem and are motivated to find new ways of thinking about things and doing things and whether they appear to trust the therapist and develop a relationships where there is a good working alliance.

On the basis of the above, and in collaboration with the child and family, the assessing therapist can suggest whether it is appropriate to offer a time-limited, mentalization-based frame for the work and, if so, provide some ideas about the potential focus for the work.

7

Working With Children on the Building Blocks of Mentalizing

In this and the following chapter, we describe the main features of the direct work with children in mentalization-based treatment for children (MBT-C), including some of the techniques that can be used in sessions with a child. As we hope we have made clear throughout this book, techniques in themselves are only a means to an end, not an end in themselves. Their effectiveness depends on the quality of the therapeutic relationship that has been formed, the capacity to use the techniques in a lively and appropriate way, sensitivity to the "emotional temperature" in the room, and the child's level of functioning. In Chapter 5 in this volume, we described the therapist's mentalizing stance and the role it plays in all mentalization-based treatment work. This is the foundation on which the rest of the work can be built. Indeed, a prerequisite for working with MBT-C is that the therapist works to maintain their own mentalizing capacity before, during, and after a session, and pays careful attention when their own mentalizing capacity breaks down. The therapist should also work to connect whatever happens in a session to the focus formulation and goals of the therapy.

All the techniques described in the following two chapters might be used with any children referred for time-limited MBT-C. The challenge is always to follow the child and work out what is most needed at each moment. However, we have tried to break up this material into two different chapters, each focusing on different aspects of direct work with children in MBT-C. Which interventions are used is based on the therapist assessing what mentalizing "level" the child is currently working at and adapting their technique accordingly. In this chapter,

https://doi.org/10.1037/0000486-008
Mentalization-Based Treatment for Children: A Time-Limited Approach, Second Edition, by N. Midgley, K. Ensink, K. Lindqvist, N. Malberg, and N. Muller
Copyright © 2026 by the American Psychological Association. All rights reserved.

we present activities and interventions focused on helping children to establish attention control and emotional regulation, which (as set out in Chapter 1, this volume) can be thought about as the "building blocks" of mentalization. These building blocks are necessary for developing the capacity for explicit mentalizing—that is, the ability to understand what we feel and why, to imagine how others might make sense of us (i.e., to see ourselves from the outside), and to imagine how others might feel (i.e., to see others from the inside). In the next chapter, we will introduce activities and interventions focused on working with the child's explicit mentalization skills, as well as exploring how the therapist works in MBT-C when the child's capacity for explicit mentalizing temporarily breaks down.

In practice, therapists tend to move between these two different levels (i.e., building blocks and explicit mentalization) from session to session and from moment to moment when working with most children. By organizing the chapters in this way, we hope to simplify and clarify the techniques used in MBT-C. Although some children may need more help with the building blocks of mentalizing and others may be able to make greater use of explicit mentalizing interventions, we would not want readers to see this separation as an indication that therapists will work exclusively in one level with any particular child. Whatever techniques are used, it is also important to keep in mind that the mentalizing stance (Chapter 5, this volume) is at the heart of the work, and that when working with school-age children, we must never forget the centrality of play.

TIME-LIMITED MENTALIZATION-BASED TREATMENT FOR CHILDREN IS PLAY CENTERED

Play is a powerful medium, providing a way to explore relationships, to learn about the world of feelings, and to find one's own psychological voice as a child. Play is a form of social learning because all kinds of experiences in daily life are rehearsed, changed, and completed and, through these means, integrated in the behavior repertoire of a child, stimulating mentalizing (Tessier et al., 2016).

- Play regulates negative affects and diminishes stress.
- Play helps metabolize major life events.
- Play integrates new information affectively and cognitively.
- Play offers a place to experiment with new behavior and new solutions.
- Play stimulates fantasy and fosters creativity.
- Play stimulates the development of empathy.

The pediatrician Donald Winnicott (1971a) spoke of the need for the child's experience of a transitional space. It is this space that is metaphorically created in the process of the child's realization that she is separate yet connected, both physically and emotionally, from the parent. Play is one of the most fertile grounds for this process to take place, and this is one of the reasons play has always been such an essential component of psychodynamic and other play-based child therapies (Kegerreis & Midgley, 2018). As described in some of the early work on the development of the capacity to mentalize (Fonagy & Target, 1996), when a child plays, they are learning to separate what they feel inside and how it is related to, yet separate from, what is in the external world. As Fonagy and Target (1998) noted, "the capacity to take a playful stance may be a critical step in the development of mentalization" (p. 108). For some of the children referred for MBT-C, however, this critical step may not yet have taken place, and so the focus shifts to helping the child develop the capacity for symbolic (i.e., pretend) play. This is done by focusing the work on the building blocks of mentalizing—in particular, the child's capacity for attention control and emotion regulation.

WHEN CHILDREN CANNOT ENGAGE IN SYMBOLIC PLAY

John, Age 8

John comes in with an angry expression. He doesn't want to, or isn't able, to tell the therapist what happened that made him so angry. In previous sessions, he always seemed to calm down while playing with clay, so the therapist asks him if he wants to use the clay, which John accepts. When the therapist and John both have a piece of clay, the therapist asks John if he wants to throw the clay on the table so it's easier to handle. Her idea (although she doesn't say this to him) is that it might help John direct his anger into throwing the clay, communicating to him in an implicit way that his anger is seen and that it is okay, as well as signaling to him that she is available and he is allowed to find a way to express some of his feelings with her.

John sighs deeply, with a mixture of despair and relief, and looks to the therapist when he throws the clay with all his force, seeming to double-check that he is not scaring her and whether expressing his anger in this way is acceptable to her. Going one step further, in response to the pleasure John seems to have in throwing the clay, the therapist suggests that he should climb up onto the table and hurl the clay onto the ground from up high. John first thinks the therapist is joking, but when he sees her smile, he looks excited and climbs up onto the table. The therapist explains that this is not something they would usually do, but she has the impression John really needs to throw his clay from a big distance today.

John is completely focused, controlling his breath, and puts all his strength into throwing the clay. When the clay hits the ground, it makes a big noise, like a fart. John laughs out loud. The therapist laughs with him. John's face starts relaxing, and he seems open and connected with the therapist. She asks him who he would like to have lying on the floor where he is throwing his clay. John responds by connecting his feelings to a frustrating incident that happened at school, saying, "Luke teased me the whole day and called me a pig, and I tried not to fight, but in the end I did, and my teacher was angry with me and not with Luke and that was so mean!"

The therapist, happy that John could tell her about his emotions, gives him the clay again and says, "Well, then, it sounds like he deserves this clay. Do you feel like giving it all you've got?"

John throws again and again and is standing on the table doing a monkey drum on his chest, feeling strong, feeling in control, and looking really pleased. The therapist says, "Sometimes, it's just so great to let it all out when you know you can't hurt anyone or get into trouble. Those situations are so frustrating when these guys set you up and provoke you, and you know they want to get you into trouble. You try your best, but in the end, they walk away while you get into trouble."

John nods and seems to relax. He starts cleaning up the mess and then adds thoughtfully, "Well, I thought you'd be proud of me—I controlled myself and only pushed him, when I actually felt like punching him right in the face!"

As with John, many children who are referred to therapy may have a limited capacity to make use of play to symbolize their thoughts and feelings. When children are traumatized, their play can become too real and inhibit their ability to play, to represent their emotions (Muller et al., 2025). For some children, physical games, such as playing with a hockey puck and sticks or with a foam swimming noodle, can be useful to practice control and care. This provides a therapeutic opportunity to think about how to keep everyone safe because either the therapist or the child may get hurt if the play becomes too rough. When a child cannot or will not participate in pretend play, activities that involve the body and movement may be helpful (Juffermans & Muller, 2021; Muller & ten Kate, 2023). Typical activities can include playing with balls (e.g., tossing balls back and forth), sword fighting, darts, playing music together, or playing in a gym.

In the preceding vignette, the therapist is aware that John has been struggling with his anger and that he is desperately afraid he will be rejected if he expresses anger, as this is what happened in his life many times. He has had few opportunities to have anger normalized by understanding that we all feel angry sometimes and that anger can be important for overcoming obstacles, coping when someone has hurt us, or protecting ourselves. However, children need to learn to use it effectively rather than be blinded or controlled by it, losing the connection with themselves or others. Furthermore, John has probably had few, if any, opportunities to talk freely about how angry he feels and to have this accepted and tolerated.

The therapist has the sense that it is important for John to learn that angry feelings are normal and can be accepted and validated so that he can learn to be less afraid of his anger and begin to see it as a feeling he can learn to control. In suggesting that John throw the clay at the floor, the therapist communicates that she is not afraid of his anger and invites John to express it in the room with her. She gives him permission to express his physical anger and frustration in a somewhat wild, but also controlled, way. The therapist is engaging with him (and even encouraging him) in this activity as a means of helping him express the feelings he is so afraid of and thinks are forbidden and unacceptable so that they can become less frightening and dangerous. Through this process, the therapist communicates through her body and facial expression in an embodied mentalizing way that she is not afraid of John's feelings even when they are "big, angry feelings," that they can be expressed without hurting others, and that it is human to feel this way. The hope is that, in this way, John might begin to feel less afraid and have a sense that his feelings can be tolerated and accepted and that he can therefore be tolerated and accepted having these feelings, paving the way for self-acceptance and self-regulation. In this way, the therapist helps John build emotion regulation skills. This could be helpful in the long term to create awareness and foster explicit mentalizing capacity about his angry feelings, including the anger about the unjust experiences he had to endure in his life.

The use of clay or a sand tray can also help establish contact with children who present as inhibited or unwilling. All these activities have in common that they do not require well-developed fine motor skills but also can be used to play with rhythm, force, and rituals. When a ball is thrown, the therapist may illustrate (mirror) with a sound the force and the course of the ball. When playing music together, the therapist can lead the way in experimenting with volume, rhythm, and tempo. Activities that stimulate the senses may be good for children not currently able to play symbolically (e.g., encouraging them to feel how the sand, water, clay, or paint feels in their hands). By drawing attention to the physical senses, John's therapist helps John build attention control.

ENSURING THAT INTERVENTIONS ARE ADAPTED TO THE RIGHT LEVEL FOR THE CHILD

Anne, Age 6

It is the 10th session, and Anne is playing with the dolls and the animals at the table, elaborating a theme that has been central throughout therapy. She returns to a game that she has played before, in which the lion cub runs away from the therapist's doll but then suddenly turns round and hits it. The therapist, mindful that they are coming toward the end of their 12 sessions, wonders aloud whether today the lion cub is unsure if she likes the doll or is angry with her. Anne tells her to shut up and play. The therapist notices Anne's agitation but continues to explore why the lion cub may be feeling grumpy like this today. Anne gets increasingly frustrated and eventually throws the lion cub into the corner of the room and screams at the therapist, "I hate you!" Before the therapist can do anything, Anne runs to the door and runs crying back to the waiting room.

In previous chapters, we spoke about the importance of not expecting children to be able to mentalize explicitly when they are in a heightened emotional state that may have led their mentalizing capacity to go "offline." A. J. E. Verheugt-Pleiter (2021) referred to this as "recognizing the child's level of mental functioning and meeting it at the same level" (p. 57), acknowledging that therapists sometimes have a tendency to speak at a level that is too abstract, assuming, for example, that a child may be able to be curious about why the therapist may have said something when, at that moment, the child is certain the therapist has said it to hurt her.

Given that high arousal is often a trigger for a breakdown in mentalizing, even in children who have developed some capacity to reflect on mental states, in the therapy room with a child, the therapist must be continually judging the "emotional temperature" and trying to ensure that their interventions meet the child at the right level. When we sometimes get this wrong, as we inevitably will, all we can do is acknowledge our mistake and try to recover. For example, in the preceding vignette, Anne's therapist is mindful that their short-term intervention is coming to an end, and before beginning the session, the therapist had gone back to remind herself what the agreed focus had been for the therapy: "Getting to know and taking care of the wild animals and the wild emotions." But in her own anxiety about ensuring that she and Anne were on track with the therapy, the therapist lost sight of Anne's emotional state in the room, inviting her to explicitly mentalize about the lion cub ("I wonder why she may be feeling like this today?") when Anne was in an agitated state (at this stage, we can only guess why), which makes this kind of controlled, reflective activity impossible. This is a common mistake among novice (and more experienced) MBT-C therapists, who may ask questions that invite explicit mentalizing (e.g., "How do you think your mum felt when you did that?" "Why are you feeling like that now?") when the child is in an emotional state in which their capacity to mentalize is "offline."

In thinking about "which intervention when," Bateman and Fonagy (2016), in the context of mentalization-based treatment for adults, introduced the idea of interventions on a spectrum according to their complexity as well as their depth and emotional intensity. These range from offering empathy and support, which they described as being "the simplest most superficial and least intensive" intervention, to mentalizing the relationship, which they described as "the most complex and, for the most part, the most emotionally intensive" intervention (p. 111). In a similar way, Jacobsen et al. (2015), describing their work with children in foster care, talked about a "mentalizing staircase," from being supportive and empathic when there are high levels of emotional intensity in the room to exploring and reflecting on the minds of self and other when the child is calmer and has the capacity to make use of explicit mentalizing. As Taylor (2012) put it, "high arousal states are responded to by simple mentalizing efforts such as support and empathy; low arousal states by high mentalizing states such as exploring and interpreting thinking" (p. 166).

As therapists, we are almost certain to get this wrong at times and pitch things at the wrong level for a child at certain moments. This is inevitable, but the important thing is to try to recognize when we do this, apologize, and try again. When in doubt, it is always best to fall back on the fundamental aspects of the mentalizing stance set out in Chapter 5 in this volume, including being curious ("Wow, what did I just do there?"), empathic ("I can see you got really upset when I asked you what it was like for your mom when you did that"), and then, in time, try to understand the misunderstanding ("Now that things are calmer, can we just go back and see what happened?"). Furthermore, it is always helpful to return to our initial clinical formulation of the child and their context in order to reassess if we are working where the child is in the developmental line of mentalizing (i.e., attention control, emotion regulation, and explicit mentalization).

BUILDING THE FOUNDATIONS OF MENTALIZING

Ruth, Age 12

Ruth is inhibited and passive; she hardly speaks to the therapist. She sits quietly, appearing almost petrified, and seems unable to express interest or choose something to do. The therapist observes her uneasiness but decides not to focus attention on it; instead, he presents Ruth with potential ways of becoming more active and resolving her unease. He asks her if she wants to make something, gently adding that she seems to find it hard to choose.

Although Ruth mostly only answers with her eyes, showing she understands what the therapist says, or replies with a simple yes or no, this time she quietly says she wants to make something. The therapist feels surprised and delighted, but tones this down to attune to Ruth and not overwhelm her. The therapist believes that making something is a task that Ruth can do alone to affirm her agency; he has a sense that his role is to observe her agentic action and that this is the priority. He asks Ruth if she wants to draw or paint or perhaps work with the clay. The therapist has the sense that he should offer some choices, so that Ruth can have the experience of choosing and working with what is best for her, but not too many options, which could overwhelm her. Ruth answers that she wants to paint. He is pleased to hear what Ruth wants, expressing that he likes to know what she likes.

The therapist takes paper and the pots of paint out of the cupboard, asking Ruth if she wants to help and put the paint on the palette. Ruth does this, and the therapist comments and affirms Ruth's skillfulness in nicely putting little portions of paint on the palette all by herself. Then, Ruth stands behind the easel with some white paper and indicates that she does not know what she should paint. The therapist tentatively asks her what comes to mind. Ruth says she doesn't know. The therapist is aware that this is a potentially important moment where Ruth is trying to take ownership of something and is anxious that it should not end up in defeat and failure. At the same time, he wonders how he can best help and support Ruth and whether he should just simply focus on helping her tolerate the anxiety about finding what she wants to do and trust that something will emerge. He wonders to himself whether he should help out more actively as one might with a younger child, but without inadvertently sabotaging this moment when something new could potentially emerge by taking control too quickly and perhaps communicating to Ruth that he does not have confidence in her ability. He decides to turn it into a guessing game, saying that he's not sure what Ruth might like to paint. Could it be a tree? Her house? Herself taking her dog for a walk? Ruth likes the third idea and seems to relax; she dips the paintbrush into the paint and starts with a surprisingly confident brushstroke.

When a child is taking their first steps toward play but is not yet able to engage in pretend or symbolic play, then, at the most basic level, the therapist's role may involve simply describing the play process. This is an active process in which the therapist summarizes and integrates all the information presented by the child during the play session (behaviors, affects, themes). For some children, this can help them to create an awareness of their own actions or simply give them a sense that what they are doing can be seen and reflected on by someone else—that the therapist is curious about what they are doing. It is also a way of building the relationship with the therapist and gaining experience of having a mind of their own.

At times, it may be necessary for the therapist to try to stimulate the play narrative by asking questions with the aim of understanding the story the child is telling during the play or what they are expressing when they are painting or drawing. This technique is the first step to understanding the play context that the child is presenting during the session and helps the therapist make sense of what is going on. Additionally, this technique encourages the child to elaborate on the stories presented during the play through gentle inquiry about the material presented and by asking for more details and descriptions. Such clarification and exploration, as Bateman et al. (2019) pointed out, is not simply to establish facts; rather, it is to encourage the capacity to play. Parallel to this gentle focus on the content, we find the process of joint attention that takes place between the therapist and the child. This experience provides the potential for coregulation as well as the modeling of thinking about the mental states behind the observable behavior in displacement.

In the preceding vignette, the therapist is actively trying to arrange the setting to facilitate Ruth's agency, supporting her and helping her feel secure and free to increasingly express herself. The therapist tries to draw her out from her passive position and help her discover that she can be more active—for example, in deciding what she wants to do—and eventually take more of an active position in relationships by expressing what she wants to do rather than simply waiting and following others' lead. This is a behavioral pattern in her life, or a coping style, which helped her to adjust to difficult life circumstances but is not so helpful anymore. The therapist thinks developmentally, mindful of how a parent may scaffold the agency of a young child by imagining what may be appropriate and giving options that the child might want to choose from. The therapist tries to be attuned to and affirm expressions of Ruth's agency and self as well as her creativity, but he is careful not to inadvertently overwhelm Ruth so that she can feel the process belongs to her. He is guided by Ruth's reactions to adjust his reaction to the right level of intensity, thus scaffolding and encouraging Ruth. The therapist tries to create a safe space and a relationship in which Ruth experiences the therapist's benign interest in her internal world. At the same time, he is also able to wait and be "at the service" of Ruth's emerging self, not overwhelming her with his own enthusiasm because he is concerned that she should not subtly feel that she is doing this only to please the therapist. In sum, the therapist creates a potential space where Ruth can emerge and discover her more active, agentive self; he is helping Ruth to establish the building blocks of the capacity for mentalization.

As we have argued previously, attention control and emotion regulation facilitate the capacity for more explicit mentalizing. These building blocks need to be established in order for a child to be able to keep in mind the thoughts and feelings of oneself and others (explicit mentalizing) and then use this ability interpersonally. When children are easily affectively dysregulated, show impulsivity, or have little capacity to think about themselves and relationships in mental-state terms, it can be therapeutic to focus on building these foundations that support mentalizing by working on capacities for basic attention control and emotion regulation. With some children, this will be the focus for much of the therapeutic work; with others, it may be possible to work simultaneously with their more explicit mentalizing skills, including more controlled, reflective exploration of the mental states of self and other or their narrative. The therapeutic work is always guided by the therapist's assessment of the child's capacity for regulation and mentalization, both globally and at a moment-by-moment level, and working to develop the building blocks of mentalizing may include the following:

- stimulating contact by working on attunement and joint attention,
- mirroring and contingent coordination,
- creating rhythm and patterns in interactions,
- enhancing attention control and self-awareness by naming and describing what is happening in the here and now,
- promoting intentionality by linking behavior to effects in the external world,
- regulating affects by exaggerating or slowing down,
- regulating attention and affects by setting and playing with limits, and
- clarifying and naming feeling states.

Working With Attention Control: Attunement, Mirroring, and Contingent Coordination

Anne, Age 6

In a session with her MBT-C therapist, Anne uses swords and hits them against each other. The therapist imitates the sound by saying, "Bam, bam, bam!" Anne laughs and hits hard. The therapist comments that Anne hits hard, and she makes loud noises! Anne then finds a kettle and wants to go and get water for it. She wants to do it herself. She fills the kettle to the brim. The therapist notes that it's very full and wonders if maybe they need to pour some out. Anne says no and insists that she will walk carefully. She does this, and the therapist comments that she is indeed very strong and can walk very carefully. Then, Anne finds a toy syringe from a doctor's kit, sucks water into the syringe, and wants to spray it out. When she wants to spray water in the doll's stroller, the therapist says no, but Anne sprays some water there anyway. The therapist says, "You know what, you can spray in the sand tray; you see here are two sand trays!"

Anne wants to spray in the tray with dry sand, but the therapist suggests that she sprays in the tray with the wet sand, and Anne follows her directions. Anne and the therapist repeat this over and over again: Anne sucks water into the syringe (which is really small) and the therapist tells her when it's full (because it's difficult to see), and then Anne sprays it in the sand. Sometimes, she pushes so hard that she sprays water on the toys on the shelves, and she laughs happily. The therapist makes sound effects when Anne pulls the syringe apart to be able to fill it with water (it makes a popping sound, and the therapist says, "POP!"). Anne laughs at it the first time, and then they say it together as she pulls it apart and when she sprays the water. Anne and the therapist walk between the table with the water and the sand tray repeatedly. When Anne sprays all over the shelf with the toys, the therapist smiles and comments that it was very far to reach the right place.

Children acquire the capacity for attention control and emotion regulation through the early experiences of caregiving (Fonagy & Target, 2002). According to Csibra and Gergely (2011), mutual gaze serves crucial communicative and affiliative functions. It informs about another person's attention directed to self, signals communicative intent, provides means of sharing positive affect, and helps to regulate an infant's emotions in moments of distress (MacLean et al., 2014; Segal & Moulson, 2024). The MBT-C therapist offers new opportunities to revisit the early experiences of attunement, mirroring, and contingent coordination in order to offer a new developmental and relational experience that expands the child's interactive expectations and their response repertoire. A range of activities and interventions can be used to support attention control (see Table 7.1). With children who have experienced relational trauma, this might be the main focus of the work in the process of building epistemic trust (Muller et al., 2025).

The sand box, particularly when used with kinetic sand, offers opportunities to reconnect with the therapist and coregulate. The sand box is helpful in meeting sensorially with a child. It also lends itself to creating a playing space when words are not necessary, in which child and therapist can cocreate rhythms of being together without the pressure of a goal (e.g., in board games).

TABLE 7.1. Activities and Interventions to Support Attention Control

Attention control	Activities and interventions
Create joint attention: rhythm, structure, and feeling of being together	Playing with sensory material or using art material: sand tray, water box, drawing, painting, clay, looking at a book or image together Music: listening to music or making music with your voice or with instruments, paying attention to following, leading, sharing; add fantasy—make a sound like an elephant or a mouse, or the rain, a storm, or thunder Movement/bodily awareness: dancing, throwing a ball, darting Movement based on image/metaphor (curl up small like a seed, now grow into a big tree); mimic animals (small and timid like a mouse to big and strong like an elephant)
Assume responsibility for structure and holding	Choosing the same time and place to do the therapy Saving everything the child has made during the therapy Doing the same exercises or working on the same project several times and being explicit about it During moments of dysregulation, connecting, coregulating, and offering ways of safely returning to emotional safety
Name and describe with explicit curiosity what child is doing / what is happening in the here and now	When the child plays with toys in the room, naming what you see them doing, showing curiosity, verbally and nonverbally
Look for / be curious about mental states (even when playing)	When noticing posture, tone of voice, or other indications of affective state in the child, explicitly showing curiosity and offering contingent marked mirroring

As psychotherapy sessions evolve with some children, the sand box may offer a contained space in which the child goes from nonsymbolic, mechanical play (e.g., making and destroying) to more symbolic use of the materials. We may observe a movement from emotional coregulation to coconstruction of narratives and more vital interpersonal exchanges with the therapist. Thus, the sand box may offer some children the opportunity of finding each other in joint attention (attention regulation) in the service of affect regulation and moving forward in safe company toward explicit mentalization.

Children who are chaotic and disorganized or who do not seem to be grounded in their bodies and are not yet able to connect with themselves or others may not have developed the foundations that can help to support symbolization or mentalizing. Some children may feel a sort of emptiness inside or, at times, they may seem unaware of what they are doing and why. It can be challenging for the therapist to make real contact. There is also a risk of turning into a "police officer," making sure that nothing in the room gets damaged. Sometimes, the first step has to do with making contact with the child, even if for fleeting moments, to let the child know that the session is a safe place and to try to increase the child's attention to aspects of her own experience. The therapist's contingent coordination with the child, drawing on nonverbal modalities such as making a soothing sound with a soft tone of voice or a facial expression full of compassion, can be important therapeutic interventions. Such interventions can help these children to attend to and process information and modulate their emotions before opening the door to developing other mentalizing abilities.

With children like Anne, much of the therapeutic process may be about "*creating patterns of being together* rather than only what is actually said" (A. J. E. Verheugt-Pleiter, 2021, p. 37, italics added). It is about trying to create rhythm, predictability, joint attention, and a feeling of togetherness. In the session with Anne just described, the therapist tries to imitate, synchronize, and make contact at a nonverbal level. At the same time, she is trying to make Anne more aware of her own body and its force. The therapist is trying to turn the child's attention inward and enhance self-awareness. This can be done, for example, by naming and describing what is happening in the here and now, such as physical states and actions ("You hit hard! You are using all your force! Bam, bam, bam!"). This work has many elements of nonverbal attunement (mirroring). The focus is on what Anne is doing, and the therapist is joining her in the play. What Anne does (banging swords, pouring water, throwing pucks) and how the therapist reacts can also be seen as introducing some affect regulation—becoming aware that one's own expressions and behaviors can be modulated, that Anne can regulate and modulate things she does and thus also modulate the effect of her behavior on the external world. The therapist links the child's behavior ("you hit hard") with the effect in the external world ("there's a loud noise"). This is the beginning of working on an implicit concept of intentional behavior. At the same time, the therapist herself is managing her own arousal level because she is worried that the play could get out of hand. In doing this, she is also trying to regulate the emotional level of the child, in an implicit and playful way, and slowly but surely introducing more rules and limits. The therapist gently introduces the idea of limits in a flexible way, not being punitive when Anne does not comply but reiterating and directing where a good place is to squirt the water until Anne is able to comply. This is much as one might do with a younger child. Offering limits is also an aspect of creating safety.

Exploring boundaries is a normal way for a child to explore the world and to put the people around them to the test. Setting and playing with limits in the therapy room also develops and practices regulatory abilities in several ways. When Anne plays at home or school, it often ends in chaos and destruction. At the beginning of therapy, she often impulsively poured liters of water on the floor in the therapy room and then worried about the mess she had made. The therapist wanted to help Anne gain a sense that she could play without things getting out control. She also regulates the emotional excitement, trying to create awareness in Anne of what she is doing, implying that she has a choice. For many boisterous children like Anne who come for treatment, developing the capacity to accept limits or develop internal control is a major challenge, and they often get punished and rejected at school and elsewhere unless they are able to develop such control. However, these children often get little help in doing so, setting off a negative spiral, with implications for their self-esteem. Practicing these kinds of negotiations and trying to regulate affects related to them can be an important aspect of the therapeutic work and can be done playfully. The experience of marked mirroring and contingency might facilitate the development of effortful control—that is, the capacity of inhibiting one's impulses in the service of safeguarding the relationship.

The therapist is also actively creating opportunities to help Anne think about the situations that pose difficulties in real life using a "school" installed in the corner of the sand tray. The two of them play with the idea, saying that sometimes it is fine to express oneself freely, but at other times and in other environments, it is important to learn to follow the rules, even when it is hard to do so. Anne seems to respond and engage with this practice with the therapist. Therapists may feel ambivalent about engaging in this type of playful practicing and be concerned that it is not traditional play therapy. However, practicing and elaborating in play the situations in which the child gets stuck can be valuable in helping her elaborate, see, and think about these difficulties creatively. It implies that the therapist has done a mental microanalysis in which the problem is broken down and each step in the sequence of events is imagined until the problem can be clearly pictured, as in a mental video. The therapist can ask the child, "Is this what happens?" or "Show me what happens now," and they can physically walk through the sequence—for example, from arriving at school, hanging up their coats. They may go on to eat their pretend snack, up to the moment when the bully approaches and provokes or teases the child, until she snaps and gets sent to the principal's office. As they go through each part, it may be possible to explore bodily sensations. Through the attention of the therapist, the child develops a growing awareness of bodily impulses and learns when to divert from an impulse or when attention can be directed to these bodily signals to inform about possible feelings. Drawing an "emotional thermometer" can be helpful to make it more concrete and visible. The ultimate intention is that the child internalizes this and can direct themselves more, which promotes self-agency. For some children, it is possible to shift to more explicit mentalizing and explore mental states in the self and other by asking questions such as "So what was going on for you right then?" or "What do you think was in her mind when she said that?" With some children, this can also be done by creating a cartoon series together.

Using play in this way can be an important stepping stone toward more sophisticated play activity. Later, as Anne's play changed and became more symbolic, she started playing more with the lion and farm animals, and the therapist was able to use this creatively. For example, they could "take the lion to school" together or teach the tiger some deep-breathing exercises when he started having roaring feelings and wanted to bite. Together, they could write a little comic book manual especially for tigers who want to start school but are afraid that they might bite someone, addressing step by step each of the difficulties that a little tiger is likely to face at school and his strategies to overcome these difficulties.

As part of this marked mirroring process, the therapist may make use of ostensive cues. This might involve calling attention to what the therapist is about to communicate (e.g., by making direct eye contact with the child while calling the child by name, or tilting the head toward the child and changing the intonation of her voice slightly). For a traumatized child, it may be important not to offer direct eye contact but rather to call the child's name and talk with her without activating a fight-or-flight response. In some cultures, it is not common to look the other in the eyes, and therefore being attuned to cultural differences using ostensive cues is also an aspect to keep in mind (Gergely, 2013). In some cases, it can be helpful for the child to have an activity that she can focus on so that the intensity of the relationship is somewhat hidden as she pays attention to the joint activity and slowly eases into the relationship. In this way, by coregulating through joint attention, the child can self-regulate and be able to receive the therapist's communication in a contained and regulated state. The possibility of new social learning emerges and, with it, the potential to experience difficult emotions by using internal resources as well as the support of a trusted adult.

In communicating in this way, the therapist's expression of emotion can be marked by modifying (e.g., exaggerating or slowing down) the display of the child's affect, such that the therapist's emotional expression not only resembles but also regulates the child's emotion simultaneously. The idea is not that the therapist should be perfectly accurate every time that she comments on what might be going on for the child but rather that the child senses that the therapist is interested in her experience and is able to follow and stay in emotional contact with her and that she experiences the therapist's presence and genuine interest in her mind.

At times, this process happens at a nonverbal level, especially for children who have little emotional vocabulary that could help them to describe their internal states. The therapist often has to be imaginative and resourceful to find a way to reach and engage children in such states. This is particularly important when working with children whose aggression easily gets out of control and whose apparent incapacity to play may represent a safety measure to protect themselves and others from the strength of their angry feelings and their perception of themselves as unable to manage these feelings. It can be equally important when children have faced almost unspeakable trauma and loss and can gradually help them build up an experience of, and attention to, subjective states: "This is me, I can have intentions, wishes, feelings, and thoughts." The child may also become more curious about the other: "There is someone out there who seems to be interested in me and wants to be in contact with me." By paying attention in this way, children learn to be attentive to themselves and to the world around them.

Working With Emotion Regulation: Helping the Child to Identify, Modulate, and Express What They Feel

Mohammed, Age 7

In one of the early sessions, Mohammed plays with a police car and a doll (see Figure 7.1). He is banging the doll and the car on the table, shouting loudly. When the therapist speaks, he ignores her. He keeps banging the doll and the car until the therapist touches his arm gently and tries to find his eyes to make sure there is some contact. "There is a lot of banging and screaming. It looks like someone may be getting hurt! Who is screaming so loudly?" she asks. "I am," Mohammed says. The therapist then comments, staying in the play, "Are you okay, or are you hurt? Or are you afraid?" "Yes," Mohammed says with a sigh, looking at his therapist for a split second.

The therapist makes sure she is mirroring the boy's expression. "Show me what happened," she says in an exaggerated, slow tone of voice, as she looks at the doll

FIGURE 7.1. Mohammed's Play

Note. Image created by Nicole Muller.

and the car in Mohammed's hands as he bashes them together and screams. She adds, "Hmm ... all that noise, with lots of people screaming and shouting. That sounds very confusing and scary" (showing with her face and bringing her hands to cover her ears). Mohammed smiles slightly and seems to be considering what to do next. The therapist comments on this: "Big feelings inside, big sounds outside?" Mohammed smiles, gets up, and runs around the room and then sits back down and seems ready to start playing again. The therapist asks, "I wonder what is happening next? What are the police doing? Do we need to call an ambulance?"

When a child has difficulties noticing, naming, and managing their emotions, they must work much harder to function in school, the home, and the world of peers. In MBT-C, the therapist can make use of a range of different activities to promote emotion regulation, and these should be used flexibly and creatively (see Table 7.2). By validating implicitly and explicitly, and by being curious and

TABLE 7.2. Activities and Interventions to Support Emotion Regulation

Emotion regulation	Activities and interventions
Be aware and curious about feelings	"Stop and rewind" and invite the child to notice when the affective tone between the two of you shifts positively or negatively, working in the here and now Use self-disclosure about what you feel when a child makes you feel something, showing the impact on others of feelings or behaviors Use books or television shows to awaken curiosity and thinking about self and others' states of mind and the impact on behavior Create a book where the child describes themselves and their friends using feelings and personality characteristics Use drawings to express feelings Make a short film to depict a character's story with a specific feeling
Identify obstacles for achieving regulation or triggers for dysregulation in the playroom and in other settings	Create phrases such as "bumpy roads" to identify sequences that tend to repeat themselves and lead to dysregulation
Regulate arousal level	Integrate mindfulness exercises such as "breathing bubbles" and use of sensory regulatory toys Playfully verbalize moments that trigger emotional dysregulation Practice embodied mentalizing to elicit experiences of contingency (e.g., sand-box chats and slime games, dancing, or moving while talking)
Play with regulation and limits	Play with regulation in the session by creating a sound at the beginning and end of the therapy Develop a predictable set of verbal and nonverbal responses that the child can use to regulate Make alternative, positive attributions of behaviors that usually draw negative attributions from adults
Stimulate pretend play	Make a game with rules created together with the child Shift tone of voice, posture, and facial expression to communicate relational safety Invite the child to play with realities in role-play or pretend play

open-minded, a therapist can give value to emotional states. Sometimes, the emotional temperature in the room can get very high or very low, and a child can challenge the emotions of a therapist. Being genuine in recognizing the emotions you as a therapist are experiencing and deciding if you can show your own emotion in a metabolized way can be helpful for a child to recognize the impact of their emotions on the relationship, which can be powerful feedback in motivating a child to change.

In the example above, the therapist notices that Mohammed is becoming dysregulated, as the play appears to be evoking some of the strong feelings linked to the car crash he experienced in real life. She notices that there is a feeling of being out of contact with Mohammed, who does not seem to be "in the room" and seems unaware of how loudly he is screaming. He seems lost in repetitive traumatic play in which he is reliving the trauma rather than mentally processing and metabolizing it by elaborating the experience in the play. Mohammed seems to dissociate as the play stirs up powerful trauma-related feelings in him. In using his name and touching him gently on the arm, the therapist brings Mohammed back into the room and into the contact with her, and interrupts the dissociative process so that he can benefit from the process of representing the trauma and developing semantic discourse about it with the scaffolding of the therapist's verbal commentary on his play rather than simply reliving the most traumatic affects. She chooses not to specifically name the feelings of fear at this point because she is not sure whether he is ready and is concerned that he will stop playing. However, at a future point when he plays this trauma-related scene again, she will talk about him having felt very scared.

Through her verbal commentary on his play, the therapist helps Mohammed elaborate the traumatic experience, put it into words, and make it into a story with a beginning, a middle, and an end that can be increasingly elaborated until it contains all the essential elements (e.g., whether the ambulance took anyone to hospital) so that Mohammed is not stuck with reliving only the most traumatic moment of the crash and the unbearable affects at that moment. This explicit coconstruction of a narrative around a traumatic event is not always achieved within time-limited therapy such as MBT-C, but where it can take place, it helps the child to integrate the experience into their narrative of self.

Noticing and naming can be directed not only to feeling and the inner world of the child but also to the inner world of the therapist. By "subtitling" yourself as a therapist, you can help the child to become aware that you have an inner world of your own, with feelings, thoughts, and wishes. Noticing, naming, and clarifying feeling states is also a way to invite the child to self-observe, to create a motivation to be curious about why they behave in a certain way. Noticing and naming can be thought of as the bridge between attention regulation and emotion regulation. When a therapist notices and names a shift in affect, it allows the child the experience of being thought and felt by another not only verbally but also in an embodied manner as the therapist notices and names changes in the child's movement, tone of voice, and posture and links it to mental states.

Helping a Child to Develop an "Emotional Vocabulary"

Anne, Age 6

During a session with Anne, the therapist feels that Anne needs help developing an emotional vocabulary. So, she decides to bring in a specific activity. She shows Anne a card with a picture of a boy peeking out from behind a sofa (see Figure 7.2) and asks her to tell a little story. "Ooh, there is a child hiding behind the couch," says Anne. The therapist encourages her to elaborate her story further to find out why he is sitting there and what he is feeling. Ann guesses that he is hiding, but she says she can't say what the boy might be feeling. "Do you think maybe he is afraid, or sad, or playing a trick on someone by hiding?" asks the therapist. Although Anne first says she doesn't know, with the therapist's encouragement to look at the boy's face, she guesses that the boy is sad, adding, "Yes, he has a sad look in his eyes."

The therapist is impressed with this comment, and Anne then starts talking about a time when she felt sad, when she was separated from her mother in an amusement park. She suddenly gives a detailed account of what happened. The therapist wonders what she felt when she couldn't find her mother, and Anne tells her that it was her own fault: "Because I wanted to play in the playground and wanted to stay there." The therapist shows empathy with how Anne felt. "Yes and then I had to cry out loud, and a lady asked me what happened, and I said, 'I don't know where my mommy is,' and then we started to look for my mom and then we saw her." The therapist asks whether Anne remembers how she felt when she saw her mother's face, and she tells her she was happy. "And your mom?" "She was happy too, but also a little angry," she replies.

For some children, it can be helpful for the therapist to bring in more structured ways of helping the child to name feelings. Asen and Fonagy (2012a) referred to these as *mentalization-enhancement activities* and give the example of a "Guess Your Feelings" game that can be used in a family session. Using pictures like that in Figure 7.2 may help children talk about feelings, especially those children who

FIGURE 7.2. A Boy Peeking Out From the Sofa

Note. Painting by Ruth Zuilhof, The Hague, The Netherlands. Reprinted with permission.

may need more scaffolding to name emotions. Alternatively, picture books or drawings can be used.

Based on a slow process of contingent coordination, the therapist in MBT-C can gradually begin to try to make connections between action and emotions, and clarify and begin to name feeling states. This might begin with the therapist simply asking the child to tell her what she wants (e.g., saying, "Today, maybe you can tell me when you are thirsty and which toys you feel like playing with"). The therapist thus scaffolds the development of the child's capacity to express agency and her feelings and to ask for what she needs in relationships. When a child expresses preferences and starts asking for particular toys, the therapist can mark this with comments such as "Look at you—you know exactly what you want!" She can also help the child become aware that she can express her feelings, sometimes through play (e.g., when playing with dolls, say, "Maybe if the baby learns to *say* she feels scared of the dark, then we will know to switch the light on in the hall so she doesn't have to cry?").

In the vignette above, the therapist used picture cards to initiate a conversation about feelings. Anne did not start talking about feelings spontaneously, but when the therapist gave some suggestions, she was able to make a good guess about the emotions of the boy behind the couch. She could also, when prompted by the therapist, link the way the boy in the picture looks to emotions, indicating that she had some understanding of emotional expressions. She was then able to tell the therapist about an incident when she felt sad. The therapist noticed Anne's emotional involvement when she told the story. She expressed sadness and fear when talking, and she had a smile on her face when she came to the end of the story; she even showed awareness of how someone could hold two different feelings simultaneously. When the therapist reacted and commented on the story, she was deliberately emotionally expressive as well.

CONCLUSION

As MBT-C is a developmental therapy, the "level" at which the therapist is working has to be adapted to the needs of each particular child based on a careful assessment of the development of a "mentalizing profile," as set out in Chapter 6 in this volume. At the same time, the therapist needs to be able to adjust their focus and the "level" of intervention on a moment-to-moment basis, responding to what the child needs at each moment. In this chapter, we have described the way in which the MBT-C therapist may focus on developing the building blocks of explicit mentalizing—in particular, the child's capacity for attention control and affect regulation. In some cases, such as with children who come to therapy with high levels of emotional dysregulation, this may be the primary focus of the work, and research has suggested that therapists who work at this level with such children are likely to have better treatment outcomes (Coşkun et al., 2024). In other cases, however, the child may already demonstrate a capacity for explicit mentalizing, even if this capacity may sometimes be temporarily lost when the child is under stress or in a state of high arousal. In the following chapter, we focus on the techniques that the MBT-C therapist may use when the child has the capacity for explicit mentalizing and on ways of responding to the different types of mentalizing breakdown.

8

Working With Children on Explicit Mentalizing and Breakdowns in Mentalizing

In the previous chapter, we set out some of the techniques that can be used in mentalization-based treatment for children (MBT-C) to help establish the "building blocks" of mentalizing—in particular, by focusing on attention control and emotion regulation. In this chapter, we describe ways of working with children when they demonstrate a capacity for explicit mentalizing. In particular, we explore how such explicit mentalizing work can take place in the context of pretend (symbolic) play, as well as in work directly exploring the relationship between the child and key people in the child's life and the "here and now" relationship between the child and the therapist.

Additionally, this chapter explains how to respond when a child who previously demonstrated a capacity for explicit mentalization loses that capacity, on either a temporary or more chronic basis. The breakdown of explicit mentalizing often takes the form of a switch away from more controlled, explicit mentalizing toward a nonmentalizing mode of functioning, usually in the context of heightened emotional states of stress or arousal or too low stress or arousal. Responding to these breakdowns may involve slowing things down before going back and reviewing what has happened ("stop and rewind"), thereby helping the child to reestablish their mentalizing capacity.

https://doi.org/10.1037/0000486-009
Mentalization-Based Treatment for Children: A Time-Limited Approach, Second Edition, by N. Midgley, K. Ensink, K. Lindqvist, N. Malberg, and N. Muller
Copyright © 2026 by the American Psychological Association. All rights reserved.

LINKING MENTAL STATES TO BEHAVIOR AND PLAYING WITH PERSPECTIVES

Anne, Age 6

During a session toward the end of Anne's therapy, her interest shifts from somewhat repetitive play with cars to a set of figures in the sand tray. Anne playacts the figures calling either her or the therapist from the sand tray to consult them in different matters—for example, about how to take care of the wild animals that are moving into their playground. Through the play, the therapist and Anne explore what it is like for different animals to be together, what wishes and needs the animals may have, and how they think and feel. A couple of wild animals are still living nearby—a lion and a wolf—but they are in a fenced-in area and are no longer roaming freely or being a threat to the other animals (see Figure 8.1). The therapist voices some worry about this through the figure of a small mouse: "Are you sure it's safe now, with the fence?" Anne reassures her: "Yes, it's safe."

Anne arranges food for the animals to eat and explores the room to find things that can be used as food and cutlery. In different ways, she shows an emerging identification with a more caring role, demonstrating her developing capacity for care, concern, and interest in the animals and their relationships. The therapist wonders whether the wild animals might sometimes want to come out of their cage and asks if they might not be feeling a bit trapped in there.

"I don't think they like the cage," says Anne, "but the mice would be scared if they were allowed out." The therapist accepts this but wonders whether they can find some way for both the wild animals and the farm animals to have some space to move about, while making sure the farm animals stay safe.

Once a child is able to engage in symbolic play in an elaborate way, the therapist can focus on explicitly mentalizing the narrative in the play context (Muñoz Specht et al., 2016). This technique involves putting into words and clarifying and exploring the stories children present in their play and facilitating an elaboration of ideas and thoughts about these stories, including the opportunity to invite the child to mentalize about what different characters in the play

FIGURE 8.1. Anne and the Wild Animals

Note. Image created by Nicole Muller.

may be thinking or feeling and, in some cases, to make a connection to their own life or situation.

Having an adult take on this function of commenting and putting into words the narrative of the play can be a powerful means of reflecting and consolidating the play ideas. This indicates that the relationship between child and therapist is one of coconstruction, sharing ideas, and listening to each other to explore and understand the story that best supports the child in what she wants to say. Sometimes, this may involve mentalizing characters and relationships in the play context (Muñoz Specht et al., 2016). In doing this, the therapist is aiming to stimulate the mentalizing capacity of the child in a playful and unthreatening way by helping the child to think in terms of mental states about the play characters and their relationships during the play therapy session. This technique has to be used carefully, adopting a "wondering" approach so that the child does not feel dismissed or forced to accept the therapist's point of view about what characters in the play are thinking. But when done in a respectful way, it can help the therapist to introduce words, more perspectives, and the connections among thoughts, feelings, and behavior. This technique also seeks to help the child express her inner world and understand the inner world of others. Symbolic play provides a powerful medium for exploring, explicitly or implicitly, difficult feelings and expressing the way a child understands and deals with the world of relationships (Halfon et al., 2019).

In Anne's play, we can observe her struggles between integrating good and bad feelings—angry crocodile feelings and mouselike vulnerable feelings. Through the use of symbolic play, Anne's therapist is able to facilitate the expression and tolerance of both feelings and to gently explore the idea that different feelings might be able to "live together." By following the child and imagining, wondering, and putting into words the way the animals may be feeling, the therapist facilitates the emergence of richer and more flexible internal representations in the mind of the child and, most importantly, helps the child develop her capacity to play and use this as a way to communicate and express an inner source of creativity. She constructs and reconstructs an image of the different figures in her mind to help Anne think in mental-state terms by exploring what the animals may think, feel, or behave. The therapist might wonder if she has to make a connection to reality—for example, by asking Anne if she sometimes feels like the crocodile. It is difficult to know when to trust the process and the impact of symbolic play and when to make a connection with reality. There is no right or wrong. For many children, it can be safer, especially in the beginning of therapy, to stay in the realm of play and express freely about their inner world instead of making connections with reality too quickly.

Valuing play implies that we are able to stay in touch with our own playfulness as therapists. Playfulness is an inner disposition to being open and experiencing freedom of thinking, feeling, and imagining; playfulness makes it possible to approach a topic or a problem from different perspectives and make contact with a child in a different way (Kolev, 2024). It implies being open-minded and curious and letting go of standard ways of thinking and observing the content

(Gluckers & Van Lier, 2011). Sometimes, holding back, letting the child experience an adult observing his play, and waiting for the story to emerge may be therapeutic. Playfulness is a way of being free and creative, and although the play in MBT-C should mostly be child led, the therapist can introduce playful or challenging elements that might help the child become freer or less inhibited. Child therapists sometimes worry if they are "just playing" (Hurry, 1998) or if they are introducing their own ideas into a play situation. However, play can be therapeutic in and of itself, and it is for that reason that Barish (2009) encouraged those working with children to "relax with child patients—to be animated and playful, at times even silly" (p. 83). However, when therapists find themselves introducing elements into the play, a self-reflexive process in which the therapist reflects on the work after the session may be particularly important. For example, the therapist may reflect on whether she contributed something meaningful by introducing a play theme or character to help the child elaborate a central issue. This is usually consciously planned, but it may also be spontaneous. Sometimes, the therapist may be modeling, at an appropriate moment, that playfulness, silliness, and fun are allowed and can be enjoyed. Thus, we suggest that therapists practice a degree of self-monitoring. This may be especially important if they are left with a sense of discomfort about their interventions after a session or when they notice that they became more active than usual or introduced new themes rather than following the child's themes. Sometimes, a child's play can have an emotional impact on the therapist, and there is a need for self-mentalization from the therapist.

MENTALIZING THE RELATIONSHIP

Ruth, Age 12

Ruth sits in the corner of the room. As she plays with the big stuffed bear, she ignores her therapist completely. When the silence continues, the therapist wonders out loud that there are "no words in the room today" and wonders what could be going on. Ruth responds by pretending to be sleeping for a while and complains out loud: "This is soooo boring." The therapist looks confused and, with a somewhat exaggerated facial expression, says, "Hmm, that's so confusing." "What?" Ruth asks. "Well," the therapist replies, "last week we had such a lot of fun together playing cards, and now you seem to feel so different. I wonder if it has something to do with the end of the session last week. When it was time to go, you seemed grumpy . . . I wonder if you might still be grumpy because we had to stop that good moment together." Ruth replies, "You just don't get it!"

The therapist asks her if they can wind things back so that he can understand what he got wrong. Ruth is hesitant at first, but after a while, she says that she realized after the last session that her therapist only plays with her because he's paid to do so. The therapist responds, "That must have been a difficult feeling and thought, thinking I don't genuinely like seeing you here in the session. Thank you for being honest about that." Then, the therapist tries to explore the situation, asking, "What makes you think that?" Ruth says that she noticed the therapist looking at his watch several times before ending the last session. "And how did this make you feel?"

> Ruth and her therapist talk this through for some time, with the therapist trying to understand how and maybe also why Ruth interpreted his behavior this way. The therapist says he understands that it is painful to feel someone you enjoy being with might be not trustworthy and might seem more concerned about the time, and perhaps this is what makes Ruth hesitant to engage today. Ruth shrugs her shoulders, but her attitude seems to have softened, indicating that she feels understood. The therapist continues and acknowledges that he was anxious about the time as the last session ended, but from his side, it was because he could see Ruth was enjoying it and wanted to make sure that he didn't interrupt things too abruptly. Ruth remains somewhat unconvinced, but she does feel seen and begins to see that there may be other reasons why her therapist looked at his watch and that it was probably not because he wanted to get rid of her. She starts to bounce the bear that was on her lap around the room and then throws it at the therapist, who replies, "Is that an invitation not to lose more of our time and just get the fun going?" Ruth smiles, "Shut up and just play! Let's do some coloring." The therapist asks what is special about coloring, and Ruth replies, "So I can calm down . . . I hate it that the time goes so fast in here and the sessions are so short. Let's play and not waste more time."

Bateman et al. (2019) explained that the aim of mentalizing the relationship is to

> focus the patient's attention on another mind, the mind of a therapist, and to assist the patient in the task of contrasting their own perception of themselves with how they are perceived by another, and thought about differently by different minds. (p. 139)

Although bearing some similarity to the work of transference interpretation, the aim is not so much to provide insight into repetitive patterns of relating but rather to give further opportunity to experience how recovering the capacity to mentalize can help interpersonal relationships.

In Ruth's case, the experiences of losing people and of seeking confirmation from grown-ups begin to show in the treatment only a few weeks after beginning therapy. She seems to enjoy her sessions, but this seems to activate the attachment system, and suddenly she is reminded of not only the pain of loss but also her feeling that she always gets the "short end of the stick." By staying with what the child brings in the here and now to the session, the therapist, once again, uses a process of stop and rewind, but he goes beyond this to try to mentalize the relationship. When the initial supportive and empathic response reduces the high arousal level and Ruth's affect is better regulated, the therapist invites some explicit mentalizing, encouraging Ruth to think about other possible reasons the therapist might have been checking his watch. This is not to find out about the truth; rather, it is a way to create a flexible mind and to play with the idea of understanding things from different perspectives. It is a way to invite explicit mentalizing about the mind of others. At a certain stage, the therapist then shares his own, different perspective on why he may have been looking at his watch. Through this slow process, Ruth is able to recover her capacity to mentalize and responds to the therapist's attempts to invite her to join in. This could have been a moment for the therapist to go on and connect what happened in the therapy to Ruth's feelings outside the room—she has been in so many places during her life that she might have gotten the feeling everyone wanted to get rid of her. This theme might connect to her feelings in her new foster home as well.

This interaction is a good example of the rupture-and-repair process that has been increasingly recognized as a core change process across a range of therapeutic approaches (Safran et al., 2011) and through which new ways of managing feelings in relationships can emerge in the context of MBT-C. By looking at what is going on in the moment, the therapist is establishing a sequence and presenting an option of how to deal with the rupture. Furthermore, it invites the child to look at herself from the outside while also trying to stay with the inside experience of the therapist, who is being open and curious. As Tronick (2007) observed, miscommunication and "messiness" are at the heart of the development of the self, and when negative experiences can be repaired in a relationship, it creates increasing levels of self-regulation. The MBT-C therapist can use rupture and repair in the relationship as opportunities to model and engage the child in mentalizing.

OBSERVING AND RESPONDING TO BREAKDOWNS IN MENTALIZING

Mohammed, Age 7

Mohammed wants to keep the ambulance car when the therapy session is over. He finds it difficult to accept the rules of the therapy and the limits that come with it because the therapist tells him he cannot take the ambulance home. He accuses his therapist of being mean and says he knows that the therapist doesn't like him. He wants to take something with him that is real: something tangible, touchable, and concrete. He also seems to want the therapist to stay with him and make extra time as "proof" of her affection toward him. The therapist tells Mohammed she understands he wants to take it home, but playfully explains that they need to keep the ambulance in the room in case other emergencies happen while he is away. She recruits his help in thinking about where to keep the ambulance safe until he returns. Mohammed seems suspicious but also intrigued by the therapist's request for help and begins to calm down. The therapist invites Mohammed to make a drawing together of the ambulance that he can take home to validate his longing for the vehicle and to help him remember the work done in the session.

Breakdowns in mentalizing are part of every human being's everyday functioning. School-age children who learn to use the support of trusting adults are generally able to develop efficient ways of facing stressful situations, but breakdowns in mentalizing are also natural. Identifying when a child's mentalizing capacity has broken down and recognizing the prementalizing functioning of a child are extremely helpful to guide the therapist's interventions. The goals of the therapist are to observe and respond to the prementalizing mode in the context of the interaction with the child and to offer new relational patterns of response to interpersonal stress.

In the above vignette with Mohammed, it seems that Mohammed's mentalizing capacity has broken down when faced with the end of the session and the frustration linked to the fact that he cannot take one of the toys home with him. The therapist recognizes that Mohammed's capacity to mentalize has temporarily broken down, and so she does not try to invite explicit mentalizing—for example, by asking Mohammed to consider other reasons why she will not let him take the ambulance home. Instead, she tries to validate this child's wish with empathy while being attentive to the wish. The therapist also reinforces Mohammed's attempts to find words for his feelings and offers ideas of how she imagines Mohammed is feeling about the rule regarding toys staying in the room. By maintaining a mentalizing stance of curiosity and empathy, the therapist provides a response not to his behavior but rather to the motivations behind his behavior. He feels seen and understood, leading to the capacity for emotion regulation and, most importantly, the experience of coregulation with a trusting adult. The therapist's verbal tone, bodily posture, and facial expression are all very important, as they communicate to the child a sense of relational safety and a new way of working through difficult emotions. By making the drawing together, she gives him a tangible concrete alternative, in a teleological way, showing his longing to take the ambulance is very understandable considering his age and where they are in the therapy process.

Responding to Children Who Are Stuck in "Pretend Mode"

Liza, Age 11

Liza comes to the session saying she had an accident this morning when she fell over. No one saw it, but an ambulance came. Liza explains, "Because I was okay, I didn't need an ambulance, so I just sent them back to the hospital."

The therapist had wondered before how to handle moments in which Liza told something that clearly wasn't true, without a sense of connectedness with her inner feelings in the way she told them or her way of dealing with reality. The therapist noticed that it felt difficult to show real empathy for Liza at these moments. Thinking about Liza's family situation with her brother, who was in trouble all the time, demanding so much of the attention of both parents, helped the therapist to always regain her empathy. This time, she decides to try to validate Liza's feelings by saying, "You must have been very startled. Gosh, it's good of you to tell me."

When that doesn't appear to have any impact, the therapist decides to use humor and make a joke about the ambulance, saying, "And the ambulance and the police and the fire squad all came to rescue you." Liza and the therapist laugh together, and Liza says, "Well, I really thought the ambulance would have to come because I really felt bad." This feels much more genuine, and the therapist can react in a more real way by responding empathically: "Yes, I can imagine you must have thought it was really serious because it felt so painful. Sometimes, it seems your feeling is so big, you make your story a little bigger too, perhaps?" Liza grins, and it feels as if there is a moment of connection.

Recognizing what a child's "preferred" prementalizing mode is, when faced by stress or high arousal, is helpful as a way to guide the therapist's intervention. Sometimes, as part of a general style of avoiding or cutting off feelings that may be especially hurtful or overwhelming, children can slip into pretend mode. In this state, the child can, for example, pretend not to care about something painful and defensively create grandiose fantasies. The therapist and child are then stuck, unable to address and metabolize the real issue.

Pretend mode can also manifest as empty and repetitive play, disconnected from anything meaningful, such as simply lining up toys or painting repetitive patterns or decorative flowers all over the page. This appears to have the function of "papering over" any feelings or thought so as not to feel or think. In these cases, the therapist can try to connect with the child by suggesting that she add specific things to the drawings or the play or by making things happen. For example, the therapist might engage the child in making a messy drawing together, or "messing around," as a way to help the child become unstuck and engaged. The therapist can also try to bring the child back into the room by commenting on her drawing technique or being interested in her way of doing things, imagining what this might be expressing or gradually pulling her actions into imagining with the therapist.

In the vignette above, Liza appears to have arrived at the session after having had some kind of fall that morning, which is likely to have activated her attachment needs. However, as a child with a more avoidant attachment style, she minimized these needs and presented the situation in an overly cognitive way, with her account lacking in emotional resonance. She then went off into a flight of fantasy, in which reality and pretending became confused. The therapist noticed how this seemed to be played out in the way the two of them interacted in the session, with the therapist herself feeling rather distant and uninvolved. Noticing this in herself, she was able to think how Liza was operating in pretend mode and that, rather than engage with her at a cognitive level (e.g., "So why do you think the ambulance came all the way out and then just went straight back?"), she was able to validate the feeling behind the story to try to bring Liza's mentalizing capacity back online. This did not happen at first. So, the therapist introduced some humor into the situation. Although it can be a little risky to challenge a child in the way that the therapist did here, the humor can allow a more real contact, which, in this case, was followed up by a recognition of the real feelings that the child was experiencing.

Supportive and empathic interventions are particularly important during moments when the child seems emotionally dysregulated; the aim is to help regulate the heightened or (as in this case) diminished affective arousal. Such interventions have an additional importance: They can help reduce a child's level of epistemic mistrust. Repeated experiences of feeling understood and supported in this way can lead a child to gradually have a sense that it may be safe to trust and therefore to begin to take on board what the other is offering. When Liza and the therapist felt a connection, the therapist could explore with Liza how to understand her urge to make things bigger and connect this to the family situation. For the first time, Liza could express her feelings toward her brother, how he made her feel, and how painful it was that her parents had no idea of her feelings.

Slowing Things Down by Using "Stop and Rewind"

Liza, Age 11

Liza is playing cards in her session. During the game, she suddenly realizes that the therapist is applying a rule, which she had forgotten to apply earlier, and in a firm tone that is unusual, given her generally timid demeanor, Liza says, "Wait, I didn't do that when it was my turn!" With this, the atmosphere of being close and complicit in playing a game together changes immediately, and Liza throws her pieces onto the table. Responding to this change, the therapist comments, "Can we just stop for a moment? What just happened there? One moment we were playing together, and suddenly it feels tense." Liza doesn't reply, but the emotional temperature in the room seems to have settled again. "Can we just go back and think what happened there?" the therapist asks again, and this time Liza nods.

After retracing what had happened step by step, the therapist suddenly hits on an idea and asks, "Did you maybe think I made you miss out on purpose?" Liza nods again, and says yes—that was exactly how she felt. The therapist is able to thank her for explaining this because now she can understand why Liza got so upset with her. "It must feel awful to think I tricked you on purpose," she says, with feeling.

At this point, Liza says they should carry on with the game, and they do. A little while later, while still playing, the therapist asks, "Liza, I'm just wondering, do you think there's any other reasons I might have not reminded you about the rule?" Liza shrugs her shoulders, and says, "Maybe you just forgot?" "Yes, I think you're right," says her therapist, "at least as far as I know. I certainly didn't mean to do it, but I'm sorry I did."

Later, they come back to this again, and the therapist is able to talk to Liza about whether this kind of thing happens elsewhere in her life and how what happened here might link to what happens in her home or at school, when she feels like a fool when others know rules but don't tell her. They then use it to their advantage to gain things she worked hard for, so she feels tricked and defeated, as if she will never know all the rules and will always lose.

Once the therapist has seen that a child's mentalizing has broken down and offered the kind of supportive and empathic response that can help to bring the capacity back online, it is possible to work together to explore and learn from such experiences, making use of more controlled, reflective thinking. To do this, it can often be helpful to slow things down, using a technique that Bateman et al. (2019) referred to as *stop and rewind*. They state that the purpose of using this strategy is

> to reinstate mentalizing when it has been lost or to promote its continuation in the furtherance of the overall goal of therapy, which is . . . to encourage the formation of a robust and flexible mentalizing capacity that is not prone to sudden collapse in the face of emotional stress. (p. 132)

By doing so, the therapist actively interrupts the nonmentalizing interaction and slows things down before asking questions with the aim of reconstructing the events that led to the mentalizing breakdown.

In the preceding example, it may not have been helpful for the therapist to explain at first, "Well, of course I didn't do it on purpose. I am here to help you." Although that may be true, it would assume that Liza had the capacity to be curious about what was in the mind of the other and to consider a different perspective. The child, in psychic equivalence mode at this time, is convinced that what she thinks is the truth and nothing but the truth. What is helpful for Liza is that her therapist shows empathy and acknowledges the reality of her internal reality and experience ("That must feel awful to think I tricked you on purpose"). In this way, Liza feels acknowledged in her experience, and trust is beginning to be established. As soon as the therapist notices that the emotional temperature had changed in the room, she stops the play and tries to help Liza to begin self-observing and thinking about what happened between the two of them. Later in the session, they explore together how this happens in other relationships as well.

The stop, rewind, and explore process is a powerful tool to address mentalizing breakdowns. In this way, the therapist makes a connection and validates the feeling and, at the same time, is facilitating a process of perspective taking by providing possible hypothesis, displaying curiosity about what Liza feels and what she thinks others feel or think and, at times, introducing different possibilities. Talking about a situation in the here and now can help generate new representations about feelings from situations outside therapy as well.

Creating Mentalizing Narratives Around Traumatic Events and Relational Trauma

Ruth, Age 12

Ruth had been witness to sexual acts in her previous foster family and was not adequately protected by the foster parents. In this particular meeting, the therapist invites Ruth to return to what they talked about in the previous session: witnessing two boys having sex in the foster home. Ruth confirms this, saying with a quiet voice and looking away from the therapist, "Yes, they were doing 'it.'" The therapist responds with the same quiet tone of voice, "In your head, you know what you saw, but maybe it is hard to say these things aloud." Ruth whispers a yes, looking uneasy. The therapist says that maybe it is hard to say things out loud because there were so many thoughts and feelings. Ruth firmly replies with a firm "yes" and puts her hands on her face: "Oh my god." The therapist repeats, "Oh my god," spontaneously mirroring Ruth's affective state but with a mix of empathy and concern and also indicating that he is thoughtful and thinking about the experience.

Ruth moves uncomfortably in her chair and is quiet. The therapist wonders whether it might be easier if she writes down some feelings and thoughts: "I imagine, Ruth, that you know well what you feel, but it seems to be embarrassing to talk about it with me—did I get it right?" Ruth nods. He suggests that Ruth draw her feelings. At first, Ruth hesitates. Then, she looks for the right color of paper to start, as if trying to avoid the task. The therapist says it probably won't be a nice drawing because difficult feelings don't feel nice. Ruth decides she needs a red piece of paper. She draws a face with big eyes and an open mouth, writing in a bubble "confused and afraid." The therapist repeats, "Confused and afraid ... yes, I can see it in your drawing."

After a short silence, the therapist wants to further explore the feelings, starting to say, "These anxious feelings...," but then Ruth suddenly writes the word "angry" and explains that is why she chose red. Then, she is silent again, and the therapist says calmly, "So some different feelings ... confused, afraid, and angry."

The therapist again asks permission to talk to Ruth about her feelings so that he can really understand her. "You write the word 'afraid.' Do you have a sense of what you were afraid of? Sometimes, children are afraid of what they have seen. Sometimes, they are afraid that it might happen to them." Ruth gets restless on her chair. "I see you are getting restless," the therapist says. Ruth reads out loud while writing "I am afraid about what will happen." "What do you mean?" the therapist asks. "I am afraid about what will happen," Ruth repeats in a louder voice. The therapist replies, "Sometimes, children are afraid of an angry reaction from the grown-ups who are there to look after them." Ruth interrupts, saying that her previous foster parents were angry when she told them. She shared that she was afraid she would be placed in yet another foster home, just like 3 years ago. "From one place to the other," says the therapist emphatically. Ruth adds, "And my brothers too." The therapist replies in a compassionate way, saying he knows that Ruth has moved many times and that it has been painful for her. Ruth is letting him know that she is afraid this will happen again. Ruth starts to cry.

Children who have experienced chronic relational trauma or traumatic events tend to display more prementalizing responses to interpersonal stressors (Muller et al., 2025; Oehlman Forbes et al., 2021). Often, their capacity for mentalizing is still underdeveloped, and they need support in managing a state of certainty about the intentions of the other (psychic equivalence) and the concrete proof that the therapist cares for them. Because of this, it is important to develop a clinical formulation of their mentalizing functioning informed by their developmental and relational history. In this way, the therapist will be able to set realistic expectations and truly attempt to meet children where they are. Often, it might be simply to focus on establishing connection by working on the basic blocks of mentalizing where the experiences of contingency and marked mirroring, alongside the therapist's mentalizing stance, provide a foundation to develop a sense of trust and safety.

In the vignette above, Ruth demonstrates that she is capable of staying in touch with the therapist and using his help to express her feelings about what she has seen. She can then articulate her deeper concerns about what this might mean in terms of what is an even deeper trauma for her—that of potentially losing yet another foster family. In putting her feelings into words, she opens the door to being potentially less confused about what happened. For children like Ruth, part of the value of therapy may be the opportunity to create a narrative about her life and traumatic experiences and integrate this into her autobiographical sense of self. Children might have multiple fantasized stories about the conception, birth, trauma, or previous circumstances of their lives, especially when they are an adopted, fostered, or traumatized child. Their ideas, and the ideas of parents, may be both unconscious and conscious and, at times, incompatible. At the same time, some children with a difficult start in life or who have experienced trauma find it difficult to integrate these experiences emotionally because they have not had the opportunity and help to put their stories into words. Constructing a coherent narrative about their lives, the trauma, and their family or families can help children to explore their experiences in current relationships as well as their narrative about past relationships.

When working with fostered or adopted children, after they have established some capacity for joint attention and affect regulation, the therapist may use questions such as "Do you feel at home?" "What does the word 'home' mean to you?" "In what way do you feel that your family belongs together?" "What does the word 'family' mean to you?" "How often do you think about your birth parents?" or "What do you call your birth parents?" (Muller et al., 2012). The children, too, may have questions about the trauma, such as "Why did this happen to me?" or "Do my parents still love me?" Exploring such questions can help children to discover a sense of self and other, thereby increasing the capacity to mentalize explicitly and helping them tell a coherent "what makes me" story. It is also a way to give meaning to feelings of mourning or sadness, which might be hidden behind an aggressive attitude.

CONCLUSION

MBT-C involves a process of fluid scaffolding in which the therapist works at a level that is appropriate to the child and seeks to offer the child a new developmental experience in the presence of a therapist who is responsive and guided by curiosity and a genuine attempt to connect. Meeting children where they are—developmentally, cognitively, and emotionally—is central to all the techniques of MBT-C. Especially for children who have had few opportunities to learn about their minds and that of others, a relationship with a therapist who provides a potential space where they can discover who they are and how their minds work may help them open the door to seeing themselves and others in a new way. The journey of psychotherapy, just like the process of development, consists of a fluid and ever-changing road.

Child therapists can sometimes feel that they are doing "real" mentalization-based work when they are able to make use of symbolic play to explicitly explore the thoughts and feelings of the child, or inviting the child to explore the thoughts and feelings of others. This is certainly an aspect of MBT-C work, as illustrated in the first part of this chapter. But as Zevalkink et al. (2012) put it,

> What is therapeutic in MBT-C is 1) the identification of the *loss of mentalizing* as it occurs in the here and now of the session and 2) not allowing the child to continue in a non-mentalizing mode for too long but accepting non-mentalizing whilst offering to replace it with more adaptive modes of thinking about self and others in a social (attachment) context. (p. 143, italics added)

In other words, to offer an alternative way of response in the context of a safe and trusting relational environment.

For the psychotherapist who chooses a relationally based approach such as MBT-C, the most important skill is their own capacity to remain curious and genuine and thus provide the child with an experience in feelings, thoughts, and behaviors are freely expressed and looked at from both inside and out.

9

Working With Parents From a Mentalization-Based Framework

In Chapter 1 in this volume, we described the qualities and features of a reflective parenting stance and how this is evident both in the way that parents are able to imagine the child's perspective (particularly thinking of their child's behaviors as motivated by mental states) and in their ability to interact with the child as a reflective parent from a stance of genuine curiosity, playfulness, and with an awareness of the "opacity" of other people's minds. We also described the empirical research that has demonstrated that when parents can take such a reflective stance, it is likely to support their children in terms of emotional growth, security of attachment, and the child's own capacity to thrive. In Chapter 2 in this volume, we outlined and provided examples of failures and breakdowns in mentalizing in parents, the kind of "vicious cycles of nonmentalizing" that can happen so easily under the pressures of family life and when facing situations or problems that stretch or exceed the abilities even of parents who, in other contexts, have a high capacity to be reflective. In this chapter, we focus on the work with parents that is offered alongside the child's therapy in time-limited mentalization-based treatment for children (MBT-C).

BALANCING STRUCTURE WITH FLEXIBILITY

As we described in Chapter 4 in this volume, regular meetings with the parents or caregivers are always scheduled alongside the direct work with children as part of time-limited MBT-C. When possible, work with parents take place at the

https://doi.org/10.1037/0000486-010
Mentalization-Based Treatment for Children: A Time-Limited Approach, Second Edition, by N. Midgley, K. Ensink, K. Lindqvist, N. Malberg, and N. Muller
Copyright © 2026 by the American Psychological Association. All rights reserved.

same time as the child's meetings but with a separate therapist. Sometimes, when resources are limited, the same therapist works with both the child and the parents. This is often the case for therapists working in private practice. Whatever the arrangement, it is important that the therapist has a structured framework guiding the process of parent work.

In delineating our approach, we draw on our own experience and on models of working with parents elaborated by colleagues (e.g., Asen & Fonagy, 2012a, 2012b; Cooper & Redfern, 2015; Etezady & Davis, 2012; Rexwinkel & Verheugt-Pleiter, 2021; N. Suchman et al., 2013); we have taken particular inspiration from the pioneering work of Slade (2005, 2008). More recently, N. Malberg et al. (2023) proposed a structured model of working with parents that expands on the mentalization-based approach to working with parents, exploring this work as an intervention in and of itself rather than as an addendum to child psychotherapy.

We consider that in working with parents, the concept of reasoned flexibility is particularly relevant (Slade, 2008). By this, Slade meant recognizing that when working with parents, it is not always possible to hold to a pure approach, with a fixed, predetermined structure. Depending on the situation, it may be necessary to see the parents more (or less) often; to offer phone calls or other contact in between meetings, or to set boundaries that limit contact; to see parents only if they come together, or to propose that they might work better if they come apart; or to arrange for joint parent–child sessions, or to work only with the parents and not bring the child into the room at all. This potential variability can make working with parents seem messy, but as long as the therapist holds on to the purpose and aims of parent work, Slade reminds us that it remains reasoned flexibility rather than a chaotic response to one crisis after another. (Although, of course, the work can sometimes feel like that too.) Minding parents also means being flexible and responsive to their crises and needs, even when these may be quite different from what the therapist or team might think the focus should be. Especially when working with vulnerable parents who face overwhelming circumstances, such flexibility is essential.

WHY WORK WITH PARENTS?

As this chapter will make clear, the work with parents in MBT-C is not done to support the child's therapy alone; rather, it is seen as an integral part of the intervention. Ideally, the sessions should be sufficiently regular so that they are not simply an opportunity to catch up about the child but instead provide a space in which some ongoing work and thinking can be done together. The general aim of this aspect of the MBT-C work is to help parents develop a reflective stance, with the following specific goals:

- helping them develop or regain the capacity to look past the child's behavior to his or her internal psychological experience and mind;

- becoming aware of their own affects and behavior, especially in contexts of conflict when they may lose their mentalizing capacities, which may, in turn, undermine their child's self-regulation and mentalizing; and
- encouraging parent–child interactions in which the child feels secure and understood and that facilitate motivation, self-regulation, basic self-knowledge, and mentalizing.

Airplane safety instructions remind parents that, in the case of an emergency, they should put on their own oxygen mask first before helping their children with theirs. Likewise, when a child is referred for therapy, it is essential that we do not neglect the parents' needs. This is not only because the parents play an important role in helping their child but also because any changes that children make in therapy will be maintained only if the environment in which they spend most of their day helps sustain the changes.

In their reframing of therapeutic change in terms of restoring epistemic trust, Fonagy and Allison (2014) made the important point that the emergence of robust mentalizing in therapy is only the start of the process of change. In the context of adult therapy, they wrote,

> In the past modifications of the patient's social world were felt to fall outside the concerns of therapy. It is possible, however, that effective treatments depend as much on ensuring that the patient's social environment is benign as on ensuring a similar emotional tone in the consulting room. (p. 378)

To the extent that this is true of work with adults, it is even more so when working with children and their parents, given that ensuring that children's home environments are benign can radically impact their development. Helping parents improve mentalizing capacities under relational stress supports the development of children generally and is essential for establishing secure attachments and mentalizing capacities in children. In this chapter, we hope to illustrate ways in which MBT-C therapists can promote parents' scope to support children's renewed capacity to learn from the significant adults in their lives.

Our basic assumption at the outset is that most parents have a deep wish to do right by their children, to be the best parents they can be, regardless of their own difficulties, whether these be financial stress, psychological difficulties, or their own childhood histories of relational trauma or neglect. However, many parents struggle despite their best intentions not to fall back and repeat patterns from the past, and they often need help to become the parents they wish to be and develop skills in thinking and relating to their children in ways that can help their children develop and flourish. Parenting is arguably one of the most important and challenging, and also one of the most rewarding and meaningful, human endeavors; however, parents of children who have been referred to clinical services frequently require help to develop ways of relating to their children and supporting their development. This can be especially true when parents did not experience such relationships as children and thus have few, if any, internal role models to guide them.

To add to the challenge, it may be more difficult for parents of children with emotional or behavioral difficulties to mentalize about their child because such difficulties can evoke uncomfortable and sometimes overwhelming affects, such as anger or helplessness, that interfere with the parent's capacity to mentalize. A child's temperament may be very different from that of the parent or the child's siblings, making it hard for the parent to identify and understand how the child experiences the world. Sometimes, this contributes to a perception that the child is purposely behaving badly simply to be naughty or provoke the people around them.

Troubled and externalizing children can strain even the most thoughtful and loving parents. It can also erode couple relationships, especially when one parent shoulders a larger burden of care or when parents disagree about how to respond to the child's difficulties. Negative feelings toward one's own child can be seen as taboo—difficult to admit even to oneself. Guilt about such "forbidden feelings" can lead to denial, hindering mentalization and constructive problem solving. Therefore, an important aim of the work with parents is to help them mentalize about their own feelings to better understand their reactions to their child and to become more flexible and open. Part of this process might be helping parents identify what kind of prementalizing responses they might characteristically use. For example, some parents may have a tendency to mostly use a "teleological mode," where they focus overly on the child's behaviors and may try to quickly move to solving an emotional problem through direct action. In cases where children display oppositional behavior, teleological interventions aimed at making the child stop behaviors, showing them the consequences or "teaching" them that what they did was wrong, can lead to escalating cycles of dysregulation and violence. Helping these parents develop new skills in mentalizing their reactions to inhibit nonoptimal verbal and behavioral reactions may help to stop behaviors escalating further. Such parents may be helped by developing the capacity to disengage from using behavioral responses. Other parents may need to work toward recognizing the negative attributions about the child that can inhibit their capacity to exercise their reflective capacities.

THE MENTALIZING STANCE IN WORK WITH PARENTS

Belinda, Age 7

Belinda's mother, Mrs. C, comes to an individual session with the therapist to discuss difficulties she is experiencing in her relationship with her daughter. She tells the therapist that she just needs ways of talking to Belinda that are effective, and confides that she frequently fears she is going to "lose her mind" with Belinda, especially when she can't get her out of the house in the morning. The therapist empathically validates how awful it must feel when Mrs. C feels she's losing her mind. Mrs. C agrees but then insists that what she needs urgently is not sympathy but strategies to work with Belinda. The therapist accepts this, apologizes, and agrees that it is important for Mrs. C to leave the session feeling she has some better ideas to handle the morning situation. He asks whether Mrs. C would find it helpful to tell him about

> one of the times recently when things have been hard, and then they could think about it together and see if they can come up with some ideas for what would help next time. Mrs. C says that yes, that would be helpful and starts telling the therapist about a difficult incident from that morning.
>
> As the therapist listens, he sometimes clarifies and slows things down, asking Mrs. C to talk him through it one step at a time, and checks out what was going on for Mrs. C at a given moment. Sometimes, he interjects with supportive comments, such as, "Yes, that does sound tough!" or "Yes, parents often say they struggle when their children do that." As they continue and begin to make sense of what happened that day, Mrs. C seems calmer and more relaxed, and her voice becomes less insistent and panicky. The therapist also stimulates Mrs. C's mentalizing about the internal experience of her daughter by expressing some curiosity about what Mrs. C thinks was going on with her daughter at the time: "So, when you said that, how did she respond?" or "What do you think she felt when you said that?" Mrs. C gradually starts to become a little more reflective, and she and the therapist continue to think together about that morning's events.

In Chapter 5 in this volume, we spoke about the importance of the therapist's mentalizing stance, including the basic therapeutic presence of the therapist (i.e., a basic helping orientation; authenticity; being nonjudgmental, genuine, and accepting); an interest in the mind, not just behavior; curiosity and the not-knowing (or inquisitive) stance; and the importance of monitoring misunderstandings. All these are equally relevant to our work with parents as they are to our work with children in therapy, but some aspects of the mentalizing stance are especially important or may take on particular significance in this part of the work.

First of all, it must be acknowledged that many parents do not bring their child to therapy because they want the child to "become more reflective." This is not necessarily high on parents' agenda when they are struggling to look after a child who may be having tantrums, is not sleeping at night, cannot get on with peers, is constantly in tears, or struggles every morning to get out of bed and get on the bus to school. In most cases—and quite rightly so—parents are likely to be seeking professional help because they want help changing their child's behavior or reducing distress, or at the very least, they are seeking solid, professional advice on how they can better manage the situation. When Mrs. C starts the session just described by talking about the difficulties she is having getting her daughter to school in the morning, she appears to find it irritating when the therapist simply empathizes with her feelings. The therapist quickly appreciates that he needs to take this concern seriously and apologizes for getting it wrong. (This is not to say that being empathic is wrong but that, at that moment, he had not offered what Mrs. C needed.) The therapist needs to help Mrs. C feel that her worries are being heard and that coming to therapy can make a difference in the problems at home. In suggesting that they focus on a particular incident, the therapist is trying, in the first instance, to help regulate Mrs. C's affect and to come alongside her, using the word "we" to make clear that the two of them will collaborate together to come up with solutions. Once Mrs. C feels her concerns are being taken seriously, she calms down, and at that stage, a more reflective atmosphere is created.

Slade (2008) suggested that the first aim of work with parents from a mentalizing perspective is the creation of a play space, an environment where the parent can "feel safe enough to mentalize, to envision, name, and play with mental states" (p. 221). Doing so relies on our communicating to parents the importance that they have in supporting their child and our respect for their experiences as a parent. Paradoxically, it may sometimes require us to start by focusing on behavior, if that is what the parent is struggling with, as a basis for creating a context in which the parent feels heard and safe enough to become curious about mental states. Considering culture-based expectations of parenting is very relevant here, and doing so is essential for the development of epistemic trust during the initial period of engagement, where the MBT-C therapist is explicitly curious about parenting expectations as they relate to the parent's own past experiences of relationships and their cultural context. Therapists can use the mentalizing stance to model the process of stopping, thinking, and wondering for parents. Parents also need to feel understood and taken seriously in their concerns and their struggles. It is important to model and offer a not-knowing and curious stance toward parents in order to motivate them to be open to new social learning within the therapeutic relationship.

Pally and Popek (2012) wrote that the therapist needs to hold a delicate balance, "*emphasizing* a parent's strengths and *empathizing* with weaknesses" (p. 53, italics in original). With regard to the latter, this may mean that there are times when we do not confront what we may consider "bad" parenting practices, even when we may have concerns about how they are affecting the child. For example, when a parent tells us that her daughter "gave me a look I knew was disrespectful, so I grounded her for a week," we may have our own ideas about whether the mother has interpreted her child's behavior correctly and might have our own views on whether the punishment she imposed was appropriate. However, our initial response may need to empathize with how awful it is as a parent when you feel that your child does not show respect. Such a response helps to validate the parent's experience and will hopefully make her feel heard, recognized, and supported. It may only be sometime later that we can then come back to the incident itself and work together to think about other possible meanings of the child's "disrespectful" look and explore alternative ways the parent could have responded.

This example speaks to the issue of how a therapist working with parents in MBT-C can hold a not-knowing position, especially in the face of requests for advice or when hearing about parenting behaviors that do not seem productive. In such situations, we, as therapists, may feel a strong pull to make suggestions or to come up with an "expert" view on what a child needs to support his development. As described in Chapter 5 in this volume, the not-knowing stance is not the same as knowing nothing: As therapists, we have expertise and experience, and sharing our knowledge and making suggestions is a perfectly valid aspect of working with parents in MBT-C. But it is only done at the point when the parents' mentalizing is online so that these ideas can be accepted as another perspective, one that can be thought about, explored, and either accepted or rejected. If expert advice is offered when the parents' mentalizing is offline, and they are perhaps demanding that you come up with an immediate solution (teleological mode) or telling you that they know exactly why their child behaved in a certain way (psychic equivalence), then the advice is unlikely to be of much help. Furthermore, as Rexwinkel and Verheugt-Pleiter (2021) recognized, when parents are operating in a prementalizing mode, "they often follow child-rearing advice much too literally because, although their need for advice is great, the framework for applying it as it was meant to be applied is not there" (p. 74). The parent therapist in MBT-C is therefore encouraged to resist the temptation to jump in and problem solve, while validating the parents' wish to find an answer about what they should do (Pally & Popek, 2012).

Many parents come to therapy with a fear that a therapist is going to point out their failures as a parent—something they may already feel guilty about. We need to work to avoid confirming these preconceptions if we are going to help foster a reflective stance in which parents can experience the way that developing curiosity about their child's mind and behaviors will help them build a stronger relationship with their child and find creative solutions to the practical challenges of being a parent.

There is also a risk that, with MBT-C, it may sound as if we are only interested in thoughts and feelings and that behavior does not matter. This is not what we mean when we describe the importance of maintaining a mentalizing stance. At the end of the day, the work with parents is not going to be successful if the parents do not come away from it feeling that it has helped them with the difficulties that first spurred them to seek help. To make sure this is kept in mind, we have found it can be helpful to use a therapeutic strategy suggested by Haugvik (2013), who, at the end of each session, asked parents two questions: "What do you feel has been most important for you in our talk today?" and "What do you feel has been most important in relation to the child in this session?" (p. 507). Haugvik pointed out that, in addition to providing an opportunity to check that the work being done with the parents is relevant and meaningful to them, these questions are also a way of stimulating mentalizing capacity in the parents by encouraging them to think about what has gone on in that day's session—from both their own perspective and that of their child. And of course, if the answer to these questions is "nothing," then this is extremely important feedback for the therapist, who will need to acknowledge this failure and invite the parents to work together next time to ensure that the same thing does not happen again.

WORKING WITH STRENGTHS, ENCOURAGING OBSERVATION, AND PROMOTING PLAY

Mohammed, Age 7

Mohammed's father, Mr. D, comes to the second parent meeting with his new partner, Ms. L. Since Mohammed's accident, she has been his primary caregiver when he is staying with them, with Mr. D getting involved mostly as a disciplinarian.

For this reason, the therapist suggested at the previous meeting that Mr. D try to find half an hour during the week to sit down with Mohammed and play with him. She suggested that Mr. D simply follow the play and not try to steer it or make the game "educational." She asked him to observe as closely as possible and come back this week and tell her how it went and what he noticed.

Ms. L begins by teasingly saying that it took several reminders on her part for Mr. D to find the time to do this, but in the end, Mr. D sat down with Mohammed over the weekend, and they had played with some LEGO blocks together. "In my family, my father would never have sat down and played with me!" laughs Mr. D, and when the therapist hears this, she acknowledges that she doesn't know how fathers are expected to be in Mr. D's family and asks if he would be able to help her understand that a bit more. Mr. D talks about some of the differences between how he has brought up and how he'd like to be as a father himself. He says he sometimes feels as if parenting is "my wife's job," but that he was happy to be asked to sit down and find time to play with Mohammed. When the therapist asks what it was like for him to do this, he says that it felt odd at first, but in the end, he enjoyed it. He explains how they built two spaceships and then had some races around the room. "I didn't know how much Mohammed knows about science and space travel—he's a real expert." He goes on to say that the play got a little bit overheated, especially when the spaceships crashed into the furniture, but he remembered what the therapist had said last week and tried not to tell Mohammed to stop.

"How do you think that was for Mohammed?" asks the therapist, and Mr. D says that he seemed to have enjoyed it—"He's probably used to me telling him off recently, so I guess it was nice for him that I wasn't just doing that . . . and nice for me too, to be honest."

The therapist compliments Mr. D on his sensitivity to what this had been like for Mohammed and asks whether Ms. L had noticed a difference that day. Ms. L says that after the game, they'd actually had a peaceful evening. Asked if she had any thoughts about why that might be, Ms. L says, "Well, it just changed the atmosphere in the house a bit—and I guess playing at spaceship crashes isn't a thousand miles from car crashes, so maybe it was good for Mohammed to play out some of his worries." Mr. D looks surprised and says he hadn't thought of it that way at all. He asks the therapist, with genuine curiosity, if she thinks Mohammed's play was connected to the car accident.

The work with parents in the MBT-C model is, as much as possible, a strengths-based approach, starting with confirming and validating what parents are doing well. Reinforcing parents' attempts to understand their child during the session helps them to feel at ease and understood, in turn fostering an atmosphere of mutual collaboration and exploration. This can make it possible for parents to develop increased curiosity about their children's inner worlds. For example, when working with a young single mother who spends hours helping her son with homework after a long day's work, even though this often leads to arguments, it can help to start by commenting on the conscientiousness and effort this takes on the mother's part. Starting in this way may not only help her be more receptive to thinking with the therapist but also affirm her strengths, help her feel capable, and engage with the side of her that is resourceful. The mother may then work with the therapist, helping her discover and develop her other capacities as a mother, for example, to become more thoughtful about her son and to explore what is leading the two of them to end up arguing so often.

The parent therapist takes an active stance to support the parent and works alongside, or "behind," the parent, trying to see things from their perspective (Lieberman et al., 2005). The therapist does not hesitate to share information when this can be helpful to the parent. The therapist is mindful of what the parent will be receptive to and be able to use and takes care to work in the parent's zone of proximal development (Vygotsky, 1978). By this, we mean trying to offer only what the parent is able to make use of at that moment or intervening only one step ahead of where she is currently operating, helping her to achieve what is within her reach. The therapist takes care to build on the strengths of the parent and make sure that she feels her efforts and struggles are acknowledged. The therapist also highlights successful mentalizing, ensuring that parents see how doing this well makes a difference to their relationship with their child.

In the vignette with Mr. D, the therapist actively "marks" the moment when Mr. D shows curiosity about his child's experience and reflects on what it may have felt like for him to be engaging with Mohammed in a way that was more playful—especially when coming from a family culture where this may not have been considered part of the role of fathers. The therapist had suggested that they find time to play together because she hoped this would create a different kind of interaction between father and son during a period when Mr. D had been spending a lot of time taking on the role of disciplining Mohammed for his aggressive outbursts. As described in earlier chapters, this joint play would also provide Mohammed with opportunities to develop his own mentalizing capacities, facilitate their attachment relationships, and, as Ms. L perceptively realized, also to revisit, in a safe context, those experiences that had been upsetting and distressing. By the end of this brief review of the play activity, Mr. D was demonstrating a genuine curiosity about his son's mind in a way that boded well for the ongoing work in therapy.

By suggesting to Mr. D that he should not direct the play with Mohammed but simply try to follow his son's lead, the therapist was also trying to invite this boy's father to develop his own curiosity about his son's experiences. In so doing, Mr. D was able to see an aspect of his son that he did not usually notice and also found time to reflect on what it was like for him as a father to have this different kind of interaction—one that had not been part of his own experience of being parented as a child. One effective way in which MBT-C therapists can help this process of self-observation in the parent is by helping the parent take a developmental perspective—that is, encouraging and reinforcing attempts in parents that indicate a curiosity and awareness of the role of maturation and experience in learning to think, perceive, and feel about relationships in more complex ways.

Cooper and Redfern (2015), in their book for parents on reflective parenting, described what they call the "Parent App," which they suggested can be helpful for parents who want to attune to their child's experience and improve their relationship. This Parent App is not something to download onto your phone (or at least not yet!) but rather a stance that parents are encouraged to take, made up of three components:

- Attention: To become curious about a child's behavior, a parent first needs to pay attention, stepping back to watch, listen, and be curious about the child.
- Perspective taking: Instead of assuming that the child sees the world in the same way as his parents, the parents try to step back and imagine how the child may be seeing things. As Cooper and Redfern (2015) put it, "Your child may be behaving in a way that is unreasonable, but for a reason that is entirely reasonable" (p. 76).
- Providing empathy: This involves imaginatively standing alongside the child, showing that you are able to connect with their experience of an event.

In the preceding vignette, Mr. D's therapist is, in essence, trying to work with him to promote this stance. Finding creative ways to help parents become attentive to their child in itself stimulates curiosity. As Cooper and Redfern (2015) put it, "The impact of being attentive to what your baby or child is doing, thinking and feeling cannot be overestimated" (p. 71) because learning to observe and become curious about a child's behavior is the first step toward being able to understand it better. Once parents are curious about their child, they are likely to become less critical and less absolute in their understanding of what may be going on. At this stage, the therapist can actively encourage parents to explore situations from different perspectives. This does not only have to include the child's perspective. For example, some parents find it a very powerful experience to be asked, "If your best friend / your own parent were here now, what do you think she would say about what is going on?" Asking parents to step out of their own shoes and look at a situation from another perspective often has therapeutic value in and of itself. It can then be much easier for parents to be empathic with their child, even if they may not like or agree with what the child is doing.

One way of inviting a different perspective is to explore the parent's own experience of being a child, as Mr. D did spontaneously when he commented on how his father would never have played with him in this way. There is some debate in the literature about how appropriate or necessary it is, when working with parents, to actively explore the parents' own experiences of being parented as part of the process of increasing self-awareness and self-observation (Whitefield & Midgley, 2015). In time-limited MBT-C, there is no requirement or expectation that parents be asked to speak about their own childhood experiences, but there are times when a parent may spontaneously refer to his own experience of being parented or the therapist may choose to ask about such experiences. This may be the first time parents have the opportunity to think about themselves as parents and what role models they had in this capacity and can allow an open exploration of different family cultures and how these have shaped expectations around being a parent. It may help them to articulate what they struggle with and what kind of parent they want to be, as well as to think about this from an intergenerational perspective and in terms of the stories of their lives (Siegel & Hartzell, 2014). Sometimes, it may help parents with difficult attachment histories and trauma to have a therapist who is perceptive and compassionate regarding their struggles to be resilient as parents to address both the "ghosts in the nursery" that may cast doubts about their parenting (Fraiberg et al., 1975) and the "angels" that are there to help them (Lieberman et al., 2005). It can also provide opportunities to think about ways in which their own child may be different from what they were like as children, especially if there is a strong overidentification with the child's experiences. In having such discussions, however, the focus remains on helping to support parental reflective functioning in the here and now.

IDENTIFYING TRIGGERS FOR STRONG EMOTIONS

Anne, Age 6

The previous week, Anne's mother, Mrs. H, had been describing how difficult dinnertime was at home and had said to the parent therapist, "If you could see it, you'd understand what I mean." The therapist had been curious about what Mrs. H thought he might see that he didn't get from Mrs. H describing the situation, but after exploring this further, he had suggested that if it would be helpful, Mrs. H would be welcome to video one of the meals at home and bring it to review together at their next meeting. Mrs. H had said that she'd find this helpful.

The following week, Anne's mother brings a recording of the two of them eating together, and the therapist suggests she pick a short extract to show him, which sums up what she wants the therapist to know about the difficulties they have. He asks if it is okay for either of them to pause the video at any time when they think something important happened, and Mrs. H agrees to this. The two of them sit together and watch, and at certain moments, either Mrs. H or the therapist presses pause. At first, Anne's mother does this to make comments focusing on Anne such as, "Look, that's what she's always doing!" or "Can you see how rude she's being?" The therapist responds by empathizing with the difficulty of the situation, adding that if he were the parent at that moment, he might also really struggle to keep his cool.

At one point, the therapist observes a shift in Mrs. H's affect, so he pauses and wonders about it. Mrs. H speaks of noticing that Anne was trying to get her attention the whole time, commenting that this "always winds me up." The two of them go back and replay that sequence, and the therapist notices that, at first, Anne seems to have found something she's interested in that she wants to show Mrs. H. When she doesn't get her mother's attention right away, her voice becomes whinier, and then Mrs. H gets annoyed. "Yes, that's what happens all the time!" exclaims Mrs. H.

The therapist helps Mrs. H explore her own reaction to this, and then asks her what face she thinks Anne sees when her mother gets wound up like this? Mrs. H says that she's not sure—probably a pretty exhausted one. The therapist says, "I imagine this was at the end of your working day, and I can understand that you were probably very tired."

Mrs. H goes back to the video and plays it back once again. "You know, I didn't really have the energy to speak to Anne right then, but she probably just wanted to show me something." The therapist stays with this and, a little later, asks Mrs. H what face she'd want Anne to see when she looks up at her. Mrs. H isn't sure and says that when she's that tired, she can't find the right words to say anything. She asks the therapist if he can suggest something. The therapist says that some parents he has spoken to, when they are just too exhausted to speak, have tried to make contact with their children by just touching them. He explains that touching is sometimes more important than words. Mrs. H agrees to give this a try, adding that this is very different from the way her own mother used to handle things.

> At the next session, Anne's mother comes in with a big smile on her face. She tells the therapist that a miracle happened: When Anne started demanding her attention, Mrs. H made contact with her by touching her arm. She then told Anne that she'd give her attention when the food was ready and they were sitting down at the table. Anne stopped whining and had even waited a minute before trying to get her attention again. In response, Mrs. H could caress her hair and thank her for being patient, and they both felt connected.

In their book on working with parents from a mentalization-based framework, N. Malberg et al. (2023) highlighted four key techniques for working with powerful emotions in parent work:

- A focus on slowing down, emphasizing the importance for the therapist of gaining all of the information necessary to understand the situation and see the parents' perspective. Example: "I can see that this is a difficult topic for both of you, am I right? I wonder if we could slow down a little to look at this difficult topic together. It will really help me to help you think about this."
- The use of ostensive cues and curiosity about the parents' own minds (what they think) and internal experiences. Example: The therapist adjusts their tone of voice, facial expression, and posture in response to how the parents present to send the explicit message that they are trying to "stay with" the parents and understand them.
- Empathic validation, including a focus for the therapist to (a) validate the basic emotions (e.g., anger, sadness, fear, happiness) and more complex emotions that underlie the parents' behaviors and (b) to understand, where possible, the contexts in which they make sense. Example: "If I were you, I would probably feel very tired and frustrated.... What do you usually do when those feelings get too much?"
- Capacity to name, notice, and repair ruptures in the working relationship in the here and now of the session. Example: "You know ... it might just be my impression, but I noticed that when I asked you about your relationship with your other child, you got silent. Was there something about my question that was difficult or annoying? I am sorry if there was."

Identifying the usual "bumpy roads" (N. T. Malberg, 2015) or "hot spots" (Slade, 2008) that are the common battlegrounds where children and parents seem to have the most difficulty in their interactions is of great value in work with parents. Although parents may sometimes want to speak in generalities ("my child always does X" or "what usually happens is Y"), getting down to the nitty-gritty and exploring a particular incident where things have been difficult can pave the way and help the therapist and parents develop an understanding of how and when mentalizing breaks down. These incidents often turn out to be examples of the vicious cycles of nonmentalizing that we described in Chapter 2 in this volume, where parents and child enter patterns of relating in which nonmentalizing in one arouses nonmentalizing in the other. Examining a specific example is usually more therapeutically productive than speaking about how this happens in general or "all the time."

Often, the first step in reviewing these "hot-spot" moments involves a process of sequencing or microanalysis in which the parent and therapist jointly reconstruct what happened. Prompted by the therapist's interest and request for clarification (e.g., "And then what happened?" "Let me see whether I have this right"), the therapist and parent clarify and elaborate the emotional and behavioral sequence in the interactions until they have a clear picture and frame-by-frame, slow-motion movie of exactly what triggers and escalates interpersonal breakdowns. Slowing down interactions that are often so affectively charged that they are remembered as a blur helps parents mentally observe their own behavior from the outside and think about their child's reactions, thus paving the way to understand breakdowns and behaviors that "happen for no reason." This can be a springboard for the therapist to invite curiosity about what was going on for all of the people involved in the interaction.

By inviting parents to "stop and rewind" in this way (a technique we described in Chapter 8, this volume), the therapist helps them understand the sequence underlying repeated or common cycles of nonmentalizing in their family. This is the first step in helping them regulate and adjust their own behavior and then being able to catch themselves when they react in a way that will escalate the child's dysregulation rather than help them to regulate. The therapist can also bring in her own thoughts and perspectives on what may have been going on, checking with the parents and asking them to consider these different perspectives from an inquisitive and curious position. In this way, the therapist also models the path to mentalizing and thinking together about why each person reacts a certain way and noticing where mentalizing breaks down.

Verbal accounts of incidents from outside the session can be used with the stop-and-rewind technique, but in some cases, it can be powerful to work with video material. Video is now widely used in many intervention approaches, especially in parent–infant psychotherapy and attachment-based interventions with high-risk parent–child dyads, but it may not be the right strategy for all parents. When parents are fragile and have a great deal of guilt and paranoia regarding inadequate parenting, some work on building their sense of competence or helping them with immediate difficulties may be a priority; video may be too exposing and threatening. Likewise, there is a risk that parents may want to use video as a way of showing up or humiliating their child (e.g., by showing the therapist how awful their child's behavior really is). When used in this way, it is unlikely to be helpful.

THE USE OF VIDEO INTERVENTIONS WITH PARENTS IN MENTALIZATION-BASED TREATMENT FOR CHILDREN

Belinda, Age 7

Belinda has been attending weekly MBT-C sessions for a month. Her therapist has had two parallel sessions with Mrs. C. During these sessions, Mrs. C reports feeling disconnected from her child and disliking some aspects of Belinda's personality because they remind her of her child's father. In addition, she speaks about not knowing what to do when Belinda becomes distressed about "silly things" and makes regular comments about how useless she is as a parent. At times, Mrs. C also becomes demanding of the therapist, asking for tools and saying she does not know if this MBT thing is what her daughter needs.

Following the last parent session, the therapist seeks supervision due to feeling stuck in the process and decides to introduce video intervention to Mrs. C. He explains that sometimes it helps to look at ourselves and our child from the outside and imagine what is going on from the inside with the support of a therapist. In fact, quite often when using video intervention (the therapist tells Mrs. C), many parents report discovering that they are not doing things so badly. After all, being tough on oneself is a common issue for many parents. Finally, the therapist explains how he would like to ask Mrs. C and Belinda to engage in an activity together for about 20 minutes and videotape it. Following this, the therapist and Mrs. C would meet and observe, feel, and think together about what they could see in the video. The therapist explains this is not an evaluation and that Mrs. C should try to enjoy the activity and do what she would usually do. Mrs. C is satisfied with the explanation. Although a bit anxious, she agrees to give it a try, and arranges a time to meet with the therapist together with her daughter.

When Belinda and Mrs. C meet him, the therapist suggests the squiggle task (as explained in Chapter 6, this volume) as an activity. After introducing it to both Belinda and Mrs. C, the therapist sits back and observes them play, and he videotapes the interaction. During the task, the therapist observes moments of mutual enjoyment as well as moments of rupture. For instance, when Belinda erases her contribution several times, Mrs. C seems annoyed and begins to speak to the therapist instead of supporting her daughter. In another instance, Belinda looks for her mother's support with a facial expression of curiosity to which Mrs. C responds by mirroring her daughter. A very funny interaction takes place with both showing enjoyment.

A week later, Mrs. C and the therapist sit to watch some clips from the video. The therapist first asks about Mrs. C's overall feeling while watching the clip. Mrs. C speaks about feeling somewhat emotional. Following this comment, the therapist invites her to tell him what she sees in herself in the video and what she sees in Belinda. The therapist supports and responds with curiosity, while reinforcing attempts to observe "ostensive cues" such as facial expressions and bodily posture. Later, the therapist invites Mrs. C to imagine what the feeling, wish, or need in her child's mind is during the observed interaction and then asks the same about Mrs. C. In this way, the therapist directs her attention to behavior as a communication and to the fact that states of mind are opaque. Furthermore, the therapist supports Mrs. C in seeing the value of small moments of vitality for the development of a healthier relationship and a greater sense of mutual emotional regulation between mother and daughter.

Video intervention has been described as a "golden tool" by clinicians and researchers for the promising impact it can have in terms of therapeutic work in different contexts, even in a small number of sessions. The key to its clinical usefulness lies in the fact that it allows the client, from the observation of recorded interactions, to approach things gradually, with greater regulation and with the support of the therapist in a collaborative role, enhancing observational and reflective skills, the recognition and attribution of mental states, as well as the identification of mutual influence. It allows the therapist to identify and enhance specific aspects of parenting by amplifying the moments of synchrony, coordination, and pleasure between parents and children, which then facilitate the approach to more difficult aspects of the interaction. All this supports the ability of parents to repair and connect with children.

In the context of working with parents in mentalization-based treatment, using video can serve as a way of explicitly helping parents increase self–other observational skills and recognize examples of positive mentalizing. This can lead to an increase in reflective functioning in the parent as well as to a feeling of mutual collaboration between the therapist and the parents. Difficult interactions, in which mentalizing may have broken down, can also be a focus for review. Video can be invaluable in providing an opportunity for parents to look at themselves from a distance in a way that is much more challenging, if not impossible, in the midst of a situation, especially if it is a highly emotional one.

The therapist can empathize with challenging situations and ask questions while watching the video—for example, "What do you think your child was trying to say with that behavior right there?" "What were you feeling when your child was behaving like that?" In this way, the therapist can shift between inviting mentalizing of self and the other. These questions help in the process of making links between what can and cannot be seen and to concretely illustrate the concept of the opacity of minds.

In MBT-C, we can use video feedback with parents to

- highlight examples of positive mentalizing, helping parents to see what they are doing well and how that can support the relationship they have with their child;
- look at "hot-spot" interactions from a distance and when parents are not so emotionally activated, using the more reflective and observing stance naturally activated by the video to increase awareness of self and other;
- increase awareness of affects and their impact, especially the parents' own negative emotions and intensity of anger that they may not have been aware of;
- increase curiosity about the child's experience underlying their behavior, thus preparing the ground for adapting parents' reactions so they can help the child regulate; and
- observe and understand the sequence of interactions that lead to increases in child dysregulation.

With some parents or in some settings, the use of video may not be possible or welcome. In these cases, a journal or self-monitoring log can be useful to facilitate the development of self-awareness and self-regulation (monitoring and reflecting). Especially in working with parents whose capacity to mentalize is easily lost, it can be helpful to keep a log that activates a self-monitoring function and engages the more cognitive, reflective part of the parent. It is useful to encourage parents to use the journal soon after a difficult moment or conflict with their child, while acknowledging the strong emotions in their perceptions of the child and themselves at that moment. It requires a good therapeutic alliance and basic trust for parents to share what they may feel are embarrassing or forbidden thoughts and feelings about themselves as parents and their children that may come up during some painful exchanges. However, looking at these entries together during a meeting can help facilitate the task of self-observation in a safe and contained environment and encourage parents' development of self-monitoring.

WORKING WITH PARENTS IN CONFLICT

Belinda, Age 7

Belinda's main caregivers, Mrs. C and grandma, are discussing her rude vocabulary. Grandma says that it isn't surprising, given that Mrs. C is not careful with the TV programs she allows Belinda to watch. This sets off Mrs. C, and she shouts at her mother that she is old-fashioned and controlling. Grandma shouts back, accusing her daughter of undermining her just to punish her. The therapist puts up his hands to indicate that they should stop, and when this is ignored, he stands up and uses his hands to indicate that they should "simmer down." With a firm voice, he interrupts the two of them and says, "I'm going to stop you there because I don't think it helps anyone if I let the two of you shout at each other."

They stop shouting, but the tension remains high. "If you think that was shouting," says Grandma, "you should hear her at home when she really shouts—Belinda goes and locks herself in the bathroom." "Well, that's helpful to know," says the therapist, "and maybe we'll need to come back later and think about what it might be like for Belinda when the two of you are arguing. Because for me, that did feel like shouting, and when it is like that, I find it difficult to think. And if I can't think properly, I'm probably not going to be able to help much."

Mrs. C and grandma look at each other, and the tension in the room decreases slightly. "So, are you two both okay," the therapist goes on, "if I step in and stop you like that when the volume goes up?" Mrs. C and grandma both nod. "Thank you," says the therapist, "and thanks also for explaining to me that compared with what goes on at home, you don't consider that shouting. . . . Is that how you see it too, Mrs. C?" Mrs. C nods again, and says that yes, at home, they sometimes shout so loud that the neighbors knock on the door and check to see if everything is okay. "Well, that's really important for me to know," says the therapist. "And is that how the two of you want it to be?" Mrs. C and grandma both shake their heads. "And is it how you want it to be for Belinda?" Again, they both shake their heads, but this time Mrs. C also looks tearful.

Conflict is inherent in humans and thus in families, but divorce and the dissolution of the original family unit often trigger deep and profound anxiety and anger around loss of and access to children, abandonment, future financial security, and division of family resources. This frequently activates nonmentalizing, coercive patterns in the separating parents (Nyberg & Hertzmann, 2014). However, it is not only in the context of divorce that therapists encounter conflict. As illustrated by the preceding vignette, conflicts around parenting often become a way in which parents and family members caring for the child can express their fears and other painful affects. When a parent is afraid, angry, or confused, her mentalizing capacity is likely to become impaired. In this section, we think about how to work with parents in conflict from a time-limited MBT-C perspective in parent sessions. This includes intergenerational conflict, as in our example, or conflict within a parental couple.

One of the main questions that emerges in the context of family conflict is how ready the parents or caregivers are to engage collectively in the process of making meaning of the child's behavior and their own. This will affect the therapeutic framework chosen for each case—namely, whether the therapist favors parallel sessions at first to explore the individual sources of conflict and the impact on the child, or whether the therapist would rather meet with both parents and other significant caregivers all at once. For example, with separated or divorced parents where there is a history of coercive mentalizing patterns, it may not be suitable to meet with both at the same time because their own relational agenda may take over. That said, witnessing and assessing such interactions is always important in the context of the initial assessment. Sometimes, it can be important for separated or divorced parents to come together and create a shared perspective of their child. The main aim always remains to find the best setting in which parents can learn to mentalize each other and the child in a way that will contribute to a more coherent and predictable relational experience for the child—one in which they can feel seen and heard.

The first step is generally to provide parents with such an experience in the context of parent sessions. For instance, during sessions with parents, feelings can become overheated, and it can be challenging to remain calm when angry parents are shouting at each other and assuming threatening postures. Trying to discuss the meaning of what is being said (e.g., grandma's comment that Mrs. C is doing this "to hurt her") is almost certain to have little value. When the level of conflict and arousal is high in the room, our own capacity for mentalizing is likely to be inhibited, so it is important to try to stop the interaction before the therapist becomes overwhelmed, sometimes using what mentalization-based treatment workers with families have called, somewhat jokingly, the "mentalizing hand" (Asen & Fonagy, 2012a). In doing so, it can be helpful to use your own experience as the therapist in the room to explain why you are trying to stop the parents and get them to "simmer down"; this can introduce the idea that behaviors have an impact on others and that others may experience our behavior very differently from how we see it ourselves.

By inviting parents to simmer down and introducing our capacity to be reflective about what is going on in the room, we try to model thinking while feeling. In retrospect, when reviewing interactions like this, the therapist can sometimes introduce an element of psychoeducation about what happens when we get into dysregulated states or use such reviewing to help the parents recognize patterns and check whether they are ones that the parents want to repeat. Parents themselves usually do not want these interactions to continue, so this can be the basis for deepening the therapeutic alliance, with a shared goal about areas that parents would like to work on.

Whenever the emotional temperature in a session becomes high, as in the preceding example, it is important to acknowledge it and, once things have simmered down, invite participants to think about what happened. The stop-and-rewind method helps to cool off the interaction so that those involved can reflect on the sequence of thoughts and feelings that emerged before and during the moment when things became heated, allowing the situation to be mentalized. In the preceding vignette, Grandma raised the issue of how Belinda reacts to the shouting in the house; as this demonstrates, it is often easy for a child to get lost in parents' minds amid an argument. Thus, having a space and an opportunity to consider what Belinda's experience might be when her mother and grandma are arguing, as well as to slow down, pause, and wonder about what is going on between them, can be extremely helpful. However, when it is clear that parental or caregiver conflict is chronic and ongoing, it is likely that time-limited work as part of MBT-C may not be sufficient, and a referral to some form of couple therapy may be required (Hertzmann et al., 2017). This can sometimes take place alongside time-limited MBT-C, so that the child's therapy is not interrupted and the MBT-C parent meetings can focus on their role as parents in mentalizing and responding to their child's needs.

WORKING WITH FOSTER PARENTS

John, Age 8

John's foster parents are speaking to the therapist about their concerns about what will happen in terms of John's permanent placement with them. His biological father has petitioned the court for visitation, and John's behavior, the foster parents say, has deteriorated since then. "It is like they don't want this boy to have peace of mind. . . . Don't they understand, they are going to drive him crazy?" The therapist asks them whether they have spoken with John about this at all. "I tried," says Mr. F, "but he told me to piss off and mind my own business—in fact, he told me that if we stopped him from seeing his mom, he'd never speak to me again."

They explain that John's social worker also spoke to them, and when they voiced their concerns, they felt that the social worker was quite critical of them and implied that they didn't know what was best for John. "I felt like telling her to come and live with John for a week," says Mrs. F, "and then tell us who knows best."

Although the approach to working with foster parents in time-limited MBT-C is like that with other parents, there are a number of specific issues that this work can raise. First of all, as described in Chapter 2 in this volume, many of the children who come into the care system have not had the experience, in their early years, of a parent who is able to notice or think about what is going on in their minds or to offer marked or contingent mirroring. As children, they may have had many experiences in which their intentions were misread, there were negative attributions about their behavior, or there was extreme inconsistency in how their attachment needs were met. In turn, these children may be avoidant of their dependency needs. They may appear highly controlling and domineering in ways that invite rejection from adults and may even be frightening, or they may be prone to hyperarousal, behave in a way that can be seen as "attention seeking," or be indiscriminate in their attachments (Taylor, 2012). These children, like John and Ruth in this book, are likely to have negative views of themselves, often believing that they are unlovable, shameful, and worthy of rejection.

Research has suggested that some foster parents may have variable levels of reflective functioning, with limitations specifically in aspects that may be most important for effective fostering (Bunday et al., 2015). It is not surprising, then, that fostered children and their carers frequently struggle to understand each other. Furthermore, foster parents may well have trouble dealing with the highly rejecting behavior that foster children may display, or struggle with their incapacity to show emotional responsiveness (Muller et al., 2012). We can imagine that it is also much more challenging to mentalize and try and understand the behavior of a child that the foster parent may not know particularly well. Some carers may struggle to set limits out of a wish to make up for the lack of love and care that they imagine the child experienced when they were younger or possibly out of fear of the child's aggression and anger. In other instances, the carers might withdraw from emotional engagement with the child in their care, dealing with them at a behavioral level, often ending up in power struggles, leading to cycles of misbehavior and punishment (Jacobsen et al., 2015). All these complex dynamics can easily get played out in the systems around the child as well, as seems to be the case with John in the preceding vignette, where there is mutual blame and anger among the child, foster parents, and social work team. In these situations, foster parents often have little choice but to accept the lack of permanency and the unexpected demands of a system that, although designed to support them, often turns to measures that result in an exacerbation of nonmentalizing responses to the needs of both carers and children. As a result, foster parents may end up feeling frustrated, angry, puzzled, or deeply distressed.

In considering how best to support foster parents in the context of a mentalizing approach, Cooper and Redfern (2015) talked about the need to have an "enhanced Parent App" (p. 126). By this, they meant a stance toward parenting with an increased focus on perspective taking, given how hard it can be for foster parents if a child sees them, as John does (at least momentarily), as uncaring or nasty or treats them with distrust and hostility. The parent therapist may therefore need to work especially hard at helping the foster parents see things from the child's perspective, and in many cases, this can be helped (if foster parents do not already have this knowledge) with a degree of psychoeducation about attachment and trauma and the impact of early maltreatment and abuse on how children see the world and relate to it.

Managing problematic behaviors is one area with which foster parents often struggle, given the extreme emotion dysregulation they are frequently challenged to respond to. They can sometimes feel caught between advice to take an entirely behavioral approach (e.g., time-outs, reward systems) or simply empathizing and seeing things from the child's perspective, but this can sometimes leave the foster parents feeling that they are giving the child carte blanche to behave as they like. Drawing on the work of Golding and Hughes (e.g., Golding, 2015; D. A. Hughes, 2000), Cooper and Redfern (2015) suggested that the concept of "Two Hands" is compatible with a mentalizing approach. The Two Hands approach involves managing behavior, on the one hand, while seeking to understand it, on the other. For example, when John was rude to his foster father and told him to "piss off," it would be possible to encourage Mr. F to consider both *whether* and *how* to respond when spoken to in this way, while remaining curious about *why* John may have spoken in that way. It is likely that an understanding response regarding John's comment can help him feel that his new foster parents are concerned about him having to make this decision. As Cooper and Redfern put it, "it is easier to influence others when they have a feeling of being understood and connected with [and] nowhere is this more important than when disciplining your child" (p. 107).

In addition to the meetings that are offered to foster parents, the parent therapist may also need to liaise with teachers, social workers, and other allied professionals. The aim of this work is to help "mentalize the system" (Bevington et al., 2015) by offering a new version of the child's and, in this case, the parents' behavior—one that introduces an inquisitive style alongside a developmental and trauma-informed perspective. As with individuals, when the members of the professional network around a child in care are under pressure, they may lose the capacity to remain reflective. If the network cannot sustain such pressure, they are likely to act out in unthinking ways, often making rash decisions that may not be based on holding in mind the child's perspective (Emanuel, 2002; Taylor, 2012). When operating in a nonmentalizing, teleological mode of this sort, there can be a powerful pressure to "do something." Although action may well be necessary, the therapist may need to make use of mentalizing techniques such as slowing down, stop and review, or simmering down with members of the network around the child to help restart more mentalizing interactions and ensure that any action taken is thoughtful and based on the capacity to take the foster child's perspective (Wood et al., 2015).

COMING TO THE END OF THE WORK WITH PARENTS

Anne, Age 6

By the time the meetings with Mrs. H come to an end, there are marked improvements in her personal and professional life, and she appears to feel much more confident about her ability to control herself and see herself as a competent parent who can understand, if not change, her daughter, Anne. However, in the review meeting, Mrs. H becomes distressed when the therapist reflects on her progress and wonders whether it is time to think of moving toward ending treatment. Mrs. H says that she can't imagine managing without the therapist's support and thinks that the therapist overestimates Mrs. H's abilities. She says that she sometimes feels like just leaving Anne at school instead of picking her up and that she does not have the courage to face the difficulties with Anne on her own.

When the therapist comments on what has just happened, Mrs. H starts to cry and says that everyone leaves her when she needs them, probably because she does not deserve to be helped. She goes on to say that her mother died when she was an adolescent, and her husband left her when Anne was so difficult. Now, the therapist wants to leave her too, and she has no idea how she will manage on her own. When the therapist responds empathically about how anxious Mrs. H is about believing she can do things on her own this time, after having been let down so painfully, Mrs. H becomes calmer. The two of them spend some time thinking together about how Mrs. H's past experiences of being left can lead to her feeling vulnerable when faced with endings. Mrs. H says that she realizes that she would be sad to not see the therapist but knows that she is able to manage on her own. She knows now that Anne's problems are not because she—Mrs. H—has done something wrong and that all she can do is do her best. And even when she does her best, she may not be able to fix everything. She knows that the best she can do is hang in there with Anne. The therapist suggests that they think together about how Mrs. H can best consolidate the changes that have taken place once they are no longer coming to therapy.

Deciding whether the parents are ready to end treatment should be guided, in part, by the ongoing assessment of their needs and developing strengths. As a general principle, the last few sessions should provide an opportunity to have an experience of an ending in which the parents and therapist can not only reflect on how to consolidate gains and maintain strengths that they have discovered but also, if needed, talk about painful past experiences of loss, separation, and individuation in the parents' lives.

Creating a narrative of the process of treatment in which the parents see themselves in the therapist's mind as agents of change for themselves and their child can help parents build on their strengths and maintain their sense of agency in the face of future challenges. Helping parents develop a balanced and realistic perception of themselves and their children and understand what can be changed and what probably cannot and will have to be accepted can help them overcome paralyzing feelings of guilt about being responsible for all of their child's difficulties. For example, if Anne continues to have behavioral difficulties at school, it can be a relief for Mrs. H to know that it is not the result of her being an inadequate parent and that nothing she can do will "make" Anne comply. For a mother overwhelmed by pressures from Anne's school, the child's distress, and her own concern, this can be of great benefit. When problems continue and the level of family need is more complex, home visits, with their ecological lens and wraparound interventions, can be particularly useful, especially to help parents maintain gains made in therapy.

CONCLUSION

The aim of working with parents in time-limited MBT-C is to help them develop their strengths and discover a reflective stance. This can help develop the kind of parent–child interactions in which children feel secure and understood, which, in turn, facilitates motivation, self-regulation, basic self-knowledge, and mentalizing. Many parents who come to consult may well have good reasons to approach therapists with a degree of uncertainty and mistrust, but when their vigilance relaxes in the context of a respectful relationship, they may be relieved and open up to new ways of understanding. As a result, parents are likely to show increased interest in the therapist's attempts to help them think about their child. Consequently, this stimulates and strengthens parents' capacity for reflective functioning.

10

Moving Toward Goodbye

Endings in Time-Limited Mentalization-Based Treatment for Children

Because mentalization-based treatment for children (MBT-C) is a time-limited therapy, its ending is kept in mind from the start of treatment. The use of a calendar helps to remind both the child and the therapist how many sessions have taken place and how many remain. Although some have argued that meaningful relationships cannot be established in short-term or time-limited psychotherapy, 3 to 6 months (which is the usual length of time-limited MBT-C) can be a significant period of time in a child's life, and we have found that children can form strong and lasting emotional attachments when working this way.

In this chapter, we present how the process of ending offers not only opportunities to explore ways of managing loss or goodbyes from a mentalizing perspective but also the chance to consolidate what has been achieved, while giving the child (and parents) the confidence to generalize what they have learned into new settings. Being able to recognize when the therapy is not progressing, or when it needs to continue further, is also essential. We explore the importance of assessing whether the child and the family are ready to end treatment or if additional (or alternative) interventions are needed. The chapter also illustrates the way in which "booster sessions" can be used as part of MBT-C, after the therapy's ending, and explores how this may fit with a mentalizing focus.

https://doi.org/10.1037/0000486-011
Mentalization-Based Treatment for Children: A Time-Limited Approach, Second Edition, by N. Midgley, K. Ensink, K. Lindqvist, N. Malberg, and N. Muller
Copyright © 2025 by the American Psychological Association. All rights reserved.

HOW THE TIME-LIMITED NATURE OF THE WORK IS INTRODUCED TO CHILDREN AND PARENTS

Thinking about time and time limitation is not just an aspect of the last phase of therapy. Every MBT-C therapeutic intervention has as its aim to encourage and increase the child and the parents' ability to mentalize and regulate emotions in relationships in a way that helps them manage their difficulties beyond the end of therapy. In this way, the end is always in mind and is strongly linked to the process of assessment, the goals, and the process of the treatment. It helps, when we introduce the time-limited model to parents and children, to explain what they can expect. We might say,

> From our experience and what we know from research, the kind of issues that have brought you to seek help can often be resolved with about 12 weekly sessions—about 3 months. That doesn't necessarily mean that everything will be completely sorted by that point, but we'd hope that we'd have made some real progress on the goals we set together and that you'd also have the skills and the confidence to continue getting help from each other and from the other important people in your lives. But each person and each family is different, so after about eight meetings, we'll sit down together and review how things are going. At that point, we can decide whether to stick with the original plan, to continue for a bit longer, or to think if there's something else that would be of help to you. I'll try and be as honest and open with you as I can in this, and I'd really appreciate it if you can be the same with me. If I am missing something or get something wrong (which is always quite likely!), it makes my job easier if you can let me know so that we can try and sort things out.

For children, it can be helpful to introduce the fixed number of sessions in order to give a sense that there is a clear start and end. Parents can sometimes react in a way that suggests they think a limited number of sessions will never be enough, or they may feel that it is far too big a commitment, especially in terms of their own involvement. However, for some parents, it is helpful to know there is a clear time frame. In the separate parent meetings, reflecting on these feelings can often open up valuable discussions regarding feelings of helplessness, hopelessness, and their own insecurities as parents. If parents are concerned that the treatment may be too short for the difficulties the child is facing, we can ask them to think about whether they have had a brief relationship in their own lives that has been defining and important for them. Was there a teacher, a coach, a best friend, or a mentor who was in their life for a relatively brief time, whose influence they carry with them to this day? We can also reassure them that we will be meeting to review progress after the first eight sessions, and that in cases where it is felt that more time is needed, this is something that can be negotiated.

When discussing a parent's worry about the time limitation, the therapist should ideally focus on both the emotional content (e.g., fear of dependency in therapy), as described above, as well as give realistic information regarding the structure and length of the treatment. The therapist can be open about saying that, in our experience, many children profit from working within this time frame, but in some cases, time-limited work is not enough. Having the possibility in a service to make the choice to extend a therapy can be reassuring to both professionals as well as to parents.

KEEPING ENDINGS IN MIND DURING THE PROCESS OF TIME-LIMITED THERAPY

Anne, Age 6

Mrs. H, Anne's mother, has arrived consistently late with Anne since their first appointment. Regardless of the therapist's attempts to stress the importance of punctuality and the impact that it has when Anne has less time, Mrs. H has not changed this pattern of behavior. Different excuses are given each time. After a particularly difficult session in which Anne showed her anger because the therapist stopped a game that Anne had just started, as the session had to come to an end, the therapists decide that the parent therapist will address the issue with Mrs. H during the next parent session. He reminds Mrs. H of Anne's behavior in the waiting room at the end of the session and points out that it is difficult for Anne to have so little time. He invites Mrs. H to imagine what this means for her daughter. Quite unapologetically, Mrs. H expresses her belief that the therapists could run over a bit more if they wanted to. The therapist says that he can appreciate that Mrs. H may feel like she's being told to do all the hard work, and that other people, including the therapists, don't seem to offer much flexibility. (The therapist is mindful that Mrs. H and her husband are divorced.) Mrs. H says, "Well yes, I certainly don't get any help from my ex-husband in getting Anne to her sessions on time." The therapist shows some sympathy with this, and Mrs. H visibly relaxes and is a little tearful. After a bit, the therapist goes back to the issue of punctuality, and risks saying that perhaps, given all that has happened, Mrs. H wants to teach Anne something about people . . . Mrs. H smiles and adds, "Like people leave you or let you down when you least expect it?" Then she adds, "It is never enough for her."

The vignette above illustrates the multiple meanings of behavior around time and how important it is to invite parents to reflect and try to understand their child's experience from an inquisitive stance. Although Mrs. H at first indicates that the problem is the therapists' inflexibility, once the therapist responds in a nondefensive way, she is able to recognize that her stress is stopping her from being able to look at the meaning of being late from her daughter's perspective. We might say that Mrs. H is at first operating in a more teleological mode—that is, thinking that the solution would be for the therapists to do something different by extending the length of the sessions. The therapist recognizes that the first task is to help Mrs. H feel understood and supported, so that her capacity for mentalizing can come back online. In being able to speak to Mrs. H's own feelings of frustration and loneliness when confronted with the behavioral challenges of a 6-year-old without the support of a partner, the therapist shows a capacity to think about things from Mrs. H's perspective. Possibly due to shame, Mrs. H was not able to express these feelings openly, and instead they were expressed by disrupting Anne's time with her therapist. Perhaps fearing her child's and her own attachment to the therapist, she had found a way to stay emotionally distant by rendering the therapists ineffective and seemingly greedy with their time in her mind and that of her child.

Once Mrs. H felt understood (and not judged), the therapist was able to help her to get in touch with her daughter's experience of missing time with her therapist, and following this meeting, Mrs. H was more careful to bring Anne on time.

In time-limited work, the aspect of time is present in each session, keeping time, recording progress, and trying to keep the goals in mind. For children, working with the calendar not only makes the planning of the therapy visible (see also Chapter 4, this volume) but also acts a reminder of the time-limited nature of the therapy. Children with separation anxiety problems, histories of loss, or trauma and children with attachment problems often find it difficult to end sessions (Gil & Crenshaw, 2016). As described in Chapter 2 in this volume, we might come to understand this in the light of their attachment patterns and their mentalizing capacity.

The moment of saying goodbye at the end of a session is often an opportunity to learn about and support the child's capacity to mentalize. For example, some children run off immediately, whereas other children want to give the therapist a hug or even a kiss. Sometimes, children feel so close to the therapist that they fantasize about them becoming a part of the family. Being sensitive to the meaning of the way a child says goodbye or what the therapist feels when saying goodbye and trying to use this information in therapy to explore the longings, wishes or blank spots in a child's mind can help to understand how the child deals with closeness and attachment needs. But even more importantly, it might open a dialogue about what they miss or how they experience the important people around them. Exploring what happens in the here and now between therapist and child and what kind of feelings you as a therapist are left with at the end of each session can give information about the implicit relational processes and can become an important basis for further therapeutic work.

DECIDING WHEN IT IS TIME TO STOP—OR CARRY ON

Belinda, Age 7

Belinda cannot sit on a chair during the review session. She stands in a corner of the room, playing with a plastic dog. She doesn't want to answer any question herself. She seems to listen to her mother and the therapist, but only says that she wants to go to her own session to play. When the parents and the therapist agree that she needs 12 more sessions, she is happy.

In the second review session, midway through the second block of 12 sessions, Belinda once more finds it hard to join the conversation but is willing to sit on a chair, paying real attention to what everyone is saying and reacting to it nonverbally. Again, her parents and the therapist decide she needs 12 more sessions, which will be the last set of 12. She seems to be better able to control her levels of arousal in this review session but still finds it difficult to contribute her own thoughts and feelings to the meeting.

As discussed in Chapter 4 in this volume, in MBT-C, the therapist creates a calendar with each child. During the last few minutes of each session, the therapist invites the child to draw something on the calendar as a way to document whatever the child is thinking about and to mark how many sessions they have remaining

FIGURE 10.1. Belinda's Calendar

Note. From a child seen at YOUZ (formally known as DeJutters CAMHS) Clinic in the Netherlands. Reprinted with permission.

together in the time-limited work. In the review session, Belinda sits in her chair and discusses some of the drawings in her calendar (see Figure 10.1). She says to the therapist and her mother that she knows she is sometimes a "refusing horse" and sometimes a "wild horse," but that there are reins and she can be the jockey sitting on the horse with the reins in her hand. She sits in her chair proudly, as if sitting atop a horse, and everyone in the room agrees that Belinda is now in the right place for therapy to come to an end.

As described in Chapter 4 in this volume, at the beginning of the treatment, the therapist explains that after the first eight meetings, there will be a review session in which parents, child, and therapist(s) look back over the work together and decide whether to move toward ending the therapy or to prolong the therapy with 12 more sessions, up to a maximum of three sets of 12 sessions. Alternatively, the therapist and family may decide that a different kind of intervention or support is needed.

The decision to stop or carry on with the therapy depends on a number of factors, including:

- Whether the problems that brought the child to therapy have diminished and the goals set by the family have been met, and whether the child, the therapist, and family feel that continuing with therapy further would help to achieve this.
- Whether the child has (re)gained a capacity to play, if this was inhibited, and to modulate and regulate their emotions—or use an adult's support in dyadic regulation—in an age-appropriate way.
- The resilience of both the parents and child.
- The quality of the calendar drawings. For example, with Belinda's calendar, the change in the images can be used to reflect on her experiences over time, and in this case is a sign of her greater self-coherence and ownership of her own narrative.
- Whether the family and wider social context is supportive, and the parents are able to provide the necessary emotional care for the child and the child is able to make use of this.

Given that this is a time-limited treatment, it is important to note that we do not always see that the problems sought for have completely gone away at the end of treatment. If not, it may be helpful to revisit the process of addressing these problems in the family. We may look at whether the parents are able to better mentalize the child, and if so, how this enables them to respond to the child adequately during difficult times. If some key shifts have taken place, we may feel that the family has developed enough resources to keep working with these problems independently. Related to this is the parents' capacity to cope. We can explore how they are able to mentalize and regulate themselves in difficult situations, and how they are able to use support if needed. This can partly be assessed in discussion with the parents. However, we know that endings often cause feelings of self-doubt and worry, meaning that we cannot expect families to independently assess their own readiness entirely or always expect parents to express that they feel "done."

Deciding when to end a treatment is always a challenging aspect of being a practitioner, as many of us are driven partly by our need to support and help and our belief that there is often "something more that can be done" (Fragkiadaki & Strauss, 2012). Sometimes, ending the therapy evokes strong feelings in the therapist of loss, guilt, inadequacy, or, on some occasions, relief and freedom, especially when dealing with complex and challenging families or children. In response, the therapist might sometimes find themselves being more teleological in their actions—for example, by allowing the child to take a toy from their consulting room or giving more time to parents during the last sessions. Some therapists, especially those not used to working in a time-limited way, can find it difficult to know that the therapy has a fixed length before they even begin. This may also have the impact of them being reluctant to invest wholeheartedly in the therapy or allowing for a deeper bond to develop. In these situations, supervision can be helpful to reflect on the therapist's ambivalent feelings and doubts around working in a time-limited time frame or about ending therapy. Therapists can use this information constructively to know whether there is something urgent that still needs to be addressed or to accept the limitations and frustrations of time-limited work without depreciating the value it may have.

PREPARING THE CHILD AND PARENTS FOR THE REVIEW SESSION

Ruth, Age 12

Ruth has now completed seven sessions of MBT-C. During this time, Ruth has learned to show herself, to express herself a bit more, and to develop an understanding of "this is me from the outside and this is me from the inside."

As with Belinda's case, during the last few minutes of Ruth's session, the therapist has invited Ruth to draw something on the calendar (see Figure 10.2). In the first session, Ruth is hardly able to draw anything, tentatively drawing three little lines. In the second session, she draws herself with open eyes as if saying "Yes, I can see you." After a few sessions, Ruth spontaneously starts to experiment with drawing faces and begins expressing an understanding of how she sometimes feels things on the inside that she doesn't express on the outside. She realizes that despite having severe emotional problems, she always seems to smile at everyone rather

FIGURE 10.2. Ruth's Calendar

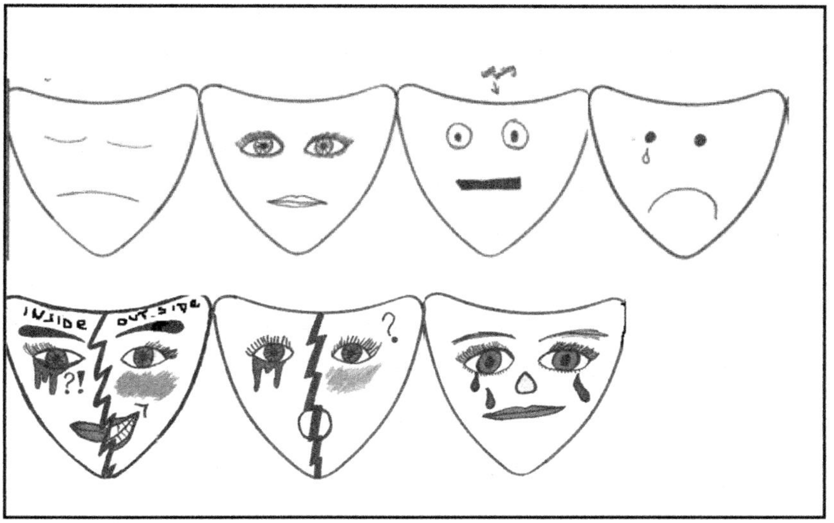

Note. From a child seen at YOUZ (formally known as DeJutters CAMHS) Clinic in the Netherlands. Reprinted with permission.

> than show her feelings. After a few sessions, she takes the colored pencils and writes "inside/outside." An important theme in her therapy is that she doesn't feel seen by her foster carers. At the end of her fifth and sixth sessions, she puts question marks in her drawings as if she is wondering "what do people see when they look at me?" She then seems to start discovering and realizing that other people cannot know what she is feeling unless she can express something about it rather than pushing everyone away. In the last of these seven drawings, she shows her inner feelings, as if she is ready to look at her inside feelings and thoughts and is developing a sense of confidence about expressing them.
>
> As part of their preparation for the review meeting, during their eighth meeting, Ruth and her therapist look back at the way she has made the calendar and use it as a way of reviewing what has happened so far in the therapy. The therapist is able to check out some of his own thoughts about Ruth's progress, and this opens up a discussion about whether they should be looking to end after 12 sessions, as they had originally planned. They don't make any definite decision about this, but agree to take some of what they were thinking about together into the review meeting with her foster carers and social worker.

The review session serves as an opportunity to solidify the child's sense of agency regarding the process of the therapy. Therefore, it is important to try to prepare for this session with the child. Sometimes, the calendar can be helpful to talk about the therapeutic progress with the child. In the example above, preparing for the review session with Ruth, the therapist reflected with her on her drawings to clarify the meaning of the changes in them. Ruth could see that she was learning to trust others and started to understand that if she could express what she felt to others around her, then she could get something from them in return. (The therapist noted to himself that this seemed to reflect an increase in trust, suggesting that Ruth would be able to continue to make use of other relationships to learn and grow, even if the therapy ended.) The therapist asked her if she was willing to share these insights with her foster carers and social worker at the review meeting the following week, and she agreed.

The review session often presents the challenge of discussing matters while safeguarding the child's confidentiality. This can prove especially challenging when there are cultural beliefs regarding the (lack of) rights of children to their own privacy. Discussions about this with parents present an opportunity to explore the idea that the child is an individual with their own thoughts and feelings and private internal world within the context of a specific cultural group (Gil & Drewes, 2005).

Preparing children for the review session and asking them what is okay and not okay to share is considered good practice and can help to build trust in the child that the therapist is considering things from their point of view. During this conversation with the child, it is important to acknowledge external reality—for example, by letting the child know if there has been any contact with the school and whether the teacher noticed any changes in the child's behavior.

In preparing for the review session with parents, they are usually asked what they have learned so far about themselves or about their child, serving as a way to help the parents verbalize and consolidate their developing understanding of the child. They are also asked what they think they might need in the near future to be able to hold on to the progress that has been made. Sometimes, the therapist may be concerned that parents will not come back, even if this is needed, because they have concerns about being weak or failing if they have to ask for further help. It is important to explore whether there are feelings like this and what they mean to the parents, as it is easier to end therapy when there is a reciprocal faith about letting each other go, knowing the therapist will be there when needed.

As part of the discussion with parents in preparation for the joint review meeting, it can also be helpful to ask what they think should be shared with their child from their own meetings and what would not be appropriate. For some parents, this question can be a useful way to think about things from the child's perspective, including what aspects of the parental situation may not be appropriate to share.

THE REVIEW MEETING

Mohammed, Age 7

Mohammed, his father (Mr. D), and his father's new partner (Ms. L) are present in the review session with their therapist. Mohammed looks anxious. Mr. D smiles at him in a reassuring way. He seems relaxed himself. Ms. L is sitting silently but smiling. The therapist starts the session by reflecting that Mr. D and Ms. L seems more relaxed and able to reassure Mohammed. Ms. L nods. When asked why she nodded, she tells the therapist that she is very happy with how things are going at the moment. She feels Mohammed and his father have got over everything that happened with the car accident and things are beginning to be normal again. When asked what she means by "normal," she laughs and says, "A fish is not aware of the water in which he swims unless it is taken away from him." Everyone laughs in the room because of the way Ms. L is expressing her thoughts. Mr. D explains they were not so used to talking about what they feel but that he has learned so much about doing that and it has helped him to be able to understand Mohammed better. Mohammed is asked if he sees things in the same way as Mr. D. does. Mohammed nods. He is asked about the focus statement: "Finding out what will help you to feel in control again." Mohammed says, "I am a fish, and I need water, and because of the accident, my bowl was broken—but I know now I need water to feel happy." The therapist laughs and says that she can see that this is a family of poets! Then, Mohammed, his father, and Ms. L talk together about what has been helpful in the therapy and how things have changed for the best. There seems to be a strong, shared view that the work of therapy is coming to an end.

The central aim of the review session is to provide an opportunity to discuss the question of the progress of the work to date and clarify the aims of the remaining part of the intervention. By the end of the review meeting, a decision will usually be made about whether they will be moving toward an ending, whether another set of 12 sessions is needed, or whether some other form of intervention is required—for example, parent–child therapy or family therapy. Going back to the goals that were set at the beginning of therapy helps to remind everyone where things were at the beginning of the work and whether each person feels that progress has been made (Law & Wolpert, 2014). In settings where other empirical measures of progress are used, these may also be consulted.

At the same time, the review session is a good opportunity to observe the parents' capacity to facilitate the child's participation and include the child while protecting them from information that may be hurtful or damaging to them. It is a good moment to reinforce the important role of parents in supporting the child's mentalizing capacities, keeping in mind where the child is at in the development of mentalization. For example, does the child need more support at home with attention control and emotion regulation, or is the child ready to practice explicit mentalization at home? The vignette above illustrates how the atmosphere in a session can reflect the changes that have taken place. A mentalizing stance from the therapist includes curiosity about all the different perspectives that people in the room may have. For some young children, it is difficult to express their view, since they have learned or have been instructed to listen to the grown-ups in the room. In this context, the way the child's contributions regarding the ending are allowed, considered, and thought about establishes the groundwork for any explicit mentalizing around issues of separation and loss. Furthermore, the ways in which the child and parents reacts to such a discussion in which the child's therapy is being discussed can provide further information regarding the parents' and child's current reflective capacity.

Opportunities offered by the review session in time-limited MBT-C include the chance to

- reevaluate initial therapeutic goals in the context of current functioning;
- explore the meaning of ending;
- provide an opportunity for the child and the parents to express their unique perspectives regarding the process of psychotherapy in a secure environment where multiple perspectives are encouraged and respected;

- increase the child's and the parents' sense of ownership over the process of therapy; and
- practice communication about problems in a constructive way together as a family.

In these review meetings, it is especially important to keep in mind that information about the process can be shared, but the content of the child's and the parents' therapy is confidential. Sometimes, talking with the child about an upcoming session with the parents can be an opportunity for reflecting together, thinking about what would be helpful for a parent to know about, from both the child's and the parents' perspective. The therapist can tell the child that the session is coming up and ask the child if there is anything in particular they would want the therapist to tell or show the parents. The decision to end or continue with the therapy depends on how quickly the problems diminish and goals are met, and if they are not, whether the child, family, and therapists consider that continuing therapy further can help to achieve these goals. Negotiating this decision is itself part of the work of promoting mentalizing, aiming to explore the situation from multiple perspectives, before making a final decision.

As part of the review process, it may also be important to check in with the school regarding the child's progress and bring this to the review meeting to be shared and reflected upon in the context of the question: How are we doing in here and outside? Parents and schools (and therapists) can sometimes measure the success of a therapeutic intervention in very different ways. It can be challenging at times to bring forward these different viewpoints and agendas, holding on to the value of what we have observed in therapy but without assuming that we have a more accurate view than anyone else. As therapists, we only see the changes taking place inside the therapy setting and may have less perspective on how this relates to the way the child is managing in other contexts. Thus, the review session helps the therapist to see things "from the outside," and the therapist can help the parents and external agencies to see things "from the inside." The review meeting is an opportunity to return to the coconstructed goals of treatment and to see how things have progressed—and to assess the capacity of the people around the child to support any gains that have been made. This meeting is another opportunity to reinforce a message about the importance of those around the child in helping them to generalize new ways of managing and responding to the emotional impact of life events.

THE LAST PHASE OF THERAPY

Belinda, Age 7

Belinda arrives at her therapist's office. The therapist is aware that there are only two more sessions before their goodbye. Belinda is looking around the room and seems quite solemn. Her therapist notices her facial expression and says something about it: "You seem a bit lost as to what to do in here today. Did I get that right?"

> Belinda smiles and replies, "I am going to miss playing with the sand tray. . . . And you." "I will miss you too, Belinda," her therapist responds. Belinda begins to draw and tells her therapist that she is beginning dance classes next month. She also talks about a playdate she has got set up for the following week. The therapist comments that it is sad to say goodbye, but it is happy to think about all the new things she will be doing now that she feels stronger inside.

Once a decision has been made to move toward ending therapy, we may hope to see a shift regarding the role of the therapy in the child's life. The child may gradually explore ways in which external life feels safer now and may speak of ways in which this takes over what will be the empty space left by the ending of therapy. For other children, deciding to hate both the therapy and the therapist and turning them into something useless and ineffective in their mind is a way to let go. All of these ways of managing the pain of separation and loss regarding ending therapy may not only reflect existing and remaining difficulties but also represent opportunities to face such experiences in the context of a planned ending.

In general, the last few sessions with both the parents and the child should potentially provide the opportunity for

- a developmental experience of a meaningful goodbye;
- an opportunity to explore experiences of loss in both the child and the parents' lives;
- a chance to explore issues of separation within the context of each person's family and larger culture; and
- an opportunity to think about gains and how to follow up and consolidate what has been learned in the context of treatment, with a particular focus on how the child and parents can make use of relationships in their daily life to support them.

Creating a narrative of the process of treatment with the parents, one in which the parents can witness themselves as agents of change for themselves and their child, can prove an extremely powerful motivation for further change and strength in the context of current and future contextual stressors. In the same way, creating a balanced (strengths and weaknesses) profile of the parents, their child, and their relationship communicates to the parents a belief that they can be the "experts" from now on.

In MBT-C, the therapist may actively introduce some activity with the child that helps to prepare for the ending. Some therapists might want to create a small box and place pictures and any other items the child and the therapist have created together and let the child take it home after the last session (*creating a container of experience*). Others may create a song or a funny story about their therapeutic journey together (*creating a common link*). We can speak about other times when the child has said goodbye and link them to the way they have felt (*creating an opportunity for revisiting*). Some therapists write an ending letter for the child, in which they share with them some of their own views on the work that has been done together. All of these can be important ways to mark the ending, although as therapists we need to be careful not to force a "good" ending, when sometimes the child may actually be feeling angry or hurt and need to express that in the way they leave (Blake, 2008). In such cases, the therapist may have to allow the child to end therapy without the kind of positive feelings that Belinda expresses in the vignette above.

For children who already have experienced multiple losses in their lives, this phase can prove extremely painful. The work of the therapist in these cases will include psycho-education with parents/caregivers in order to understand behaviors that may emerge in response to the ending of treatment. In this way, while working with school and home, we increase the chance that these children will continue to experience adults who are trying to support and understand their challenging or simply puzzling behaviors as communications of their pain and fear, and not necessarily seeing it simply as defiance or being oppositional.

For other children with more internalizing tendencies, as endings approach, we might observe a withdrawn style of interaction and a general tendency toward avoidance (Gil & Crenshaw, 2016). The challenge here is for the therapist to help these children explore and express their feelings regarding the ending. Many times, therapists find themselves with a wall of avoidance as the final session approaches. Suddenly, the symbolic play stops, and the child engages in mind-numbing activities. The therapist feels shut out in the relationship. Using those feelings to guide their ability to explore the child's experience proves invaluable.

In the final meetings with parents, it can be helpful to think with them about how they can balance their focus on their child and on themselves—for example, by thinking about what gives them the energy to hold on in very stressful lives. This can be asking for help in their own network, or when they need to have a break or some fresh air. It means talking about how to stay open in relationships within and outside the family and avoid harsh self-judgments and isolation. Sometimes, we can create a "first aid kit" in the form of a letter in which the therapist and parents write down together what they have found out about how to manage challenging situations. This can be helpful in understanding their difficulties in dealing with their child and knowing what the "banana peels" may be that they can expect to slip on. This helps to convey the message that problems and setbacks will inevitably continue to happen, but that the parents should hopefully have increased resources to cope with them.

AFTER THE END OF THERAPY: "BOOSTER SESSIONS"

John, Age 8

John's foster parents come back for a booster session 3 months after ending therapy. They enter the room with big smiles on their faces. The therapist comments on their relaxed appearance and asks them how things are going with them, John, and their family. Mrs. K answers that she is really happy. John is doing fine, and her worries about whether therapy was long enough are discussed. Earlier, she stopped working because of all the problems at home and is now thinking about applying for a new job. Mr. K is a man of little words, but he says, "I am really happy with our little chimpanzee in the house. I always wanted a son, and it really feels like he belongs with us now."

Once therapy has ended, we recommend offering *top-up or booster sessions* in MBT-C. This can be arranged in a number of ways, but the general aim is the same. Knowing that there is another meeting planned where the family and the therapists will see each other again to talk about progress, or to identify ongoing or new difficulties, can contribute to a continued feeling of being kept in mind. When the child or parents can ask themselves "I wonder what the therapists will say about this when we meet for the booster session?" this can help them to keep in mind what they have learned in therapy and to maintain a reflective and curious stance. It can also contribute to a sense of safety, thereby reducing stress and anxiety, or when things have deteriorated, it offers an opportunity to reconsider what kind of support the child and family may need.

One way of organizing this is to plan a booster/top-up session with a set date 3 to 12 months after the final therapy session. The appropriate length for the follow-up time depends on the needs of the family and the outcome of treatment and can be negotiated. When suspecting that you may need to plan for further clinical interventions, the follow-up time may need to be shorter (and sometimes even shorter than 3 months) compared with when working with families that do not report a lot of problems at the point at which therapy is ending.

An alternative approach to organizing the booster sessions, which leaves more responsibility with the family, is using the "voucher model." In this approach, the family is told that they have a certain number of "vouchers" (typically one to three) to use for booster sessions when needed. It is up to the child and family to decide when (or if) to use these, giving them greater freedom to reflect on what their needs are and to have more control over how they engage with services.

Which of these two models to use may be based not only on what is possible for the therapists (e.g., whether you be able to offer a booster session within a reasonable time if the family calls using the voucher model) but also on an assessment of the needs of the family. This is something that can be discussed with the family as the work is coming to an end, and models an open-minded and collaborative approach that characterizes MBT-C. With high-functioning families with the ability for self-observation and agency, the voucher model may be a good choice, since it stimulates agency, leaving the responsibility to them to decide when they need help. Thinking about when to use the vouchers can stimulate mentalizing as well as self-observation in the family. For families that are unlikely to use the vouchers when needed, or who need more continuity, it may be more suitable to plan a date for a review or booster session before ending.

Sometimes, it is most appropriate to have the entire booster session together with the child and the parents in the same room, or if two therapists have worked separately with the child and parents, they may want to have some time apart and then all come together. Especially for older children, it can help the family reflect together about their process and possible obstacles they have encountered. The therapist can use the calendar to look back on the therapy with the child and find out how things have been going for them since they last met.

When things have been difficult since the therapy ended, helping parents regain a mentalizing stance, as described in Chapter 9 in this volume, is an important aim of this session. Sometimes, parents come back to booster sessions with an urgent wish to resume treatment. One way of handling this is to schedule a few sessions for the parents initially not only to discuss the pros and cons of this but also to see if it is possible to help the parents get back on track independently before planning further interventions.

WHEN THERAPY ENDS UNEXPECTEDLY

There are many reasons why endings may sometimes be abrupt or unplanned, although one of the advantages of time-limited work is that it tends to reduce the level of premature termination. Nevertheless, there will be times when, for a range of reasons, therapy has to stop before the planned ending. That does not mean that these endings cannot still be opportunities to validate and empathize with a difficult external reality, which often renders therapist, the child, and the family feeling helpless and frustrated.

The most common reason why children stop attending therapy abruptly is because parents decide to stop bringing them. Parents may say this is because they feel that the therapy is not helpful (or that it is making things worse) or that it is too great a burden to bring the child. Sometimes, parents want to end treatment because they cannot take more time off from work, because other children in the family need their care, or for financial reasons. These concerns should always be taken seriously, and the reality of external circumstances recognized. In some cases, such concerns can offer an important opportunity to explore something that has gone wrong and to understand misunderstandings.

However, when faced with a family who has determined that they cannot come anymore, the therapist in MBT-C should attempt to manage some kind of planned ending—one that includes acknowledging the loss and saying goodbye. In this context, the goal is to have at least one session where the child is able to say goodbye and the parents are able to return without fear of retaliation and where they can experience that their wish to end the treatment is understood and respected. Such situations can be difficult, especially when the therapist may feel angry about the child's therapy ending or that the decision is a bad one. In these situations, the MBT-C therapist will try to acknowledge the external and the internal realities and help to verbalize other feelings associated with the process of saying goodbye. It can be useful to return to the original focus formulation and go over the gains and the areas where there is still vulnerability, and revisit what brought the family and the therapist together in the first place. In this way, the door can always stay open for further therapeutic support while honoring the fact that this phase of the work is ending.

Sometimes, a child does not want to continue with therapy because of a healthy desire to use the time to be at school or with friends or as a way of avoiding the discomfort and pain emerging from the sessions. It is difficult for therapists to know when a child's desire to leave treatment should be discouraged or followed. Because we work with the parents on a frequent basis, the therapist can discuss the question of a child wanting to stop in the review session. She can also tell the child she really wants to understand and explore their wish to stop therapy.

When a child is unable to commit to therapy but the problems are getting worse, it is also necessary to consider whether the child needs more intensive treatment or whether some other kind of approach needs to be considered. It might be appropriate to switch to another treatment modality with less frequency, for a different therapist to work with the child, or simply to focus on parent work for a while. Discussions around these options can also be a port of entry to invite parents to mentalize the reasons behind their child's opposition or refusal to attend psychotherapy.

CONCLUSION

One of the key features of any time-limited approach to therapy is a mindfulness of endings, from the very start of the work. In this chapter, we have tried to describe how the therapist in MBT-C can work with endings, not only throughout the therapy but also during the final phase of treatment. The process of ending is a time of consolidating therapeutic gains and internalizing the accomplishments in the context of saying goodbye (Novick & Novick, 2005). There is always more to do, but MBT-C aims to plant the seeds of curiosity and genuine empathy, providing enough source of "emotional oxygen" to both child and parents that they can face the pleasures and challenges of life beyond therapy with hope. We begin with a focus formulation, an invitation to coconstruct how everyone understands the reasons for the work and what they hope to get from it; we end by revisiting that starting point, reflecting on the gains and remaining challenges. In this way, we try to keep a mentalizing stance—one of curiosity and genuine flexibility until the end of the work.

11

A Case Study

In this chapter, we present an account of a 24-session treatment (two blocks of 12 sessions) with Lulu, a 6-year-old, adopted girl. We hope to illustrate the process of time-limited mentalization-based treatment for children (MBT-C) and to show how the mentalizing frame and stance of the MBT-C therapists allow for a process of emotional coregulation, feedback, and developmental restoration to take place. This case illustrates the work with the child and the parents, as well as some of the interactions between the two therapists and their peer supervision that contributed to their work with the family.

REFERRAL AND INTAKE INFORMATION

Lulu was adopted from China at two and a half years of age by a middle-aged couple from Europe with two older biological children. Both parents were White and cisgender. Mrs. and Mr. S contacted the clinic, motivated by their feelings of exhaustion and helplessness in parenting their two older children while, at the same time, adequately supporting their adopted child, who they felt tested them beyond their limits with her demands. During the first telephone contact with Mrs. S, she described Lulu as having frequent violent outbursts in which she seemed completely unreachable, followed by excessive clinging behavior toward her. Early in this conversation, Mrs. S began to cry, saying that she was at a loss as to how to manage Lulu.

Case examples are composites of real clients. Details have been changed to ensure patient confidentiality.

https://doi.org/10.1037/0000486-012
Mentalization-Based Treatment for Children: A Time-Limited Approach, Second Edition, by N. Midgley, K. Ensink, K. Lindqvist, N. Malberg, and N. Muller
Copyright © 2026 by the American Psychological Association. All rights reserved.

ASSESSMENT SESSION WITH THE FAMILY

The clinical team decided that two therapists would work collaboratively with the family: one with the parents and one with Lulu. This was because the problems of the child and family appeared to be complex, and working with two therapists offered the possibility not only of sharing different perspectives but also of sharing the responsibility and pressure that the initial referral suggested could be put on the shoulders of just one therapist. Following the initial meeting with the parents, both therapists invited the whole family for a joint assessment session. They had planned to begin by asking the family members to each introduce the person sitting next to them. This proved difficult to do, as the family immediately started to show some of the difficulties that had brought them to therapy by the way they interacted in the room, which led the therapists to realize that some flexibility was needed. The following is a description of the beginning of that initial meeting from the perspective of the therapist who would later work with the parents:

> What first caught my attention was how striking Lulu's special position in the family was, as she demanded her mother's constant attention by pulling at her and whining, not leaving room for anyone else. The session started with everyone choosing a place to sit and Lulu immediately demanding, "I want to sit next to mommy!" Both her sister (age 8) and her brother (age 9) also wanted to sit next to their mother, so what seemed like a common struggle ensued. When I curiously asked the mother what it was like for her to have all three children wanting to sit on her lap or close to her, she did not reply directly to me but explained to the other two children and me that Lulu had missed so many "mama hours." Because of that, she had to give Lulu more attention and that she expected the other children to understand this and be sweet about it. The mother seemed to be under so much pressure, she couldn't join me in any reflection around the situation. Lulu's siblings looked furious with her, and it seemed to me the situation was almost unbearable for them. I noticed their facial expressions and said that they looked angry and then checked if my impression was correct. They started to tell me immediately that it was always like this. Lulu always wanted mama, but she was their mommy as well! Mr. S explained that he tried to make up for this imbalance in the family by taking the oldest two children out to play outside or for special activities, but everyone seemed to feel alone, "on their own island." The older children seemed to agree.

In order to try and create some space for curiosity about each person's experience, the therapists talked with each other out loud during the session about how they experienced the atmosphere in the room. They especially noticed the interactions between the children as they struggled to listen to each other's different perspectives. Both Lulu and her older brother seemed highly distractible and restless, moving around and not being able to sit in their chairs. Noticing this, the parent therapist spoke to her colleague directly and wondered if it could be a good idea to shift the format of the session by engaging in something more active than the usual activity of choosing animals for the family members. The child therapist replied to her colleague by saying she had also noticed that the kids seemed to be having a hard time joining the interaction, and then checked with the family and asked whether they had noticed correctly? The children seemed intrigued, and the parents relieved. The child therapist then noticed that the children were looking at the drums in the corner of the room. She wondered whether they could try and do a music exercise together. The children responded enthusiastically, and the child therapist smiled and replied in a playful and inviting way: "Then let the music begin!" The children's curiosity and attention had been activated.

At this point, everyone got their own percussion instrument. Music exercises can be used to try to enhance attunement and to experience the difference between "me, you, and us together." The parent therapist played a rhythm, and everyone tried to join and imitate her. She tried to help the family harmonize by paying attention to each other and by taking turns in deciding the rhythm and direction of the music. She experimented with playing loud and soft, quick and slow. Then, someone in the family was asked to play a rhythm, and the others followed. How does one follow? How does one lead? Who is followed in the family? The therapists paid attention to whether different family members could play a rhythm that could be followed by the others or if they played something far too difficult. Could they think about what others are able to do or not? Were they able to mentalize each other at an implicit level by the way they engaged in this joint task?

What happened next surprised the mother and the children, as Mr. S took the lead and was very present in playing the basic rhythm. When talking about this afterwards, they explained to the therapists that this was a new experience for this family, as Mrs. S had the leading role almost all of the time. The children seemed to be having fun together. The atmosphere in the room changed, from one of hostility to one of cooperation and mutual regulation and attention. Lulu was able, in an age-appropriate manner, to show with her facial expression her concern about not daring to take the lead: When she was asked to play a rhythm, she said she didn't dare. The child therapist reflected on her age and how sometimes not being able to do the things her older siblings were able to do may feel frustrating. Lulu's siblings seemed to be able to listen to this and, when asked about it, gave examples of their own experiences when they were younger and felt frustrated or ashamed because they were not able to do things that others seemed to be able to do easily. During this exercise, the therapists were able to observe some of the strengths of this family, and they spoke openly about them. One noticed out loud how the older siblings seemed to, for a moment, see Lulu as an insecure little girl instead of a "monster," and how this seemed to have some impact on their interactions during the session. She continued, commenting that it seemed that Lulu's siblings were flexible, curious, and open to new ideas and behaviors. She observed that it was a good indicator of the way they had felt thought about and supported by their parents throughout development and was a potential protective factor for them and Lulu.

ASSESSMENT MEETINGS WITH THE PARENTS

During this first meeting, Lulu's parents told the therapist that they adopted Lulu out of their desire to give a home to a child in need, as they felt so blessed with their two biological children. They went on to describe how they were unprepared and overwhelmed by Lulu's extreme rivalry and jealousy toward her two siblings. They were distressed by her "hoarding" behavior and her tendency to steal things from her siblings as well as other children. They were concerned that Lulu had a negative self-image and was very isolated, with no friends in school or on the street where they lived. Furthermore, they described how she was often controlling and insensitive toward other children at school as well as her siblings, and this contributed to her becoming unpopular and being rejected by her peers and caused conflict with her siblings.

This meeting with the parents conveyed the frustration, helplessness, and loneliness they experienced in dealing with their 6-year-old daughter while also trying to take care of the needs of their other two children. The parent therapist sought to validate and normalize the parents' feelings by speaking of what she imagined was their desire for a happy family, as well as how their sadness and frustration with the current situation were understandable and common. She also shared her experience regarding the process of adaptation that adoptive parents commonly go through. In addition, the therapist tried to infuse some realistic hope by talking about the importance of the fact that Lulu was still young and developing and by focusing on some of the strengths of Lulu and her family, such as the parents' real interest and curiosity about Lulu's behavior and how her early experience might have influenced the way she was now.

The therapist had videotaped the family session, so at this point, she invited both parents to look at the first 5 minutes of it and share their thoughts and feelings about what had happened. She asked them to look at the faces of the children and invited them to comment on what they might have been feeling or thinking. The parents were able to reflect about what it meant for their two other children that Lulu got more "mama hours" and thought about how this might have impacted family dynamics. Mrs. S reflected on her reasons for feeling that she needed to be constantly available for Lulu. She commented that she had experienced the adoption as a huge and important responsibility to take on and how she desperately wanted to make Lulu happy in order to feel that the adoption was a success. However, at the same time, she felt very guilty for what she felt amounted, at times, to "borderline neglect" of her biological children, as she felt consumed by Lulu's emotional and other needs. Mr. S referred to Lulu as "the queen of the house," who completely controlled the family routines and schedule. Mrs. S concluded by saying that she felt exhausted, and Mr. S added that although he could see how demanding this was for his wife, he could not help feeling left out. When they felt overwhelmed by these feelings, it was difficult to reflect and mentalize. Despite this, when feeling supported and thought about by the therapist, they could begin to explore the needs and wishes behind their children's behaviors. At these moments, their capacity for explicit mentalizing was high. On one hand, they were able not only to reflect on the feelings of exclusion their biological children likely felt but also to accept the therapist's attempts to normalize the fact that sibling rivalry is common in most families. This opened the door toward an emerging balance between emotions and cognitions, and they started considering new possibilities and new ideas for ways of supporting the children that emerged in the conversation.

At the same time, both parents were able to reflect on Lulu's incapacity to accept the normal frustrations of having to share her parents with the two other children. Perhaps, the therapist said, Lulu feels like she isn't quite a full member of the family and therefore needs constant reassurance that this is her "forever family." Mr. and Mrs. S and both their biological children were White with blond hair, and all were very tall. The therapist wondered out loud if maybe the physical differences between Lulu and the other members of her family might increase her feeling of being different and not belonging. Mr. S at first said that he didn't like to focus on any differences between them, as they were all one family, but when the therapist acknowledged that this was important, Mr. S became thoughtful. He reflected on the possibility of Lulu having a feeling of being different not just at home but also at school where she, possibly, felt different both as an adopted child and as someone who also looked different from most of the other children in her class because of her ethnic background. Mrs. S responded spontaneously that Lulu's teacher mentioned to them that other children had asked Lulu why she doesn't look like her mom and that this had upset Lulu. The therapist invited the parents to think about ways in which the family could support Lulu in acknowledging the differences between them and, at the same time, look for ways to increase feelings of belonging and togetherness. This seemed to be a challenge for the whole family and something that they said they hadn't talked about much together.

Later on, Lulu's parents came back to the issue of Lulu's anger. Both the therapist and Lulu's parents tried to think of various different ways to understand this anger, which was often expressed in unexpected and inadequate ways. The aim was not to find the "real" meaning of her behavior but rather to introduce the idea that the same behavior (anger) could be understood in many different ways. In order to support their curiosity about Lulu's mental states, the therapist asked the parents about Lulu's early development and what they knew about her life before she came to live with them. Not much information had been given to the parents regarding Lulu's early life and family history when they adopted her. Mr. and Mrs. S were told that Lulu had been abandoned by her biological parents at a market and then taken to a private orphanage, where several children lived under the care of one woman. At the time of adoption, Lulu was overweight, which made Mr. and Mrs. S suspect that the children were given food as a source of comfort and in order to keep them quiet. In the early stages after the adoption, Lulu had severe aggressive outbursts, and she seemed to be unable to connect with other children. She also seemed unable to develop a normal eating pattern. This led the therapist to explore what had been similar or different in their experience of parenting their other children, as well as their own experiences of being parented as children.

It is often helpful to reflect on and think about the parents' own relational and cultural history. This can be an aid in assessing their reflective functioning, as well as an opportunity to explore how their own past relationships and socioeconomic and cultural upbringing influence how they cope with and respond to their children's behaviors. Lulu's father said that he was an only child, raised in a fairly rich family, and he reflected on how this could be linked to his difficulties managing the liveliness and conflicts of his now larger family, with three children always begging for attention. Mrs. S, on the other hand, had grown up in a larger, middle-class family with four siblings and therefore felt quite used to dealing with conflict and chaos. Mr. S even said that he got a feeling that there was a side of Mrs. S that thought that the chaos in their family was a normal state. Together, they could reflect on how their different backgrounds influenced their perspective on the current situation and also the way they understood and communicated with each other about it.

Regardless of all the frustration both parents felt, they exhibited a kind and generous demeanor when speaking of all their children, and Lulu in particular. They also showed a great deal of curiosity as well as a capacity to respond to the therapists' playful comments and invitations to reflect about themselves as parents. All of these characteristics helped the therapists to come up with a preliminary impression of these parents' reflective functioning as quite well developed. At the end of the assessment with the parents, the therapist asked them about their needs and what they wished the goals of the treatment to be. The parents expressed that they really wanted to focus on thinking of ways they could promote a healthier atmosphere between their three children and working toward feeling more unified as a family, where they could support their children to express themselves while respecting each other. They hoped that Lulu could feel safe and connected in the family with all the family members and could develop a narrative about who she was and how she came to be adopted. They realized that they hadn't wanted to think much about Lulu's Chinese cultural heritage, but they said that as she grew up, this was something they would need to think about more—and they hoped one day to visit China together so she could learn more about where she came from. They also expressed their hope that she could regulate her anger in a better way and normalize her eating pattern.

The therapists concluded this session by acknowledging how hard Lulu's parents were working to think about the different aspects of Lulu's development, and that they could use this space together to start thinking about some of these things, taking things one step at a time. As a starting point, the therapist encouraged Lulu's parents to introduce activities in which the three children could play and have fun together while supporting each other because joy increases attachment bonds. The aim was to help Lulu learn to feel connected in a positive way to her brother and sister, feeling safe enough to experiment and learn about how to ask for help and how to belong. The parents agreed that this would be a good first step, and they decided to buy a video game console with three controllers for the family for Christmas. They also decided to start going to the local bowling alley on Sundays and to begin to find out a bit more about the Chinese community in the city where they lived to see if there were some cultural activities that Lulu and the whole family could get involved with.

ASSESSMENT MEETINGS WITH LULU

The following is the therapist's description of the beginning of her first assessment session with Lulu:

> Lulu was not easy to establish rapport with. She was rejecting of any direct contact (verbal or nonverbal) with me at the beginning. She started the assessment by sitting in a corner with her back turned toward me. I wondered silently to myself if she was concerned for her safety—that I could turn out to be someone who could hurt or betray her. I decided to let her know that she could decide the pace, and I tried to invite her to look around the room. I was aware of the way I looked at her and moved around, not too actively but gently, showing patient curiosity. I played casually with some sand in my hand as I observed her explore the room quietly. I would name some of the things she was looking at and made some simple comments such as, "Hmm ... yes, those are my cars. Some are fast and some are slow." She began to look at me with a quick glance and smiled shyly.

The therapist noted that Lulu presented as hypervigilant and very restless, only touching the play materials but not engaging with them properly, much more so than would be expected for a child of her age. As a result, her ability to play seemed inhibited. However, she could recognize and name emotions when prompted, which suggested that some of the building blocks of mentalizing were in place. When presented with a chart with faces, she was able to identify and name most of the emotions, but she seemed unable to think of times and situations where she felt sad or angry and didn't seem aware of her own emotions as they emerged in interaction with the therapist in the session. For example, when the therapist asked her if she could give an example of things that made her sad or angry or think of a time when she felt these feelings, she couldn't, and even though she became quite angry with the therapist during some points in the session, it seemed as if she was entirely unaware of this. When the therapist asked about the change in her face and wondered whether she was maybe feeling a little angry, Lulu shrugged and rejected this idea, saying that she was not and, in a categorical and authoritative tone, that angry feelings were not a problem for her. During the assessment sessions, the therapist noticed that Lulu didn't seem to feel comfortable in her body: carrying her hand stiffly, always hungry and wanting to eat during the session, and presenting as very tense, especially when her sense of safety seemed threatened by the therapist's words or actions, which often seemed to be the case.

The therapist introduced the "family constellation exercise," where Lulu was asked to choose shells representing her family. Lulu chose three shells for her three mothers, explaining in a matter-of-fact way that she had a birthmother in China, a mother in China who looked after her in the orphanage, and her current mother in this country. The therapist asked her where she wanted to place each of these mother shells. She didn't know. Lulu wanted all three shells near to her shell. Meanwhile, the shells of the other two children in the family had to lie in a corner of the room. She didn't want to share the table with them. She chose only one "father shell," representing her adoptive father. When asked to say something about how it felt to make this story, she looked at the therapist without answering, as if the question wasn't meant for her or did not make sense for her.

Lulu struggled to settle on playing with anything in particular, repeatedly wanting to go out of the room and run in the corridor. It seemed that rather than being hyperaroused and reactive to external stimuli, Lulu was driven more by an inner sense of unease that was probably amplified rather than contained by being in the room with a person she had not yet established a relationship of trust with. The therapist, after reflecting on the context, decided to focus first on the fact that being with someone whom she did not know might be stressful. The therapist said that she thought Lulu was showing her how difficult it was for her to be in the room, in the clinic, with someone she did not know or trust. Lulu liked to draw, and this had a regulating effect on her. Lulu made a drawing of a beautiful flower, still under the ground, saying that it was the national flower of her adoptive country. After this, Lulu drew an airplane. The therapist casually commented on the pictures, saying it seemed like the little flower was still underground, waiting to become a beautiful flower after flying to this new place in a plane. This was the first moment Lulu could express in a symbolic way something about her inner world, and it appeared to be the starting point of her narrative about herself. It also seemed important that the flower was a symbol of her adoptive country, suggesting a wish to feel that she "belonged" in this country. However, she ignored the therapist completely while drawing and didn't seem to hear her comments about the little flower still being underground.

SHARING THE ASSESSMENT AND DEVELOPING A FOCUS FORMULATION

Based on her individual meetings and a range of other standardized assessment procedures and questionnaires, it appeared that Lulu met many of the criteria for reactive attachment disorder. She also had symptoms of attention-deficit/hyperactivity disorder, and the child therapist discussed with her colleagues whether these symptoms could be part of the attachment problems or might be influenced neurologically by aspects unknown to the adoptive parents, such as fetal alcohol syndrome. The child therapist considered how the duration and severity of the traumatic losses in her life might be playing a role in the current problems. The fact that Lulu exhibited a growing attachment toward her adoptive parents (especially in wanting to cuddle, looking for affection, and asking for comfort from Mrs. S when she was upset), rather than looking for affection from others indiscriminately, seemed to be evidence of her resilience. It seemed that she could potentially make use of an MBT-C intervention, even if the focus was likely to be on helping her to establish some of the building blocks of mentalizing rather than on the use of explicit mentalizing per se. The parents showed increasing insight in the family dynamics after only three assessment sessions, giving the clinical team the impression that it was likely that they would also profit from further MBT-treatment. During the feedback session, both therapists spoke to Lulu and her parents about time-limited MBT-C. They provided the family with a general explanation of MBT-C and the rationale behind it, as well as how they felt this approach related to their family and specifically to Lulu's needs. The family accepted, and after establishing a basic social contract around the structure of treatment (day, time, frequency), the idea of a focus formulation was introduced as the first step in the process of intervention itself.

When trying to look for a focus formulation with Lulu and her parents, Lulu still did not say much. She gave the impression that she most of all wanted to be left alone, and she still didn't express any hopes or wishes of getting any help. It occurred to the therapist that this seemed to be a common relational pattern for her where she pulled back and retreated from relationships rather than sharing her feelings, wishes, or ideas, perhaps because she had little experience of doing so. Based on Lulu's behavior during the assessment, the child therapist had formulated an impression that Lulu thought of the world as unsafe, and she had little sense that adults could be trusted or attuned to her or that they might be willing to see and hear her. In response to her passivity, it seemed to the therapist, adults tried to take control in order to support her, but Lulu interpreted this as them not acknowledging her wishes and needs, strengthening her belief that adults were not interested in what she thought or felt. The therapist and the parents had thought together about an appropriate focus formulation for Lulu's therapy. Together, they came up with the image of a caterpillar changing into a beautiful butterfly.

Lulu's parents were very pleased with the drawing of the flower when they saw it and commented that Lulu too was like a beautiful little flower. Lulu responded by angrily saying that she wasn't a flower at all! It seemed as if she felt mocked and could not trust that her parents were genuinely complimenting her, seeing her this way and loving her in spite of her "thorny parts." The parents responded to this in a playful but serious way, saying that maybe Lulu was a caterpillar, always wanting to eat, often wrapped up in her own cocoon of anger, fear, or sadness, not being able to make contact with them when she needed them most—but that they thought that there was a wonderful colorful butterfly inside of her. They also expressed their hope that the therapy could help her to become this beautiful butterfly, who could learn how to handle her big angry feelings and practice playing with others and feeling more connected, not having to stay inside the cocoon. Lulu listened with great attention. There was a feeling of confidence and openness between the parents, Lulu, and the therapist. The therapist experienced this as both helpful and hopeful. The parents explained to Lulu that they also needed to learn more about how to be good parents for all their children. The parents and the therapist proposed together that the focus formulation for the therapy could be "Caterpillar on a journey." Lulu was okay with this and even offered a shy smile.

THE BEGINNING PHASE

Work With Lulu

During the first MBT-C session, the therapist and Lulu started by creating something that was linked to the agreed-upon focus formulation as a way of further establishing the focus and increasing ownership over it for Lulu. Together, they made a clay caterpillar. While working with the clay, Lulu made angry faces. The therapist observed Lulu's body language, facial expression, and moments of greater tension, trying to get a better understanding of this nonverbal communication. The therapist mentioned in a casual and playful way that she noticed how Lulu was really good at following her instructions when working with the clay, but that she was not sure that Lulu was really enjoying it, and that Lulu's body and face seemed to be saying that. She checked with Lulu if she was getting it right, but Lulu ignored her, seemingly disconnected from both the therapist and herself. Toward the end of the first session, Lulu suddenly took a stuffed monkey, smashed it against the wall and said with a different tone of voice, "You have to die!" She looked at the therapist in a challenging way as if asking, "What do you have to say about this?" The therapist got the sense that this was the first instance of a genuine feeling and action coming from Lulu. She said, "Monkey, I have no idea what you have done, but it seems to me that Lulu does not like you and wants you to disappear or die." Then, shifting her attention to Lulu, she said, "I sure would like to understand why you have such big feelings and want Monkey to die!" Lulu's body and face relaxed for the first time, as if the therapist had managed to make contact with her (possibly by speaking about the feelings a toy may have) followed by a direct inquisitive acknowledgment of the emotional experience Lulu was expressing, said in a nonjudgmental, curious tone of voice.

Following this session, the therapist decided to work with Lulu more physically, trying to give her space to follow her impulses and express herself in a physical way, allowing her to feel free to express her "big feelings." It felt as if a more physical focus could help Lulu to develop the building blocks of mentalizing, such as joint attention and a level of affect regulation. So, the therapist set up a special corner in the playroom with mattresses, pillows, curtains, kangaroo balls, boxing material, and other resources, inviting both motoric and sensory exploration. Lulu engaged with these materials enthusiastically but constantly tested the boundaries in the room—her own and those of the therapist. For example, one rule in the playroom was that they were not allowed to walk in that corner with their shoes on, but Lulu completely refused to take off her shoes during the beginning phase. Furthermore, she started each session by climbing up a big pile of mattresses, trying to sit on top or glide away or in between them. The therapist found herself put in the position of reminding Lulu constantly that she had to keep her safe in the room and that Lulu therefore needed to come down from the pile. When observing Lulu, it seemed like she didn't care about herself with her reckless and accident-prone behavior. She often wanted to run out of the room, as she had tried before, and the therapist firmly reminded her that they had agreed on staying in the room during their session time. When in session with Lulu, the therapist tried to name what she thought was Lulu's longing to test her physical boundaries, as if she tried to find out "this is me." The capacity of the therapist to keep Lulu safe was also tested, as she struggled to simultaneously keep Lulu in mind while not taking over the activity.

During team supervision, the therapist "marked the task" as reflecting on how she could balance keeping Lulu safe in the room without turning into a policeman. The supervisory team were curious about the therapist's own feelings when this was happening, and she shared her annoyance and frustration regarding this matter and reported feeling drawn toward coercive behavioral strategies to stop the defiant adventures of her patient. As she spoke, the therapist realized how difficult it was to keep mentalizing herself while being challenged all the time. She felt, at times, both annoyed and anxious about Lulu's behavior. The therapeutic team then invited the therapist to imagine Lulu's experience. What could she be saying or asking with her behavior? The therapist thought Lulu's question in the relationship with her was something like "What do you do when I am in danger? Do you look after me? Do you care about me at all?" The MBT-C team reflected on the sense that Lulu was operating at a prementalizing level, looking for constant evidence from the therapist that she could keep her safe, would respond predictably, and had the capacity to survive her attempts for destruction. It was not difficult to understand how the therapist felt drawn into the same behavioral rather than mentalizing stance, wanting to take physical action. In "returning to task," the therapist reflected that it probably was important for Lulu to see that her therapist would actively intervene to keep her safe but that she needed to keep in mind that Lulu was probably operating in a prementalizing mode because of her levels of anxiety and relational distrust, and that keeping this in mind would help her as a therapist to manage the demands Lulu put on her better.

During the sessions during this midphase of the therapy, Lulu and her therapist were trying to create a place where they could be together, where it felt safe enough to experiment and where Lulu was in control but aware that she was looked after and kept safe, and that she could begin to build trust in the therapist as someone who was interested not only in how she behaved but also in what was going on inside of her. Lulu's therapist would closely follow her in her movements while reflecting out loud on her own experience of Lulu's behavior. For example, she spoke about how she felt very afraid of Lulu falling, and she wondered what it was like for Lulu when she took these physical risks. Increasingly when the therapist made these comments, Lulu would stop her play and listen. She became more present, and this was evident in her body posture, level of activity, and willingness to meet her therapist "half way." Often, her therapist would verbally track the sequence of events in the session and reflect on her own increased anxiety or capacity to feel more relaxed in relation to Lulu's behaviors and responses. It seemed that Lulu was feeling helped, and increased feelings of agency and positive self-image were starting to emerge. The therapist got the sense that Lulu started feeling and knowing "I am Lulu. I have a body with muscles. I can influence the situation, my feelings are important, I am worth noticing and getting attention, my behavior has an effect on others."

In the following sessions, Lulu repeatedly killed the stuffed monkey in different ways—slapping him, riding over him with a huge Kangaroo ball, screaming and saying he had to die. Her therapist observed and commented on what was going on, simply narrating and accepting Lulu's anger. The therapist thought that this allowed Lulu to experience herself as a physical agent, expressing anger and destructiveness toward the monkey in a safe and contained environment with the supportive presence of the therapist. She tried to help Lulu by narrating what she observed, linking it to what she thought might be going on inside her; it seemed very important to Lulu that she could use her whole body to destroy the monkey. It was as if she was expressing a profound rage that inhabited her. The therapist thought that what seemed most important was for her to be able to express this in a relationship, as well as have the experience that it could be tolerated and not reacted to as if it was real in the same way as if she was actually murdering the monkey but instead tolerated as an expression of her internal reality and drama and that it was okay to pretend to the kill the toy monkey and express her psychic reality in this way.

The therapist tried to remain nonjudgmental about Lulu playing out such a murderous scene. However, after reading a book by Xinran (2011) about what happened to Chinese girls during the time of the one-child policy in China, the therapist thought of this play in a new light. In this book, Xinran explains that many Chinese girls were, in fact, murdered, and many adoptive Chinese baby girls had been rescued from this situation because boys were more wanted in Chinese families. The therapist, who at the time was working with several girls adopted from China, had noticed that several of these children often had nightmares or acted out in play sessions the experience of being murdered, even by their own family. Knowing that even babies can have these experiences stored in their body and memory made this play of Lulu even more meaningful. There seemed to be an implicit "knowing," a wordless memory, reinforcing her sense of "being" and of "being with the other," which was felt in the relationship. Although the therapist did not know what Lulu's early experiences had been, being mindful of this historical and cultural context helped the therapist to be present in the moment, empathic on a deeper level, and to help Lulu express her feelings in her actions against the monkey. Although these thoughts were in the therapist's mind, she did not say anything directly to Lulu about the possible circumstances in which she was born.

Lulu's violent games continued for some while. At times, the therapist validated the physical strength of Lulu; at other times, she took on the role of the toy monkey, trying to express what she thought its feelings were: "Aw, this hurts, wow I can feel the pain, I am afraid, she is trying to destroy me. She wants me to die, I don't understand why." In this way, the therapist attempted to help Lulu develop a self-image rooted in her body and, at the same time, label the emotions she thought the monkey would have. This was to help Lulu find the words and create representations of her emotions as she understood Lulu's play. Lulu ignored this. The therapist then changed her tone and tried to match Lulu's affective tone of excitement by mirroring her expression as if the therapist was the television reporter of an important match, expressing aahs and oohs: "Yes, what a power you have. You are so strong." The therapist was trying to establish an environment of mutual regulation and emotional feedback to promote mutuality, a sense of weness, while encouraging agency. She attempted this by trying to mirror Lulu's play in a marked and contingent way and by sharing her reactions in a direct manner using words but also her nonverbal communications in the here and now. All these can be thought about as the building blocks for the development of more explicit mentalizing capacities.

Working with children who express aggression often impacts on the therapist's own mentalizing capacity. Peer supervision is extremely helpful in this context. This was certainly the case for Lulu's therapist, who, in meetings with her team, expressed how anxious she felt witnessing Lulu's aggression in killing the monkey. At times, she said, she had difficulties thinking and staying in the here and now in the therapy room, as she felt concerned that she was not doing enough for Lulu and her family. The parent therapist then shared with the team that Lulu's parents were reporting an improvement in Lulu's capacity to contain her aggression at home and school. This indication that they were on track seemed to help the child therapist to restore faith in the therapeutic process, helping her to stay present and think when confronted with Lulu's aggressive behaviors. In addition, the therapist had the impression that Lulu was playing out something around the experience of rejection and the hatred that she felt for this scared and distressed part of herself, and that this was not simply a repetitive expression of a cruel and sadistic part of herself.

After about five sessions, Lulu took the monkey and laid him down with her own teddy, putting a little blanket on top of them. The therapist asked the teddy, "What happened? Lulu is so gentle and careful today?" Lulu picked up on the therapist's question and answered with a dark teddy voice: "Yes, I told her that maybe the monkey is a bit tired today, and so am I, so we need a day off." The therapist thanked the teddy for explaining and asked the teddy how it could tell it was tired. Lulu answered, "No idea." She then wanted to lift the foam rubber blocks and asked the therapist to time how many seconds it took her to move the blocks from one side of the room to the other. The therapist felt there was more contact between her and Lulu and was happy with this tiny conversation with the teddy and Lulu displaying some playfulness in her voice while answering as the teddy. Lulu now seemed to tolerate the therapist looking at her, answering simple questions, and she even asked her to be part of her play by timing the activity. The therapist continued to work on this new joint focus of attention by giving words to what she observed Lulu doing and, where possible, checking what she thought and asking for clarification and encouraging elaboration. She responded positively when Lulu displayed efforts to establish boundaries, both mentally and physically, between her and the therapist by making nonjudgmental comments. In this way, the therapist tried to help Lulu focus her attention on her physical experiences as part of improving embodied mentalizing and help her to be more attentive toward what was happening inside her: "Your face turned red . . . . What do you think is happening to you? This exercise seems to make you warm. You are out of breath, do you notice that? You are very quick and strong!" The therapist tried to validate her ideas and enjoy them with her.

The therapist was surprised by Lulu's attempts to test her strength despite her small frame. In peer supervision, she told her colleagues about how Lulu was moving the blocks, and her search for the meaning of this play. A colleague shared an association she had, which was that it seemed as if Lulu was moving her two worlds—her homeland and her adoptive one—in a superfast way. Hearing the different perspectives of colleagues helped the therapist to try to keep mentalizing about what might have happened in the sessions, knowing these associations, interpretations, or hypotheses could help in trying to better understand Lulu's actions when she herself so often lacked words to describe her experiences. The implicit and explicit mentalizing of the therapist in and after the sessions seemed to have a huge impact on the therapeutic process with Lulu.

During this phase of the therapy, there was a focus on Lulu's sense of self and self-agency, with an emphasis on connecting her inner and outer worlds, her body and mind. There was also a shift in opening up to another person and trying to connect and meet with "another mind." Lulu responded positively to this and seemed to begin to enjoy contact with the therapist more and more, moving away from simply engaging in a repetitive physical activity where she moved blocks from one side of the room to another, which seemed to have a self-soothing and protective function. She reacted to the therapist's encouragement and seemed pleased by her enthusiasm about her physical strength. After exercising, her therapist encouraged her to stop and relax, beginning to introduce a focus on affect regulation. One exercise that really relaxed Lulu was blowing bubbles—an activity that the therapist introduced in order to help Lulu become able to regulate her breathing and focus on something that made her feel calm. Being able to create the beautiful bubbles and watch them float away seemed to give Lulu a sense of calmness and control that she seldom felt. The therapist commented on the bubble-blowing feeling and said that Lulu looked as if she was able to deal with anything. She marked the feeling by mirroring Lulu's calm, in control, and slightly blissful look, as she felt that Lulu needed some mirroring of herself in this positive state. Working on the calendar at the end of the session also had a regulating effect on Lulu.

At this point, the monkey was no longer thrown away at the end of each session. Instead, Lulu put him in a corner, sitting with the other teddy bears, and told him she would be back next time. These comments made the therapist think that Lulu was developing a sense of herself and her relationship with the therapist as something that would endure over time. She now trusted that they would meet again and that the relationship would endure the time away from each other. At the same time, it seemed as if she was now taking on a more caring role in relation to the rejected teddy part of self that she previously seemed to have such hateful feelings toward.

At the beginning of therapy, the therapist felt that Lulu had very little sense of continuity and predictability, and therefore used the calendar as a help with this, talking to Lulu about how they were going to meet next week and how many sessions they had left, as well as looking back at previous sessions while Lulu was filling in the calendar. After initially seeming quite uninterested in these conversations, as time passed, Lulu started taking more interest when the therapist talked about this, and after a while, she would make comments on previous and coming sessions as well. Then, Lulu began to take the initiative by playing games she had seen on TV. One of her favorites was a quiz for children, where they had to answer questions to test their knowledge while hanging on a climbing wall, testing their physical endurance at the same time. Lulu explained that she loved this quiz and hoped one day to be in it. The therapist asked her what made her like it so much, and Lulu answered that she wanted to be "strong in her head and in her arms." This was new, as she was articulating and communicating something about herself and what she wanted. In addition, this was the first time she made any attempt to connect the world in the therapy room with the outside world. She continued to challenge herself physically, asking the therapist to count how many seconds she could hang on the door frame. Lulu pushed beyond her physical limits: Her muscles trembled and her hands were red and looked in pain, but as usual, she did not really seem connected with her physical sensations or willing to use them to guide her actions. The prevalence of avoidance strategies in developmental trauma makes it necessary to actively look at what is not talked about or played out in therapy. The child might have learned to survive by becoming unaware of connections between their body and their mind. So, the therapist validated her longing, spoke about how she seemed to need to feel strong and in control and focused on her urge to go far. After playing like this for a few sessions, it seemed as if Lulu was able to connect her bodily sensations, feelings, and expressions a little bit more, stopping earlier when feeling her arms starting to tremble but still expressing how strong she was with a certain sense of pride.

Work With Lulu's Parents

During the treatment, the parent therapist worked in parallel with Lulu's parents. She started by explaining how the therapy with Lulu would be working and explored their thoughts and feelings regarding the process of the individual therapy. Lulu's mother expressed her concerns regarding Lulu's delight in provoking the cats at home by trying to squeeze them or pull their tails, and wondered if this was an early sign that Lulu lacked empathy and the capacity to care for others. Lulu had told her mom about the killing of the monkey in the therapy, and Mrs. S expressed serious worry that Lulu hadn't developed a conscience. She felt anxious and believed she was failing as a mother, or that Lulu's "damage" was so deep that nothing they could do would "fix" it. Lulu's father, on the other hand, reported that he found Lulu less aggressive at home since the therapy started. He reflected on the possibility that the start of her life may have been painful or that she might have experienced aggression in the orphanage, but that she now was feeling safe to express these feelings in the treatment. The fact that they didn't know much about the first period of Lulu's life was very frustrating for both parents. The therapist tried to help the them reflect on what Lulu was trying to communicate with her behavior. They started to think together about this implicit information, and both parents started to consider other possible explanations for the things that Lulu sometimes did or said. Furthermore, the therapist explained about disorganized attachment, which was helpful for both parents, as it helped them to feel that some of their daughter's behavior had a sense to it, even if it felt, at times, as if it was nonsensical. Mr. and Mrs. S were asked to observe and try to notice shifts in their behavior and also to try to do the same for Lulu. Where possible, they were also encouraged to help give words to some of the feelings that Lulu might be experiencing at home—but doing so in a tentative way that did not assume they knew for sure what Lulu was feeling. The therapist thought this might help Lulu in developing her capacity to recognize feelings in herself and others, finding words for inner experiences while also seeing that her parents respected that her mind and experiences were separate from theirs.

Later in the therapy, as a result of Lulu's newfound interest in physical expression, her parents enrolled her in badminton at school, and she seemed to have a talent for this. Lulu's parents commented that they had been watching the Olympics on TV with Lulu, and Lula had got excited by the Chinese women's team, who had won the gold medal. They felt that perhaps this might be a way to help her feel proud of her cultural roots. Parallel to this, the therapist had asked both parents to keep a mentalizing log, which resulted in them realizing that Lulu's outbursts often occurred when Mrs. S wasn't home. This made the therapist and parents reflect together on the interactions between Mr. S and Lulu. Mr. S felt that he had difficulties showing his love for Lulu, since she appeared to be so clear about preferring Mrs. S, and this made him feel redundant and insecure. The therapist invited both parents to consider whether there might be other reasons Lulu behaved like this, and this led them to wonder whether Lulu had ever experienced two adults caring for her together, or what experience she had had of male caregivers. This led Mr. S to consider whether his relationship with Lulu was perhaps more important than he had realized. When asked about what he liked about Lulu, he had a hard time coming up with something, and this shocked him. The therapist asked him to think of something he had liked doing himself with his parents when he was young. He remembered that he loved to visit soccer games with his father and decided to take Lulu alone to the next match, as he sometimes did with the other children.

During this phase of the MBT-C intervention, the therapist also contacted Lulu's school, realizing it could be helpful to work with the wider network. Lulu's teacher had questions about how she could stay better attuned to Lulu. The therapist gave some psycho-education about attachment disorders and how these might lead to behavior and interactional problems at school. The therapist also addressed the topic about Lulu "looking different" from other children in the class (where there was not a lot of ethnic diversity) and asked about the comments made by some of the children in class about why Lulu didn't look like her mother, curious how the school and teacher were responding to this. The teacher admitted that this wasn't a topic she felt comfortable speaking about with the class, as she wanted all of the children to be "equal." The therapist asked if it would be okay for Lulu to be "equal" to the other children in the class without being "the same"? The teacher agreed that this would be helpful, and the two of them began to think about how she could approach situations differently when they came up again in future. Specifically, the therapist encouraged Lulu's teacher to pay more attention to her own reactions to Lulu, as well as helping Lulu to express more about her feelings by being curious and presenting her with tentative explanations and helping her to notice and become curious about the feelings of others. The teacher and therapist agreed to stay in touch, mostly by email, establishing, in this way, an environment of collaboration in which the valuable roles of both teacher and therapist were acknowledged.

REVIEW SESSION

During the review session, which took place after eight sessions, Lulu said that she liked attending therapy and expressed her wish to continue. Both parents were surprised to hear Lulu stating her feelings as clearly as this. Although there had not been a great deal of change in the rating of the behavior checklist that had first been used when Lulu started therapy, her parents said that they noticed Lulu being more at ease at home and less angry. They also felt that they had made some progress in their own goal of creating a healthier atmosphere between their three children and commented that their other two children were no longer feeling as if Lulu took up all of their parents' attention. The parent therapist asked what they thought their other children might have said had they been there. Mrs. S said that she thought they would agree that their parents were being more careful about not making them feel Lulu got all the attention, and that this had actually improved their relationship with their adoptive sister. Mr. S reflected that the siblings may experience it in different ways, reflecting on the perspectives of each one of them. The parent therapist noted how carefully they were thinking about the experience of each of their children, and then wondered what other people who knew them might say about how Lulu was doing. Mrs. S said that the school had told them that she was not trying to eat all the time as she had done before, and that she seemed a bit more relaxed, even if she had not yet managed to make any close friends and could still be quite a handful in class. The child therapist asked Lulu about school, and she said that she didn't like it when she had to sit outside the classroom on her own for a time-out.

Having spent some time reviewing how things were, both the therapists and Mr. and Mrs. S felt that Lulu needed to consolidate her new strengths, as they were not yet sure that Lulu was able to generalize what she was learning in therapy and use it to make good use of other key relationships (e.g., with teachers and peers). Lulu had limited epistemic trust, something the therapist had thought about from the start of the treatment when considering whether a single block of 12 sessions would be sufficient. At the end of the meeting, there was therefore a mutual decision to go on for another 12 sessions after the first block of 12 sessions came to an end.

THE MIDDLE PHASE

After this first period, Lulu started to engage more in pretend play. She had a fantasy where she was a queen of "the other world" and she and her teddy bear could not feel any pain. Up until then, she had been very much in a teleological or psychic equivalence mode, where her feelings could become "too real" and overwhelming. However, she started to experiment, first in a controlling way, telling the therapist exactly what to do. Gradually, she began to accept the therapist's invitations to "be together," where she tried to stay in contact with Lulu in the play, following her lead while retaining her own boundaries regarding safety, wondering, often out loud, about what Lulu and she herself were experiencing in their bodies—what each of them might be feeling and thinking.

The therapist felt Lulu remained quite rigidly stuck in either fantasy or reality, with no evidence of age-appropriate flexibility. For example, she started to make a throne using rubber blocks, wanting to be the queen far above everyone and in control. This was somewhat hazardous and Lulu repeatedly nearly fell from her throne of blocks, testing the attentiveness of the therapist. Lulu seemed to be playing out her own game, with the therapist only allowed to be a spectator. She rejected or ignored any attempts of the therapist to engage in the play and did not respond to suggestions or questions from her. She seemed unable to accommodate the perspective of others in her play and showed very limited explicit mentalizing, especially for considering the thoughts and feelings of the other. However, Lulu was also beginning to express her own feelings in a more contained fashion with the support of her therapist, who tried to provide a safe context. Gradually, play started becoming more reciprocal, which allowed the therapist to find a balance between keeping it challenging and playful at the same time.

A few sessions later, Lulu's play took a turn, as she decided she wanted to take the queen's role and wanted the therapist to play a baby lying on the ground with a nappy on. She said that she wanted to "dump" the baby. When the therapist asked her what "dumping" meant, Lulu shrugged her shoulders and ran around repeating the word over and over again in a loud tone. The therapist named the fact that Lulu's feelings had suddenly gotten big, and she wondered what had happened. She asked her if they could stop and think together for a minute. Guided by her awareness of how difficult it is to think when you are in a high level of emotional and bodily arousal, the therapist didn't try to immediately review what had happened. Instead, she invited Lulu to follow her in "pretending to blow bubbles," a variation on really blowing bubbles that had relaxed Lulu in earlier sessions but now operating at a more symbolic level. This calmed Lulu down a bit, and when she was calmer, Lulu wanted to reengage in pretend play with the therapist. In the story, the therapist was lying on the ground being a baby with a nappy on getting "dumped." Lulu tried to cover the therapist with several blankets, roll balls over her, and put the foam rubber blocks around her, hitting her with a soft ball. However, Lulu's level of regulation had improved and so had her capacity to stay in contact with the therapist. She could now accept the therapist's limits when she said that she did not want Lulu to roll the Kangaroo ball over her head. The therapist tried to keep talking to Lulu with different tones of voices: a voice of the baby being dumped, a voice of herself as the therapist setting limits, a voice of the therapist empathically subtitling what Lulu seemed to be doing. Considering Lulu's tendency to be overwhelmed by fantasy or play, slipping into the prementalizing mode of psychic equivalence, the therapist thought of this as a way of further helping Lulu to stay in the play by marking what was fantasy and reality in a concrete way with different voices. At the same time, the therapist had to contain her own emotions because the play made her feel anxious and deeply sad.

When making notes about the session after Lulu had gone, the child therapist noted how this session literally took her breath away. She felt Lulu's fierceness and power in wanting to harm the baby, and imagined that she was, in part, expressing her hatred of this abandoned part of her. Writing this down helped her to mentalize Lulu's experience of feeling "dumped" as an abandoned child, and she understood this as a way for Lulu to actively manage the narrative of her early life and feel in control of it by being the one dumping the baby. She thought that it might be important for her to share this with the parent therapist, as she might want to let the parents know that Lulu was now actively exploring her own experience of being adopted, and invite them to pay attention to whether there were any differences in how she was at home. She felt that sharing with the parents her thoughts and feelings about the process of the child therapy could be very helpful, although she was careful not to go into too much detail about what had been said or done, so as to respect Lulu's privacy and right to confidentiality.

In the next session, Lulu seemed reluctant to talk about what had happened the previous week. Guided by her awareness that it might help Lulu to make the implicit more explicit and to construct a coherent narrative, the therapist decided to draw a little book trying to make up a story about "a little caterpillar on a journey," arriving in an upside down world full of monkeys and meeting a queen who was very strong and fierce. She had made some drawings that could be finished together with Lulu, trying to make it a book of them together. The therapist had put all her creativity into the little book, feeling that she wanted to give Lulu the best she had, motivated by the strong feelings she had felt in her role as the dumped baby and thinking how this was probably a taste of the rejection and sadness that Lulu herself might have felt as a baby. This was so intense that the therapist found herself powerfully hoping that the therapy could help Lulu to feel seen and mentalized and that it would help her to overcome her destructive feelings and finally be able to mourn.

The therapist presented the book to Lulu, who refused to even look beyond the first page. Instead, Lulu became very dysregulated, running around the room and trying to escape out into the corridor. She screamed, "I hate caterpillars! I hate your book and I hate you!" and she began to kick and push the therapist, who struggled to continue mentalizing, not understanding this strong reaction of Lulu, while feeling under physical attack by this very angry little girl. The therapist lowered her body, took Lulu's hands and said she could tell she had made a serious mistake, thereby taking responsibility, even if she did not yet understand quite what she had done wrong. Lulu did not seem to respond much to what the therapist said, but the body posture and calm voice of the therapist seemed to have a calming effect on her. The therapist reflected to herself that Lulu needed help with very basic self-regulation before they could think together about what had happened. She tried to remain calm and signaled to Lulu with her hands and her tone of voice that they needed to simmer down. She told Lulu it was okay to be angry but that, at the same time, she wanted it to be safe for her and for the therapist.

The therapist was taken by surprise when, all of a sudden, Lulu collapsed on the cushions in the room and began to cry. The therapist kept talking to her with a soothing, low voice, trying to keep in contact with her. Then, Lulu suddenly stood up, took a pin from the bulletin board, and stabbed herself, saying, "Bad Lulu!" Her therapist stopped her and reminded her that she would always keep her safe, but that she could see she felt something inside and was looking for ways to communicate what she felt. In the moment, it was difficult for the therapist to make sense of what had happened, but she understood this as Lulu regressing to a teleological mode, where only an action (stabbing herself) could be used to manage strong feeling states. However, at this point, the priority was to help Lulu become less dysregulated. So, the therapist simply spoke to her in a soothing, empathic way, expressing her own view that she didn't think Lulu was bad but acknowledging that she seemed upset and felt misunderstood. The therapist continued that it was sometimes so difficult to understand each other and to know what was the right thing to do—like today, where she had clearly got something wrong and was really sorry.

In peer supervision, the therapist was angry with herself and expressed her sense that she had crossed a line in trying to explicitly connect the child's play and fantasy too early, knowing that she couldn't integrate them before, wanting to give her a really special homemade book. However, there was a space for mentalizing, leading to reparation after what she felt had been a painful rupture for both child and therapist. Once the group had helped the therapist to regain her own mentalizing capacity, the therapist was able to think together with her colleagues about what might have been the reason for this powerful reaction from Lulu. Although at the time everything happened too fast for her to think it through and make sense of it, the therapist now had a sense that Lulu felt betrayed by her, perhaps because Lulu had started to trust her as a helpful and respectful facilitator of her emerging sense of agency and sense of herself, and that creating and giving the book to Lulu had somehow surprised and overwhelmed her. The book, which the therapist had meant to further validate Lulu's story (the therapist's intention), was experienced as somehow doing the opposite. Or it might have been that by making the play too tangible, realistic, and concrete by putting it in a book, Lulu connected for the first time in an explicit way with her own life experiences, which seemed too unbearable to handle. The therapist realized in peer supervision that her own mentalizing capacity had been influenced by her desire to rescue this child, feeling so sorry for her and, at the same time, feeling powerless in really taking away Lulu's pain. In a similar way to the parents, who sometimes felt let down and helpless by Lulu's inability to use their containing and loving efforts, the therapist had reacted to the same feeling of helplessness by providing something concrete too quickly, acting somewhat in teleological mode. During meetings with the parents, this episode was used to explore the feelings Lulu's parents experienced and the shame they felt. The therapist's use of self (mentalizing her own experience in the session) while sharing with the parent therapist, who communicated to the parents her colleague's experience, seemed to help these parents to mentalize further their shame and anger toward their child and reflect on the impact it had on their parenting. The parents told the therapists that "a miracle" had happened after Lulu's emotional outburst in her last session: Lulu was relaxed, playing with the construction material with her brother and eating well for the first time in many months.

THE ENDING PHASE

After the difficult session with the caterpillar story, Lulu's mother joined the next session together with Lulu and the therapist, invited by the therapist to do so, as it was felt that this might help in restoring a sense of safety in the room. A conversation ensued in which Mrs. S, Lulu, and the therapist could mentalize about the relationship between Lulu and her therapist. Lulu could tell the therapist that she was neither a caterpillar nor a queen—she was just Lulu. The therapist apologized once more, and Lulu seemed calm and listening. She said she didn't want to play today and asked if they could draw something together as they had done at the start of the therapy. The therapist agreed, and Mrs. S sat by the side and watched for a while until Lulu turned to her and said, "You can go and see Mrs. A [the parent therapist] now."

Once the paper and materials were out, Lulu wanted to paint a panda. The therapist asked if there was a reason why she wanted to paint a panda, aware of the fact that the panda is an important symbol in China. Lulu replied that it was her favorite animal and also that her parents had recently taken her to see two pandas that the local zoo had received from China. The therapist felt the deeper meaning for the choice of the panda. Lulu asked the therapist if she could help her by drawing the outline so she could color it. Afterwards, she wanted to glue a little monkey in the picture. It seemed to the therapist that Lulu wanted to make her own story, her own narrative, with her own symbols in it, being the one to choose and decide. She expressed again that she didn't want a caterpillar on her painting, as she didn't like them. Lulu started to explicitly talk about what she liked and what she wanted. For the first time, she also started to tell the therapist what she knew about China and also about some nice things that had happened recently at school and at home.

The creation of Lulu's painted story took a few sessions. The painting expanded: She wanted more paper glued to the first one. During these sessions, the therapist felt surprised as she observed an emerging sense of self and self-agency and Lulu's verbalizing of feelings. The therapeutic work with Lulu now felt as if it had moved to a different level, where the creation of the story about the panda made it possible to explore a wide range of thoughts and feelings, connecting different cultural and emotional parts of her narrative. Neither Lulu nor the therapist linked the story back to her own experiences explicitly, but there was a strong sense that they were working on something that was emotionally significant and that the act of creation had a powerful internal drive to it. For the first time, the therapist was able to make use of techniques for promoting explicit mentalizing, such as mentalizing the characters and relationships in the play context. Drawing on a popular television series that she had seen, Lulu told the story of a panda who went to a new zoo in another country, having new adventures, seeking something he had lost, looking for new friends, and searching for food. The therapist's role was to support the telling of this story, sometimes drawing figures, taking on specific roles, and sometimes asking questions about the thoughts, fantasies, wishes, and feelings of the main characters. At times, the panda met other characters, and the therapist and Lulu were able to use these narratives to explore a range of feelings and experiences, including new themes that seemed to play an important role in her life now. These included curiosity and difficulties about playing together, sharing, wanting to belong, and wanting to be special, even as an "outsider."

The Second Review Session and Working Toward an Ending

The therapists, parents, and Lulu met for a second review session after a total of 20 sessions. By this stage there was a noticeable improvement on the behavior checklist, especially for items related to behavior with peers. More importantly, Lulu's parents reported that she seemed to allow herself to enjoy the intimacy with her parents and siblings. At school, her teacher had become really fond of Lulu. In therapy, Lulu had managed to repair her sense of safety with her therapist, who wanted to help her understand herself in this new world. The world of adults seemed to begin to feel safe and helpful for Lulu, and with it came an increased capacity to manage her "big feelings" and, most importantly, try to understand them with the support of those who loved her. She seemed to have found some way to recognize the reality of being adopted, aware of her differences but, on the other hand, being just one of the children, both at home and in school. It was agreed by all that the therapy should come to an end after the second block of 12 sessions was over.

During the last phase of the contact with the parents, they reported seeing changes in Lulu, which made them happy and hopeful. Mr. S had gone to a soccer match with her. Lulu had enjoyed it but, at the same time, had been a bit overwhelmed by the huge stadium, searching for his hand all the time and sitting on his lap during the match. For the first time, he said, he felt that he was her father, feeling how she could relax against his body, feeling the warmth of sitting there with his daughter, being able to protect her and offer her an exciting new experience. With the rest of the family, the situation had changed as well. Mrs. S felt less exhausted and freer to be the mother of all three of her children. At school, Lulu started to make friends with other children and was invited to a birthday party for the first time. There were no longer extreme violent outbursts, and both parents and teacher continued to reinforce Lulu's attempts to calm down and tried to always be curious and "wait it out" with Lulu instead of trying to fix things right away.

The therapist discussed with Lulu if they could think of something to do together in the last sessions and wondered out loud if the focus formulation, "Caterpillar on a journey," should be a part of these last sessions or not. She remembered aloud what had happened before when she had got it wrong and brought in the book about the caterpillar. Lulu answered that she didn't like the caterpillar but she liked butterflies. She found a wooden picture frame in the therapist's cupboard with space for two pictures. She chose to paint this frame during the last two sessions and brought a picture of herself and her (adoptive) mother to the last session to put in the frame. The therapist asked why she wanted her mother in the frame with her. Lulu answered that she loved her mother very much, and although she had two other mothers somewhere in China, this mother was going to stay! In the last session, the therapist gave Lulu a postcard on which she had written a few lines about how she had seen Lulu change during the sessions and about how much she had learned in working with Lulu, saying that she would never forget her. Lulu gave the therapist a beautiful drawing in a somewhat tough but, at the same time, shy way.

CONCLUSION

The MBT-C treatment provided Lulu with a safe space where she could experience and express her anger, fear, mistrust, happiness, confusion, and sadness while feeling supported. During the first phase of therapy (the first block of 12 sessions), the focus was primarily on building the foundations for mentalizing, with a particular focus on joint attention and affect regulation. Much of the work was carried out at a physical level, helping Lulu to feel "at home" in her body, and with the therapist offering an experience of contingent and marked mirroring. Midway through this first phase, the therapist felt that she and Lulu had a real "moment of meeting" after a significant rupture and that, following this, the work had been able to move to another level, where the focus could be on more explicit mentalizing and the creation of a trauma narrative around her early experiences of loss and the beginnings of a narrative around her identity across different cultures. The parent therapist worked on mentalizing the system by offering a containing and nonjudgmental space to Lulu's parents. Furthermore, the parallel collaboration between both therapists while being supported by the therapeutic team provided a mentalizing space when confronted with the feelings of helplessness in response to the child's anger and the parents' frustration. Finally, by starting the therapeutic work with a focus on attention regulation followed by an emphasis on affect regulation, Lulu's mentalizing capacity began to emerge and develop, which helped her to regulate her emotions and increase her attention control, which, in turn, helped her explicit mentalizing capacity to develop further. By the end of the 24 sessions, Lulu and her family had gained enough from the therapy to be able to continue the work themselves, but with an understanding that, at later stages of her development, as new issues might emerge for Lulu, they would have the option to come back to the service, knowing it was a space where they could feel supported, heard, and cared for.

Conclusion

Looking Forward

In writing this book, we have tried to crystalize the key notions and present the time-limited mentalization-based treatment with children (MBT-C) model that has emerged over the years as practiced by ourselves and that we consider builds on the concepts and approaches of mentalization-based treatment (MBT) as developed by Peter Fonagy, Anthony Bateman, and their collaborators. After reading this book, some readers may feel that much of what is described in this book is close to what you are already doing when working with children in therapy. If this is the case, we hope you take this as a compliment and take this opportunity to reflect with us on the extent to which mentalization is a common factor in psychotherapy. As we noted at the outset, MBT is, in many ways, an integrative therapy, which draws on elements from a number of existing therapies and aims to enhance our focus on one element (mentalizing) that may well be a common factor in a number of evidence-based interventions (Goodman et al., 2015).

Since the publication of the first edition of this book, interest in adapting and integrating the principles of mentalization-based thinking into work with children, young people, and families has continued to grow, and the book has been translated into several languages and formed the basis for training that has been delivered around the world, with practitioners in different countries reflecting on how the model can be adapted in different cultural contexts. (For a casebook of how MBT has been used with children in various different countries, all of whom have experienced early relational trauma, see Muller et al., 2025.) As Chapter 3 in this volume illustrates, there have been many developments in the evidence base for MBT for children and young people since the first edition of

https://doi.org/10.1037/0000486-013
Mentalization-Based Treatment for Children: A Time-Limited Approach, Second Edition, by N. Midgley, K. Ensink, K. Lindqvist, N. Malberg, and N. Muller
Copyright © 2026 by the American Psychological Association. All rights reserved.

this book. An international conference about MBT for children and young people took place in Barcelona in 2023, and a second one in Chile in 2025.

Developments in the practice of MBT-C have included thinking about the adaptation of MBT-C for particular populations, including neurodiverse children (N. T. Malberg, 2021), care-experienced children (Dalgaard et al., 2023; Hagelquist et al., 2023), and children who have experienced early relational or developmental trauma (Muller et al., 2025). Greater attention has been given to specific elements of the model, such as work on nonverbal communication and the role of "embodied mentalization" (Shai et al., 2022), as well as how a multicultural orientation (Owen et al., 2011) can be fully integrated with the mentalizing stance, especially when working cross-culturally. Different applications of the MBT model have been given specific attention, such as the work with parents (N. T. Malberg, 2024) or in schools (Lombardi et al., 2022). At the same time, there has been continued interest in exploring whether MBT-C can act as a transdiagnostic approach, especially for the large number of children who present to services with a mixed picture of emotional and behavioral difficulties, and whether MBT-C can be delivered by a broad range of mental health professionals, beyond those with a specialist psychotherapy background (see Halfon et al., 2024; Midgley et al., 2023). More broadly, mentalization-based interventions for children and young people have expanded into children's social care settings, as well as schools and other educational settings, where there is interest in thinking how the way of working can be used by the wider children's workforce (teachers, social workers, etc.) to support the well-being of children and young people (Chelouche-Dwek & Fonagy, 2025; Domon-Archambault et al., 2020; Hagelquist et al., 2023).

We believe that the guiding light for working with children and families, and training students and future therapists to do this work, is a respect for and interest in psychological experience and a curiosity about the way that different people's thoughts and feelings inform how they behave. This brings us to the training and conditions that we think are necessary to successfully work in this way. Emerging from a psychodynamic tradition, we hope that the time-limited model of MBT-C can be practiced by a wide range of child therapists and psychological practitioners working with children. Those wishing to do so would need a basic training in conducting psychotherapy with children and families but would also benefit from specific training in the practice and techniques of MBT-C, with a particular focus on working with the "mentalizing stance." This is similar to the situation for MBT for adults, where core therapeutic expertise is complemented by MBT-specific training. Furthermore, we consider that ongoing supervision, especially of challenging cases, is necessary to provide the best service and to continue to develop further as therapists.

Although we have described a basic MBT-C approach, including principles and techniques that we believe are applicable clinically to the treatment of children presenting with a wide range of psychological difficulties, much remains to be done. In addition to the creative work that is always necessary to adapt any model or approach in a way that is optimal for each individual patient, it is certain that, looking forward, work in a number of areas would be important.

First, further work is still needed to adapt time-limited MBT-C and optimize it for specific populations. For example, for children with serious externalizing difficulties, MBT-C may need to be adapted to more specifically address the difficulties and needs these children and their families have. This will require elaborating a model of the key mentalizing problems and associated interventions to specifically address these difficulties, as well as establishing what kind of training and supervision is needed to support the adaption of these approaches. It may be that this will require an integration of certain aspects of MBT-C with other types of interventions, such as art therapy, cognitive behavioral therapy, eye movement desensitization and reprocessing, or mindfulness-based approaches. Just as MBT itself emerges from the integration of knowledge from different fields, so too the future of MBT may involve its integration with other approaches to psychological therapies.

Second, we believe that some of the learning that has emerged from MBT with children could be helpfully integrated into MBT work with adolescents and adults. Too often, therapy with children is simply seen as an "adaptation downward" from therapy with grown-ups, but there are opportunities for those therapists working with older people to learn from child therapy. For example, the focus within time-limited MBT-C on the "building blocks" of mentalizing has not yet been fully taken on board by MBT practitioners working with adolescents and adults. How might it change that work if this developmental perspective were considered more fully? Are there developments in technique with adults that can be made on the basis of what has been learned by working with younger children? How, for example, should the learning about the importance of working with the network around the child inform the way MBT is delivered when working with adults?

Third, although the evidence base for this work has made significant strides forward (see Chapter 3, this volume), much remains to be known in terms of the empirical evidence for the work. Who are the children who can most benefit from time-limited MBT-C (and those who cannot)? When is a single block of 12 sessions sufficient, and when is there a need for a more extended period of MBT-C? What kind of practitioners and what kind of training or supervision is needed to ensure that MBT-C is delivered effectively? And can we establish more clearly which elements of time-limited MBT-C are the "change mechanisms" that make the work effective and which elements are not necessary or positively unhelpful? The logic of focusing on promoting mentalizing in children and parents has considerable empirical support, but we still need to understand more about what works for whom, under what circumstances, and when. As always when it comes to something as vital as addressing the mental health needs of children and families, much work remains to be done.

APPENDIX A

Measures of Mentalization in Children and Parents

The following clinical research assessments have been developed and validated to assess mentalization for research purposes, but they are also widely used (and adapted) by clinicians because of their clinical utility. To meet the standards of being able to publish in peer-reviewed journals using these assessments, training is provided by the developers to assure that coders are fully familiar with the concepts and are able to reliably code the interviews. However, these interviews, or short versions of these interviews or questions from them, are widely integrated into clinical assessments. There is little doubt that it is ideal and also very stimulating to enroll for the full training where the background to the development of the measures, the theoretical principles and assumptions on which they are based, and the nuances of coding and interpretation are explained. However, in many clinical settings, as well as universities and training institutions, the essence of these approaches has been integrated into clinical assessment protocols.

When it comes to measures of the capacity to mentalize in adults, there is a wide range of assessment tools that can be selected (for a review, see C. Shaw et al., 2020). For school-age children, however, the options are more limited, and researchers often rely on "proxy" measures, such as the child's theory of mind or affective understanding (see Vrouva et al., 2012).

ASSESSMENT OF PARENTAL MENTALIZING / REFLECTIVE FUNCTIONING

A number of approaches to assessing parental mentalizing have been developed using interviews, self-report questionnaires, and observational assessments. Although most research on parental mentalizing has been done in the context of infants and babies, there is now a range of measures (and studies using those measures) focusing on parents of school-age children.

Parent Developmental Interview—Reflective Functioning Scale

The reflective functioning coding on the Parent Development Interview is generally considered the "gold standard" measure of parental mentalizing, but it is quite time-intensive and requires specific training in coding. The Parent Development Interview has also been used in clinical settings as a clinical interview.

Key References

Slade, A., Aber, J. L., Bresgi, I., Berger, B., & Kaplan, M. (2004). *The Parent Development Interview—Revised* [Unpublished manuscript]. The City University of New York.

Sleed, M., Slade, A., & Fonagy, P. (2020). *Parent Development Interview–Reflective Functioning Scale (PDI-RF)* [Database record]. APA PsycTests. https://doi.org/10.1037/t76587-000

Slade, A., & Sleed, M. (2024). Parental reflective functioning on the parent development interview: A narrative review of measurement, association, and future directions. *Infant Mental Health Journal, 45*(4), 464–480. https://doi.org/10.1002/imhj.22114

Contact Person

Arietta Slade (https://pditraininginstitute.com)

Parental Reflective Functioning—Trauma Focused

The concept of trauma-specific reflective functioning was developed to assess the complexity of thought processes regarding trauma.

Key References

Berthelot, N., Ensink, K., Bernazzani, O., Normandin, L., Luyten, P., & Fonagy, P. (2015). Intergenerational transmission of attachment in abused and neglected mothers: The role of trauma-specific reflective functioning. *Infant Mental Health Journal, 36*(2), 200–212. https://doi.org/10.1002/imhj.21499

Berthelot, N., Ensink, K., Normandin, L., & Fonagy, P. (2015). *Trauma reflective functioning coding manual* [Unpublished manuscript]. Department of Nursing Sciences, Université du Québec à Trois-Rivières.

Berthelot, N., Garon-Bissonnette, J., Muzik, M., Simon, V., Menke, R., Stacks, A. M., & Rosenblum, K. L. (2025). Resolving trauma: The unique contribution of trauma-specific mentalization to maternal insightfulness. *Development and Psychopathology, 37*(3), 1280–1293. https://doi.org/10.1017/S095457942400110X

Ensink, K., Berthelot, N., Bernazzani, O., Normandin, L., & Fonagy, P. (2014). Another step closer to measuring the ghosts in the nursery: Preliminary validation of the Trauma Reflective Functioning Scale. *Frontiers in Psychology, 5*, Article 1471. https://doi.org/10.3389/fpsyg.2014.01471

Contact Person

Nicolas Berthelot (nicolas.berthelot@uqtr.ca)

The Parental Reflective Functioning Questionnaire

This self-report measure assesses parents' ability to understand their child's behavior in terms of mental states. It has been validated for use with parents of children and adolescents.

Key Reference

Luyten, P., Mayes, L. C., Nijssens, L., & Fonagy, P. (2017). The Parental Reflective Functioning Questionnaire: Development and preliminary validation. *PLOS ONE, 12*(5), Article e0176218. https://doi.org/10.1371/journal.pone.0176218

Contact Person

Patrick Luyten (patrick.luyten@kuleuven.be)

Reflective Parenting Assessment Coding

The aim of this coding was to develop a reliable and valid assessment of reflective parenting implicit in interaction with school-age children using an adaptation of the Squiggle paradigm developed by the child psychoanalyst and pediatrician, D. W. Winnicott.

Key References

Ensink, K., Leroux, A., Normandin, L., Biberdzic, M., & Fonagy, P. (2017). Assessing reflective parenting in interaction with school-aged children. *Journal of Personality Assessment, 99*(6), 585–595. https://doi.org/10.1080/00223891.2016.1270289

Normandin, L., Leroux, A., Terradas, M. M., Fonagy, P., & Ensink, K. (2015). *Reflective Parenting Assessment Coding manual* [Unpublished manual]. University Laval.

Contact Persons

Lina Normandin (lina.normandin@psy.ulaval.ca) and Karin Ensink (karin.ensink@psy.ulaval.ca)

Parental Observational Tool for Mentalization

Although not yet as widely used as interview-based or self-report measures, there is a clear need to be able to assess the parent's capacity for mentalizing "live," during their actual interactions with a child. Such measures are beginning to appear.

Key References

Decker, L. B., Stob, V., Woolston, J., Conway, C. A., & Slade, A. (2025). *Psychometric validation of the SPOT-ME—A multi-dimensional clinician-observation measure of parental mentalizing and non-mentalizing* [Under review].

Sprecher, E., Cresswell, C., Kerr-Davis, A., Sleed, M., & Midgley, N. (2023). Caregiver mentalizing and child emotional regulation: A novel approach to examining bidirectional impact, *Journal of Infant, Child, and Adolescent Psychotherapy, 22*(4), 358–374. https://doi.org/10.1080/15289168.2023.2274200

Stob, V., Brotnow, L., Adnopoz, J., Woolston, J., & Slade, A. (2020). *Coding manual: Short parental observational tool for mentalization* [Unpublished manual]. Yale Child Study Center.

Contact Persons

Line Decker (line.decker@yale.edu), Victoria Stob (victoria.stob@yale.edu), and Eva Sprecher (eva.sprecher@ucl.ac.uk)

Parental Mentalizing Questionnaire

This newer measure evaluates parental mentalizing across four dimensions: self-mentalizing, child mentalizing, effort, and curiosity. It has shown good validity and reliability in preliminary studies.

Key Reference

Teräsahjo, T., Turunen, T., Lahtinen, O., & Salmivalli, C. (2024). A preliminary validation of PMQ—A four-factor questionnaire measuring parental mentalizing. *Frontiers in Psychology, 15,* Article 1250092. https://doi.org/10.3389/fpsyg.2024.1250092

Maternal Mind-Mindedness

Maternal mind-mindedness refers to a caregiver's ability to perceive and treat their child as an individual with their own thoughts, feelings, and intentions. As such, it has a close relationship to the concept of parental reflective functioning, and there is a well-developed coding system based on linguistic markers in the caregiver's speech.

Key Reference

McMahon, C. A., & Bernier, A. (2017). Twenty years of research on parental mind-mindedness: Empirical findings, theoretical and methodological challenges, and new directions. *Developmental Review, 46,* 54–80. https://doi.org/10.1016/j.dr.2017.07.001

ASSESSMENT OF CHILD MENTALIZING / REFLECTIVE FUNCTIONING

Compared with the assessment of parental mentalizing, fewer measures have been developed to assess the capacity to mentalize in children, especially in school-age children. As self-report measures in middle childhood are of limited value, the measures listed here use a mixture of interview and projective testing. For a wider range of measures for school-age children assessing related concepts, such as "theory of mind" and "affective understanding," see Vrouva et al. (2012).

Child Attachment Interview

This semi-structured interview assesses children's attachment representations and includes questions that probe their understanding of mental states. When used in the context of the assessment of mentalizing, it can be used in combination with the Child Reflective Functioning Questionnaire (see below).

Key References

Bizzi, F., Locati, F., Parolin, L., Yael, S. G., & Brusadelli, E. (2022). Advancement in the child attachment interview and the Child and Adolescent Reflective Functioning Scale using a PDM-2 framework: Case reports. *Research in Psychotherapy: Psychopathology, Process and Outcome, 25*(1), 57–71. https://doi.org/10.4081/ripppo.2022.586

Shmueli-Goetz, Y., Target, M., Fonagy, P., & Datta, A. (2008). The Child Attachment Interview: A psychometric study of reliability and discriminant validity. *Developmental Psychology, 44*(4), 939–956. https://doi.org/10.1037/0012-1649.44.4.939

Target, M., Fonagy, P., Shmueli-Goetz, Y., Datta, A., & Schneider, T. (1999). *The Child Attachment Interview (CAI) protocol.* University College London.

Child Reflective Functioning Scale

This scale is adapted from the adult version and assesses children's capacity to reflect on their own and others' mental states.

Key References

Bizzi, F., Charpentier-Mora, S., Cavanna, D., Borelli, J. L., & Ensink, K. (2022). Testing children's mentalizing in middle childhood: Adopting the Child and Adolescent Reflective Functioning Scale with clinical and community children. *Journal of Child and Family Studies, 31*, 114–127. https://doi.org/10.1007/s10826-021-02057-4

Ensink, K., Normandin, L., Target, M., Fonagy, P., Sabourin, S., & Berthelot, N. (2015). Mentalization in children and mothers in the context of trauma: An initial study of the validity of the Child Reflective Functioning Scale. *British Journal of Developmental Psychology, 33*(2), 203–217. https://doi.org/10.1111/bjdp.12074

Ensink, K., Target, M., & Oandasan, C. (2013). *Child Reflective Functioning Scale scoring manual: For application to the Child Attachment Interview* [Unpublished manuscript]. Anna Freud Centre, University College London.

Contact Person

Karin Ensink (karin.ensink@psy.ulaval.ca)

The Story Stem Assessment Profile

This tool uses story stems to elicit children's narratives, which are then analyzed for mentalizing abilities.

Key References

Hillman, S. (2011). *The standardization and validation of the Story Stem Assessment Profile (SSAP): A clinical narrative-based assessment for children* [Unpublished dissertation]. University College London.

Contact Person

Saul Hillman (saul.hillman@annafreud)

APPENDIX B

The Mentalization-Based Treatment for Children Adherence Scale

The MBT-C Adherence Scale was developed by Jordan Bate, Norka Malberg, and Nick Midgley as a tool for research and training purposes to assess adherence to the time-limited mentalization-based treatment for children (MBT-C) model. For an example of its use in research studies, see Halfon et al. (2024). Although the scale was developed as an observation-based research tool to be rated based on watching a video-recorded MBT-C session, it can also be used as a self-report tool by practitioners as a way of encouraging reflection on their practice. This scale can serve as a guide to help each clinician focus on their strengths and areas for development that arise in supervision, training, and self-reflection. The aim is for them to learn to apply with fidelity the model, stance, and MBT-C techniques in practice.

The terms "adherence," "fidelity," "competence," and so forth have different meanings; however, all are related. In this scale, the term "adherence" is used to describe not only the use of specific techniques but also the capability to hold the core elements of a "mentalizing stance" and the quality of the way in which the model is applied. A core feature of MBT-C is the development of the children's sense of self, which also has different needs. Each clinician, in turn, also has a different style and a sense of "self." So, although the MBT-C Adherence Scale sets out the core principles and techniques that are expected to be present in an MBT-C session "according to the model," these may be different for each child–therapist dyad at different times.

When used by therapists or supervisors as an aid in developing fidelity to the MBT-C approach, it is recommended that the therapist spend 5 to 10 minutes reviewing this scale after each MBT-C session with a child, assessing the presence and skill level that, "according to the model," was presented in the session. The scale is not focused on what was done "right or wrong" but rather is a process of reflecting on the work with each child, where clinicians and supervisors can make the implicit explicit (i.e., what they did or did not do) and attend to and explore the thoughts, feelings, and intentions that underlie their behavior as clinicians and those that may have been underlying the child's behavior in the session.

We are all likely to fall into nonmentalizing modes when working with children who are emotionally dysregulated and who are themselves nonmentalizing. Therefore, it may be useful to make use of the scale during supervision, since a function of relationships of this type is to restore and facilitate the therapist's own mentalizing. By practicing restoring our mentalizing functions in the context of supervision, we become more able to restore our own mentalizing when we are in session with children, allowing us to help them develop or restore their mentalizing abilities.

Each item on this scale requires the assessor to assess whether the stance or technique was present. If it is considered present, the skill level should be assessed (on a scale of 1–5) based on the therapist's demonstration of

- expertise/experience, competence, and commitment;
- willingness to take well-considered relational risks;
- adequacy in timing and pace of intervention;
- adaptation to the fluctuating mentalizing state of the child/parent; and
- response to where the child or parents are going at specific times.

The skill level is not the same as the efficacy of the intervention. A clinician may perform an intervention with a high level of skill; however, it may not have an immediate noticeable effect for a number of reasons. The skill level of each item includes the following:

1. Frequency (the number of discrete times the clinician performs the intervention)
2. Extensiveness (the depth or detail with which the clinician performs a given intervention)
3. Appropriateness (the degree to which the intervention is adapted to the proper level for the given context)

A highly skilled clinician performs interventions with a frequency and extensiveness appropriate to each situation. Therefore, when interventions are performed too infrequently / insufficiently frequently or too minimally / inappropriately extensive, they should receive a lower skill rating as a result.

Please note that use of the MBT-C Adherence Scale for research purposes requires training to ensure appropriate use, and the full manual, providing detailed guidance on scoring, is only available to those who undertake training. (Please contact nick.midgley@annafreud.org for further details.) However, practitioners and supervisors are invited to use the scale in a clinical setting to help reflect on their own practice, without needing specific training.

TABLE B.1. MBT-C Adherence and Competence Scale

MBT-C stance and core principle	Presence (adherence) Check only when present	Skill (competence) Indicate level on scale of 1–5
1. Adaptation to the child's developmental level	☐	
2. Nonjudgmental stance	☐	
3. "Not knowing" mentalizing stance	☐	
4. Playful stance	☐	
5. Make implicit explicit	☐	
6. Use of self	☐	
MBT-C technique	**Presence**	**Skill**
Attention control interventions		
Create joint attention: rhythm, structure, and feeling of being together	☐	
Assume responsibility for the structure and for holding	☐	
Name and describe what the child is doing / what is happening at the present time	☐	
Look for / be curious about mental states (even when playing)	☐	
Other characteristic attention control interventions:	☐	
Emotion regulation interventions		
Awareness and curiosity about perception and feelings	☐	
Identify obstacles for achieving regulation or triggers for dysregulation	☐	
Regulation of arousal level	☐	
Play with regulation and limits	☐	
Offer support and empathy when facing mentalizing breakdowns	☐	
Other characteristic emotional regulation interventions:	☐	
Explicit mentalizing interventions		
Link mental states to behavior	☐	
Play with perspective	☐	
Mentalize the relationship	☐	
Other characteristic explicit mentalizing interventions:	☐	

Note. MBT-C = mentalization-based treatment for children.

REFERENCES

Abrines-Jaume, N., Midgley, N., Hopkins, K., Hoffman, J., Martin, K., Law, D., & Wolpert, M. (2016). A qualitative analysis of implementing shared decision making in Child and Adolescent Mental Health Services in the United Kingdom: Stages and facilitators. *Clinical Child Psychology and Psychiatry, 21*(1), 19–31. https://doi.org/10.1177/1359104514547596

Adkins, T., Reisz, S., Hasdemir, D., & Fonagy, P. (2022). Family minds: A randomized controlled trial of a group intervention to improve foster parents' reflective functioning. *Development and Psychopathology, 34*(3), 1177–1191. https://doi.org/10.1017/S095457942000214X

Ainsworth, M. D. S., Blehar, M., Waters, E., & Wall, S. (1978). *Patterns of attachment: A psychological study of the strange situation.* Lawrence Erlbaum.

Aival-Naveh, E., Rothschild-Yakar, L., & Kurman, J. (2019). Keeping culture in mind: A systematic review and initial conceptualization of mentalizing from a cross-cultural perspective. *Clinical Psychology: Science and Practice, 26*(4), Article e12300. https://doi.org/10.1111/cpsp.12300

Allen, B. (2008). An analysis of the impact of diverse forms of childhood psychological maltreatment on emotional adjustment in early adulthood. *Child Maltreatment, 13*(3), 307–312. https://doi.org/10.1177/1077559508318394

Allen, J. G., & Fonagy, P. (Eds.). (2006). *Handbook of mentalization-based treatment.* Wiley.

Allen, J. G., Fonagy, P., & Bateman, A. W. (2008). *Mentalizing in clinical practice.* American Psychiatric Association.

Allen, J. G., O'Malley, F., Freeman, C., & Bateman, A. W. (2012). Brief treatment. In A. W. Bateman & P. Fonagy (Eds.), *Handbook of mentalizing in mental health practice* (pp. 159–197). American Psychiatric Association.

Aras, A., Fonagy, P., Campbell, C., & Rosan, C. (2024). What do we know about parental embodied mentalizing? A systematic review of the construct, assessment, empirical findings, gaps and further steps. *Attachment & Human Development, 26*(6), 588–624. https://doi.org/10.1080/14616734.2024.2421432

Armitage, J. M., Newlove-Delgado, T., Ford, T., McManus, S., & Collishaw, S. (2024). Characteristics of children with a psychiatric disorder in 1999, 2004 and 2017: An analysis of the national child mental health surveys of England. *Journal of Child Psychology and Psychiatry, 66*(2), 167–177. https://doi.org/10.1111/jcpp.14040

Asen, E., & Fonagy, P. (2012a). Mentalization-based family therapy. In A. W. Bateman & P. Fonagy (Eds.), *Handbook of mentalizing in mental health practice* (pp. 107–128). American Psychiatric Association.

Asen, E., & Fonagy, P. (2012b). Mentalization-based therapeutic interventions for families. *Journal of Family Therapy, 34*(4), 347–370. https://doi.org/10.1111/j.1467-6427.2011.00552.x

Asen, E., & Fonagy, P. (2021). *Mentalization-based treatment with families.* Guilford Press.

Asen, E., & Midgley, N. (2025). Working with families. In A. Bateman & P. Fonagy (Eds.), *Handbook of mentalizing in mental health practice* (pp. 135–149). American Psychiatric Association Publishing. https://doi.org/10.1176/appi.books.9781615379019.lg08

Atkins, D., Uskul, A. K., & Cooper, N. R. (2016). Culture shapes empathic responses to physical and social pain. *Emotion, 16*(5), 587–601. https://doi.org/10.1037/emo0000162

Bain, K. (2014). "New beginnings" in South African shelters for the homeless: Piloting of a group psychotherapy intervention for high-risk mother–infant dyads. *Infant Mental Health Journal, 35*(6), 591–603. https://doi.org/10.1002/imhj.21457

Ballespí, S., Vives, J., Sharp, C., Chanes, L., & Barrantes-Vidal, N. (2021). Self and other mentalizing polarities and dimensions of mental health: Association with types of symptoms, functioning and well-being. *Frontiers in Psychology, 12,* Article 566254. https://doi.org/10.3389/fpsyg.2021.566254

Banaschewski, T., Hage, A., Hohmann, S., & Mechler, K. (2023). Perspectives on ADHD in children and adolescents as a social construct amidst rising prevalence of diagnosis and medication use. *Frontiers in Psychiatry, 14,* Article 1289157. https://doi.org/10.3389/fpsyt.2023.1289157

Banerjee, R. (2008). Social cognition and anxiety in children. In C. Sharp, P. Fonagy, & I. Goodyer (Eds.), *Social cognition and developmental psychopathology* (pp. 239–269). Oxford University Press. https://doi.org/10.1093/med/9780198569183.003.0009

Baradon, T., Fonagy, P., Bland, K., Lénárd, K., & Sleed, M. (2008). New beginnings—An experience-based programme addressing the attachment relationship between mothers and their babies in prisons. *Journal of Child Psychotherapy, 34*(2), 240–258. https://doi.org/10.1080/00754170802208065

Barish, K. (2009). *Emotions in child therapy.* Oxford University Press.

Barnicot, K., Redknap, C., Coath, F., Hommel, J., Couldrey, L., & Crawford, M. (2022). Patient experiences of therapy for borderline personality disorder: Commonalities and differences between dialectical behaviour therapy and mentalization-based therapy and relation to outcomes. *Psychology and Psychotherapy: Theory, Research and Practice, 95*(1), 212–233. https://doi.org/10.1111/papt.12362

Baron-Cohen, S. (2009). Autism: The empathizing–systemizing (E–S) theory. *Annals of the New York Academy of Sciences, 1156*(1), 68–80. https://doi.org/10.1111/j.1749-6632.2009.04467.x

Baron-Cohen, S., Leslie, A. M., & Frith, U. (1985). Does the autistic child have a "theory of mind"? *Cognition, 21*(1), 37–46. https://doi.org/10.1016/0010-0277(85)90022-8

Bateman, A., & Fonagy, P. (2004). Mentalization-based treatment of BPD. *Journal of Personality Disorders, 18*(1), 36–51. https://doi.org/10.1521/pedi.18.1.36.32772

Bateman, A., & Fonagy, P. (2008). 8-year follow-up of patients treated for borderline personality disorder: Mentalization-based treatment versus treatment as usual. *American Journal of Psychiatry, 165*(5), 631–638. https://doi.org/10.1176/appi.ajp.2007.07040636

Bateman, A., & Fonagy, P. (2009). Randomized controlled trial of outpatient mentalization-based treatment versus structured clinical management for borderline personality disorder. *American Journal of Psychiatry, 166*(12), 1355–1364. https://doi.org/10.1176/appi.ajp.2009.09040539

Bateman, A., & Fonagy, P. (2010). Mentalization based treatment for borderline personality disorder. *World Psychiatry, 9*(1), 11–15. https://doi.org/10.1002/j.2051-5545.2010.tb00255.x

Bateman, A., & Fonagy, P. (2013). Mentalization-based treatment. *Psychoanalytic Inquiry, 33*(6), 595–613. https://doi.org/10.1080/07351690.2013.835170

Bateman, A., & Fonagy, P. (2016). *Mentalization-based treatment for personality disorders: A practical guide*. Oxford University Press. https://doi.org/10.1093/med:psych/9780199680375.001.0001

Bateman, A., Fonagy, P., Campbell, C., Luyten, P., & Debbané, M. (2023). A history of mentalizing and mentalization-based treatment. In A. Bateman, P. Fonagy, C. Campbell, P. Luyten, & M. Debbané (Eds.) *Cambridge guide to mentalization-based treatment (MBT)* (pp. 1–3). Cambridge University Press. https://doi.org/10.1017/9781108896054

Bateman, A., Unruh, B., & Fonagy, P. (2019). Individual therapy techniques. In A. Bateman & P. Fonagy (Eds.), *Handbook of mentalizing in mental health practice* (2nd ed., pp. 103–115). American Psychiatric Association.

Bazzi, M., Sadeghi, M., & Mohammadi, A. (2024). The structural relationship between insecure attachment styles and self-harm: The mediating roles of resilience and mentalization. *Research in Cognitive and Behavioral Sciences, 13*(2), 41–56 https://doi.org/10.22108/cbs.2024.140193.1867

Beck, E., Bo, S., Jørgensen, M. S., Gondan, M., Poulsen, S., Storebø, O. J., Fjellerad Andersen, C., Folmo, E., Sharp, C., Pedersen, J., & Simonsen, E. (2020). Mentalization-based treatment in groups for adolescents with borderline personality disorder: A randomized controlled trial. *Journal of Child Psychology and Psychiatry, 61*(5), 594–604. https://doi.org/10.1111/jcpp.13152

Beebe, B., Lachmann, F., & Jaffe, J. (1997). Mother–infant interaction structures and presymbolic self- and object representations. *Psychoanalytic Dialogues, 7*(2), 133–182. https://doi.org/10.1080/10481889709539172

Beebe, B., Lachmann, F. M., Markese, S., Buck, K. A., Bahrick, L. E., Chen, H., Cohen, P., Andrews, H., Feldstein, S., & Jaffe, J. (2012). On the origins of disorganized attachment and internal working models: Paper II. An empirical microanalysis of 4-month mother–infant interaction. *Psychoanalytic Dialogues, 22*(3), 352–374. https://doi.org/10.1080/10481885.2012.679606

Bellis, M. A., Hughes, K., Ford, K., Ramos Rodriguez, G., Sethi, D., & Passmore, J. (2019). Life course health consequences and associated annual costs of adverse childhood experiences across Europe and North America: A systematic review and meta-analysis. *The Lancet Public Health, 4*(10), e517–e528. https://doi.org/10.1016/S2468-2667(19)30145-8

Benbassat, N., & Priel, B. (2012). Parenting and adolescent adjustment: The role of parental reflective function. *Journal of Adolescence, 35*(1), 163–174. https://doi.org/10.1016/j.adolescence.2011.03.004

Berk, L. E., Mann, T. D., & Ogan, A. T. (2006). Make-believe play: Wellspring for development of self-regulation. In D. G. Singer, R. M. Golinkoff, & K. Hirsh-Pasek (Eds.), *Play = learning: How play motivates and enhances children's cognitive and social-emotional growth* (pp. 74–100). Oxford University Press.

Bernier, A., McMahon, C. A., & Perrier, R. (2017). Maternal mind-mindedness and children's school readiness: A longitudinal study of developmental processes. *Developmental Psychology, 53*(2), 210–221. https://doi.org/10.1037/dev0000225

Berthelot, N., Ensink, K., Bernazzani, O., Normandin, L., Luyten, P., & Fonagy, P. (2015). Intergenerational transmission of attachment in abused and neglected mothers: The role of trauma-specific reflective functioning. *Infant Mental Health Journal, 36*(2), 200–212. https://doi.org/10.1002/imhj.21499

Berthelot, N., Garon-Bissonnette, J., Muzik, M., Simon, V., Menke, R., Stacks, A. M., & Rosenblum, K. L. (2024). Resolving trauma: The unique contribution of trauma-specific mentalization to maternal insightfulness. *Development and Psychopathology, 37*(3), 1280–1293. https://doi.org/10.1017/s095457942400110x

Berthelot, N., Paccalet, T., Gilbert, E., Moreau, I., Mérette, C., Gingras, N., Rouleau, N., & Maziade, M. (2015). Childhood abuse and neglect may induce deficits in cognitive precursors of psychosis in high-risk children. *Journal of Psychiatry and Neuroscience, 40*(5), 336–343. https://doi.org/10.1503/jpn.140211

Bevington, D., & Fuggle, P. (2012). Supporting and enhancing mentalization in community outreach teams working with hard-to-reach youth: The AMBIT approach. In N. Midgley & I. Vrouva (Eds.), *Minding the child: Mentalization-based interventions with children, young people and their families* (pp. 163–186). Routledge.

Bevington, D., Fuggle, P., & Fonagy, P. (2015). Applying attachment theory to effective practice with hard-to-reach youth: The AMBIT approach. *Attachment & Human Development, 17*(2), 157–174. https://doi.org/10.1080/14616734.2015.1006385

Bianco, F., Levante, A., Petrocchi, S., Lecciso, F., & Castelli, I. (2021). Maternal psychological distress and children's internalizing/externalizing problems during the COVID-19 pandemic: The moderating role played by hypermentalization. *International Journal of Environmental Research and Public Health, 18*(19), Article 10450. https://doi.org/10.3390/ijerph181910450

Bifulco, A., Moran, P. M., Ball, C., & Bernazzani, O. (2002). Adult attachment style. I: Its relationship to clinical depression. *Social Psychiatry and Psychiatric Epidemiology, 37*(2), 50–59. https://doi.org/10.1007/s127-002-8215-0

Bizzi, F., Charpentier-Mora, S., Bastianoni, C., Ensink, K., Cavanna, D., & Borelli, J. L. (2022). Attachment representations and mentalizing in middle childhood across one year: A preliminary pilot longitudinal study. *Psychoanalytic Psychology, 39*(1), 69–73. https://doi.org/10.1037/pap0000379

Bizzi, F., Charpentier-Mora, S., Cavanna, D., Borelli, J. L., & Ensink, K. (2022). Testing children's mentalizing in middle childhood: Adopting the child and adolescent reflective functioning scale with clinical and community children. *Journal of Child and Family Studies, 31*(1), 114–127. https://doi.org/10.1007/s10826-021-02057-4

Blake, P. (2008). *Child and adolescent psychotherapy.* Karnac.

Bo, S., Sharp, C., Beck, E., Pedersen, J., Gondan, M., & Simonsen, E. (2017). First empirical evaluation of outcomes for mentalization-based group therapy for adolescents with BPD. *Personality Disorders: Theory, Research, and Treatment, 8*(4), 396–401. https://doi.org/10.1037/per0000210

Bogdanović, A., Radev, M. T., & Stanojević, T. S. (2023). Disorganized attachment, mentalization and dissociation in context of childhood trauma: Implications for depressive symptoms. *Child Abuse Review, 32*(2), Article e2798. https://doi.org/10.1002/car.2798

Borelli, J. L., Cohen, C., Pettit, C., Normandin, L., Target, M., Fonagy, P., & Ensink, K. (2019). Maternal and child sexual abuse history: An intergenerational exploration of children's adjustment and maternal trauma-reflective functioning. *Frontiers in Psychology, 10,* Article 1062. https://doi.org/10.3389/fpsyg.2019.01062

Bruha, L., Spyridou, V., Forth, G., & Ougrin, D. (2018). Global child and adolescent mental health: Challenges and advances. *London Journal of Primary Care, 10*(4), 108–109. https://doi.org/10.1080/17571472.2018.1484332

Bukatko, D., & Daehler, M. W. (2004). *Child development: A thematic approach* (5th ed.). Houghton Mifflin.

Bunday, L., Dallos, R., Morgan, K., & MacKenzie, R. (2015). Foster carers' reflective understandings of parenting looked after children: An exploratory study. *Adoption & Fostering, 39*(2), 145–158. https://doi.org/10.1177/0308575915588730

Burson, S. L., & Castelli, D. M. (2022). How elementary in-school play opportunities relate to academic achievement and social-emotional well-being: Systematic review. *Journal of School Health, 92*(10), 945–958. https://doi.org/10.1111/josh.13217

Byrne, G., Murphy, S., & Connon, G. (2020). Mentalization-based treatments with children and families: A systematic review of the literature. *Clinical Child Psychology and Psychiatry, 25*(4), 1022–1048. https://doi.org/10.1177/1359104520920689

Byrne, G., Sleed, M., Midgley, N., Fearon, P., Mein, C., Bateman, A., & Fonagy, P. (2019). Lighthouse parenting programme: Description and pilot evaluation of mentalization-based treatment to address child maltreatment. *Clinical Child Psychology and Psychiatry, 24*(4), 680–693. https://doi.org/10.1177/1359104518807741

Caldarera, A. M., Vitiello, B., Turcich, C., Bechis, D., & Baietto, C. (2022). The association of attachment, mentalization and reflective functioning with mental health in gender diverse children and adolescents: A systematic review. *Clinical Child Psychology and Psychiatry, 27*(4), 1124–1140. https://doi.org/10.1177/13591045221075527

Camoirano, A. (2017). Mentalizing makes parenting work: A review about parental reflective functioning and clinical interventions to improve it. *Frontiers in Psychology, 8,* Article 14. https://doi.org/10.3389/fpsyg.2017.00014

Capobianco, J., & Farber, B. A. (2005). Therapist self-disclosure to child patients. *American Journal of Psychotherapy, 59*(3), 199–212. https://doi.org/10.1176/appi.psychotherapy.2005.59.3.199

Caspi, A., Houts, R. M., Ambler, A., Danese, A., Elliott, M. L., Hariri, A., Harrington, H., Hogan, S., Poulton, R., Ramrakha, S., Rasmussen, L. J. H., Reuben, A., Richmond-Rakerd, L., Sugden, K., Wertz, J., Williams, B. S., & Moffitt, T. E. (2020). Longitudinal assessment of mental health disorders and comorbidities across 4 decades among participants in the Dunedin Birth Cohort Study. *JAMA Network Open, 3*(4), Article e203221. https://doi.org/10.1001/jamanetworkopen.2020.3221

Caspi, A., Houts, R. M., Belsky, D. W., Goodman-Mellor, S. J., Harrington, H., Israel, S., Meier, M. H., Ramrakha, S., Shalev, I., Poulton, R., & Moffitt, T. E. (2014). The p factor: One general psychopathology factor in the structure of psychiatric disorders? *Clinical Psychological Science, 2*(2), 119–137. https://doi.org/10.1177/2167702613497473

Cassidy, K. W., Werner, R. S., Rourke, M., Zubernis, L. S., College, B. M., & Balaraman, G. (2003). The relationship between psychological understanding and positive social behaviors. *Social Development, 12*(2), 198–221. https://doi.org/10.1111/1467-9507.00229

Centifanti, L. C. M., Meins, E., & Fernyhough, C. (2016). Callous-unemotional traits and impulsivity: Distinct longitudinal relations with mind-mindedness and understanding of others. *Journal of Child Psychology and Psychiatry, 57*(1), 84–92. https://doi.org/10.1111/jcpp.12445

Charki, A., & Adnane, E. (2024). Affective mentalizing in children with and without autism spectrum disorder at school age. *Acta Neuropsychologica, 22*(4), 531–543. https://doi.org/10.5604/01.3001.0054.8514

Charpentier Mora, S., Bastianoni, C., Koren-Karie, N., Cavanna, D., Tironi, M., & Bizzi, F. (2022). Parental mentalizing during middle childhood: How is the adoption of a reflective stance associated with child's psychological outcomes? *International Journal of Environmental Research and Public Health, 19*(10), Article 6205. https://doi.org/10.3390/ijerph19106205

Chazan, S., Kuchirko, Y., Beebe, B., & Sossin, K. M. (2016). A longitudinal study of traumatic play activity using the Children's Developmental Play Instrument (CDPI). *Journal of Infant, Child, and Adolescent Psychotherapy, 15*(1), 1–25. https://doi.org/10.1080/15289168.2015.1127729

Chelouche-Dwek, G., & Fonagy, P. (2025). Mentalization-based interventions in schools for enhancing socio-emotional competencies and positive behaviour: A systematic review. *European Child & Adolescent Psychiatry, 34*(4), 1295–1315. https://doi.org/10.1007/s00787-024-02578-5

Chiesa, M., & Fonagy, P. (2014). Reflective function as a mediator between childhood adversity, personality disorder and symptom distress. *Personality and Mental Health, 8*(1), 52–66. https://doi.org/10.1002/pmh.1245

Chronaki, G., Hadwin, J. A., Garner, M., Maurage, P., & Sonuga-Barke, E. J. (2015). The development of emotion recognition from facial expressions and non-linguistic vocalizations during childhood. *British Journal of Developmental Psychology, 33*(2), 218–236. https://doi.org/10.1111/bjdp.12075

Cicchetti, D. (2016). Socioemotional, personality, and biological development: Illustrations from a multilevel developmental psychopathology perspective on child maltreatment. *Annual Review of Psychology, 67*(1), 187–211. https://doi.org/10.1146/annurev-psych-122414-033259

Cicchetti, D., & Banny, A. (2014). A developmental psychopathology perspective on child maltreatment. In M. Lewis & K. D. Rudolph (Eds.), *Handbook of developmental psychopathology* (3rd ed., pp. 723–741). Springer. https://doi.org/10.1007/978-1-4614-9608-3_37

Cooper, A., & Redfern, S. (2015). *Reflective parenting: A guide to understanding what's going on in your child's mind.* Routledge. https://doi.org/10.4324/9781315764108

Coşkun, A., Halfon, S., Bate, J., & Midgley, N. (2024). The use of mentalization-based techniques in online psychodynamic child psychotherapy. *Psychotherapy Research, 34*(7), 1005–1017. https://doi.org/10.1080/10503307.2023.2245962

Coughlan, B., Duschinsky, R., Bakermans-Kranenburg, M. J., Bakkum, L., Skinner, G. C. M., Markham, A., Beckwith, H., & van IJzendoorn, M. J. (2023). *Sequelae of child maltreatment: Umbrella synthesis on mental health correlates in over 11 million participants.* PsyArXiv. https://doi.org/10.31234/osf.io/zj7kb

Csibra, G., & Gergely, G. (2009). Natural pedagogy. *Trends in Cognitive Sciences, 13*(4), 148–153. https://doi.org/10.1016/j.tics.2009.01.005

Csibra, G., & Gergely, G. (2011). Natural pedagogy as evolutionary adaptation. *Philosophical Transactions of the Royal Society of London. Series B, Biological Sciences, 366*(1567), 1149–1157. https://doi.org/10.1098/rstb.2010.0319

Dalgaard, N. T., Villumsen, A. M. A., Sørensen, K. M., Midgley, N., Væver, M. S., Almlund, M., & Pontoppidan, M. (2023). Holding a foster child's mind in mind: Study protocol for a cluster-randomized controlled trial of mentalization-based therapy (MBT) for foster families. *BMC Psychology, 11*(1), Article 62. https://doi.org/10.1186/s40359-023-01103-8

Danielsdottir, H. B., Aspelund, T., Shen, Q., Halldorsdottir, T., Jakobsdottir, J., Song, H., Lu, D., Kuja-Halkola, R., Larsson, H., Fall, K., Magnusson, P. K. E., Fang, F., Bergstedt, J., & Valdimarsdottir, U. A. (2024). Adverse childhood experiences and adult mental health outcomes. *JAMA Psychiatry, 81*(6), 586–594. https://doi.org/10.1001/jamapsychiatry.2024.0039

Davis, D. E., DeBlaere, C., Owen, J., Hook, J. N., Rivera, D. P., Choe, E., Van Tongeren, D. R., Worthington, E. L., & Placeres, V. (2018). The multicultural orientation framework: A narrative review. *Psychotherapy, 55*(1), 89–100. https://doi.org/10.1037/pst0000160

Denham, S. A., Bassett, H. H., Way, E., Kalb, S., Warren-Khot, H., & Zinsser, K. (2014). "How would you feel? What would you do?" Development and underpinnings of preschoolers' social information processing. *Journal of Research in Childhood Education, 28*(2), 182–202. https://doi.org/10.1080/02568543.2014.883558

DePasquale, C. E., Handley, E. D., & Cicchetti, D. (2019). Investigating multilevel pathways of developmental consequences of maltreatment. *Development and Psychopathology, 31*(4), 1227–1236. https://doi.org/10.1017/S0954579418000834

Dodge, K. A., Laird, R., Lochman, J. E., & Zelli, A. (2002). Multidimensional latent-construct analysis of children's social information processing patterns: Correlations with aggressive behavior problems. *Psychological Assessment, 14*(1), 60–73. https://doi.org/10.1037/1040-3590.14.1.60

Dollberg, D. G., & Hanetz-Gamliel, K. (2023). Therapeutic work to enhance parental mentalizing for parents with ACEs to support their children's mental health:

A theoretical and clinical review. *Frontiers in Child and Adolescent Psychiatry, 2,* Article 1094206. https://doi.org/10.3389/frcha.2023.1094206

Dollberg, D. G., Harlev, Y., Malishkevitch, S., & Leitner, Y. (2022). Parental reflective functioning as a moderator of the link between prematurity and parental stress. *Frontiers in Psychiatry, 13,* Article 804694. https://doi.org/10.3389/fpsyt.2022.804694

Domon-Archambault, V., Terradas, M. M., Drieu, D., De Fleurian, A., Achim, J., Poulain, S., & Jerrar-Oulidi, J. (2020). Mentalization-based training program for child care workers in residential settings. *Journal of Child & Adolescent Trauma, 13*(2), 239–248. https://doi.org/10.1007/s40653-019-00269-x

Dorahy, M. J., Lewis-Fernández, R., Krüger, C., Brand, B. L., ar, V., Ewing, J., Martínez-Taboas, A., Stavropoulos, P., & Middleton, W. (2016). The role of clinical experience, diagnosis, and theoretical orientation in the treatment of posttraumatic and dissociative disorders: A vignette and survey investigation. *Journal of Trauma & Dissociation, 18*(2), 206–222. https://doi.org/10.1080/15299732.2016.1225626

Downes, C., Kieran, S., & Tiernan, B. (2022). "Now I know I'm not the only one": A group therapy approach for adoptive parents. *Child Care in Practice, 28*(1), 43–51. https://doi.org/10.1080/13575279.2019.1664992

Drozek, R. P., & Unruh, B. T. (2022). Mentalization-based treatment for a physician with borderline personality disorder. *American Journal of Psychotherapy, 75*(1), 51–54. https://doi.org/10.1176/appi.psychotherapy.20210019

Dunn, J., & Brown, J. (1994). Affect expression in the family, children's understanding of emotions, and their interactions with others. *Merrill-Palmer Quarterly, 40*(1), 120–137.

Eggum, N. D., Eisenberg, N., Kao, K., Spinrad, T. L., Bolnick, R., Hofer, C., Kupfer, A. S., & Fabricius, W. V. (2011). Emotion understanding, theory of mind, and prosocial orientation: Relations over time in early childhood. *The Journal of Positive Psychology, 6*(1), 4–16. https://doi.org/10.1080/17439760.2010.536776

Emanuel, L. (2002). Deprivation X 3. *Journal of Child Psychotherapy, 28*(2), 163–179. https://doi.org/10.1080/00754170210143771

Enav, Y., Erhard-Weiss, D., Kopelman, M., Samson, A. C., Mehta, S., Gross, J. J., & Hardan, A. Y. (2019). A non-randomized mentalization intervention for parents of children with autism. *Autism Research, 12*(7), 1077–1086. https://doi.org/10.1002/aur.2108

Ensink, K., Bégin, M., Martin-Gagnon, G., Biberdzic, M., Berthelot, N., Normandin, L., Fonagy, P., Bernazzani, O., & Borelli, J. L. (2023). Post-traumatic-stress in the context of childhood maltreatment: Pathways from attachment through mentalizing during the transition to parenthood. *Frontiers in Psychology, 14,* Article 919736. https://doi.org/10.3389/fpsyg.2023.919736

Ensink, K., Bégin, M., Normandin, L., Biberdzic, M., Vohl, G., & Fonagy, P. (2016). Le fonctionnement réflexif maternel et les symptômes intériorisés et extériorisés d'enfants victimes d'une agression sexuelle [Maternal reflective functioning and child internalizing and externalizing difficulties in the context of child sexual abuse]. *Revue Québécoise de Psychologie, 37*(3), 117–133. https://doi.org/10.7202/1040163ar

Ensink, K., Bégin, M., Normandin, L., & Fonagy, P. (2016). Maternal and child reflective functioning in the context of child sexual abuse: Pathways to depression and externalising difficulties. *European Journal of Psychotraumatology, 7*(1), Article 30611. https://doi.org/10.3402/ejpt.v7.30611

Ensink, K., Bégin, M., Normandin, L., & Fonagy, P. (2017). Parental reflective functioning as a moderator of child internalizing difficulties in the context of child sexual abuse. *Psychiatry Research, 257*, 361–366. https://doi.org/10.1016/j.psychres 2017.07.051

Ensink, K., Bégin, M., Normandin, L., Godbout, N., & Fonagy, P. (2017). Mentalization and dissociation in the context of trauma: Implications for child psychopathology. *Journal of Trauma & Dissociation, 18*(1), 11–30. https://doi.org/10.1080/15299732.2016.1172536

Ensink, K., Berthelot, N., Bernazzani, O., Normandin, L., & Fonagy, P. (2014). Another step closer to measuring the ghosts in the nursery: Preliminary validation of the Trauma Reflective Functioning Scale. *Frontiers in Psychology, 5*, Article 1471. https://doi.org/10.3389/fpsyg.2014.01471

Ensink, K., Berthelot, N., Biberdzic, M., & Normandin, L. (2016). The mirror paradigm: Assessing the embodied self in the context of abuse. *Psychoanalytic Psychology, 33*(3), 389–405. https://doi.org/10.1037/pap0000018

Ensink, K., Borelli, J. L., Roy, J., Normandin, L., Slade, A., & Fonagy, P. (2019). Costs of not getting to know you: Lower levels of parental reflective functioning confer risk for maternal insensitivity and insecure infant attachment. *Infancy, 24*(2), 210–227. https://doi.org/10.1111/infa.12263

Ensink, K., Leroux, A., Normandin, L., Biberdzic, M., & Fonagy, P. (2017). Assessing reflective parenting in interaction with school-aged children. *Journal of Personality Assessment, 99*(6), 585–595. https://doi.org/10.1080/00223891.2016.1270289

Ensink, K., Normandin, L., Plamondon, A., Berthelot, N., & Fonagy, P. (2016). Intergenerational pathways from reflective functioning to infant attachment through parenting. *Canadian Journal of Behavioral Science / Revue canadienne des sciences du comportement, 48*(1), 9–18. https://doi.org/10.1037/cbs0000030

Ensink, K., Normandin, L., Target, M., Fonagy, P., Sabourin, S., & Berthelot, N. (2014). Mentalization in children and mothers in the context of trauma: An initial study of the validity of the Child Reflective Functioning Scale. *British Journal of Developmental Psychology, 33*(2), 203–217. https://doi.org/10.1111/bjdp.12074

Ensink, K., Target, M., Oandasan, C., & Duval, J. (2015). *Child Reflective Functioning Scale scoring manual: For application to the Child Attachment Interview* [Unpublished manuscript]. University College London.

Etezady, M. H., & Davis, M. (Eds.). (2012). *Clinical perspectives on reflective parenting: Keeping the child's mind in mind.* Jason Aronson.

Fearon, R. M. P., & Belsky, J. (2004). Attachment and attention: Protection in relation to gender and cumulative social-contextual adversity. *Child Development, 75*(6), 1677–1693. https://doi.org/10.1111/j.1467-8624.2004.00809.x

Fischer-Kern, M., Fonagy, P., Kapusta, N. D., Luyten, P., Boss, S., Naderer, A., Bluml, V., & Leithner, K. (2013). Mentalizing in female inpatients with major depressive disorder. *The Journal of Nervous and Mental Disease, 201*(3), 202–207. https://doi.org/10.1097/NMD.0b013e3182845c0a

Fishburn, S., Meins, E., Fernyhough, C., Centifanti, L. C. M., & Larkin, F. (2022). Explaining the relation between early mind-mindedness and children's mentalizing abilities: The development of an observational preschool assessment. *Developmental Psychology, 58*(1), 17–31. https://doi.org/10.1037/dev0001272

Foley, S., Hughes, C., & Fink, E. (2022). Expectant mothers' not fathers' mind-mindedness predicts infant, mother, and father conversational turns at 7 months. *Infancy, 27*(6), 1091–1103. https://doi.org/10.1111/infa.12498

Fonagy, P. (1991). Thinking about thinking: Some clinical and theoretical considerations in the treatment of a borderline patient. *International Journal of Psychoanalysis, 72*(4), 639–656.

Fonagy, P. (2004). Early-life trauma and the psychogenesis and prevention of violence. *Annals of the New York Academy of Sciences, 1036*(1), 181–200. https://doi.org/10.1196/annals.1330.012

Fonagy, P. (2015). Mutual regulation, mentalization and therapeutic action: A reflection on the contributions of Ed Tronick to developmental and psychotherapeutic thinking. *Psychoanalytic Inquiry, 35*(4), 355–369. https://doi.org/10.1080/07351690.2015.1022481

Fonagy, P., & Allison, E. (2012). What is mentalization? The concept and its foundations in developmental research. In N. Midgley & I. Vrouva (Eds.), *Minding the child: Mentalization-based interventions with children, young people and their families* (pp. 11–34). Routledge.

Fonagy, P., & Allison, E. (2014). The role of mentalizing and epistemic trust in the therapeutic relationship. *Psychotherapy, 51*(3), 372–380. https://doi.org/10.1037/a0036505

Fonagy, P., & Allison, E. (2023). Beyond mentalizing: Epistemic trust and the transmission of culture. *Psychoanalytic Quarterly, 92*(4), 599–640. https://doi.org/10.1080/00332828.2023.2290023

Fonagy, P., & Bateman, A. W. (2007). Mentalizing and borderline personality disorder. *Journal of Mental Health, 16*(1), 83–101. https://doi.org/10.1080/09638230601182045

Fonagy, P., & Campbell, C. (2015). Bad blood revisited: Attachment and psychoanalysis, 2015. *British Journal of Psychotherapy, 31*(2), 229–250. https://doi.org/10.1111/bjp.12150

Fonagy, P., Campbell, C., Constantinou, M., Higgitt, A., Allison, E., & Luyten, P. (2022). Culture and psychopathology: An attempt at reconsidering the role of social learning. *Development and Psychopathology, 34*(4), 1205–1220. https://doi.org/10.1017/S0954579421000092

Fonagy, P., Campbell, C., & Luyten, P. (2023). Attachment, mentalizing and trauma: Then (1992) and now (2022). *Brain Sciences, 13*(3), Article 459. https://doi.org/10.3390/brainsci13030459

Fonagy, P., Gergely, G., Jurist, E., & Target, M. (2002). *Affect regulation, mentalization and the development of the self.* Other Press.

Fonagy, P., Gergely, G., & Target, M. (2007). The parent–infant dyad and the construction of the subjective self. *Journal of Child Psychology and Psychiatry, 48*(3–4), 288–328. https://doi.org/10.1111/j.1469-7610.2007.01727.x

Fonagy, P., Luyten, P., & Allison, E. (2015). Epistemic petrification and the restoration of epistemic trust: A new conceptualization of borderline personality disorder and its psychosocial treatment. *Journal of Personality Disorders, 29*(5), 575–609. https://doi.org/10.1521/pedi.2015.29.5.575

Fonagy, P., Luyten, P., Allison, E., & Campbell, C. (2016). Reconciling psychoanalytic ideas with attachment theory. In J. Cassidy & P. R. Shaver (Eds.), *Handbook of attachment* (3rd ed., pp. 780–804). Guilford Press.

Fonagy, P., Luyten, P., Allison, E., & Campbell, C. (2017a). What we have changed our minds about: Part 1. Borderline personality disorder as a limitation of resilience. *Borderline Personality Disorder and Emotion Dysregulation, 4*(1), Article 11. https://doi.org/10.1186/s40479-017-0061-9

Fonagy, P., Luyten, P., Allison, E., & Campbell, C. (2017b). What we have changed our minds about: Part 2. Borderline personality disorder, epistemic trust and the developmental significance of social communication. *Borderline Personality Disorder and Emotion Dysregulation, 4*, Article 9. https://doi.org/10.1186/s40479-017-0062-8

Fonagy, P., Luyten, P., Allison, E., & Campbell, C. (2019). Mentalizing, epistemic trust and the phenomenology of psychotherapy. *Psychopathology, 52*(2), 94–103. https://doi.org/10.1159/000501526

Fonagy, P., Luyten, P., Allison, E., & Campbell, C. (2024). Taking stock to move forward: Where the field of developmental psychopathology might be heading. *Development and Psychopathology, 36*(5), 2056–2065. https://doi.org/10.1017/S0954579424000312

Fonagy, P., Steele, M., Steele, H., Higgitt, A., & Target, M. (1994). The Emanuel Miller Memorial Lecture 1992. The theory and practice of resilience. *Journal of Child Psychology and Psychiatry, 35*(2), 231–257. https://doi.org/10.1111/j.1469-7610.1994.tb01160.x

Fonagy, P., Steele, M., Steele, H., Moran, G. S., & Higgitt, A. C. (1991). The capacity for understanding mental states: The reflective self in parent and child and its significance for security of attachment. *Infant Mental Health Journal, 12*(3), 201–218. https://doi.org/10.1002/1097-0355(199123)12:3<201::Aid-Imhj2280120307>3.0.Co;2-7

Fonagy, P., & Target, M. (1996). Playing with reality: I. Theory of mind and the normal development of psychic reality. *International Journal of Psychoanalysis, 77*(2), 217–233.

Fonagy, P., & Target, M. (1997). Attachment and reflective function: Their role in self-organization. *Development and Psychopathology, 9*(4), 679–700. https://doi.org/10.1017/S0954579497001399

Fonagy, P., & Target, M. (1998). Mentalization and the changing aims of child psychoanalysis. *Psychoanalytic Dialogues, 8*(1), 87–114. https://doi.org/10.1080/10481889809539235

Fonagy, P., & Target, M. (2002). Early intervention and the development of self-regulation. *Psychoanalytic Inquiry, 22*(3), 307–335. https://doi.org/10.1080/07351692209348990

Fonagy, P., & Target, M. (2007a). Playing with reality. *International Journal of Psychoanalysis, 88*(4), 917–937. https://doi.org/10.1516/ijpa.2007.917

Fonagy, P., & Target, M. (2007b). The rooting of the mind in the body: New links between attachment theory and psychoanalytic thought. *Journal of the American Psychoanalytic Association, 55*(2), 411–456. https://doi.org/10.1177/00030651070550020501

Fotopoulou, A., & Tsakiris, M. (2017). Mentalizing homeostasis: The social origins of interoceptive inference. *Neuropsychoanalysis, 19*(1), 3–28. https://doi.org/10.1080/15294145.2017.1294031

Foulkes, L., & Andrews, J. L. (2023). Are mental health awareness efforts contributing to the rise in reported mental health problems? A call to test the prevalence inflation hypothesis. *New Ideas in Psychology, 69,* Article 101010. https://doi.org/10.1016/j.newideapsych.2023.101010

Foulkes, L., & Andrews, J. L. (2024). Accounting for the adolescent social context in school mental health interventions. *European Child & Adolescent Psychiatry, 34*(2), 803–805. https://doi.org/10.1007/s00787-024-02439-1

Fragkiadaki, E., & Strauss, S. (2012). Termination of psychotherapy: The journey of 10 psychoanalytic and psychodynamic therapists. *Psychology and Psychotherapy: Theory, Research and Practice, 85*(3), 335–350. https://doi.org/10.1111/j.2044-8341.2011.02035.x

Fraiberg, S., Adelson, E., & Shapiro, V. (1975). Ghosts in the nursery: A psychoanalytic approach to the problems of impaired infant–mother relationships. *Journal of the American Academy of Child Psychiatry, 14*(3), 387–421. https://doi.org/10.1016/S0002-7138(09)61442-4

Fredrickson, B. L. (2001). The role of positive emotions in positive psychology: The broaden-and-build theory of positive emotions. *American Psychologist, 56*(3), 218–226. https://doi.org/10.1037/0003-066x.56.3.218

Freud, A. (1966). *Normality and pathology in childhood.* Hogarth Press.

Gagne, J. R., Liew, J., & Nwadinobi, O. K. (2021). How does the broader construct of self-regulation relate to emotion regulation in young children? *Developmental Review, 60,* Article 100965. https://doi.org/10.1016/j.dr.2021.100965

Gagné, K., Lemelin, J. P., & Tarabulsy, G. M. (2021). Non-verbal and verbal parental mentalization as predictors of infant attachment security: Contributions of parental embodied mentalizing and mind-mindedness and the mediating role of maternal sensitivity. *Infant Behavior and Development, 65,* Article 101622. https://doi.org/10.1016/j.infbeh.2021.101622

Garon-Bissonnette, J., Duguay, G., Lemieux, R., Dubois-Comtois, K., & Berthelot, N. (2022). Maternal childhood abuse and neglect predicts offspring development in early childhood: The roles of reflective functioning and child sex. *Child Abuse & Neglect, 128,* Article 105030. https://doi.org/10.1016/j.chiabu.2021.105030

Geller, S. M. (2013). Therapeutic presence: An essential way of being. In M. Cooper, P. F. Schmid, M. O'Hara, & A. C. Bohart (Eds.), *The handbook of person-centred psychotherapy and counselling* (2nd ed., pp. 209–222). Palgrave.

George, C., Kaplan, N., & Main, M. (1996). *Adult Attachment Interview Protocol* (3rd ed.) [Unpublished manuscript]. Department of Psychology, University of California, Berkeley.

Gergely, G. (2013). Ostensive communication and cultural learning: The natural pedagogy hypothesis. In J. Metcalfe & H. S. Terrace (Eds.), *Agency and joint attention* (pp. 139–151). Oxford University Press. https://doi.org/10.1093/acprof:oso/9780199988341.003.0008

Gergely, G., & Watson, J. S. (1996). The social biofeedback theory of parental affect-mirroring: The development of emotional self-awareness and self-control in infancy. *International Journal of Psychoanalysis, 77*(6), 1181–1212.

Gergely, G., & Watson, J. S. (1999). Early socio-emotional development: Contingency perception and the social-biofeedback model. In P. Rochat (Ed.), *Early social cognition: Understanding others in the first months of life* (pp. 101–136). Lawrence Erlbaum.

Gervinskaitė-Paulaitienė, L., Byrne, G., & Barkauskienė, R. (2023). Mentalization-based parenting program for child maltreatment prevention: A pre–post study of 12-week lighthouse group program. *Children, 10*(6), Article 1047. https://doi.org/10.3390/children10061047

Gil, E., & Crenshaw, D. A. (2016). *Termination challenges in child psychotherapy*. Guilford Press.

Gil, E., & Drewes, A. A. (2005). *Cultural issues in play therapy*. Guilford Press.

Gilbert, R., Widom, C. S., Browne, K., Fergusson, D., Webb, E., & Janson, S. (2009). Burden and consequences of child maltreatment in high-income countries. *The Lancet, 373*(9657), 68–81. https://doi.org/10.1016/S0140-6736(08)61706-7

Gleason, T. R., & White, R. E. (2023). Pretend play as abstraction: Implications for early development and beyond. *Neuroscience & Biobehavioral Reviews, 147*, Article 105090. https://doi.org/10.1016/j.neubiorev.2023.105090

Gluckers, G., & Van Lier, L. (2011). Beeld en betekenis. Sleutelscènes uit de opleiding tot kindertherapeut [Image and meaning. Key scenes from the training of child therapists]. *Tijdschrift voor Psychoanalyse, 17*(3), 150–163.

Gölcük, M., & Berument, S. K. (2021). The relationship between negative parenting and child and maternal temperament. *Current Psychology, 40*(7), 3596–3608. https://doi.org/10.1007/s12144-019-00307-9

Golding, K. S. (2015). Connection before correction: Supporting parents to meet the challenges of parenting children who have been traumatised within their early parenting environments. *Children Australia, 40*(2), 152–159. https://doi.org/10.1017/cha.2015.9

Goodman, G., Midgley, N., & Schneider, C. (2016). Expert clinicians' prototypes of an ideal child treatment in psychodynamic and cognitive-behavioral therapy: Is mentalization seen as a common process factor? *Psychotherapy Research, 26*(5), 590–601. https://doi.org/10.1080/10503307.2015.1049672

Goodman, G., Reed, P., & Athey-Lloyd, L. (2015). Mentalization and play therapy processes between two therapists and a child with Asperger's disorder. *International Journal of Play Therapy, 24*(1), 13–29. https://doi.org/10.1037/a0038660

Goodman, G., Stroh, M., & Valdez, A. (2012). Do attachment representations predict depression and anxiety in psychiatrically hospitalized prepubertal children? *Bulletin of the Menninger Clinic, 76*(3), 260–289. https://doi.org/10.1521/bumc.2012.76.3.260

Gray, P., Lancy, D. F., & Bjorklund, D. F. (2023). Decline in independent activity as a cause of decline in children's mental well-being: Summary of the evidence. *The Journal of Pediatrics, 260*, Article 113352. https://doi.org/10.1016/j.jpeds.2023.02.004

Greenspan, S. I. (1997). *Developmentally based psychotherapy*. International Universities Press.

Gutman, L. M., Joshi, H., Parsonage, M., & Schoon, I. (2015). *Children of the new century: Mental health findings from the Millennium Cohort Study*. Centre for Mental Health. https://www.centreformentalhealth.org.uk/wp-content/uploads/2018/09/newcentury.pdf

Hagell, A., & Maughan, B. (2017). Epidemiology: Are mental health problems in children and young people really a big issue? In N. Midgley, J. Hayes, & M. Cooper (Eds.), *Essential research findings in child and adolescent counselling and psychotherapy* (pp. 14–31). SAGE Publications.

Hagelquist, J. O., Jensen, C. H., Bloch, M. S., & Rasmussen, H. (2023). A mentalization-based approach to healing children exposed to adverse experiences: Tools for residential care. *Bulletin of the Menninger Clinic, 87*(1), 83–103. https://doi.org/10.1521/bumc.2023.87.1.83

Haidt, J., & Allen, N. (2020). Scrutinizing the effects of digital technology on mental health. *Nature, 578*(7794), 226–227. https://doi.org/10.1038/d41586-020-00296-x

Halfon, S., & Besiroglu, B. (2021). Parental reflective function and children's attachment-based mental state talk as predictors of outcome in psychodynamic child psychotherapy. *Psychotherapy, 58*(1), 81–94. https://doi.org/10.1037/pst0000347

Halfon, S., Beşiroğlu, B., Bulut, P., Epözdemir, ., Aydın, G. ., Koç, H. B., Sözüer, B., Özsoy, Ö., Tulum, O., Tülü, S., & Midgley, N. (2024). The efficacy of mentalization-based treatment (MBT-C) for children with internalizing and externalizing problems: A randomized controlled trial. *Journal of the American Academy of Child & Adolescent Psychiatry*. Advance online publication. https://doi.org/10.1016/j.jaac.2024.12.006

Halfon, S., & Bulut, P. (2019). Mentalization and the growth of symbolic play and affect regulation in psychodynamic therapy for children with behavioral problems. *Psychotherapy Research, 29*(5), 666–678. https://doi.org/10.1080/10503307.2017.1393577

Halfon, S., Yılmaz, M., & Çavdar, A. (2019). Mentalization, session-to-session negative emotion expression, symbolic play, and affect regulation in psychodynamic child psychotherapy. *Psychotherapy, 56*(4), 555–567. https://doi.org/10.1037/pst0000201

Hanlon, P., McCallum, M., Jani, B. D., McQueenie, R., Lee, D., & Mair, F. S. (2020). Association between childhood maltreatment and the prevalence and complexity of multimorbidity: A cross-sectional analysis of 157,357 U.K. Biobank participants. *Journal of Comorbidity, 10*, 1–12. https://doi.org/10.1177/2235042X10944344

Happé, F., & Frith, U. (2014). Annual research review: Towards a developmental neuroscience of atypical social cognition. *Journal of Child Psychology and Psychiatry, 55*(6), 553–577. https://doi.org/10.1111/jcpp.12162

The Harris Poll. (2024, September 10). *What Gen Z thinks about its social media and smartphone usage*. https://theharrispoll.com/briefs/gen-z-social-media-smartphones/

Harter, S. (2012). *The construction of the self: Developmental and sociocultural foundations*. Guilford Press.

Harvey, L. J., White, F. A., Hunt, C., & Abbott, M. (2023). Investigating the efficacy of a dialectical behaviour therapy-based universal intervention on adolescent social and emotional well-being outcomes. *Behaviour Research and Therapy, 169*, Article 104408. https://doi.org/10.1016/j.brat.2023.104408

Haslam-Hopwood, G. T. G., Allen, J. G., Stein, A., & Bleiberg, E. (2006). Enhancing mentalizing through psycho-education. In J. G. Allen & P. Fonagy (Eds.), *Handbook of mentalization-based treatment* (pp. 249–267). Wiley. https://doi.org/10.1002/9780470712986.ch13

Haugvik, M. (2013). Structured parallel therapy with parents in time-limited psychotherapy with children experiencing difficult family situations. *Clinical Child*

Psychology and Psychiatry, 18(4), 504–518. https://doi.org/10.1177/1359104512460859

Haugvik, M., & Johns, U. (2008). Facets of structure and adaption: A qualitative study of time-limited psychotherapy with children experiencing difficult family situations. *Clinical Child Psychology and Psychiatry, 13*(2), 235–252. https://doi.org/10.1177/1359104507088345

Henrich, J., Heine, S. J., & Norenzayan, A. (2010). The weirdest people in the world? *Behavioral and Brain Sciences, 33*(2–3), 61–83. https://doi.org/10.1017/S0140525X0999152X

Hertzmann, L., Abse, S., Target, M., Glausius, K., Nyberg, V., & Lassri, D. (2017). Mentalisation-based therapy for parental conflict—Parenting together; an intervention for parents in entrenched post-separation disputes. *Psychoanalytic Psychotherapy, 31*(2), 195–217. https://doi.org/10.1080/02668734.2017.1320685

Hertzmann, L., Target, M., Hewison, D., Casey, P., Fearon, P., & Lassri, D. (2016). Mentalization-based therapy for parents in entrenched conflict: A random allocation feasibility study. *Psychotherapy, 53*(4), 388–401. https://doi.org/10.1037/pst0000092

Hodges, J., Steele, M., Hillman, S., Henderson, K., & Kaniuk, J. (2003). Changes in attachment representations over the first year of adoptive placement: Narratives of maltreated children. *Clinical Child Psychology and Psychiatry, 8*(3), 351–367. https://doi.org/10.1177/1359104503008003006

Huang, Y. L., Fonagy, P., Feigenbaum, J., Montague, P. R., Nolte, T., & the London Personality and Mood Disorder Research Consortium. (2020). Multidirectional pathways between attachment, mentalizing, and posttraumatic stress symptomatology in the context of childhood trauma. *Psychopathology, 53*(1), 48–58. https://doi.org/10.1159/000506406

Hughes, D. A. (2000). *Facilitating developmental attachment: The road to emotional recovery and behavioral change in foster and adopted children*. Jason Aronson.

Hughes, D. A. (2004). An attachment-based treatment of maltreated children and young people. *Attachment & Human Development, 6*(3), 263–278. https://doi.org/10.1080/14616730412331281539

Hughes, C., & Ensor, R. (2008). Social cognition and disruptive behavior disorder in young children: Families matter. In C. Sharp, P. Fonagy, & I. Goodyer (Eds.), *Social cognition and developmental psychopathology* (pp. 115–140). Oxford University Press. https://doi.org/10.1093/med/9780198569183.003.0005

Hurry, A. (Ed.). (1998). *Psychoanalysis and developmental therapy*. Karnac.

Invitto, S., & Moselli, P. (2024). Exploring embodied and bioenergetic approaches in trauma therapy: Observing somatic experience and olfactory memory. *Brain Sciences, 14*(4), Article 385. https://doi.org/10.3390/brainsci14040385

Jacob, J., Edbrooke-Childs, J., Flannery, H., Segal, T. Y., & Law, D. (2023). Goal-based measurement in paediatric settings: Implications for practice. *Archives of Disease in Childhood, 108*(5), 344–348. https://doi.org/10.1136/archdischild-2021-322761

Jacobsen, M. N., Ha, C., & Sharp, C. (2015). A mentalization-based treatment approach to caring for youth in foster care. *Journal of Infant, Child, and Adolescent Psychotherapy, 14*(4), 440–454. https://doi.org/10.1080/15289168.2015.1093921

Jessurun, H. (2021). An introduction to mentalizing theory. In T. Rossouw, M. Wiwe, & I. Vrouva (Eds.), *Mentalization-based treatment for adolescents. A practical treatment guide* (pp. 11–24). Routledge.

Johns, J. (2008). Clinical supervision as a key metaphor in reflective practice. In J. Johns (Ed.), *Becoming a reflective practitioner* (3rd ed.). Blackwell Publishing.

Johnson, D. E. (2002). Adoption and the effect on children's development. *Early Human Development, 68*(1), 39–54. https://doi.org/10.1016/S0378-3782(02)00017-8

Johnson, B. N., Kivity, Y., Rosenstein, L. K., LeBreton, J. M., & Levy, K. N. (2022). The association between mentalizing and psychopathology: A meta-analysis of the reading the mind in the eyes task across psychiatric disorders. *Clinical Psychology: Science and Practice, 29*(4), 423–439. https://doi.org/10.1037/cps0000105

Juffermans, M., & Muller, N. (2021). Case-study: Mentalization-based treatment, a time-limited approach, for a boy with a mild intellectual disability and trauma. *Global Journal of Intellectual & Developmental Disabilities, 7*(2), Article 555706. https://doi.org/10.19080/GJIDD.2020.07.555706

Jurist, E. L. (2005). Mentalized affectivity. *Psychoanalytic Psychology, 22*(3), 426–444. https://doi.org/10.1037/0736-9735.22.3.426

Kazda, L., Bell, K., Thomas, R., McGeechan, K., Sims, R., & Barratt, A. (2021). Overdiagnosis of attention-deficit/hyperactivity disorder in children and adolescents: A systematic scoping review. *JAMA Network Open, 4*(4), Article e215335. https://doi.org/10.1001/jamanetworkopen.2021.5335

Keaveny, E., Midgley, N., Asen, E., Bevington, D., Fearon, P., Fonagy, P., Jennings-Hobbs, R., & Wood, S. (2012). Minding the family mind: The development and initial evaluation of mentalization based treatment for families. In N. Midgley & I. Vrouva (Eds.), *Minding the child: Mentalization-based interventions with children, young people and their families* (pp. 98–112). Routledge.

Kegerreis, S., & Midgley, N. (2018). Psychodynamic approaches to counselling children and young people. In M. Robson & S. Pattison (Eds.), *Sage handbook of counselling children and young people* (2nd ed., pp. 45–58). SAGE Publications.

Kelly, K. R., & Bailey, A. L. (2021). Narrative story stem methodologies: Use and utility of quantitative and qualitative approaches across the lifespan. *Narrative Inquiry, 31*(1), 163–190. https://doi.org/10.1075/ni.20088.kel

Kochanska, G., Coy, K. C., & Murray, K. T. (2001). The development of self-regulation in the first four years of life. *Child Development, 72*(4), 1091–1111. https://doi.org/10.1111/1467-8624.00336

Kolev, M. V. (2024). Playfulness and adolescence: Mentalization and neuropsychoanalysis perspective. *Frontiers in Psychology, 15*, Article 1371747. https://doi.org/10.3389/fpsyg.2024.1371747

Kovács, Á. M., Téglás, E., & Endress, A. D. (2010). The social sense: Susceptibility to others' beliefs in human infants and adults. *Science, 330*(6012), 1830–1834. https://doi.org/10.1126/science.1190792

Kumpasoğlu, G. B., Saunders, R., Campbell, C., Nolte, T., Montague, R., Pilling, S., Leibowitz, J., & Fonagy, P. (2025). Mentalizing, epistemic trust and interpersonal problems in emotion regulation: A sequential path analysis across common mental health disorders and community control samples. *Journal of Affective Disorders, 372*, 502–511. https://doi.org/10.1016/j.jad.2024.12.050

Lanyado, M. (2012). Transition and change: An exploration of the resonance between transitional and meditative states of mind and their roles in the therapeutic process. In A. Horne & M. Lanyado (Eds.), *Winnicott's children: Independent psychoanalytic approaches with children and adolescents* (pp. 123–139). Routledge.

Laurenssen, E. M., Hutsebaut, J., Feenstra, D. J., Bales, D. L., Noom, M. J., Busschbach, J. J., Verheul, R., & Luyten, P. (2014). Feasibility of mentalization-based treatment for adolescents with borderline symptoms: A pilot study. *Psychotherapy, 51*(1), 159–166. https://doi.org/10.1037/a0033513

Laurent, G., Hecht, H. K., Ensink, K., & Borelli, J. L. (2020). Emotional understanding, aggression, and social functioning among preschoolers. *American Journal of Orthopsychiatry, 90*(1), 9–21. https://doi.org/10.1037/ort0000377

Law, D., & Wolpert, M. (Eds.). (2014). *Guide to using outcomes and feedback tools with children, young people and families* (2nd ed.). CAMHS Press.

Li, A., Wang, S., Paetzold, R. L., Rholes, W. S., & Liu, X. (2023). Childhood trauma and its link to adult dissociation: The role of mentalizing and disorganized attachment in a Chinese adult sample. *Journal of Trauma & Dissociation, 24*(5), 559–574. https://doi.org/10.1080/15299732.2023.2195395

Lieberman, A. F., Padrón, E., Van Horn, P., & Harris, W. W. (2005). Angels in the nursery: The intergenerational transmission of benevolent parental influences. *Infant Mental Health Journal, 26*(6), 504–520. https://doi.org/10.1002/imhj.20071

Lindblom, J., Pajulo, M., Nolvi, S., Tervahartiala, K., Karlsson, H., Karlsson, L., & Korja, R. (2022). Early pathways of maternal mentalization: Associations with child development in the FinnBrain birth cohort study. *Frontiers in Psychology, 13*, Article 855190. https://doi.org/10.3389/fpsyg.2022.855190

Liu, S., Wang, Y., & Song, Y. (2023). Atypical facial mimicry for basic emotions in children with autism spectrum disorder. *Autism Research, 16*(7), 1375–1388. https://doi.org/10.1002/aur.2957

Lombardi, E., Valle, A., Bianco, F., Castelli, I., Massaro, D., & Marchetti, A. (2022). Supporting mentalizing in primary school children: The effects of thoughts in mind project for children (TiM-C) on metacognition, emotion regulation and theory of mind. *Cognition and Emotion, 36*(5), 975–986. https://doi.org/10.1080/02699931.2022.2067521

Longhi, E., Murray, L., Wellsted, D., Hunter, R., MacKenzie, K., Taylor-Colls, S., Fonagy, P., & Fearon, P. (2020). *Minding the baby home-visiting programme for vulnerable young mothers*. National Society for the Prevention of Cruelty to Children.

Luyten, P., Campbell, C., Moser, M., & Fonagy, P. (2024). The role of mentalizing in psychological interventions in adults: Systematic review and recommendations for future research. *Clinical Psychology Review, 108*, Article 102380. https://doi.org/10.1016/j.cpr.2024.102380

Luyten, P., & Fonagy, P. (2015a). Psychodynamic treatment for borderline personality disorder and mood disorders: A mentalizing perspective. In L. W. Choi-Kain & J. G. Gunderson (Eds.), *Borderline personality and mood disorders: Comorbidity and controversy* (pp. 223–251). Springer.

Luyten, P., & Fonagy, P. (2015b). The neurobiology of mentalizing. *Personality Disorders: Theory, Research, and Treatment, 6*(4), 366–379. https://doi.org/10.1037/per0000117

Luyten, P., Lemma, A., & Target, M. (2019). Depression. In A. Bateman & P. Fonagy (Eds.), *Handbook of mentalizing in mental health practice* (2nd ed., pp. 387–402). American Psychiatric Association.

Luyten, P., Malcorps, S., & Fonagy, P. (2021). Adolescent brain development and the development of mentalizing. In T. Rossouw, M. Wiwe, & I. Vrouva (Eds.), *Mentalization-based treatment for adolescents: A practical treatment guide* (pp. 25–40). Routledge/Taylor & Francis Group. https://doi.org/10.4324/9780429323928-2-4

Luyten, P., Malcorps, S., Fonagy, P., & Ensink, K. (2019). Assessment of mentalizing. In A. Bateman & P. Fonagy (Eds.), *Handbook of mentalizing in mental health practice* (2nd ed., pp. 37–62). American Psychiatric Association.

Luyten, P., Nijssens, L., Fonagy, P., & Mayes, L. C. (2017). Parental reflective functioning: Theory, research, and clinical applications. *Psychoanalytic Study of the Child, 70*(1), 174–199. https://doi.org/10.1080/00797308.2016.1277901

Lyons-Ruth, K., Bruschweiler-Stern, N., Harrison, A. M., Morgan, A. C., Nahum, J. P., Sander, L., Stern, D. N., & Tronick, E. Z. (1998). Implicit relational knowing: Its role in development and psychoanalytic treatment. *Infant Mental Health Journal, 19*(3), 282–289. https://doi.org/10.1002/(SICI)1097-0355(199823)19:3<282::AID-IMHJ3>3.0.CO;2-O

MacIntosh, T., Hernandez, M., & Mehta, A. S. (2022). Identifying, addressing, and eliminating microaggressions in healthcare. *HCA Healthcare Journal of Medicine, 3*(3), 189–196. https://doi.org/10.36518/2689-0216.1418

MacLean, P. C., Rynes, K. N., Aragón, C., Caprihan, A., Phillips, J. P., & Lowe, J. R. (2014). Mother–infant mutual eye gaze supports emotion regulation in infancy during the still-face paradigm. *Infant Behavior and Development, 37*(4), 512–522. https://doi.org/10.1016/j.infbeh.2014.06.008

Malberg, N. T. (2015). Activating mentalization in parents: An integrative framework. *Journal of Infant, Child, and Adolescent Psychotherapy, 14*(3), 232–245. https://doi.org/10.1080/15289168.2015.1068002

Malberg, N. T. (2021). Working with autistic children and their families from a mentalization based therapy for children (MBT-C) approach. *Psychoanalytic Perspectives, 18*(1), 22–42. https://doi.org/10.1080/1551806X.2021.1845033

Malberg, N. T. (2024). Working with parents: A mentalization-based framework. *Psychodynamic Psychiatry, 52*(4), 473–489. https://doi.org/10.1521/pdps.2024.52.4.473

Malberg, N. T., & Gori, I. (2024). Epistemic justice and neurodiversity: Mentalization-based treatment with children in the autistic spectrum from a dimensional perspective. *Journal of Infant, Child, and Adolescent Psychotherapy, 23*(1), 56–71. https://doi.org/10.1080/15289168.2024.2306460

Malberg, N., Jurist, E., Bate, J., & Dangerfield, M. (2023). *Working with parents in therapy: A mentalization-based approach.* American Psychological Association. https://doi.org/10.1037/0000341-000

Mariz, C., Souza Cruz, O., & Moreira, D., (2022). The influence of environmental and genetic factors on the development of psychopathy: A systematic review. *Aggression and Violent Behavior, 62,* Article 101715. https://doi.org/10.1016/j.avb.2021.101715

Martin-Gagnon, G., Normandin, L., Fonagy, P., & Ensink, K. (2023). Adolescent mentalizing and childhood emotional abuse: Implications for depression, anxiety, and borderline personality disorder features. *Frontiers in Psychology, 14,* Article 1237735. https://doi.org/10.3389/fpsyg.2023.1237735

Mason, B. (1993). Towards positions of safe uncertainty. *Human Systems: Therapy, Culture and Attachments, 4*(3–4), 189–200. https://doi.org/10.1177/26344041211063125

McLaughlin, C., Holliday, C., Clarke, B., & Ilie, S. (2013). *Research on counselling and psychotherapy with children and young people: A systematic scoping review of the evidence for its effectiveness from 2003–2011*. British Association for Counselling and Psychotherapy. https://www.bacp.co.uk/media/1978/bacp-research-on-counselling-psychotherapy-with-children-young-people-systematic-review-2013.pdf

McMahon, L. (2009). *The handbook of play therapy and therapeutic play* (2nd ed.). Routledge.

Meins, E., Fernyhough, C., Wainwright, R., Das Gupta, M., Fradley, E., & Tuckey, M. (2002). Maternal mind-mindedness and attachment security as predictors of theory of mind understanding. *Child Development, 73*(6), 1715–1726. https://doi.org/10.1111/1467-8624.00501

Midgley, N. (2024). The unbroken circle: From child analysis to mentalization-based treatment (MBT) with children, adolescents, and families. *Psychodynamic Psychiatry, 52*(4), 452–472. https://doi.org/10.1521/pdps.2024.52.4.452

Midgley, N., Besser, S. J., Fearon, P., Wyatt, S., Byford, S., & Wellsted, D. (2019). The Herts and Minds study: Feasibility of a randomised controlled trial of mentalization-based treatment versus usual care to support the wellbeing of children in foster care. *BMC Psychiatry, 19*(1), Article 215. https://doi.org/10.1186/s12888-019-2196-2

Midgley, N., Cirasola, A., Austerberry, C., Ranzato, E., West, G., Martin, P., Redfern, S., Cotmore, R., & Park, T. (2019). Supporting foster carers to meet the needs of looked after children: A feasibility and pilot evaluation of the Reflective Fostering Programme. *Developmental Child Welfare, 1*(1), 41–60. https://doi.org/10.1177/2516103218817550

Midgley, N., Irvine, K., Rider, B., Byford, S., Cirasola, A., Ganguli, P., Katangwe-Chigamba, T., Murdoch, J., Pond, M., Pursch, B., Redfern, S., Richards, Z. L., Shepstone, L., Sims, E., Smith, C., Sprecher, E., Swart, A. M., Wyatt, S., & Wellsted, D. (2021). The Reflective Fostering Programme—Improving the well-being of children in care through a group intervention for foster carers: A randomised controlled trial. *Trials, 22*(1), Article 841. https://doi.org/10.1186/s13063-021-05739-y

Midgley, N., Mortimer, R., Carter, C., Casey, P., Coffman, L., Edbrooke-Childs, J., Edridge, C., Fonagy, P., Gomes, M., Kapoor, A., Marks, S., Martin, P., Moltrecht, B., Morris, E., Pokorna, N., & McFarquar, T. (2023). Emotion regulation in children (ERiC): A protocol for a randomised clinical trial to evaluate the clinical and cost effectiveness of mentalization based treatment (MBT) for school-age children with mixed emotional and behavioural difficulties. *PLOS ONE, 18*(8), Article e0289503. https://doi.org/10.1371/journal.pone.0289503

Midgley, N., Mortimer, R., Cirasola, A., Batra, P., & Kennedy, E. (2021). The evidence-base for psychodynamic psychotherapy with children and adolescents: A narrative synthesis. *Frontiers in Psychology, 12*, Article 662671. https://doi.org/10.3389/fpsyg.2021.662671

Midgley, N., Sprecher, E. A., & Sleed, M. (2021). Mentalization-based interventions for children aged 6–12 and their carers: A narrative systematic review. *Journal of Infant, Child, and Adolescent Psychotherapy, 20*(2), 169–189. https://doi.org/10.1080/15289168.2021.1915654

Midgley, N., & Vrouva, I. (Eds.). (2012). *Minding the child: Mentalization-based interventions with children, young people and their families*. Routledge.

Mikulincer, M., & Shaver, P. R. (2007). *Attachment in adulthood: Structure, dynamics, and change*. Guilford Press.

Moore, C., & Dunham, P. (1995). *Joint attention: Its origins and role in development.* Lawrence Erlbaum.

Morken, K. T. E., Binder, P. E., Arefjord, N. M., & Karterud, S. W. (2019). Mentalization-based treatment from the patients' perspective—What ingredients do they emphasize? *Frontiers in Psychology, 10,* Article 1327. https://doi.org/10.3389/fpsyg.2019.01327

Morris, J. (2024, April 4). *The rapidly growing waiting lists for autism and ADHD assessments.* Nuffield Trust. https://www.nuffieldtrust.org.uk/news-item/the-rapidly-growing-waiting-lists-for-autism-and-adhd-assessments

Muller, N., & Bakker, T. (2009). Oog voor de ouders: Diagnostiek van de hechtingsrelatie tussen ouders en kinderen en het mentaliserend vermogen van ouders [An eye for the parents: Diagnosis of the attachment relationship between parents and children and the mentalizing capacity of parents]. *Tijdschrift voor Kinder en Jeugdpsychotherapie, 39*(3), 65–79.

Muller, N., Gerits, L., & Siecker, I. (2012). Mentalization-based therapies with adopted children and their families. In N. Midgley & I. Vrouva (Eds.), *Minding the child: Mentalization-based interventions with children, young people and their families* (pp. 113–130). Routledge.

Muller, N., & Midgley, N. (2015). Approaches to assessment in time-limited mentalization-based therapy for children (MBT-C). *Frontiers in Psychology, 6,* Article 1063. https://doi.org/10.3389/fpsyg.2015.01063

Muller, N., & Midgley, N. (2020). The clinical challenge of mentalization-based therapy with children who are in "pretend mode". *Journal of Infant, Child, and Adolescent Psychotherapy, 19*(1), 16–24. https://doi.org/10.1080/15289168.2019.1701865

Muller, N., Morris, E., & Midgley, N. (2025). *Mentalization-based treatment for developmental trauma.* Routledge. https://doi.org/10.4324/9781032713441

Muller, N., & ten Kate, C. (2008). Mentaliseren bevorderende therapie in relaties en gezinnen [Mentalization-promoting therapy in relationships and families]. *Tijdschrift voor Systeemtherapie, 20*(3), 117–132.

Muller, N., & ten Kate, C. (2023). Lichaamsgerichte MBT bij getraumatiseerde kinderen en adolescenten [Body-oriented MBT in traumatized children and adolescents]. *Tijdschrift voor Psychotherapie, 49*(4), 266–281.

Muñoz Specht, P., Ensink, K., Normandin, L., & Midgley, N. (2016). Mentalizing techniques used by psychodynamic therapists working with children and adolescents. *Bulletin of the Menninger Clinic, 80*(4), 281–315. https://doi.org/10.1521/bumc.2016.80.4.281

Music, G. (2011). *Nurturing natures: Attachment and children's emotional, sociocultural and brain development.* Psychology Press.

Nelson, C. A., Scott, R. D., Bhutta, Z. A., Harris, N. B., Danese, A., & Samara, M. (2020). Adversity in childhood is linked to mental and physical health throughout life. *The BMJ, 371,* Article m3048. https://doi.org/10.1136/bmj.m3048

Newlove-Delgado, T., Marcheselli, F., Williams, T., Mandalia, D., Dennes, M., McManus, S., & Ford, T. (2023, November 21). *Mental health of children and young people in England, 2023.* NHS England. https://digital.nhs.uk/data-and-information/publications/statistical/mental-health-of-children-and-young-people-in-england/2023-wave-4-follow-up#

Newlove-Delgado, T., Russell, A. E., Mathews, F., Cross, L., Bryant, E., Gudka, R., Ukoumunne, O. C., & Ford, T. J. (2023). Annual research review: The impact of

COVID-19 on psychopathology in children and young people worldwide: Systematic review of studies with pre- and within-pandemic data. *Journal of Child Psychology and Psychiatry, 64*(4), 611–640. https://doi.org/10.1111/jcpp.13716

NHS Digital. (2025, October 2). *Mental health services monthly statistics, performance.* https://digital.nhs.uk/data-and-information/publications/statistical/mental-health-services-monthly-statistics

Nieto-Retuerto, M., Torres-Gomez, B., & Alonso-Arbiol, I. (2025). Parental mentalization and children's externalizing problems: A systematic review and meta-analysis. *Development and Psychopathology, 37*(4), 1804–1820. https://doi.org/10.1017/s0954579424001391

Nijssens, L., Vliegen, N., & Luyten, P. (2020). The mediating role of parental reflective functioning in child social–emotional development. *Journal of Child and Family Studies, 29*(8), 2342–2354. https://doi.org/10.1007/s10826-020-01767-5

Normandin, L., Bate, J., Bégin, M., Fonagy, P., & Ensink, K. (2023). Play completion predicts fewer child psychological difficulties: A longitudinal study of mentalizing processes. *International Journal of Play Therapy, 32*(2), 122–133. https://doi.org/10.1037/pla0000195

Northrup, J. B., & Iverson, J. M. (2020). The development of mother–infant coordination across the first year of life. *Developmental Psychology, 56*(2), 221–236. https://doi.org/10.1037/dev0000867

Novick, K. K., & Novick, J. (2005). *Working with parents makes therapy work.* Rowman & Littlefield.

Nyberg, V., & Hertzmann, L. (2014). Developing a mentalization-based treatment (MBT) for therapeutic intervention with couples (MBT-CT). *Couple and Family Psychoanalysis, 4*(2), 116–135. https://doi.org/10.33212/cfp.v4n2.2014.116

Oehlman Forbes, D., Lee, M., & Lakeman, R. (2021). The role of mentalization in child psychotherapy, interpersonal trauma, and recovery: A scoping review. *Psychotherapy, 58*(1), 50–67. https://doi.org/10.1037/pst0000341

Orben, A., & Przybylski, A. K. (2019). The association between adolescent well-being and digital technology use. *Nature Human Behaviour, 3*(2), 173–182. https://doi.org/10.1038/s41562-018-0506-1

Ostler, T., Bahar, O. S., & Jessee, A. (2010). Mentalization in children exposed to parental methamphetamine abuse: Relations to children's mental health and behavioral outcomes. *Attachment & Human Development, 12*(3), 193–207. https://doi.org/10.1080/14616731003759666

Owen, J. J., Tao, K., Leach, M. M., & Rodolfa, E. (2011). Clients' perceptions of their psychotherapists' multicultural orientation. *Psychotherapy, 48*(3), 274–282. https://doi.org/10.1037/a0022065

Pajulo, M., Pyykkönen, N., Kalland, M., Sinkkonen, J., Helenius, H., Punamäki, R. L., & Suchman, N. (2012). Substance-abusing mothers in residential treatment with their babies: Importance of pre- and postnatal maternal reflective functioning. *Infant Mental Health Journal, 33*(1), 70–81. https://doi.org/10.1002/imhj.20342

Pally, R., & Popek, P. (2012). CRP direct services and training programs. In M. H. Etezady & M. Davis (Eds.), *Clinical perspectives on reflective parenting: Keeping the child's mind in mind* (pp. 31–58). Jason Aronson.

Panksepp, J., & Biven, L. (2012). *The archaeology of mind: The neuroevolutionary origins of human emotions.* W. W. Norton.

Parada-Fernández, P., Herrero-Fernández, D., Oliva-Macías, M., & Rohwer, H. (2021). Analysis of the mediating effect of mentalization on the relationship between attachment styles and emotion dysregulation. *Scandinavian Journal of Psychology, 62*(3), 312–320. https://doi.org/10.1111/sjop.12717

Paul, S. E., Boudreaux, M. J., Bondy, E., Tackett, J. L., Oltmanns, T. F., & Bogdan, R. (2019). The intergenerational transmission of childhood maltreatment: Nonspecificity of maltreatment type and associations with borderline personality pathology. *Development and Psychopathology, 31*(3), 1157–1171. https://doi.org/10.1017/S095457941900066X

Penner, F., Gambin, M., & Sharp, C. (2019). Childhood maltreatment and identity diffusion among inpatient adolescents: The role of reflective function. *Journal of Adolescence, 76*(1), 65–74. https://doi.org/10.1016/j.adolescence.2019.08.002

Pollak, S. D. (2024). Continuing the momentum of developmental psychopathology: Lessons learned from the seminal contributions of Dante Cicchetti. *Development and Psychopathology, 36*(5), 2051–2055. https://doi.org/10.1017/s0954579424001755

Pons, F., Harris, P. L., & de Rosnay, M. (2004). Emotion comprehension between 3 and 11 years: Developmental periods and hierarchical organization. *European Journal of Developmental Psychology, 1*(2), 127–152. https://doi.org/10.1080/17405620344000022

Premack, D., & Woodruff, G. (1978). Does the chimpanzee have a theory of mind? *Behavioral and Brain Sciences, 1*(4), 515–526. https://doi.org/10.1017/S0140525X00076512

Raissouni, M., Benhammou, S., & Belbachir, S. (2023). The place of EMDR in children: A review of the literature. *European Psychiatry, 66*(S1), S734–S734. https://doi.org/10.1192/j.eurpsy.2023.1541

Rexwinkel, M. J., & Verheugt-Pleiter, A. J. E. (2021). Helping parents to promote mentalization. In A. Verheugt-Pleiter & J. Zevalkink (Eds.), *Mentalizing in child therapy: Guidelines for clinical practitioners* (2nd ed., pp. 45–70). Routledge.

Riazi, S. S., & Manouchehri, M. (2024). The mediating role of mentalization and integrative self-knowledge in the relationship between childhood trauma and fear of intimacy. *Frontiers in Psychology, 15,* Article 1384573. https://doi.org/10.3389/fpsyg.2024.1384573

Robinson, P., & Skårderud, F. (2019). Assessment of mentalizing. In A. Bateman & P. Fonagy (Eds.), *Handbook of mentalizing in mental health practice* (2nd ed., pp. 369–386). American Psychiatric Association.

Røed Hansen, B. (2012). *I dialog med barnet: Intersubjektivitet i utvikling og i psykoterapi* [In dialogue with the child: Intersubjectivity in development and in psychotherapy]. Gyldendal.

Rogers, C. R. (1957). The necessary and sufficient conditions of therapeutic personality change. *Journal of Consulting Psychology, 21*(2), 95–103. https://doi.org/10.1037/h0045357

Rosenfeld, S. K., & Sprince, M. P. (1965). Some thoughts on the technical handling of borderline children. *Psychoanalytic Study of the Child, 20*(1), 495–517. https://doi.org/10.1080/00797308.1965.11823247

Rossouw, T. (2012). Self-harm in young people. Is MBT the answer? In N. Midgley & I. Vrouva (Eds.), *Minding the child: Mentalization-based interventions with children, young people and their families* (pp. 131–144). Routledge.

Rossouw, T. I., & Fonagy, P. (2012). Mentalization-based treatment for self-harm in adolescents: A randomized controlled trial. *Journal of the American Academy of Child & Adolescent Psychiatry, 51*(12), 1304–1313.e3. https://doi.org/10.1016/j.jaac.2012.09.018

Rutherford, M. B. (2011). *Adult supervision required: Private freedom and public constraints for parents and children.* Rutgers University Press.

Ryan, R. M., Deci, E. L., & Vansteenkiste, M. (2016). Autonomy and autonomy disturbances in self-development and psychopathology: Research on motivation, attachment, and clinical process. In D. Cicchetti (Ed.), *Developmental psychopathology. Vol. 1: Theory and method* (3rd ed., pp. 385–438). Wiley.

Sadler, L. S., Slade, A., Close, N., Webb, D. L., Simpson, T., Fennie, K., & Mayes, L. C. (2013). Minding the baby: Enhancing reflectiveness to improve early health and relationship outcomes in an interdisciplinary home visiting program. *Infant Mental Health Journal, 34*(5), 391–405. https://doi.org/10.1002/imhj.21406

Safran, J. D., & Muran, J. C. (2000). *Negotiating the therapeutic alliance: A relational treatment guide.* Guilford Press.

Safran, J. D., Muran, J. C., & Eubanks-Carter, C. (2011). Repairing alliance ruptures. *Psychotherapy, 48*(1), 80–87. https://doi.org/10.1037/a0022140

Santoro, G., Midolo, L. R., Costanzo, A., & Schimmenti, A. (2021). The vulnerability of insecure minds: The mediating role of mentalization in the relationship between attachment styles and psychopathology. *Bulletin of the Menninger Clinic, 85*(4), 358–384. https://doi.org/10.1521/bumc.2021.85.4.358

Schmidt-Persson, J., Rasmussen, M. G. B., Sorensen, S. O., Mortensen, S. R., Olesen, L. G., Brage, S., Kristensen, P. L., Bilenberg, N., & Grontved, A. (2024). Screen media use and mental health of children and adolescents: A secondary analysis of a randomized clinical trial. *JAMA Network Open, 7*(7), Article e2419881. https://doi.org/10.1001/jamanetworkopen.2024.19881

Schore, A. N. (1994). *Affect regulation and the origin of the self.* Lawrence Erlbaum.

Schore, A. N. (2003). *Affect regulation and the repair of the self.* W.W. Norton.

Schwarzer, N. H., Nolte, T., Fonagy, P., Feigenbaum, J., King-Casas, B., Rüfenacht, E., Gingelmaier, S., Leibowitz, J., Pilling, S., Montague, P. R., & the London Personality and Mood Disorder Research Network. (2024). Linking mentalizing capacity, shame, and depressive symptoms in the context of childhood maltreatment. *Children and Youth Services Review, 163,* Article 107787. https://doi.org/10.1016/j.childyouth.2024.107787

Scott, S., & Dadds, M. R. (2009). Practitioner review: When parent training doesn't work: Theory-driven clinical strategies. *Journal of Child Psychology and Psychiatry, 50*(12), 1441–1450. https://doi.org/10.1111/j.1469-7610.2009.02161.x

Segal, S. C., & Moulson, M. C. (2024). The effectiveness of maternal regulatory attempts in the development of infant emotion regulation. *Infancy, 29*(5), 672–692. https://doi.org/10.1111/infa.12594

Shai, D., & Belsky, J. (2011). Parental embodied mentalizing: Let's be explicit about what we mean by implicit. *Child Development Perspectives, 5*(3), 187–188. https://doi.org/10.1111/j.1750-8606.2011.00195.x

Shai, D., & Belsky, J. (2017). Parental embodied mentalizing: How the nonverbal dance between parents and infants predicts children's socio-emotional functioning. *Attachment & Human Development, 19*(2), 191–219. https://doi.org/10.1080/14616734.2016.1255653

Shai, D., & Fonagy, P. (2014). Beyond words: Parental embodied mentalizing and the parent-infant dance. In M. Mikulincer & P. R. Shaver (Eds.), *Mechanisms of social connection: From brain to group* (pp. 186–203). American Psychological Association. https://doi.org/10.1037/14250-011

Shai, D., Laor Black, A., Spencer, R., Sleed, M., Baradon, T., Nolte, T., & Fonagy, P. (2022). Trust me! Parental embodied mentalizing predicts infant cognitive and language development in longitudinal follow-up. *Frontiers in Psychology, 13*, Article 867134. https://doi.org/10.3389/fpsyg.2022.867134

Shai, D., & Meins, E. (2018). Parental embodied mentalizing and its relation to mind-mindedness, sensitivity, and attachment security. *Infancy, 23*(6), 857–872. https://doi.org/10.1111/infa.12244

Sharp, C., & Bevington, D. (2022). *Mentalizing in psychotherapy: A guide for practitioners*. Guilford Press.

Sharp, C., Pane, H., Ha, C., Venta, A., Patel, A. B., Sturek, J., & Fonagy, P. (2011). Theory of mind and emotion regulation difficulties in adolescents with borderline traits. *Journal of the American Academy of Child & Adolescent Psychiatry, 50*(6), 563–573.e1. https://doi.org/10.1016/j.jaac.2011.01.017

Sharp, C., & Vanwoerden, S. (2015). Hypermentalizing in borderline personality disorder: A model and data. *Journal of Infant, Child, and Adolescent Psychotherapy, 14*(1), 33–45. https://doi.org/10.1080/15289168.2015.1004890

Sharp, C., & Venta, A. (2012). Mentalizing problems in children and adolescents. In N. Midgley & I. Vrouva (Eds.), *Minding the child: Mentalization-based interventions with children, young people and their families* (pp. 35–53). Routledge.

Shaw, B., Bicket, M., Elliott, B., Fagan-Watson, B., Mocca, E., & Hillman, M. (2015). *Children's independent mobility: An international comparison and recommendations for action*. Policy Studies Institute. https://westminsterresearch.westminster.ac.uk/item/98xyq/children-s-independent-mobility-an-international-comparison-and-recommendations-for-action

Shaw, C., Lo, C., Lanceley, A., Hales, S., & Rodin, G. (2020). The assessment of mentalization: Measures for the patient, the therapist and the interaction. *Journal of Contemporary Psychotherapy, 50*(1), 57–65. https://doi.org/10.1007/s10879-019-09420-z

Shin, H., Bjorklund, D. F., & Beck, E. F. (2007). The adaptive nature of children's overestimation in a strategic memory task. *Cognitive Development, 22*(2), 197–212. https://doi.org/10.1016/j.cogdev.2006.10.001

Shmueli-Goetz, Y., Target, M., Fonagy, P., & Datta, A. (2008). The Child Attachment Interview: A psychometric study of reliability and validity. *Developmental Psychology, 44*(4), 939–956. https://doi.org/10.1037/0012-1649.44.4.939

Siegel, D. J., & Hartzell, M. (2014). *Parenting from the inside out: How a deeper self-understanding can help you raise children who thrive* (10th anniversary ed.). Scribe.

Skenazy, L. (2021). *Free-range kids: How parents and teachers can let go and let grow* (2nd ed.). Jossey-Bass.

Slade, A. (2005). Parental reflective functioning: An introduction. *Attachment & Human Development, 7*(3), 269–281. https://doi.org/10.1080/14616730500245906

Slade, A. (2006). Reflective parenting programs: Theory and development. *Psychoanalytic Inquiry, 26*(4), 640–657. https://doi.org/10.1080/07351690701310698

Slade, A. (2008). Working with parents in child psychotherapy: Engaging the reflective function. In F. N. Busch (Ed.), *Mentalization: Theoretical considerations, research findings, and clinical implications* (pp. 207–234). Analytic Press.

Slade, A., Aber, J. L., Bresgi, I., Berger, B., & Kaplan, M. (2004). *The Parent Development Interview–Revised* [Unpublished protocol]. Department of Psychology, The City University of New York.

Slade, A., Holland, M. L., Ordway, M. R., Carlson, E. A., Jeon, S., Close, N., Mayes, L. C., & Sadler, L. S. (2020). Minding the baby: Enhancing parental reflective functioning and infant attachment in an attachment-based, interdisciplinary home visiting program. *Development and Psychopathology, 32*(1), 123–137. https://doi.org/10.1017/S0954579418001463

Slade, A., & Sleed, M. (2024). Parental reflective functioning on the parent development interview: A narrative review of measurement, association, and future directions. *Infant Mental Health Journal, 45*(4), 464–480. https://doi.org/10.1002/imhj.22114

Sleed, M., Baradon, T., & Fonagy, P. (2013). New beginnings for mothers and babies in prison: A cluster randomized controlled trial. *Attachment & Human Development, 15*(4), 349–367. https://doi.org/10.1080/14616734.2013.782651

Slijper, F. M. E. (2021). Treatment in practice. In A. J. E. Verheugt-Pleiter, J. Zevalkink, & M. G. J. Schmeets (Eds.), *Mentalizing in child therapy: Guidelines for clinical practitioners* (2nd ed.). Karnac.

Sotomayor-Enríquez, K., Di Folco, S., & Schwannauer, M. (2024). *Emotion regulation mediates the association between hypermentalizing and interpersonal difficulties in young people.* PsyArXiv. https://doi.org/10.31234/osf.io/65squ

Southam-Gerow, M. A., & Kendall, P. C. (2002). Emotion regulation and understanding: Implications for child psychopathology and therapy. *Clinical Psychology Review, 22*(2), 189–222. https://doi.org/10.1016/S0272-7358(01)00087-3

Sprecher, E. A., Cresswell, C., Kerr-Davis, A., Sleed, M., & Midgley, N. (2023). Caregiver mentalizing and child emotional regulation: A novel approach to examining bidirectional impact. *Journal of Infant, Child, and Adolescent Psychotherapy, 22*(4), 358–374. https://doi.org/10.1080/15289168.2023.2274200

Stallard, P. (2022). Evidence-based practice in cognitive-behavioural therapy. *Archives of Disease in Childhood, 107*(2), 109–113. https://doi.org/10.1136/archdischild-2020-321249

Staun, L., Kessler, H., Buchheim, A., Kächele, H., & Taubner, S. (2010). Mentalisierung und chronische depression [Mentalization and chronic depression]. *Psychotherapeut, 55*(4), 299–305. https://doi.org/10.1007/s00278-010-0752-9

Stern, D. (1985). *The interpersonal world of the infant: A view from psychoanalyses and developmental psychology*. Basic Books.

Stern, D. (1992). *Diary of a baby: What your child sees, feels, and experiences.* Basic Books.

Stern, D. (2004). *The present moment of psychotherapy and everyday life.* W. W. Norton.

Stern, D. (2010). *Forms of vitality.* Oxford University Press.

Stuhrmann, L. Y., Göbel, A., Bindt, C., & Mudra, S. (2022). Parental reflective functioning and its association with parenting behaviors in infancy and early childhood: A systematic review. *Frontiers in Psychology, 13,* Article 765312. https://doi.org/10.3389/fpsyg.2022.765312

Suchman, N., DeCoste, C., Castiglioni, N., Legow, N., & Mayes, L. (2008). The Mothers and Toddlers Program: Preliminary findings from an attachment-based parenting intervention for substance-abusing mothers. *Psychoanalytic Psychology, 25*(3), 499–517. https://doi.org/10.1037/0736-9735.25.3.499

Suchman, N. E., DeCoste, C., Leigh, D., & Borelli, J. (2010). Reflective functioning in mothers with drug use disorders: Implications for dyadic interactions with infants and toddlers. *Attachment & Human Development, 12*(6), 567–585. https://doi.org/10.1080/14616734.2010.501988

Suchman, N. E., DeCoste, C. L., McMahon, T. J., Dalton, R., Mayes, L. C., & Borelli, J. (2017). Mothering from the inside out: Results of a second randomized clinical trial testing a mentalization-based intervention for mothers in addiction treatment. *Development and Psychopathology, 29*(2), 617–636. https://doi.org/10.1017/S0954579417000220

Suchman, N., Pajulo, M., & Mayes, L. (Eds.). (2013). *Parenting and substance addiction: Developmental approaches to intervention*. Oxford University Press.

Svendsen, B., Tanum Johns, U., Brautaset, H., & Egebjerg, I. (2012). *Utviklingsrettet intersubjektiv psykoterapi med barn og unge* [Developmentally oriented intersubjective psychotherapy with children and adolescents]. Fagbokforlaget.

Talbot, L. (2023). Creating and supporting a team around the worker. In P. Fuggle, L. Talbot, C. Campbell, P. Fonagy, & D. Bevington (Eds.), *Adaptive mentalization-based integrative treatment (AMBIT) for people with multiple needs: Applications in practise* (pp. 217–240). Oxford University Press. https://doi.org/10.1093/med-psych/9780198855910.003.0009

Tanzilli, A., Di Giuseppe, M., Giovanardi, G., Boldrini, T., Caviglia, G., Conversano, C., & Lingiardi, V. (2021). Mentalization, attachment, and defense mechanisms: A Psychodynamic Diagnostic Manual-2-oriented empirical investigation. *Research in Psychotherapy: Psychopathology, Process, and Outcome, 24*(1), Article 531. https://doi.org/10.4081/ripppo.2021.531

Target, M., Fonagy, P., & Shmueli-Goetz, Y. (2003). Attachment representations in school-age children: The development of the Child Attachment Interview (CAI). *Journal of Child Psychotherapy, 29*(2), 171–186. https://doi.org/10.1080/0075417031000138433

Tarsha, M. S., & Narvaez, D. (2022). Effects of adverse childhood experience on physiological regulation are moderated by evolved developmental niche history. *Anxiety, Stress, & Coping, 35*(4), 488–500. https://doi.org/10.1080/10615806.2021.1989419

Taylor, C. (2012). *Emphatic care for children with disorganized attachments: A model for mentalizing, attachment and trauma-informed care*. Jessica Kingsley Publishers.

Ten Kate, C. A., Weijers, J. G., & Smit, W. M. A. (2016). Mentaliseren bevorderende therapie voor non-affectieve psychotische stoornissen [Mentalization-promoting therapy for non-affective psychotic disorders]. *PsyXpert, 1*, 42–50.

Tessier, V. P., Normandin, L., Ensink, K., & Fonagy, P. (2016). Fact or fiction? A longitudinal study of play and the development of reflective functioning. *Bulletin of the Menninger Clinic, 80*(1), 60–79. https://doi.org/10.1521/bumc.2016.80.1.60

Thompson, R. A., Meyer, S., & McGinley, M. (2006). Understanding values in relationship: The development of conscience. In M. Killen & J. Smetana (Eds.), *Handbook of moral development* (pp. 267–297). Lawrence Erlbaum.

Thorén, A., Lindqvist, K., Nemirovski, J. P., & Mechler, J. (2025). Short-term mentalization-based therapy for common childhood mental disorders—A pilot quasi-randomised controlled trial. *Clinical Child Psychology and Psychiatry, 30*(2), 436–451. https://doi.org/10.1177/13591045251316619

Timimi, S. (2002). *Pathological child psychiatry and the medicalization of childhood*. Brunner-Routledge.

Trevarthen, C., Aitken, K. J., Vandekerckove, M., Delafield-Butt, J., & Nagy, E. (2006). Collaborative regulations of vitality in early childhood: Stress in intimate relationships and postnatal psychopathology. In D. Cicchetti (Ed.), *Developmental psychopathology. Vol. 2: Developmental neuroscience* (2nd ed., pp. 65–126). Wiley.

Tronick, E. (2007). *The neurobehavioral and social-emotional development of infants and children.* W. W. Norton.

Trzesniewski, K. H., Kinal, M., & Donnellan, M. B. (2010). Self-enhancement and self-protection in developmental context. In M. Alicke & C. Sedikides (Eds.), *The handbook of self-enhancement and self-protection* (pp. 341–357). Guilford Press.

Twenge, J. M., Haidt, J., Joiner, T. E., & Campbell, W. K. (2020). Underestimating digital media harm. *Nature Human Behaviour, 4*(4), 346–348. https://doi.org/10.1038/s41562-020-0839-4

Vaish, A., Grossmann, T., & Woodward, A. (2008). Not all emotions are created equal: The negativity bias in social–emotional development. *Psychological Bulletin, 134*(3), 383–403. https://doi.org/10.1037/0033-2909.134.3.383

Valentino, K., Cicchetti, D., Toth, S. L., & Rogosch, F. A. (2011). Mother–child play and maltreatment: A longitudinal analysis of emerging social behavior from infancy to toddlerhood. *Developmental Psychology, 47*(5), 1280–1294. https://doi.org/10.1037/a0024459

van Aalst, E., Muller, N., & Feenstra, D. (2023). Mentalization-based treatment bij kinderen (MBT-K) met complexe problematiek en hun ouders [Mentalization-based treatment for children (MBT-K) with complex problems and their parents]. *Tijdschrift voor Psychotherapie, 49*(5), 331–347.

van IJzendoorn, M. H., & Kroonenberg, P. M. (1988). Cross-cultural patterns of attachment: A meta-analysis of the strange situation. *Child Development, 59*(1), 147–156. https://doi.org/10.2307/1130396

Verheugt-Pleiter, A. J. E. (2021). Intervention techniques: Attention regulation. In A. Verheugt-Pleiter & J. Zevalkink (Eds.), *Mentalizing in child therapy: Guidelines for clinical practitioners* (2nd ed., pp. 114–133). Routledge.

Verheugt-Pleiter, A., & Zevalkink, J. (2021). *Mentalizing in child therapy: Guidelines for clinical practitioners* (2nd ed.). Routledge. https://doi.org/10.4324/9781003167242

Verheugt-Pleiter, A. J. E., Zevalkink, J., & Schmeets, M. G. J. (Eds.). (2008). *Mentalizing in child therapy: Guidelines for clinical practitioners.* Karnac Books.

Viana, K. M. P., Zambrana, I. M., Bølstad, T. G., & Pons, F. (2023). "Are we both right?" relations between theory of mind and epistemic humility in dyadic cooperative problem-solving in 5- to 9-year-old children. *Journal of Applied Developmental Psychology, 87,* Article 101561. https://doi.org/10.1016/j.appdev.2023.101548

Vogt, K. S., & Norman, P. (2019). Is mentalization-based therapy effective in treating the symptoms of borderline personality disorder? A systematic review. *Psychology and Psychotherapy: Theory, Research and Practice, 92*(4), 441–464. https://doi.org/10.1111/papt.12194

Volkert, J., Taubner, S., Byrne, G., Rossouw, T., & Midgley, N. (2022). Introduction to mentalization-based approaches for parents, children, youths, and families. *American Journal of Psychotherapy, 75*(1), 4–11. https://doi.org/10.1176/appi.psychotherapy.20210020

Vrouva, I., Target, M., & Ensink, K. (2012). Measuring mentalization in children and young people. In N. Midgley & I. Vrouva (Eds.), *Minding the child: Mentalization-based interventions with children, young people and their families* (pp. 54–77). Routledge.

Vrtička, P., Andersson, F., Grandjean, D., Sander, D., & Vuilleumier, P. (2008). Individual attachment style modulates human amygdala and striatum activation during social appraisal. *PLOS ONE, 3*(8), Article e2868. https://doi.org/10.1371/journal.pone.0002868

Vygotsky, L. S. (1978). *Mind in society: The development of higher psychological processes.* Harvard University Press.

Wagner-Skacel, J., Riedl, D., Kampling, H., & Lampe, A. (2022). Mentalization and dissociation after adverse childhood experiences. *Scientific Reports, 12*(1), Article 6809. https://doi.org/10.1038/s41598-022-10787-8

Weimer, A. A., Sallquist, J., & Bolnick, R. R. (2012). Young children's emotion comprehension and theory of mind understanding. *Early Education and Development, 23*(3), 280–301. https://doi.org/10.1080/10409289.2010.517694

Whitefield, C., & Midgley, N. (2015). 'And when you were a child?': How therapists working with parents alongside individual child psychotherapy bring the past into their work. *Journal of Child Psychotherapy, 41*(3), 272–292. https://doi.org/10.1080/0075417X.2015.1092678

Widen, S., & Russel, J. (2008). Children acquire emotion categories gradually. *Cognitive Development, 23*(2), 291–312. https://doi.org/10.1016/j.cogdev.2008.01.002

Winnicott, D. W. (1967). Mirror-role of the mother and family in child development. In P. Lomas (Ed.), *The predicament of the family: A psycho-analytical symposium* (pp. 26–33). Hogarth Press/Institute of Psycho-Analysis.

Winnicott, D. W. (1971a). *Playing and reality.* Penguin.

Winnicott, D. W. (1971b). *Therapeutic consultations in child psychiatry.* Hogarth Press/Institute of Psycho-Analysis.

Winnicott, D. W. (1996). *Thinking about children.* Karnac.

Wolf, K., & Schmitz, J. (2024). Scoping review: Longitudinal effects of the COVID-19 pandemic on child and adolescent mental health. *European Child & Adolescent Psychiatry, 33*(5), 1257–1312. https://doi.org/10.1007/s00787-023-02206-8

Wood, S., Brasnett, H., Lassri, D., Fearon, P., & Midgley, N. (2015). *Mentalization based treatment for children looked after and their carers (MBT-Fostering): Treatment manual for use in the "Herts and Minds" study* [Unpublished manuscript]. Anna Freud Centre.

Xinran, X. (2011). *Message from an unknown Chinese mother: Stories of loss and love.* Vintage.

Yang, L., & Huang, M. (2024). Childhood maltreatment and mentalizing capacity: A meta-analysis. *Child Abuse & Neglect, 149*, Article 106623. https://doi.org/10.1016/j.chiabu.2023.106623

Zandpour, M., Hasani, J., Russo, L. N., Sharp, C., Lind, M., & Borelli, J. L. (2023). Mentalization in typically and atypically developing Iranian children and its associations with age, sex, and externalizing/internalizing symptoms. *Children, 10*(4), Article 657. https://doi.org/10.3390/children10040657

Zevalkink, J., Verheugt-Pleiter, A., & Fonagy, P. (2012). Mentalization-informed child psychoanalytic psychotherapy. In A. Bateman & P. Fonagy (Eds.), *Handbook of mentalizing in mental health practice* (pp. 129–158). American Psychiatric Association.

Zhou, H., Tian, C., Hong, L., Fan, Z., & Chen, W. (2025). Relationship between parenting style and peer relationships during early adolescence: The mediating role of parental mentalizing. *Journal of Genetic Psychology, 186*(2), 144–161. https://doi.org/10.1080/00221325.2024.2413488

INDEX

A

B

C

D

E

F

G

H

ABOUT THE AUTHORS

Nick Midgley, PhD, is a child and adolescent psychotherapist and professor of psychological therapies with children and young people at University College London and at the Anna Freud Centre in London, where he is director of the Child Attachment and Psychological Therapies Research Unit. Nick has been involved in the development of mentalization-based treatments for children and families and has conducted a number of research studies evaluating different types of mentalization-based interventions with children and families in both mental health and children's social care settings. He has written and coedited various books, including *Minding the Child: Mentalization-Based Interventions With Children, Young People and Their Families* and *Mentalization-Based Treatment for Developmental Trauma: A Casebook for Working With Children and Their Families.*

Karin Ensink, PhD, is a professor of child and adolescent psychology at the University Laval in Quebec, Canada, and teaches mentalization-based therapy and psychodynamic psychotherapy with children, adolescents, and parents. She completed her PhD under the direction of Mary Target and Peter Fonagy. Her research and clinical work continues to focus on the development and assessment of mentalization in children, adolescents, and parents. She has a particular interest in understanding failures of mentalization in the context of parent–child interactions and how this relates to psychopathology, personality, and treatment.

Karin Lindqvist, MSc, PhD, is a clinical psychologist and psychotherapist with a PhD in clinical psychology from Stockholm University. She is trained in mentalization-based work with children and parents at the Erica Foundation in Stockholm. Karin's research concerns different areas of psychodynamic psychotherapy with children, adolescents, and adults.

Norka Malberg, PhD, is an adult, child, and adolescent psychoanalyst and psychotherapist who trained at the Anna Freud Centre in London and the Western New England Psychoanalytic Institute in New Haven, Connecticut. She obtained her clinical doctorate at University College London for her adaptation of mentalization-based treatment (MBT) to adolescent group work in a pediatric hospital setting. She is an assistant clinical professor at Yale's Child Study Center in New Haven, Connecticut, and clinical instructor at the Fundación Vidal y Barraquer Institute of Ramon Llul University in Barcelona, Spain. She is the founder and director of IMAGINA: Centro de Aplicaciones de la Mentalización in Barcelona, Spain, a teaching and private practice organization. She is a trainer and supervisor for MBT for children, adolescents, and families. Most recently, she has developed and published proposed modifications to MBT for children, working with children with autism spectrum disorder and their families. Malberg is a coauthor of *Working With Parents in Therapy: A Mentalization-Based Approach.*

Nicole Muller, MSc, is a child and adolescent psychotherapist and family therapist at Centrum Hecht in Holland, a specialist center for the treatment of children, youth, and their families with attachment and trauma problems. She is a mentalization-based treatment practitioner with children and young people and a supervisor and trainer for the Anna Freud Centre in London. With her colleagues, she runs Centrum Hecht Opleidingen in Holland, a training center specializing in mentalization-based treatment for children and young people. She has written many articles on mentalization-based treatment and is coeditor of *Mentalization-Based Treatment for Developmental Trauma: A Casebook for Working With Children and Their Families.*